D0721893

Semantic Web
and Peer-to-Peer

Steffen Staab · Heiner Stuckenschmidt (Eds.)

Semantic Web and Peer-to-Peer

Decentralized Management and Exchange of Knowledge and Information

With 89 Figures and 15 Tables

 Springer

Editors

Steffen Staab

University of Koblenz
Institute for Computer Science
Universitaetsstr. 1
56016 Koblenz, Germany
staab@uni-koblenz.de

Heiner Stuckenschmidt

University of Mannheim
Institute for Practical Computer Science
A5, 6
68159 Mannheim, Germany
heiner@informatik.uni-mannheim.de

Library of Congress Control Number: 2005936055

ACM Computing Classification (1998): C.2.4, H.3, I.2.4

ISBN-10 3-540-28346-3 Springer Berlin Heidelberg New York
ISBN-13 978-3-540-28346-1 Springer Berlin Heidelberg New York

Springer is a part of Springer Science+Business Media

springeronline.com

© Springer-Verlag Berlin Heidelberg 2006
Printed in Germany

Typeset by the authors
using a Springer TEX macro package
Production: LE-TEX Jelonek, Schmidt & Vöckler GbR, Leipzig
Cover design: KünkelLopka Werbeagentur, Heidelberg

Printed on acid-free paper   45/3142/YL - 5 4 3 2 1 0

To our families

Preface

The Semantic Web and Peer-to-Peer are two technologies that address a common need at different levels:

- The *Semantic Web* addresses the requirement that one may model, manipulate and query knowledge and information at the conceptual level rather than at the level of some technical implementation. Moreover, it pursues this objective in a way that allows people from all over the world to relate their own view to this conceptual layer. Thus, the Semantic Web brings new degrees of freedom for changing and exchanging the conceptual layer of applications.
- *Peer-to-Peer* technologies aim at abandoning centralized control in favor of decentralized organization principles. In this objective they bring new degrees of freedom for changing information architectures and exchanging information between different nodes in a network.
- *Together*, Semantic Web and Peer-to-Peer allow for combined flexibility at the level of information structuring and distribution.

Historical Remarks and Acknowledgements

How to benefit from this combined flexibility has been investigated in a number of research efforts. In particular, we coordinated the EU IST research project "SWAP — Semantic Web and Peer-to-peer" (http://swap.semanticweb.org) that led to many chapters of this book[1] and, also, to a 15,000 Euro doIT software innovation award for the work on Bibster (see Chap. 18) from the local government of the German state of Baden-Württemberg. Thus, we are very much indebted to the EU for generously funding this project.

Obviously this book contains many other chapters — and for very good reasons: First, we profited enormously from tight interaction with colleagues in other projects, such as the Italian-funded project Edamok (Fausto Giunchiglia, Paolo Bouquet, Matteo Bonifacio and colleagues) and the German-funded project Edutella (Wolfgang Nejdl and colleagues) — just to name the two most influential, as we cannot name

---

[1] Chapters 1,5,6,7,11,14,15,17,18.

all the giants on the shoulders of whom we stand. Second, though we could have easily filled all the pages of a thick book just with research contributions from the SWAP project, it was not our primary goal to do a book "on SWAP", but a book on the "Semantic Web and Peer-to-Peer" and the many different aspects that this conjunction brings along. This, clearly, fell outside of the possibilities of SWAP, but it was easily possible with the help of many colleagues who worked on shaping the joint area of Semantic Web and Peer-to-Peer.

We thank all of these numerous colleagues within SWAP and outside. Special thanks go to Thomas Franz for integrating the contributions into a common LaTeX document.

Purpose of This Book

It is the purpose of this book to acquaint the reader with the needs of joint Semantic Web and Peer-to-Peer methods and applications, in particular in the area of information sharing and knowledge management where we see their immediate use and benefit.

For this purpose, we start with an elaborate introduction to the overall topic of this book. The introduction surveys the topic and its subtopics, represented by four major parts of this book, and briefly sorts all individual contributions into a global perspective. The global perspective is refined in an introductory section at the beginning of each part.

In the core of the book, the contributions discuss major aspects of Semantic Web and Peer-to-Peer-based systems, including parts on:

1. Data storage and access;
2. Querying the network;
3. Semantic integration; and
4. Methodologies and applications.

Together these contributions shape the picture of a comprehensive lifecycle of applications built on Semantic Web and Peer-to-Peer. Its success stories include high flying applications, such as applications for knowledge management like KEx (Chap. 16), for knowledge sharing in virtual organizations (cf. Xarop in Chap. 17) as well as for information sharing in a global community (cf. Bibster in Chap. 18).

The Future of Semantic Web and Peer-to-Peer

We see a far-ranging future for Semantic Web and Peer-to-Peer technologies. Industry discovers P2P technologies not just for document-oriented information sharing, but also for recent communication channels like voice-over-IP (internet telephony) or instant messaging. At the same time the need to structure communication and information content from many channels and information repositories grows further and underlines the need for the combined technologies of *Semantic Web and Peer-to-Peer*. Recent research efforts target and extend this area from the perspective of social networks and semantic desktops and we expect a lot of impetus from this work. *Web services* and *Grid* infrastructures rely on Peer-to-Peer service communication and the only way to discover appropriate services and exchange meaningful content is to join *Semantic Web and Peer-to-Peer*.

Hence, we invite you to ride the first wave of *Semantic Web and Peer-to-Peer* here in this book. The next big one is sure to come.

June 2006

Steffen Staab, Koblenz, Germany
Heiner Stuckenschmidt, Amsterdam, The Netherlands

Contents

Peer-to-Peer and Semantic Web

Heiner Stuckenschmidt[1], Frank van Harmelen[1], Wolf Siberski[2], Steffen Staab[3]

[1] Vrije Universiteit Amsterdam, The Netherlands,
   {heiner,Frank.van.Harmelen}@cs.vu.nl
[2] L3S Research Center, Hannover, Germany, siberski@l3s.de
[3] ISWeb, University of Koblenz-Landau, Koblenz, Germany, staab@uni-koblenz.de

Summary. Just as the industrial society of the last century depended on natural resources, today's society depends on information. A lack of resources in the industrial society hindered development just as a lack of information hinders development in the information society. Consequently, the exchange of information becomes essential for more and more areas of society: Companies announce their products in online marketplaces and exchange electronic orders with their suppliers; in the medical area patient information is exchanged between general practitioners, hospitals and health insurances; public administration receive tax information from employers and offer online services to their citizens. As a reply to this increasing importance of information exchange, new technologies supporting a fast and accurate information exchange are being developed. Prominent examples of such new technologies are so-called *Semantic Web* and *Peer-to-Peer technologies*. These technologies address different aspects of the inherit complexity of information exchange. Semantic Web Technologies address the problem of *information complexity* by providing advanced support for representing and processing information. Peer-to-Peer technologies, on the other hand, address *system complexity* by allowing flexible and decentralized information storage and processing.

1 The Semantic Web

The World Wide Web today is a huge network of information resources, which was built in order to broadcast information for human users. Consequently, most of the information on the Web is designed to be suitable for human consumption: The structuring principles are weak, many different kinds of information co-exist, and most of the information is represented as free text (including HTML).

With the increasing size of the web and the availability of new technologies such as mobile applications and smart devices, there is a strong need to make the information on the World Wide Web accessible to computer programs that search, filter, convert, interpret, and summarize the information for the benefit of the user. The Semantic Web is a synonym for a World Wide Web whose accessibility is similar to a deductive database where programs can perform well-defined operations on well-defined data, check for the validity of conditions, or even derive new information from existing data.

1.1 Infrastructure for Machine-Readable Metadata

One of the main developments connected with the Semantic Web is the resource description framework (RDF). RDF is an XML-based language for creating metadata about information resources on the Web. The metadata model is based on a resource that could be any piece of information with a unique name called uniform resource identifier (URI). URIs can either be unique resource locators (URLs) — well known from conventional web pages — but also tagged information contained on a page or on other RDF definitions. The structure of RDF is very simple: a set of statements forms a labelled directed graph where resources are represented by nodes, and relations between resources by arcs. These are labelled with the name of the relation.

RDF as such only provides the user with a language for metadata. It does not make any commitment to a conceptual structure or a set of relations to be used. The RDF schema model defines a simple frame system structure by introducing standard relations like inheritance and instantiation, standard resources for classes, as well as a small set of restrictions on objects in a relation. Using these primitives it is possible to define terminological knowledge about resources and relations mentioned in an RDF model.

An increasing number of software tools available supporting the complete life-cycle of RDF models. Editors and converters are available for the generation of RDF schema representations from scratch or for extracting such descriptions from database schemas or software design documents. Storage and retrieval systems have been developed that can deal with RDF models containing millions of statements, and provide query engines for a number of RDF query languages. Annotation tools support the user in the task of attaching RDF descriptions to web pages and other information sources either manually or semi-automatically using techniques from natural language processing. Finally, special purpose tools support the maintenance of RDF models in terms of change detection and validation of models.

1.2 Representing Local and Shared Meaning

The aim of the Semantic Web is to make information on the World Wide Web more accessible using machine-readable meta-data. In this context, the need for explicit models of semantic information (terminologies and background knowledge) in order to support information exchange has been widely acknowledged by the research community. Several different ways of describing information semantics have been proposed and used in applications. However, we can distinguish two broad approaches which follow somehow opposite directions:

1. Ontologies are shared models of some domain that encode a view which is common to a set of different parties.
2. Contexts are local (where local is intended here to imply not shared) models that encode a party's view of a domain.

Thus, ontologies are best used in applications where the core problem is the use and management of common representations. Many applications have been developed, for instance in bio-informatics, or for knowledge management purposes inside organizations. Contexts, instead, are best used in those applications where the core problem is the use and management of local and autonomous representations with a need for a limited and controlled form of globalization (or, using the terminology used in the context literature, maintaining locality still guaranteeing semantic compatibility among representations). Examples of uses of contexts are the classifications of documents, distributed knowledge management, the development and integration of catalogs and semantics based Peer-to-Peer systems.

As a response to the need for representing shared models of web content, the Web ontology language OWL has been developed. OWL, which meanwhile is a W3C recommendation, is an RDF based language that introduces special language primitives for defining classes and relations as well as necessary (Every human has exactly one mother) and sufficient (Every woman who has a child is a mother) conditions for class membership as well as general constraints on the interpretation of a domain (the successor relation is transitive). RDF data can be linked to OWL models by the use of classes and relations in the metadata descriptions. The additional definitions in the corresponding OWL model imposes further restrictions on the validity and interpretation of the metadata. A number of reasoning tools have been developed for checking these constraints and for inferring new knowledge (i.e. class membership and subclass relations). In connection with the standardization activities at W3C and the Object Management Group OMG the connection between UML and the proposed Web Ontology Language (OWL) has been studied and UML-based tools for handling OWL are developed establishing a connection between software engineering and Semantic Web technologies.

2 Peer-to-Peer

The need for handling multiple sources of knowledge and information is quite obvious in the context of Semantic Web applications. First of all we have the duality of schema and information content where multiple information sources can adhere to the same schema. Further, the re-use, extension and combination of multiple schema files is considered to be common practice on the Semantic Web. Despite the inherently distributed nature of the Semantic Web, most current RDF infrastructures store information locally as a single knowledge repository, i.e., RDF models from remote sources are replicated locally and merged into a single model. Distribution is virtually retained through the use of namespaces to distinguish between different models. We argue that many interesting applications on the Semantic Web would benefit from or even require an RDF infrastructure that supports real distribution of information sources that can be accessed from a single point. Beyond the argument of conceptual adequacy, there are a number of technical reasons for real distribution in the spirit of distributed databases:

Freshness. The commonly used approach of using a local copy of a remote source suffers from the problem of changing information. Directly using the remote source frees us from the need of managing change as we are always working with the original.

Flexibility. Keeping different sources separate from each other provides us with a greater flexibility concerning the addition and removal of sources. In the distributed setting, we only have to adjust the corresponding system parameters.

The term "Peer-to-Peer" stands for an architecture and a design philosophy that addresses the problems of centralized applications. From an architectural point of view, Peer-to-Peer is a design where nodes in a network operate mostly autonomously and share resources with other nodes without central control. The design philosophy of Peer-to-Peer systems is to provide users with a greater flexibility to cooperate with other users and to form and participate in different communities of interest. In this second view Peer-to-Peer technology can be seen as a means to let people cooperate in a more efficient way. We can define Peer-to-Peer in the following way:

> The term "Peer-to-Peer" describes systems that use a decentralized architecture that allows individual peers to provide and consume resources without centralized control.

Peer-to-Peer solutions can be characterized by the degree of decentralization and the type of resources shared between peers. Looking at the degree of centralization, we can say that there are degrees of decentralization, ranging from host based and client-server architectures to publish-subscribe and Peer-to-Peer architectures, where most existing systems are somewhere between the latter two. Concerning the kind of resources shared, we can distinguish the following types of Peer-to-Peer systems:

- Applications where peers share computational resources, also known as *Grid Computing*
- Applications where peers share application logic also known as *Service-Based Architectures*
- Applications where peers share information

The last type of Peer-to-Peer system can be seen as a *classical Peer-to-Peer system*. In this book we focus on this last type of Peer-to-Peer solutions. Discussing the use of Semantic Web technologies to support the other types of systems surely requires more books to be written.

2.1 Peer-to-Peer and Knowledge Management

The current state-of-the-art in Knowledge Management solutions still focuses on one or a relatively small number of highly centralized knowledge repositories with Ontologies as the conceptual backbone for knowledge brokering. As it turns out, this assumption is very restrictive, because, (i), it creates major bottlenecks and entails significant administrative overheads, especially when it comes to scaling up to large and complex problems; (ii), it does not lend itself to easy maintenance and the dynamic updates often required to reflect changing user needs, dynamic enterprise processes or new market conditions.

In contrast, Peer-to-Peer computing (P2P) offers the promise of lifting many of these limitations. The essence of P2P is that nodes in the network directly exploit resources present at other nodes of the network without intervention of any central server. The tremendous success of networks like Napster and Gnutella, and of highly visible industry initiatives such as Sun's JXTA, as well as the Peer-to-Peer Working Group including HP, IBM and Intel, have shown that the P2P paradigm is a particularly powerful one when it comes to sharing files over the Internet without any central repository, without centralized administration, and with file delivery dedicated solely to user needs in a robust, scalable manner. At the same time, today's P2P solutions support only limited update, search and retrieval functionality, e.g. search in Napster is restricted to string matches involving just two fields: "artist" and "track." These flaws, however, make current P2P systems unsuitable for knowledge sharing purposes.

Figure 1 illustrates the comparison. It depicts a qualitative comparison of benefits (time saved or redundant work avoided in Euro) won by using a KM system depending on the amount of investment (money spent on setting up the system).

P2P based KM systems show their benefits just by installing the client software, viz. immediate access to knowledge stored at peers. Nevertheless, the benefits to be gained from such software levels off at the point where users of the system can no longer cope with the plentitude of information returned from keyword-based queries.

Ontology-based KM systems offer — at least in principle — the possibility for rich structuring and, hence, easy access to knowledge. Their disadvantage is that an initial set-up of the system tends to be expensive *and* individual users must actively contribute into a centralized repository. Hence, the investment into the KM system requires a long time of usage to pay off — for the organization and, in particular, for the individual user.

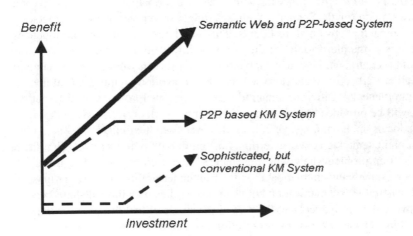

Benefit

Semantic Web and P2P-based System

P2P based KM System

Sophisticated, but conventional KM System

Investment

Fig. 1. Qualitative Comparison of Benefits resulting from Investments in KM Systems

Systems that are based on Semantic Web and Peer-to-Peer technologies promise to combine the advantages of the two mechanisms. Whereas the underlying architecture allows for instantaneous gratification by Peer-to-Peer-, keyword-based search, the possibility to provide semantic structuring provide the possibility for maintaining large and complex-structured systems. One may note here that in the combined paradigm a conventional knowledge management repository will still appear as just another powerful peer in the network. Hence, a combined Semantic Web and P2P solution may always outperform the sophisticated, but conventional, centralized system.

2.2 Peer-to-Peer and the (Semantic) Web

When we look at the current World Wide Web, we see in fact a mixed architecture, that is partly client/server-based, and partly P2P. On the one hand, each node in the network can directly address every other node in the network in a single, flat, world-wide address space, giving it the structure typical of many P2P networks. On the other hand, in practice there is currently a strong asymmetry between nodes in this address space that act as content-servers, and nodes that act as clients. Recent estimates indicate the presence of 50 million web-servers, but as many as 150 million clients. On the scale of the World Wide Web, any form of centralization would create immediate bottlenecks, in terms of network throughput and server capacity.

This need for a flat, non-server-centered architecture will be even stronger on the Semantic Web. Of course, the same physical load-balancing arguments hold as on the current Web, but the Semantic Web adds a new argument in favor of a P2P-style argument. On the Semantic Web, any server-centered architecture will not only create physical bottlenecks, but as communication relies on the use of ontologies will also create *semantic bottlenecks*. Since the semantics of information will be explicit (or at least more explicit) on the Semantic Web, any single server will in a way "impose" a particular semantic view on all its clients. This will have undesirable consequences, both in terms of the pluriformity of the available information, as well as in terms of the size of the central ontology that such information-servers would have to maintain.

Instead, a P2P-style architecture will be able to avoid both the physical and the semantic bottlenecks. Different semantic views, expressed in terms of different ontologies, will be provided by many peers in a flat network of peers, each employing their own local, small ontology. Of course, this increased flexibility comes at a price: such "different semantic views, in terms of different ontologies" create a significant data-integration problem: how will these peers be able to communicate if they do not share the same view on their data? In the remainder of this paper, we propose an approach where the communication between peers relies on a limited shared vocabulary between them. This replaces the role of the single virtual database schema that is the traditional basis for solving information exchange problems.

3 Aspects of Semantics-Based Peer-to-Peer Systems

We have argued above that the combination of Semantic Web and P2P technologies is ideally suited to deal with the problem of knowledge sharing and knowledge management, in particular in distributed or in inter-organizational settings. Concrete applications and scenarios, however, come with certain requirements and constraints that require different decisions with respect to the design of the system. In the remainder of this article, we discuss the different dimensions of semantics-based P2P systems in which design decisions have to be made to meet the application requirements. For this purpose we identify the different aspects that characterize a particular system. These aspects fall into four main topics — and roughly correspond to the four parts of this book:

1. technology used to store and access data in each source,
2. properties of the logical network that connects the different information sources and forwards queries to the appropriate information source,
3. mechanisms used to ensure interoperability of information across the network, and
4. methods to build and maintain concrete P2P applications.

In the context of ontology-based P2P systems we are especially interested in the role ontologies play in these different areas. For each of these general topics we can identify further aspects that influence the behavior of the system, characterize it and make it more suitable for one or the other application scenario. In the following we discuss these aspects and mention some typical design decisions often made in existing systems.

3.1 Data Storage and Access

An important factor in each knowledge management system is how relevant information can be searched for. This process is significantly influenced by the way the data is represented as well as the language used to formulate queries. These two aspects have also been identified as important design dimensions for P2P systems in (Nejdl et al. 2003) [6]. We add the choice of a particular engine for answering queries which may also depend on the application scenario.

Query Language

The expressiveness of the query language supported by the system is an important aspect of Peer-to-Peer information sharing. Daswani et al. [2] distinguish key-based, keyword-based and schema-based systems. In key-based systems, information objects can be requested based on a unique hash-key assigned to it. This means that documents, for example, have to be requested based on their name. Keyword-based systems extend this to the possibility to look for documents based on keywords, e.g. occurring in the title, subject description or even full text. This means that we do not have to know the document we are looking for, but can ask for all documents relevant to particular topics. More sophisticated keyword approaches rank documents based on their relevance depending on document statistics.

Schema-based systems support query languages that refer to elements of a schema used to structure the information. These systems support queries similar to queries to a traditional database. In such systems, we could, for example, ask for documents based on metadata such as the author and date of creation. Systems using schema-based query languages have the advantage that they support the exchange of structured information rather than simple data objects. This ability is essential in many application domains. A further increase of expressiveness is provided by systems that support queries enriched by deduction rules. This allows the user to explicitly state background knowledge and to introduce new terminology when querying the system. This ability can, for example, be used to automatically enrich user queries with information from a user profile to support personalization.

Data Model

The data model used to store information is tightly connected to the aspect of the query language. Many data models have been proposed for storing data and we are not able to discuss them all in detail. We rather want to mention some basic distinctions with respect to the data model that influences the ability of the system. The most basic way of storing data is in terms of a fixed, standardized schema that is used across the whole system. Further, simple storage models like the one used in key or keyword based systems can also be seen as a fixed schema. In the first case, the schema consists of a single data field that contains the hash key, in the later case it is a list of keywords. Despite the obvious limitations, fixed schema approaches are often observed in Peer-to-Peer systems because this eliminates the problem of schema interoperability. Interoperability is a problem in systems that allow the user to define and use a local schema. This not only asks for a suitable integration method, but it also leads to maintenance problems because local schemas can evolve and new schemas can be added to the system when new peers join. Another level of expressiveness and complexity is added by the use of ontologies as a schema language that allows the derivation of implicit information by means of reasoning. Ontologies are often encoded using concept-based formalisms that support some form of inheritance reasoning. In particular, the use of ontologies as a schema language for describing information is gaining importance. The expressiveness of the respective formalisms ranges from simple classification hierarchies to expressive logical formalisms.

Query Engine

The link between the query language and the data model used is created by a query engine that interprets the query expression and extracts data from the underlying data model. Naturally, the properties and abilities of the query engine depend on the choice of query and schema language. Nevertheless, the choice of a particular engine is an important aspect of the system, because the engine does not necessarily have to support the full query language or the complete semantics of data model. In such cases only parts of the derivable answers can be queried.

Part I: RDF Data Storage & Access

We adopt a Semantic Web perspective for data modelling and querying, i.e. we see the need to represent and query conceptual information in a flexible and yet scalable manner because of the semantic heterogeneity of different peers. Hence, the discussion in Part I (Chap. 1 to 3) is based on RDF as an underlying representation paradigm. It answers questions about:

- How an appropriate query language for querying conceptual information may look (Chap. 1);
- How a traditional architecture allows for distributed query processing of RDF using centralized control (Chap. 2);
- How query processing of P2P-distributed RDF works given the information of where which kind of information may be found (Chap. 3).

The latter issue still abstracts from a concrete mechanism that determines which peer to query in the network. This issue constitutes a core aspect of semantic P2P systems to be considered next.

3.2 Querying the Network

The way the P2P network is organized and used to locate and access information is an important aspect of every P2P system. Daswani et al. [2] identify the following aspects with respect to the localization of data in the network.

Data Placement

The data placement aspect is about where the data is stored in the network. Two different strategies for data placement in the network can be identified: placement according to ownership and placement according to search strategy. In a Peer-to-Peer system it seems most natural to store information at the peer which is controlled by the information owner. And this is indeed the typical case. The advantage is that access and modification are under complete control of the owner. For example, if the owner wants to cease publishing of its resources, he can simply disconnect his peer from the network. In the owner-based placement approach the network is only used to increase access to the information. In the complementary model (see [1] for survey) peers do not only cooperate in searching information, but also in storing the information. Then the network as a whole is like a uniform facility to store and retrieve information. In this case, data is distributed over the peers so that it can be searched for in the most efficient manner, i.e. according to the search strategy implemented in the network. Thus, the network may be searched more efficiently, but the owner has less control and peers frequently joining or leaving the network may incur a lot of update traffic [5]. Both variants can be further improved in terms of efficiency by the introduction of additional caching and replication strategies. Note that while this improves the network retrieval performance, it may still further reduce the owner's control of information.

Topology and Routing

Of course, a computer has to be connected to a physical network (e.g. the Internet) to participate as peer in a logical Peer-to-Peer network. However, in the Peer-to-Peer network the peer forms logical connections to other peers which need not correspond to its physical network connections. This is why Peer-to-Peer networks are (a special kind of) overlay networks. The structure these overlay networks can adopt is called topology. We can distinguish two fundamentally different approaches to network topology: *structured networks* and *unstructured networks* (cf. [1]).

In structured networks, a regular structure is predetermined and the network is always maintaining this structure. Of course, if peers leave unexpectedly, the network structure becomes imperfect for a moment. But after a short while connections are readjusted to reach the desired structure again. Similarly, if new peers join, they are assigned a position in the network which does not violate the foreseen structure.

Unstructured networks follow a completely different organization principle. New peers initially select just some other peers to which they connect, either randomly or guided by simple heuristics (e.g. locality in the underlying physical network or similarity of the topics they are interested in). Thus, the topology does not take the form of a regular structure. If nodes leave the network, no specific reorganization activity is conducted. Structured and unstructured networks have complementary advantages and disadvantages. The predetermined structure allows for more efficient query distribution in a structured network, because each peer "knows" the network structure and can forward queries just in the right direction. But this only works if the data is distributed among the peers according to the anticipated search strategy. Also, it often requires the restriction of query complexity. In unstructured networks, peers do not know exactly in which direction to send a query. Therefore, requests have to be spread within the network to increase the probability of hitting the peer(s) having the requested resource, thus decreasing network efficiency. On the other hand, requests may come in more or less any form, as long as each peer is able to match its resources against the request. This tends to make unstructured networks more suitable for ontology-based approaches where support for complex queries is essential.

In each network, the connected computers do have different capabilities regarding processing power, storage, bandwidth, availability, etc. Thus, to treat all peers equally would result in overloading small peers while not exploiting the capabilities of the more powerful peers. To avoid this, so-called super-peer networks have been developed; where powerful and highly available peers form a network backbone to which all other peers connect. The super-peers become responsible for specific tasks like maintaining indexes, assigning peers to appropriate locations, etc. This approach is used in popular file sharing P2P networks as Kazaa or BitTorrent, but also in P2P networks for Semantic Web applications [7]. When ontologies are used to categorize information, this can be exploited in a super-peer network. Each super-peer becomes responsible for one or several ontology classes. Peers are clustered at these super-peers according to the classes of information they provide. Thus, an efficient structured network approach can be used to forward a query to the right super-peer, which distributes it to all relevant peers [4].

Part II: Querying the Network

In Part II, we consider both types of networks, structured and unstructured. In Chap. 4, the authors give a comprehensive framework to characterize structured networks that is able to elucidate some of their strengths and weaknesses wrt. efficiency of communication.

Unstructured networks did not seriously consider efficiency in the past. As a consequence, a peer had to send a query essentially to all his neighbors, these to their neighbors, and so on. This distribution process is called network flooding. Unfortunately this approach works for small networks only, and very soon leads to network congestion if the network grows larger. To reduce query distribution, peers can apply filter on their connections for each query and send the query only to relevant peers. The relevancy may be estimated either based on a content summary provided by each peer (see Chap. 6) or based on the results of previous query evaluations. A further optimization for peers is to not only filter, but also readjust their connections based on the request history. Here each peer tries to diminish its distance to the peers which have resources most frequently requested by this peer. Such networks are called short-cut networks, because they always try to short-cut request routes (see Chap. 5).

Interestingly, specific reconnection strategies can lead to the emergence of regular topologies, although not enforced by the network algorithms [8]. This is characteristic for self-organizing systems in other areas (like biology) too, and seems to be one promising middle way between pure structured and pure unstructured networks. Another middle way currently under investigation is the construction of an unstructured network layer for increasing flexibility above a structured network layer for managing efficient access (cf. [11]).

Further means to tailor semantic querying of the network may require adaptations motivated by specific applications. We consider two examples here: First, *personalization* (cf. Chap. 7) may adapt network structures to specific needs of individual peers rather than to a generic structure. Second, *publish/subscribe* mechanisms support continuous querying in order to observe the content available in the network without flooding the network (Chap. 8).

3.3 Integration Mechanism

In a distributed system it often cannot be guaranteed that the information provided by different sources is represented in the same way. This leads to the need of providing integration mechanisms able of transferring data between different representations. We can distinguish the following aspects of integration.

Mapping Representation

Mappings that explicitly specify the semantic relation between information objects in different sources are the basis for the integration of information from different sources. Normally, such mappings are not defined between individual data objects but rather between elements of the schema. Consequently, the nature of the mapping definitions strongly depend on the choice of a schema language. The richer the schema language, the more possibilities exist to clarify the relation between elements in the sources. However, both creation and use of mappings becomes more complex with the increasing expressiveness. There are a number of general properties mappings can have that influence their potential use for information integration:

- Mappings can relate single objects from the different information sources or connect multiple elements that are connected by operators to form complex expressions.
- Mappings can be undirected or directed and only state the relation from the point of view of one of the sources connected.
- Mappings can declaratively describe the relation between elements from different sources or consist of a procedural description of how to convert information from one source into the format of the other.
- Declarative mappings can be exact or contain some judgement of how correct the mapping reflects the real relation between the information sources.

In the context of P2P information sharing, the use of mappings is currently restricted to rather simple mappings. Most existing systems use simple equality or subsumption statements between schema elements. Approaches that use more complex mappings (in particular conjunctive queries) do not scale easily to a large number of sources. A prominent example is the Piazza approach (see Chap. 12).

Mapping Creation:

The creation of semantic mappings between different information sources is the crucial point of each integration approach. Existing work often assumes that mappings are known. It turns out, however, that the identification of semantic relationships between different information sources is a difficult problem. As a result, methods for finding semantic relations have become an important area of research. Existing methods can roughly be categorized into

- Manual approaches where only methodological guidelines for identifying mappings
- Semi-automatic approaches, where the system proposes or criticizes mappings and the user provides feedback for the method that is used in following iterations
- Automatic methods that try to find mappings without the intervention of the user at the price of possibly incorrect and incomplete mappings

The identification of semantically related elements in different information sources can be based on a number of different criteria found in the information sources to be compared. The most obvious one is to compare the names of schema elements. This kind of linguistic comparison is the basis of most approaches. On a higher level, the structure of the information can be used as a criterion (e.g. the attributes of a class). As a reaction to the known problems of name and structure based approaches in dealing with ambiguous terms, recent work focuses on matching approaches that do not only rely on the schema, but also take additional information into account. This additional information can either be the result of an analysis of instances of the schema or background knowledge about the semantic relations between terms taken from an ontology. In many cases, the availability of background knowledge is an important success factor for integration.

Integration Method

Once they have been created, mappings can be used in different ways to support the integration of information.[1] These different ways correspond to different degrees of independence of the integrated information sources. This also means that not all of the possible integration methods are suitable for Peer-to-Peer networks. The integration method that preserves the least independence of information sources is the approach of merging the representations into a single source based on the semantic relations found. This approach is used if a tight integration of sources is needed and is not suited for Peer-to-Peer information sharing solutions because it does not preserve the independence and autonomy of the sources. Another approach is to keep the schemas of the sources separate but to completely transform the data of one source into the format of the other to enable query processing over the content of both sources. This approach is less radical than the merging approach because it does not change the structure of the sources, but it also assumes a rather tight integration that is not desirable in a Peer-to-Peer setting. Besides this, the transformation approach is only feasible if there is a small number of target schemas the data has to be translated to. In a Peer-to-Peer system, however, there can be as many schemas as peers. For this reason, methods that do not require a transformation of the data are better suited. The most widely used approach in this context is query re-writing. Instead of transforming the data to be queried, these approaches transform query expressions received from external sources into the format used by the queried source using the mappings between the schemas. This approach still requires a transformation of data in order to make the result of the query compatible with the format of the querying sources, but the transformation is limited to the information that is really requested by the other source. In some situations, the nature of the application or the system does not even allow the transformation of query answers either because the mappings do not provide enough support for this task or because the owner does not allow a modification of the data. In this case, integration can also consist of a specialized representation of the content of the external source that relates it to the corresponding schema elements in the local source. This very weak integration approach can be accommodated by a visualization that shows the user the relation between the external data and the local schema.

Part III: Semantic Integration

In this part of the book, we deal mostly with rather simple mapping representations, which currently constitute the state-of-the-art in P2P research. At the same time the methods considered target multiple dimensions of difficulty, viz. pragmatics of ontology use, sloppiness of ontology mappings, scalability of mapping creation, functionality of mapping execution and evaluation of mapping quality by its use:

Chapter 9: Bouquet, Serafini and Zanobini target the mapping of concepts organized in taxonomies. In their approach they try to encounter the problem that the se-

---

[1] In traditional, practical approaches information integration mostly refers to approaches such as (or less sophisticated than) the ones from Chap. 2 and 3.

14 Heiner Stuckenschmidt, Frank van Harmelen, Wolf Siberski, Steffen Staab

mantics of an ontology must not be completely dissolved from the pragmatics of its use. Their method considers a situation that is frequently encountered for light-weight organizational structures, such as folder hierarchies. In such a situation, if "Italy" is a subterm of "Photos" and "Europe" is a subterm of "Photos" this is not meant to say that this conflicts with Italy being part of Europe, but rather that this occurrence of "Europe" (as a string) here is meant to refer to its pragmatic meaning, viz. "Europe with the exception of Italy".

Chapter 10: Aleksovski and ten Kate pursue an approach that builds on Chap. 9. However, they discuss the effect that in the real world labels do not come in a clean form and some degree of sloppiness actually helps to improve the performance of (semi-)automatic mapping creation between taxonomies of concepts.

Chapter 11: Ehrig and Staab tackle further dimensions of difficulty in creating ontology mappings. First, they include instance information as well as ontology relations into their account. Secondly, they consider the situation that two peers try to come to a terminological agreement. In practice, this may involve the automatic comparison of 10^5 concepts on each peer. In domains of such problem sizes, however, runtime matters. Their approach is therefore targeting a satisficing (from satisfying and sufficient; [12]) solution, which gives up on some accuracy in favor of improved runtime performance.

Chapter 12: Ives, Halevy, Mork and Tatarinov present their Piazza approach. Piazza pursues a functional approach to transform query expressions and thus to bridge between different semantic vocabularies.

Chapter 13: Aberer, Cudre-Mauroux and Hauswirth provide a mixed model of mapping creating and use, where the success of mapping creation is discovered by the use of mappings in a self-organizing manner.

3.4 Building and Maintaining Semantic P2P Applications

Intelligent systems that are built on Semantic Web and Peer-to-Peer applications exhibit a number of properties that make them *technologically suitable* for such tasks as intelligent information sharing or knowledge management.

However, one of the hard learned lessons of intelligent systems has been that their success depends only to a very limited extent on the technical properties of such a system. Rather what becomes a major issue is the *organizational dimension* of an intelligent system (cf. [9]) and the stakeholders of its ontology (cf. [3]) exert an overwhelming influence on how such a system must or must not be shaped to fulfill users needs.

Correspondingly, we here present three successful Semantic Web and Peer-to-Peer applications that make use of much of the technology presented in Chap. 1 to 18, but in addition take care of

- Users' interface needs,
- Their organizational interactions and limitations,
- The processes that make up their information sharing and knowledge management tasks.

Part IV: Methodology and Systems

At an abstract level the experiences from the case studies of these applications have been collected in two methodologies:

The **Hope** methodology considers the knowledge management task that needs to be solved and the organizational constraints under which it is placed (cf. Chap. 14); while

The **Diligent** methodology addresses the need for a *collaborative ontology engineering efforts* that must be met under real-world constraints, such as distributed expert groups, limited efforts of time and costs and user-initiated feedback to the ontology (cf. Chap. 15).

Finally, Chap. 16 to 18 present the concrete applications that have been built by their authors and tested in the field: KEx, Xarop and Bibster.

3.5 Other Issues

Data Publishing

Another relevant aspect of Peer-to-Peer data sharing systems is the way they support the publishing of data in the network. This aspect includes technical aspects as well as questions of privacy, security and trust. It is also tightly related to the integration aspects because the system might force the sources to adhere to a specific schema or provide integration methods that in turn have certain requirements with respect to the way the data is made available. Unfortunately, the aspect of data publishing has not really been discussed intensively in the literature on P2P information sharing. It seems to be widely regarded as a practical problem with less scientific implications. When we look at the other aspects discussed so far, however, we see that all of them are closely related to the data publishing mechanism. Issues like topology, data placement and data model are interdependent with this aspect.

Security

Security requirements vary widely dependent on the application. A simple file-sharing network doesn't need access control, etc. However, if information is to be shared in a restricted context — as often the case with knowledge management systems — then security is an important factor. To encrypt information in a P2P system without central key management, several algorithms have been devised. For example, the Secret Sharing Scheme (SHA, Schamir 1979) [10] allows to distribute data over peers so that it stays reproducible for the key owner even if a large percentage of the peers drop out. For access control, no pure P2P solution has been found yet. A pragmatic approach is to employ a hybrid approach where a central certification authority is responsible for key assignment, but the complete information management is done in the P2P system. Two applications presented in this book have taken security considerations seriously having adapted existing solutions to their application needs (see Chapters 16 and 17).

4 Conclusions

In this introduction we have sketched the two technologies that underly work in this book:

Semantic Web

&

Peer-to-Peer

We have surveyed what makes each of the two technologies attractive to use *on their own* and we have described their potential for information sharing and knowledge management when they are *joined together*. Along this way we have seen a number of aspects, most of which are discussed by the following contributions to this book, some of which we mostly had to ignore because of their intrinsic complexity (e.g. security) and some of which we simply do not know how to respond to, because they require more research (e.g. data publishing).

Even when just skimming over the contributions in this book the reader will find out about the tremendous potential that the joint technologies of Semantic Web and Peer-to-Peer have to offer. Furthermore, she will find out that this potential does not lie in the distant future, but is already alive in concrete applications and waiting to get out into the full wide open. It is the objective of this book that by working through most of these aspects it becomes evident that practical methods and methodologies are available and ready for take-up — even though the topic put forward sufficient research challenges for many years to come.

References

[1] S. Androutsellis-Theotokis and D. Spinellis. A survey of peer-to-peer content distribution technologies. *ACM Comput. Surv.*, 36(4):335–371, 2004.

[2] N. Daswania, H. Garcia-Molina, and B. Yang. Open problems in data sharing peer-to-peer systems. In *Proceedings of the 9th International Conference on Database Theory (ICDT)*, Siena, Italy, 2003.

[3] A. Gomez-Perez, M. Fernandez-Lopez, and O. Corcho. *Ontological Engineering with examples from the areas of Knowledge Management, e-Commerce and the Semantic Web*. Springer, 2004.

[4] A. Loeser, M. Wolpers, W. Siberski, and W. Nejdl. Semantic overlay clusters within super-peer networks. In *Proceedings of the International Workshop on Databases, Information Systems and Peer-to-Peer Computing*, Berlin, Germany, 2003.

[5] B. Loo, J. Hellerstein, R. Huebsch, S. Shenker, and I. Stoica. Enhancing p2p file-sharing with an internet-scale query processor. In *Proc. of Int. Conf. on Very Large Databases (VLDB), Toronto, 2004*, 2004.

[6] W. Nejdl, W. Siberski, and M. Sintek. Design issues and challenges for rdf- and schema-based peer-to-peer systems. *SIGMOD Record*, September, 2003.

[7] W. Nejdl, M. Wolpers, W. Siberski, C. Schmitz, M. Schlosser, I. Brunkhorst, and A. Loeser. Super-peer-based routing strategies for rdf-based peer-to-peer networks. *Web Semantics*, 1(2):137–240, 2004.

[8] C. Schmitz. Self-organization of a small world by topic. In *Proceedings of the 1st International Workshop on Peer-to-Peer Knowledge Management*, Boston, MA, 2004.

[9] G. Schreiber et al. *Knowledge Engineering and Management — The CommonKADS Methodology*. The MIT Press, Cambridge, Massachusetts; London, England, 1999.

[10] A. Shamir. How to share a secret. *Communications of the ACM*, 22:612–613, 1979.

[11] R. Siebes. pnear: combining content clustering and distributed hash tables. In *The Second International Workshop on to-Peer Knowledge Management (P2PKM05)*, 2005. www.p2pkm.org.

[12] Herbert A. Simon. *Models of Man*. John Wiley, 1957.

Part I

Data Storage and Access

Overview: Data Storage and Access

Heiner Stuckenschmidt

As discussed in the introduction, technologies for storing and accessing data is the basic aspect of semantics-based P2P systems. While data access is often limited to key-based or keyword based queries in traditional P2P solutions, a distinguishing feature of the kind of systems discussed in this book is that they provide more sophisticated ways of storing and accessing data. These are based on the use of Semantic Web technologies in terms of languages for representing and querying semi-structured data. The focus of this book is on the use of RDF for data storage and access.

It is quite obvious that there are two sides to the use of RDF: the RDF model itself and its use for representing and storing complex information content, and the provision of a language for querying and transforming RDF data. The RDF model itself has been standardized by the W3C and is now a commonly agreed standard; we therefore do not discuss its use in more detail. Specific ways of using RDF to represent different aspects of information in P2P systems will be discussed in the individual chapters. For a general introduction the reader is referred to the official W3C documents. With respect to query languages for RDF data the situation is different. Here, no commonly agreed standard has been defined yet[1]. This leaves space for a detailed discussion of the requirements for RDF query languages in the context of P2P systems. Chapter 1 addresses the issue of querying RDF data. The chapter discusses general requirements of a query language for RDF and presents the SeRQL langauge which has successfully been used in different P2P settings many of which are reported in later chapters.

Of course the definition of an appropriate query language is only one aspect of data access relevant for semantics-based P2P systems. In fact, the query language requirements do not differ that much from centralized Semantic Web systems. The distinguishing aspect of the approaches described in this book is the system architecture, which is characterized by the lack of central control and dynamic communication. These characteristics mainly effect the query processing model needed to

---

[1] At the time of creation of most chapters, the activities of the W3C Data access working group had not yet started

ensure completeness of results and efficiency of the process. With respect to their characteristics P2P systems are an extreme case. In the area of databases and information systems distributed architectures with less extreme views on decentralization have been investigated. Chapter 2 discusses some of these architectures from an RDF perspective thereby bridging the gap between existing centralized approaches and P2P architectures that are the focus of this book. In particular, the chapter identifies and discusses advantages and disadvantages of different architectures and provides additional arguments for the benefits of completely decentralized approaches.

The benefits of completely decentralized approaches in terms of flexibility and robustness come at a price: Generating a query plan that guarantees completeness and efficient execution becomes a difficult problem. In fact, many existing systems sacrifice completeness for the sake of efficiency. The main reason for the difficulty of query planning is the lack centrally available index structures that can be used to determine an optimal plan locally and then execute it. In a decentralized setting, this central index has to be replaced by something else. One opinion is the use of so-called superpeers that provide central index structures at least for a group of peers in the network. Other options are the use of overlay networks that impose an efficient search structure on top of the actual physical implementation of the system. Chapter 3 describes an approach for query planning and execution in P2P networks based on the use of an overlay network. The approach is a good example of the use of RDF in P2P systems, because the system does not only use RDF for presenting the data to be accessed, but also uses the schema of the RDF data as semantic overlay network. Peers are located in this overlay network based on the part of the schema they provide information about.

In summary, this part of the book discusses some foundational aspects of data access in semantics-based P2P systems in particular RDF query languages, distributed architectures and their impact on data access strategies as well as the use of RDF schema information to support query planning and execution in P2P systems.

1

An RDF Query and Transformation Language

Jeen Broekstra[1,2], Arjohn Kampman[2]

[1] Vrije Universiteit Amsterdam, The Netherlands, jbroeks@cs.vu.nl
[2] Aduna BV, Amersfoort, The Netherlands,
  {jeen.broekstra,arjohn.kampman}@aduna.biz

Summary. RDF Query Language proposals are numerous. However, the most prominent proposals are query languages that were conceived as first generation tryouts of RDF querying, with little or no RDF-specific implementation and use experience to guide design, and based on an ever changing set of syntactical and semantic specifications.

In this chapter, we introduce a set of general requirements for an RDF query language. This set is compiled from discussions between RDF implementors, our own experience and user feedback that we received on our work in Sesame, as well as general principles of query language design. We go on to show how we have compiled these requirements into designing the SeRQL query language, and conclude that SeRQL can be considered a real second generation RDF querying and transformation language.

1.1 Introduction

RDF Query Language proposals are numerous. However, the most prominent proposals are query languages that were conceived as first generation tryouts of RDF querying, with little or no RDF-specific implementation and use experience to guide design, and based on an ever-changing set of syntactical and semantic specifications.

Now that the RDF specifications have reached the status of W3C Recommendation and are therefore less likely to change significantly, it is the right time to reevaluate the design of the current set of query languages.

In this chapter, we introduce the new RDF query language SeRQL. SeRQL was designed using experiences gained from design and implementation of other query languages and from feedback received from users and developers of these query languages and the systems in which they were implemented, such as Sesame [6].

SeRQL's aim is to reconcile ideas from existing proposals (most prominently RQL [12], Squish/RDQL [13, 7, 15], N-Triples [8] and N3 [3]) into a proposal that satisfies a list of key requirements, and thus offer an RDF query language that is powerful, easy to use and adresses practical problems one encounters when querying RDF.

This paper is organized as follows: in Sect. 1.2, we present a list of principles and requirements to which an RDF query language should conform. In Sect. 1.3, we introduce the syntax and design of the SeRQL query language. In Sect. 1.4, we define a formal interpretation of SeRQL. In Sect. 1.5, we discuss related work. Finally, we present our conclusions in Sect. 1.6.

1.2 Query Language requirements

In the previous section, we have introduced the basic syntax of SeRQL. In this section, we will look at some requirements that an RDF query language should fullfill and we will give examples of how SeRQL supports these requirements.

In [14], Alberto Reggiori and Andy Seaborne have collected a number of use cases and examples for RDF queries. From this report, we can distill several general requirements for RDF queries, most notably expressivity requirements. Apart from these requirements, several principles for query languages in general can be taken into account (see [1]), such as compositionality, and data model awareness.

From these sources and our experience in implementing and using first generation RDF query languages such as RQL and RDQL, we have composed a list of key requirements for RDF querying. In the next sections, we briefly discuss these requirements and show how SeRQL aims to fullfill them.

In [1], a list of requirements for query languages that deal with semistructured data is presented. We highlight a few of these requirements, and we briefly discuss each requirement and how it can be applied to query languages in general and RDF query languages in particular.

1.2.1 Expressive power

In [1] it is noted that the notion of expressive power is ill-defined in the context of semistructured data models. However, we can write down an informal list of the kinds of operations that a query language should express.

Expressiveness requirements that have come up often in dialogue with RDF developers (see also [14]) and users of the Sesame system include:

1. A convenient yet powerful path expression syntax for navigating the RDF graph.
2. Functionality for navigating the class/property hierarchy.
3. Functionality for querying reified statements.
4. Value comparison and datatype support.
5. Functionality to deal with *optional* values; properties which may or may not be present in the data for a particular resource.

Of course, this list is far from exhaustive, but these requirements illustrate practical applications of an RDF query language.

1.2.2 Schema awareness

Query languages should be schema aware. When structure is defined or inferred, a query language should be capable of exploiting the schema for type checking, optimization, and entailment.

This requirement is closely tied with the requirement for formal semantics and for expressive power. In the case of RDF, it means that the query language should be aware of the semantics for RDF and RDF Schema as they are specified by the RDF model theory.

1.2.3 Program manipulation

It is important that the query language is simple enough to allow program-generated queries. This means that it is often preferable to use a query language syntax that is easy to parse and decompose, rather than try and make it as "user-friendly" as possible (at the risk of making it ambiguous and thus harder to process). Nevertheless, there is a balance to be obtained here: a query language that is unintelligable to humans will not find acceptance, no matter how well it can be processed automatically.

Considerations to take into account with respect to this requirement include simplicity of structure and avoiding redundancy, while keeping a balance with convenience and readability.

1.2.4 Compositionality

This requirement states that the output of a query can be used as the input of another query. This is useful in situations where one wants to decompose large queries into smaller ones, or when one wants to execute several queries in series, using the output of the first as the input for the second, etc. A query language with this property will also be able to facilitate view definitions.

In the case of an RDF query language, compositionality obviously means that the result of a query should be representable as an RDF graph. The effect of this is that the query language functions as a *transformation language* on RDF graphs.

1.2.5 Semantics

Precise formal semantics of a query language are important, because without these query transformations and optimizations are virtually impossible. Moreover, formal descriptions avoid ambiguity and thus help prevent misunderstanding and different implementations of the same language interpreting queries differently.

In the case of an RDF query language, such a formal description can be achieved by providing a mapping to the formal model of RDF itself, the *RDF model theory* as specified in [10].

1.3 The Syntax of SeRQL

SeRQL (Sesame RDF Query Language, proncounced "circle") is a new RDF/RDFS
query language that was developed to address practical requirements from the
Sesame user community[1] that were not sufficiently met by other query languages.
SeRQL combines the best features of other languages and adds some of its own.

In the rest of this section, we will give an overview of the basic syntax of SeRQL.
The overview of the SeRQL language given here only covers enough for the purposes
of this paper; it is not intended to be complete. A full manual for writing SeRQL
queries that covers the complete language is available on the Web [5].

1.3.1 Path Expressions

One of the most prominent parts of SeRQL are path expressions. Path expressions
are expressions that match specific paths through an RDF graph. Most current RDF
query languages allow you to define path expressions of length 1, which can be used
to find (combinations of) triples in an RDF graph. SeRQL, like RQL, allows to define
path expressions of arbitrary length.

SeRQL uses a path expression syntax that is similar to the syntax used in RQL,
and is based on the graph nature of RDF: the path is expressed as a collection of
nodes and edges, where each node is denoted by surrounding curly brackets:

```
{node} edge {node} edge {node}
```

As an example, suppose we want to query an RDF graph for persons that work
for an IT Company. A path expression to express this could look like:

```
{Person} foo:worksFor {Company} rdf:type {foo:ITCompany}
```

Notice that resource URIs and variables are intermixed to provide a template
which is matched against the RDF graph.

Multiple path expressions can be comma-seperated. For example, we can split up
the above path expression into two simpler ones:

```
{Person} foo:worksFor {Company},
{Company} rdf:type {foo:ITCompany}
```

Notice that SeRQL allows variable repetition for node (or edge) unification.

Extended Path Expressions

As we have just seen, SeRQL has a convenient syntax for basic path expressions,
which can be composed into path expressions of arbitrary length.

Every path in an RDF graph can be expressed using these basic path expressions.
However, several extended constructions are supported to allow for more convenient
expressions of paths.

In situations where one wants to query for two or more triples with identical
subject and predicate, the subject and predicate do not have to be repeated. Instead,
a *multi-value node* can be used:

---

[1] See http://www.openrdf.org/

```
{subj1} pred1 {obj1, obj2, obj3}
```

This path expression is equivalent to:

```
{subj1} pred1 {obj1},
{subj1} pred1 {obj2},
{subj1} pred1 {obj3}
```

SeRQL also introduces the notion of *branched path expressions*. This is a construction that is useful when multiple properties that emanate from a single node are queried. The semi-column is used to denote a branch:

```
{subj1} pred1 {obj1};
        pred2 {obj2}
```

which is equivalent to:

```
{subj1} pred1 {obj1},
{subj1} pred2 {obj2}
```

Reification

RDF allows for a syntactic construction known as *reification*, where the subject or object of a statement is itself a statement. Since it is a syntactic construction it can be expressed using basic path expression syntax, as follows:

```
{statement1} rdf:type {rdf:Statement},
{statement1} rdf:subject {subj1},
{statement1} rdf:predicate {pred1},
{statement1} rdf:object {obj1},
{statement1} pred2 {obj2}
```

However, this is a cumbersome way of dealing with reification. SeRQL introduces a shorthand notation for reified statements that allows one to treat reified statements as actual statements instead of the complex syntactic structure shown above. In this notation, the above reified statement would become:

```
{{subj1} pred1 {obj1}} pred2 {obj2}
```

Class and Property Hierarchies

In the previous section we have shown how the RDF graph can be navigated through path expressions. The same principle can be applied to navigation of class and property hierarchies, since these are, of course, also graphs.

For example, to retrieve the subclasses of a particular class my:class1:

```
{subclass} rdfs:subClassOf {my:class1}
```

Or, to retrieve all instances of class my:class1:

```
{instance} rdf:type {my:class1}
```

However, an RDF class/property hierarchy encapsulates notions such as inheritance, which must be taken into account. Therefore, SeRQL applies the RDF Schema semantics when this is required. In the case of the property rdfs:subClassOf, for example, SeRQL will return all such relations, including the ones that are entailed according to the model theory.

Additionally, SeRQL support a numer of *built-ins* for expressing queries about the class hierarchy. These built-ins are "virtual properties", that is, they are used as normal properties in path expressions, but this property is not expected to actually occur in the RDF graph. Instead, the meaning of the property is pre-defined in terms of other properties.

SeRQL   supports   four   built-ins: serql:directSubClassOf, serql:directSubPropertyOf and serql:directType.

As an example, the built-in serql:directSubClassOf maps to rdfs:subClassOf edges in the graph, but only those for which the following conditions hold:

1. The nodes connected by the edge are not the same node.
2. The path between the two nodes formed by this edge is the *only* path between these nodes consisting exclusively of rdfs:subClassOf edges.

In other words: a class A is a direct subclass of a class B if A and B are not equal and there is no class C that is a subclass of B and a superclass of A.

It is important to note that these built-ins are not merely syntax shortcuts, but actually provide additional expressivity: the notion of direct subclass/property/instance can not be expressed using normal path expressions and boolean constraints only.

Optional Matches

The path expressions and boolean constraints introduced sofar provide the means to specify a template that *must* match the RDF graph in order to return results. However, since the RDF data model is in its very nature weakly structured (or *semi-structured*), it is important that an RDF query language has the means to deal with irregularities.

In contrast to query languages for strongly structured data models, such as SQL [11], RDF query languages must be able to cope with the possibility that a given value may or may not be present. In SeRQL, such values are called *optional matches*. The query language facilitates optional matches by introducing a square-bracket notation that encloses the optional part of a given path expression.

Consider an RDF graph that contains information about people that have names, ages, and optionally e-mail addresses, that is, for some people the e-mail address is known, but for others, it is not. This is a situation that is likely to be very common in RDF data. A logical query on this data is a query that yields all names, ages and, when available, e-mail addresses of people. A path expression to retrieve these values would look like this:

```
{Person} person:name {Name};
         person:age  {Age};
         person:email {EmailAddress}
```

However, using normal path expressions like in the query above, people without e-mail address will not be matched by the template specified by this path expression, and their names and ages will not be returned by the query.

With optional path expressions, one can indicate that a specific (part of a) path expression is optional. This is done using square brackets, i.e.:

```
{Person} person:name {Name};
         person:age  {Age};
         [person:email {EmailAddress}]
```

In contrast to the first path expression, this expression will also match with people without an e-mail address. For these people, the variable `EmailAddress` will not be assigned a value.

Optional path expressions can also be nested. This is useful in situations where the existence of a specific path is dependent on the existence of another path. For example, the following path expression queries for the titles of all known documents and, if the author of the document is known, the name of the author (if it is known) and his e-mail address (if it is known):

```
{Document} foo:title {Title};
           [foo:author {Author} [foo:name {Name}];
                                 [foo:email {Email}]]
```

There are a few restrictions on the use of variables in optional path expressions. Most importantly, two optional path expressions that are in parallel to each other (that is, one is not nested within the other) may only have a shared variable if that variable is constrained to a value *outside* either of the optional expressions. For example, the optional path expressions `foo:name {Name}` and `foo:email {Email}` share the subject-variable `Author`. This is allowed only because this variable is constrained by the path expression `foo:author {Author}`, that is, outside the two parallel optional path expressions.

The reason for this restriction becomes apparent when we consider the following example query[1]:

```
select *
from [{<x>} <p> {a}], [{<x>} <q> {a}]
```

In this example, the variable a is shared between two parallel optional expressions, but it is not otherwise constrained. Now, we further assume that the RDF graph contains the following two RDF statements:

```
<x> <p> <y> .
<x> <q> <z> .
```

In this setting, the variable a can be unified with the value `<y>` or with `<z>`, but not both at the same time. The query causes an ambiguity: depending on the order in which the optional expressions are evaluated, the variable gets assigned a different value. Since such order dependency is an undesirable feature in a declarative language, we restrict the language to prevent this.

---

[1] Example by Andy Seaborne and Jeremy Carrol, see http://lists.w3.org/Archives/Public/www-rdf-interest/2003Nov/0076.html

1.3.2 Filters and operators

In the preceding sections we have introduced several syntax components of SeRQL. Full queries are built using these components, and using an RQL-style `select-from-where` (or `construct-from-where`) filter. Both filters additionally support a `using namespace` clause.

Queries specified using the `select-from-where` filter return a table of values, or a set of variable-value bindings. Queries using the `construct-from-where` filter return a true RDF graph, which can be a subgraph of the graph being queried, or a graph containing information that is derived from it.

The select and construct clauses

The first clause (i.e. `select` or `construct`) determines what is done with the results that are found. In a `select` clause, one can specify which variable values should be returned and in what order, by means of a comma-seperated list of variables. Optionally, it is possible to use a `*` instead of such a list to indicate that all variables that are used should be returned, in the order in which they appear in the query.

For example, the following query retrieves all classes:

```
select C
from  {C} rdf:type {rdfs:Class}
```

In a `construct` clause, one can specify which triples should be returned. Construct queries, in their simplest form, simply return the subgraph that is matched by the template specified in the `from` and `where` clauses. The result is returned as the set of triples that make up the subgraph. For example:

```
construct *
from {SUB} rdfs:subClassOf {SUPER}
```

This query extracts all triples with a `rdfs:subClassOf` predicate from an RDF graph.

However, construct queries can also be used to do `graph transformations` or to specify simple rules. Graph transformation is a powerful tool in application scenarios where mappings between different vocabularies need to be defined.

As an example, consider the following construct query:

```
construct {Parent} foo:hasChild {Child}
from {Child} foo:hasParent {Parent}
```

This query can be interpreted as a rule that specifies the inverse of the `hasParent` relation. More generally, it specifies a graph transformation: the original graph may not know the `hasChild` relation, but the result of the query is a graph that contains `hasChild` relations between parents and children. The construct clause allows the introduction of new vocabulary, so this query will succeed even if the relation `foo:hasChild` is not present in the original RDF graph.

The from clause

The from clause always contains path expressions. It defines the paths in an RDF graph that are relevant to the query and binds variables to values.

The where clause

The where clause is optional and can contain additional boolean constraints on the values in the path expressions. These are constraints on the nodes and edges of the paths, which cannot always be expressed in the path expressions themselves.

SeRQL contains a set of operators for comparing variables and values that can be used as boolean constraints, including (sub)string comparison, datatyped numerical comparison and a number of boolean functions.

As an example, the following query uses a datatyped comparison to select countries with a population of less than 1 million.

```
SELECT Country
FROM {Country} foo:population {Population}
WHERE Population < "1000000"^^xsd:positiveInteger
```

For a full overview of the available operators and functions, see the SeRQL user manual [5].

The using namespace clause

The using namespace clause is also optional and it can contain namespace declarations; these are the mappings from prefixes to namespaces for use in combination with abbreviated URIs.

1.4 Formal Interpretation of SeRQL

1.4.1 Mapping Basic Path Expressions to Sets

The RDF Semantics W3C specification [10] specifies a model theoretical semantics for RDF and RDF Schema. In this section, we will use this model theory to specify a formal interpretation of SeRQL query constructs.

Without repeating here the entire model theory, we briefly summarize a couple of its notions for reference:

- The sets IR, IP, IC are sets of resources, properties, and classes, respectively. LV is a distinguished subset of IR and is defined as the set of literals.
- $IEXT$ is defined as a mapping from IP to the powerset of $IR \times IR$. Given $p \in IP$, $IEXT(I(p))$ is the set of pairs $\langle x, y \rangle | x, y \in IR$ for which the relation p holds, that is, for which $\langle x, p, y \rangle$ is a statement in the RDF graph.

For an *RDF interpretation*, the following semantic condition holds:[1]

---

[1] Other conditions also hold, see [10], but these are not relevant for this discussion

- $x \in IP$ if and only if $\langle x, I(\texttt{rdf} : \texttt{Property}) \rangle \in IEXT(I(\texttt{rdf} : \texttt{type}))$

Additionally, we define υ as a "null" value, that is $I(x) = \upsilon$ if no value is assigned to x in the current interpretation. We will first characterize SeRQL in terms of RDF only, i.e. give an RDF interpretation. See Table 1.1.

Table 1.1. RDF interpretation of basic path expressions

{x} p {y}	$\{\langle x, p, y \rangle \mid \langle x, y \rangle \in IEXT(I(p))\}$
{x} p {y}; q {z}	$\{\langle x, p, y \rangle \mid \langle x, y \rangle \in IEXT(I(p))\} \cup$ $\{\langle x', q, z \rangle \mid \langle x', z \rangle \in IEXT(I(q))\} \wedge x = x'$
{x} p {y,z}	$\{\langle x, p, y \rangle \mid \langle x, y \rangle \in IEXT(I(p))\} \cup$ $\{\langle x', p', z \rangle \mid \langle x', z \rangle \in IEXT(I(p'))\} \wedge x = x' \wedge p = p'$
[{x} p {y}]	$\{\langle x, p, y \rangle\}$ for which, depending on which variables are undefined, the following conditions hold: case 1: $I(x), I(p), I(y) \neq \upsilon$: $\quad \langle x, y \rangle \in IEXT(I(p))$ case 2: $I(x) = \upsilon, I(p), I(y) \neq \upsilon$: $\quad \nexists x' \mid \langle x', y \rangle \in IEXT(I(p))$ case 3: $I(x), I(p) = \upsilon, I(y) \neq \upsilon$: $\quad \exists p' \mid \langle x', y \rangle \in IEXT(I(p'))$ case 4: $I(x), I(y) = \upsilon, I(p) \neq \upsilon$: $\quad IEXT(I(p)) = \emptyset$ case 5: $I(p) = \upsilon, I(x), I(y) \neq \upsilon$: $\quad \nexists p' \mid \langle x, y \rangle \in IEXT(I(p'))$ case 6: $I(p), I(y) = \upsilon, I(x) \neq \upsilon$: $\quad \nexists p' \mid \langle x, y' \rangle \in IEXT(I(p'))$ case 7: $I(y) = \upsilon, I(x), I(p) \neq \upsilon$: $\quad \nexists y' \mid \langle x, y' \rangle \in IEXT(I(p))$

An extended interpretation takes into account RDF Schema semantics. For an *RDFS interpretation* the following semantic conditions hold in addition to those specified by an RDF interpretation (cf. [10]):

- $x \in ICEXT(y)$ if and only if $\langle x, y \rangle \in IEXT(I(\texttt{rdf} : \texttt{type}))$
- $IC = ICEXT(I(\texttt{rdfs} : \texttt{Class}))$
- $IR = ICEXT(I(\texttt{rdfs} : \texttt{Resource}))$
- $LV = ICEXT(I(\texttt{rdfs} : \texttt{Literal}))$
- if $\langle x, y \rangle \in IEXT(I(\texttt{rdfs} : \texttt{domain}))$ and $\langle u, v \rangle \in IEXT(x)$ then $u \in ICEXT(y)$
- if $\langle x, y \rangle \in IEXT(I(\texttt{rdfs} : \texttt{range}))$ and $\langle u, v \rangle \in IEXT(x)$ then $v \in ICEXT(y)$
- $IEXT(I(\texttt{rdfs} : \texttt{subPropertyOf}))$ is transitive and reflexive on IP
- if $\langle x, y \rangle \in IEXT(I(\texttt{rdfs} : \texttt{subPropertyOf}))$ then $x, y \in IP$ and $IEXT(x) \subset IEXT(y)$
- if $x \in IC$ then $\langle x, IR \rangle \in IEXT(I\texttt{rdfs} : \texttt{subClassOf})$

- $IEXT(I(\texttt{rdfs}:\texttt{subClassOf}))$ is transitive and reflexive on IC
- if $\langle x,y\rangle \in IEXT(I(\texttt{rdfs}:\texttt{subClassOf}))$ then $x,y \in IC$ and $IEXT(x) \subset IEXT(y)$
- if $x \in ICEXT(I(\texttt{rdfs}:\texttt{ContainerMembershipProperty}))$
  then $\langle x, I(\texttt{rdfs}:\texttt{member})\rangle \in IEXT(I(\texttt{rdfs}:\texttt{subPropertyOf}))$
- if $x \in ICEXT(I(\texttt{rdfs}:\texttt{Datatype}))$ and $y \in ICEXT(x)$
  then $\langle y, I(\texttt{rdfs}:\texttt{Literal})\rangle \in IEXT(I(\texttt{rdf}:\texttt{type}))$

In Table 1.2, the extensions of the interpretations of SeRQL path expressions and functions that the RDFS semantics add are shown.

At first glance, the added interpretations for properties such as rdf:type may seem redundant, in light of the fact that the case is already covered by the general path expression {x} p {y}. However, these mappings are added to make it explicit that these properties use an *RDFS* interpretation, that is, the semantic conditions regarding attributes like reflexivityäand transitivity of these particular properties are observed.

1.4.2 Functions

Datatypes, operators and functions are strongly interdependent, and to interpret function behaviour in SeRQL formally, we need to summarize how RDF itself handles datatypes. The following is summarized from [10].

RDF provides for the use of externally defined datatypes identified by a particular URI reference. In the interests of generality, RDF imposes minimal conditions on a datatype.

The semantics for datatypes as specified by the model theory is minimal. It makes no provision for associating a datatype with a property so that it applies to all values of the property, and does not provide any way of explicitly asserting that a blank node denotes a particular datatype value.

Formally, a datatype d is defined by three items:

1. A non-empty set of character strings called the lexical space of d;
2. A non-empty set called the value space of d;
3. A mapping from the lexical space of d to the value space of d, called the lexical-to-value mapping of d.

The lexical-to-value mapping of a datatype d is written as $L2V(d)$.

In stating the semantics we assume that interpretations are relativized to a particular set of datatypes each of which is identified by a URI reference.

Formally, let D be a set of pairs consisting of a URI reference and a datatype such that no URI reference appears twice in the set, so that D can be regarded as a function from a set of URI references to a set of datatypes: call this a datatype map. (The particular URI references must be mentioned explicitly in order to ensure that interpretations conform to any naming conventions imposed by the external authority responsible for defining the datatypes.) Every datatype map is understood to contain $\langle rdf:XMLLiteral, x\rangle$ where x is the built-in XML Literal datatype.

Table 1.2. RDFS interpretation of basic path expressions

Path expression	Interpretation
{x} rdf:type {y}	$\{(x,y) \mid x \in ICEXT(y)\}$
{x} serql:directType {y}	$\{(x,y) \mid x \in ICEXT(y) \wedge (\nexists z \mid z \neq y \wedge x \in ICEXT(z) \wedge (z,y) \in IEXT(I(\texttt{rdfs:subClassOf})))\}$
{x} rdfs:subClassOf {y}	$\{(x,y) \mid (x,y) \in IEXT(I(\texttt{rdfs:subClassOf}))\}$
{x} serql:directSubClassOf {y}	$\{(x,y) \mid x \neq y \wedge (x,y) \in IEXT(I(\texttt{rdfs:subClassOf})) \wedge (\nexists z \mid x \neq z \neq y \wedge (x,z),(z,y) \in IEXT(I(\texttt{rdfs:subClassOf})))\}$
{p} rdfs:subPropertyOf {q}	$\{(p,q) \mid (p,q) \in IEXT(I(\texttt{rdfs:subPropertyOf}))\}$
{p} serql:directSubPropertyOf {q}	$\{(p,q) \mid p \neq q \wedge (p,q) \in IEXT(I(\texttt{rdfs:subPropertyOf})) \wedge (\nexists r \mid p \neq r \neq q \wedge (p,r),(r,q) \in IEXT(I(\texttt{rdfs:subPropertyOf})))\}$

SeRQL supports a set of functions and operators. These functions and operators can be used as part of the boolean constraints in the where-clause. Since these functions and operators deal with literal values that can be typed, we use the notion of an *XSD-interpretation* of a vocabulary V as specified in the RDF Semantics. An XSD-interpretation of a vocabulary V is an RDFS-interpretation of V, for which the following additional constraints hold (see [10] for a detailed explanation):

- D contains contains the set of all pairs of the form $\langle http : //www.w3.org/2001/XMLSchema\#sss, sss\rangle$, where sss is a built-in datatype named sss in XML Schema Part 2: Datatypes [4], and listed in [10], Sect. 5.1.
- If $\langle a, x\rangle \in D$ then $I(a) = x$.
- If $\langle a, x\rangle \in D$ then $ICEXT(x)$ is the value space of x and is a subset of LV.
- If $\langle a, x\rangle \in D$ then for any typed literal "sss"^^ddd in V with $I(ddd) = x$, if sss is in the lexical space of x then $IL("sss"^\wedge ddd) = L2V(x)(sss)$, otherwise $IL("sss"^\wedge ddd) \notin V$
- If $\langle a, x\rangle \in D$ then $I(a) \in ICEXT(I(rdfs : Datatype))$

We provide a mapping for SeRQL functions in table 1.3.

Table 1.3. interpretation of SeRQL functions

isResource(r)	true if $I(r) \in IR$; false otherwise
isLiteral(l)	true if $I(l) \in LV$; false otherwise
label("sss")	$\{sss \mid I("sss") \in LV\}$
label("sss"@lll)	$\{sss \mid I("sss"@lll) \in LV\}$
label("sss"^^ddd)	$\{sss \mid I("sss"^\wedge ddd) \in LV\}$
datatype("sss"^^ddd)	$\{ddd \mid I("sss"^\wedge ddd) \in LV\}$
language("sss"@lll)	$\{lll \mid I("sss"@lll) \in LV\}$

1.4.3 Reducing Composed Expressions

In the previous sections we have seen how basic SeRQL expressions are formally interpreted. In this section, we show how composed path expressions can be reduced to semantically equivalent sets of basic path expressions and boolean constraints by means of a simple substitution.

Definition 1. *A path expression is of the form $\langle n_0, e_0, n_1, e_1, n_2, ...e_{i-1}, n_i\rangle$, where i is the length of the path expression, and where $n_0..n_i$ are nodes in the RDF graph and $e_0..e_{i-1}$ are directed edges. Each directed edge e_k has as source node n_k and as target node n_{k+1}.*

Definition 2. *A basic path expression is a path expression of length 1.*

As an example, the SeRQL construction $\{x\}$ p $\{y\}$ corresponds to the general form $\langle n_0, e_0, n_1\rangle$, and is a basic path expression.

A path expression of length $i > 1$ can be reduced to two path expression of, one of length $i - 1$ and one of length 1, as shown in table 1.4.

By recursively applying these substitutions to any path expression of length > 1 it is possible to reduce an arbitrary length composed path expression to a set of basic path expressions and boolean constraints. Thus, any complex SeRQL query can be

Table 1.4. Breaking up composed path expressions

Composed expression	Substituted expressions	Constraints
$\langle n_0, e_0, n_1, ..., n_{i-1}, e_{i-1}, n_i \rangle$	$\langle n_0, e_0, n_1, ..., n_{i-2}, e_{i-2}, n_{i-1} \rangle$, $\langle n'_{i-1}, e_{i-1}, n_i \rangle$	$n_{i-1} = n'_{i-1}$
$\langle n_0, e_0, n_1, e_1, n_2 \rangle$	$\langle n_0, e_0, n_1 \rangle$, $\langle n'_1, e_1, n_2 \rangle$	$n_1 = n'_1$

normalized to a form consisting only of a set of basic path expressions and boolean constraints.

Branching path expressions, multi-valued node expressions and path expressions involving reification can also always be reduced to a set of basic expressions. We will prove this for branching path expressions, the proofs for the other two forms is analogous.

Theorem 1. *Any branching path expression p of the form* {x} p {y}; q {z} *can be reduced to a semantically equivalent set of basic path expressions.*

Proof. By definition, the branching expression is syntactically equivalent to the two basic expressions {x} p {y}, {x} q {z} (see section 1.3.1). The first of these is defined as $\{\langle x, p, y \rangle | \langle x, y \rangle \in IEXT(I(p))\}$ (table 1.1). The second is defined as $\{\langle x, q, z \rangle | \langle x, z \rangle \in IEXT(I(q))\}$. The union of these two sets can be expressed as $\{\langle x, p, y \rangle | \langle x, y \rangle \in IEXT(I(p))\} \cup \{\langle x', q, z \rangle | \langle x', z \rangle \in IEXT(I(q))\} \wedge x = x'$, which is by definition (see Table 1.1) equivalent to the definition of the branching path expression.

1.5 Related work

RDQL [15] is an RDF query language that has been implemented in several system, including the Jena Toolkit [7] and Sesame [6]. It offers many attractive qualities such as an easy to use syntax format. The main advantage of RDQL is that it is simple, allowing easy implementation across platforms and still offering a measure of expressivity that is sufficient in many practical applications that deal with RDF.

However, RDQL has been deliberately designed to be a minimal language. It lacks expressive power that is, in many more complex application scenarios, required. For example, it is not possible to express disjunctive patterns in RDQL, nor can it express optional matches. It also lacks a formal semantics, which may result in different implementations of the same language giving different results.

RQL [12] is an RDF Schema query language designed by ICS-FORTH. It has been implemented in ICS-FORTH's RDFSuite [2] tool and Sesame supports a partial implementation.

RQL is a very powerful and expressive language with a thorough formal grounding. It uses a path-expression syntax that closely resembles that of SeRQL (in fact, SeRQL's syntax was based on RQL) and has a functional approach to query language design.

However, partly because of its expressivity, RQL's syntax has proven to be difficult to use and understand for human users. Also, while it has a formal model, this formal model is not based directly on the RDF Semantics, but on the authors' own formal interpretation of RDF and RDF Schema, and this formal interpretation is incompatible with RDF and RDF Schema on some key points, placing additional restrictions on the structure of the RDF graph. While this is still suitable for a large range of applications, it is prohibitive in cases where interoperability is a key issue.

As mentioned in the beginning of this chapter, there are numerous RDF query languages. In [9] a survey of several query languages, including SeRQL, is done, comparing them on expressivity requirements with respect to various use cases. Since several languages (including SeRQL itself) are still under development and newer, more powerful versions are released, an online version of the findings of the paper, updated with these latest versions, can be found at `http://www.aifb.uni-karlsruhe.de/WBS/pha/rdf-query/`.

1.6 Conclusions

In the previous sections, we have given an overview of the SeRQL query language, and we have demonstrated how SeRQL fulfills a set of key requirements for RDF query languages. We have provided the basic syntax and a formal model, and have illustrated use cases in which the different features of SeRQL are demonstrated.

SeRQL is an attempt to come to an RDF query language that satisfies necessary general requirements on such a language without adding unnecessary bloat. Specifically, SeRQL has been designed to be fully compatible with the RDF specifications, to be easy to read and write by humans while at the same being easy to process and produce in an automated fashion. Most of the features of SeRQL are not new, but we believe that SeRQL is the first proposal that combines all these requirements in a single language and the only such proposal that has been implemented succesfully and is being used succesfully.

Future work on the development of SeRQL as a language will focus on adding useful and necessary functions and operators demanded by the user community, as well as encouraging other developers to implement engines that support this language.

In the following chapters of this book, diverse use cases and examples will be given in which the SeRQL query language plays a pivotal role.

References

[1] Serge Abiteboul, Peter Buneman, and Dan Suciu. *Data on the Web: From Relations to Semistructural Data and XML*. Morgan Kaufman, 1999.
[2] Sofia Alexaki, Vassilis Christophides, Greg Karvounarakis, Dimitris Plexousakis, and Karsten Tolle. The RDFSuite: Managing Voluminous RDF Description Bases. Technical report, Institute of Computer Science, FORTH, Her-

aklion, Greece, 2000. See `http://www.ics.forth.gr/proj/isst/RDF/RSSDB/rdfsuite.pdf`.

[3] Tim Berners-Lee.   Notation 3, 1998.   See `http://www.w3.org/DesignIssues/Notation3.html`.

[4] Paul V. Biron and Ashok Malhotra. XML Schema Part 2: Datatypes. Recommendation, World Wide Web Consortium, May 2001. See `http://www.w3.org/TR/xmlschema-2/`.

[5] Jeen Broekstra and Arjohn Kampman.   The SeRQL Query Language. Technical report, Aduna, 2003. See `http://www.openrdf.org/doc/SeRQLmanual.html`.

[6] Jeen Broekstra, Arjohn Kampman, and Frank van Harmelen.   Sesame: A Generic Architecture for Storing and Querying RDF and RDF Schema. In Ian Horrocks and James Hendler, editors, *Proceedings of the first International Semantic Web Conference (ISWC 2002)*, number 2342 in Lecture Notes in Computer Science, pages 54–68, Sardinia, Italy, June 9 – 12, 2002. Springer Verlag, Heidelberg Germany. See also `http://www.openrdf.org/`.

[7] Jeremy Carrol and Brian McBride. The Jena Semantic Web Toolkit. Public api, HP-Labs, Bristol, 2001. See `http://www.hpl.hp.com/semweb/jena-top.html`.

[8] Jan Grant and Dave Beckett. RDF Test Cases. Proposed recommendation, World Wide Web Consortium, December15 2003. See `http://www.w3.org/TR/rdf-testcases/`.

[9] Peter Haase, Jeen Broekstra, Andreas Eberhart, and Raphael Volz. A Comparison of RDF Query Languages. In Sheila McIlraith, Dimitris Plexousakis, and Frank van Harmelen, editors, *The Semantic Web - ISWC 2004. Proceedings of the Third International Semantic Web Conference*, volume 3298 of *Lecture Notes in Computer Science*, Hiroshima, Japan, 2004. Springer-Verlag.

[10] Patrick Hayes. RDF Semantics. Proposed Recommendation, World Wide Web Consortium, December 2003. See `http://www.w3.org/TR/2003/PR-rdf-mt-20031215/`.

[11] ISO9075:1999. Information Technology-Database Language SQL. Standard No. ISO/IEC 9075:1999, International Organization for Standardization (ISO), 1999. (Available from American National Standards Institute, New York, NY 10036, (212) 642-4900.).

[12] Gregory Karvounarakis, Vassilis Christophides, Dimitris Plexousakis, and Sofia Alexaki. Querying community web portals. Technical report, Institute of Computer Science, FORTH, Heraklion, Greece, 2000. See `http://www.ics.forth.gr/proj/isst/RDF/RQL/rql.pdf`.

[13] Libby Miller. RDF Squish query language and Java implementation. Public draft, Institute for Learning and Research Technology, 2001. See `http://ilrt.org/discovery/2001/02/squish/`.

[14] Alberto Reggiori and Andy Seaborne. Query and rule languages use cases and examples, 2002. See `http://rdfstore.sourceforge.net/2002/06/24/rdf-query/query-use-cases.ht%ml`.

[15] Andy Seaborne. RDQL - A Query Language for RDF. W3c member submission, Hewlett Packard, January 2004. See http://www.w3.org/Submission/2004/SUBM-RDQL-20040109/.

RDF and Traditional Query Architectures

Richard Vdovjak[1], Geert-Jan Houben[1], Heiner Stuckenschmidt[2], Ad Aerts[1]

[1] Technische Universiteit Eindhoven, The Netherlands,
{richardv,ghouben,wsinatma}@win.tue.nl
[2] Vrije Universiteit Amsterdam, The Netherlands, heiner@cs.vu.nl

Summary. The Resource Description Framework (RDF) is a step towards the support for integrated and uniform access to information sources. It is designed to standardize the definition and use of metadata descriptions of Web-based resources. It is complemented with RDF Schema (RDFS) that lets developers define an extensible, object-oriented type system for RDF data models. While RDF is targeted towards representing metadata, it can represent the underlying data as well. Together, RDF and RDFS provide a sound basis for the capture of domain knowledge in a form that lends itself for automatic processing. Since the Web is inherently distributed, RDF querying systems should also be able to handle the distribution of multiple, autonomous RDF repositories. A sound approach is needed for querying distributed RDF sources to disclose the information they contain. In this chapter we examine several architectures for querying distributed RDF (meta)data and point out a number of issues that will have to be dealt with in order to provide a viable solution. The discussion traces the development of distributed applications that attempt to exploit the promises of interoperability of the Semantic Web and have to deal with the requirements that arise from that. The chapter focuses on the problems associated with the introduction of RDF (meta)data in the distributed information system arena.

2.1 Introduction

The Resource Description Framework (RDF) [15] is "thought to be a step towards the support for integrated and uniform access to information sources and services as well as for intelligent applications for information processing on the Web" [10, 11]. It is a W3C recommendation, designed to standardize the definition and use of metadata descriptions of Web-based resources. It is complemented with RDF Schema [7] (RDFS) that lets developers define an extensible, object-oriented type system for RDF data models. While RDF is targeted towards representing metadata, it can represent the underlying data as well. Together, RDF and RDFS provide a sound basis for the capture of domain knowledge in a form that lends itself for automatic processing.

The availability of such a standardized framework for the representation of Web resource descriptions has spurred quite a bit of research into the technology needed to support its usage. This has led, amongst other things, to the emergence of storage and querying systems such as Sesame [8] and RDFSuite [5] that can handle combined RDF(S) data and metadata.

RDF technology is still quite young. A number of issues, such as expressiveness, the interplay between querying and inferencing (also known as schema-aware querying), and performance, is receiving a lot of attention. Since the Web is inherently distributed, RDF querying systems should also be able to handle the distribution of multiple, autonomous RDF repositories. A sound approach is needed for querying distributed RDF sources to disclose the information they contain.

In this chapter we will examine several architectures for querying distributed RDF (meta)data and point out a number of issues that will have to be dealt with in order to provide a viable solution. The discussion traces the development of distributed applications that attempt to exploit the promises of interoperability of the Semantic Web and have to deal with the requirements that arise from that. It focuses on the problems associated with the introduction of RDF (meta)data in the distributed information system arena. The rest of this chapter is structured as follows. In Sect. 2.2 we describe the types of applications we target and motivate the need for distributed RDF querying. In Sect. 2.3 we discuss architectures relying on (a hierarchy of) mediators for the integration of knowledge repositories on the Web. We focus on issues such as the location of the information and the distribution of work involved in anwering a query. In Sect. 2.4 the further evolution towards collaboration between mediators is discussed, leading to a more equal or peer-like role in the system, focusing on query planning and optimization. In the last section we discuss some open issues as well as the commonalities and differences of the proposed architectures and P2P systems such as Gnutella [1], CAN [17], and Edutella [16]. It prepares the ground for the discussion in the later chapters of the solution specific issues that arise in pure P2P systems in the querying of distributed information and knowledge.

2.2 Motivation

On the one end of the architectural spectrum there is the integration of the standalone systems. Standalone systems are autonomous knowledge repositories that were designed with a single application in mind, such as the disclosure of a library catalog or a museum collection. These systems represent a local solution to a local problem. The system architecture, in case more repositories are queried, corresponds to that in Fig. 2.1. In this figure it is indicated that the information sources themselves are independent datastores that support a query interface. In the figure only RDF stores are shown, since this is the focus of this chapter.

After the initial experience with such systems, it was realized that more can be gained by having also the ability to access several related repositories. This has led to the portal approach to integration. In the simplest version, such a portal offers access via a single interface to a number of sources [14] via an explicit protocol, such as the Z39.50 Information Retrieval protocol. It serves as a single entry point to replace several, mutually independent entry points such as depicted in Fig. 2.1. It is typically achieved by wrapping the information sources to provide a common presentation. Such a portal typically will require manual integration of the query results by the user.

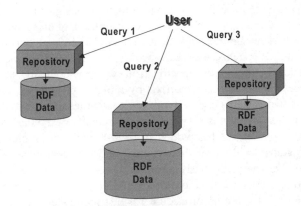

Fig. 2.1. Standalone Repositories

More advanced portals have begun to offer, albeit on a limited scale, "cross-searching" services that combine information from several sources, such as catalogs from different libraries. They present this information through a higher level interface that frees the user from the task of having to learn several interfaces [12] and do the integration of the results by hand. Such services rely on the availability of mediation services that take care of the translation of the user's question to a format acceptable for the information sources involved [21]. The mediator service also translates and integrates the answers provided by these sources to a single answer for the user. To offer these services libraries need to deal with precisely those issues that are often characterized by the term "semantic interoperability." It will allow library (and other) portals to change their scope from local to for example regional or national. Interoperability at this scale needs the solid foundation of frameworks like RDF(S) and the description formalisms built on top of these to provide the necessary expressiveness and flexibility needed for the integration.

The fact that this evolution is now within reach of the libraries has been recognized and is supported by research programs at the national and continental levels. For instance, the DELOS Network of Excellence on Digital Libraries addresses knowledge extraction and semantic interoperability in one of its new work packages. The aim to build interoperable, multimodal and multilingual services and integrated content management ranging from the personal to the global for the specialist and the general population (http://www.delos.info). Similar developments are taking place in the cultural heritage domain, where musea and archives collaborate to disclose their (digitized) collections in an integrated fashion (http://www.nwo.nl/catch). We will not discuss here the additional issues involved in these systems, such as support for personalization and human-computer interaction.

The centralized mediator architecture is just one of a number of architectures for the access of the contributing resources. On the other end of the integration spectrum are the highly decentralized P2P systems, which by design offer a high degree of interoperability and robustness. However, the description of the resources in the early P2P systems was rather limited, and consequently also their support for querying. In fact, the earliest P2P systems, such as Napster [3], were (audio) file-sharing systems that provided access through the specification of a few keywords, such as a title or an artist. These systems are characterized by a high, but varying, number of peers (nodes in the network) and a high redundancy of the files to be shared.

More advanced querying is supported in the schema-based P2P systems such as the Edutella system [9], which provides an RDF-based infrastructure. Here queries can be posed against locally available schemas and are decomposed and distributed to peers that are known (on the basis of local routing indices) to be able to contribute their information resources. Schema-aware querying is also offered in the Piazza system [13]. Here a bottom-up procedure for distributing queries is used based on the locally available mappings of the schema of the peer to those of its neigbours. The priority in query performance in schema-aware P2P systems so far has been on the reduction of the network traffic by making sure that the queries are propagated to only those peers that can be expected to provide an answer. Because of the highly dynamical character of these systems not much emphasis has yet been placed on query optimization.

In the case of integrated access to libraries or museum collections there is not much volatiltity of the contributing systems: joining and leaving of nodes in the network is not so much of an issue. However, also such systems can benefit from some of the strong points of P2P system architectures.

2.3 Hierarchical mediator architecture

The specific problem of a distributed architecture is that information relevant to a query may be distributed over the different sources. This requires the query-answering system to locate relevant information, retrieve it, and combine the individual answers. For this purpose, a mediator component [21] is introduced (compare Fig. 2.2) resulting in the mediator architecture (MA).

The rationale of this architecture is to hide from the user accessing the data the fact that the information is distributed across different sources. The user should not need to know where a particular piece of information resides. The system should behave as if all the information is available from a single source represented by the mediator. This view on the mediator as a single source also leads to an extension of the distributed architecture where the mediated sources can be mediators that again hide a set of distributed sources (see Fig. 2.3): the hierarchical mediator architecture (HMA).

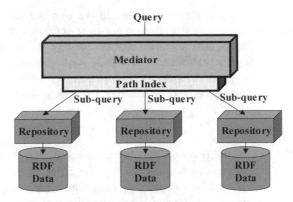

Fig. 2.2. Mediator Architecture

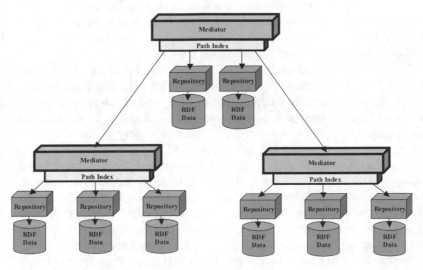

Fig. 2.3. Mediator Hierarchy Architecture

A number of problems have to be addressed when working with distributed information sources via a mediator. In particular, there are two main tasks connected with the mediator-based distribution of data and we will discuss them in the following:

Indexing The mediator has to be able to locate in the distributed system the information needed to answer a user query. In particular, it has to know which of the sources to access.

Query Planning The performance of the distributed system depends on the choice and the order of application of the different query processing operators. In the case of distributed information, the time needed to send information from the sources to the mediator becomes a major factor in choosing the right strategy.

These two problems have been studied extensively in the area of distributed database systems. The aim of this section is not to re-introduce the relevant concepts for distributed systems, but rather summarize known problems and approaches. Whenever possible the special characteristics of RDF are highlighted and results that meet the needs of these characteristics are pointed to. We will assume that RDF (meta)data exists in the stores in the form of subject-property-object triples.

2.3.1 Indexing Sources

In order to make use of the optimization mechanisms of underlying repositories themselves, complete queries can be forwarded to the different repositories. In the case of multiple external models, the query process can be further sped up by only pushing down queries to information sources that can be expected to contain an answer. The ultimate goal is to push down to a repository exactly that part of a more complex query for which a repository contains an answer. This part can range from a single statement template to the complete query. The situation can thus arise where a subset of the query result can directly be extracted from one source, and the rest has to be extracted and combined from different sources.

The majority of work in the area of object-oriented databases is focused on indexing schema-based paths in complex object models. This work can be used in the context of the graph-based interpretation of RDF models. More specifically, every RDF model can be seen as a graph where nodes correspond to resources and arcs to properties linking these resources. The result of a query to such a model is a set of subgraphs corresponding to a path expression[1]. A path expression does not necessarily describe a single path. In general, it describes a tree that can be created by joining a set of paths. A path expression then is decomposed into a set of expressions describing simple paths, the simpler path expressions are forwarded to sources that contain the corresponding information using a path-based index structure, and the retrieved answers are joined to create the result. This constitutes the main part of the query processing; Figure 2.4 shows a message sequence chart for a scenario where the top mediator has two sources one of which is again a mediator, which in turn retrieves data from its two subordinate sources.

Since the information that makes up a path may be distributed across different information sources, an index structure has to be used that also contains information about sub-paths without loosing the advantage of indexing complete paths. An index structure that combines these two characteristics is the join index hierarchy proposed in [22]. This approach is taken as a basis for defining a *source index hierarchy* [20].

2.3.2 Index Creation and Maintenance

The mediator normally constructs the index during its first startup process. This automatic index construction works fairly well for small and medium sized repositories. For large data sources the construction of the index by querying all information

---

[1] At this point additional constraints such as equality and inequality constraints are ignored that are supported by some query languages.

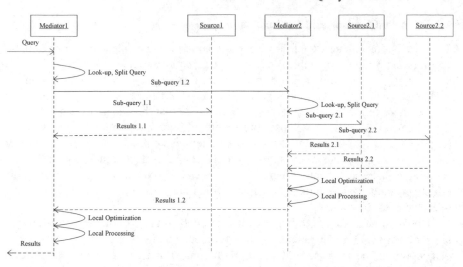

Fig. 2.4. Query processing and optimization message sequence in a distributed setting

sources for the number of occurrences of statements will take too long. The problem with the straightforward creation of the index table is that querying the remote sources for data of a certain type will result in the transmission by the source of all of that data to the mediator[1]. Transmitting data over the network, however, is a very expensive operation, especially in a distributed scenario with high communication costs. In order to avoid this problem index information is created "locally" at the side of the data source. Instead of sending the complete data, the local source only sends the index information.

If the mediators are organized into a tree hierarchy, the creation of the index table at the higher levels is made easier. The mediators at the higher levels can send a special request to mediators at lower levels, and ask those to send their own local index table. After this step, the received local indexes can be used in order to create the global index table. With this technique, the network traffic can be significantly reduced since instead of transferring all data through the network, only an aggregated data set (the index) needs to be transferred.

Compared to instance-level indexing, our approach does not require creating and maintaining oversized indices since there are far fewer sources than there are instances. Instance indexing scales much harder in the Web environment and as mentioned above in many cases it would not even be applicable, e.g. when sources do not allow replication of their data (which is what instance indices essentially do).

---

[1] Note that well a established technology such as SQL offers aggregation statements for counting tuples that have been widely implemented. Such facilities cannot be assumed in general.

2.3.3 Query Planning and Optimization

The distribution of data often follows certain patterns or dependencies. Some of them are imposed by the geographical nature of distribution, some are introduced due to the diversity of source domains. For instance, one source may focus on a domain A whereas another source focuses on a domain B. If there is no overlap between the instances of the two domains one can conclude that there is no overlap between the schema paths covered by those sources either. Such information, when available (e.g. by analyzing the content of the index structures), can be used by the optimizer and the path expressions from the two sources can be evaluated independently from each other, using a set union operation at the end to produce the final result. This effectively reduces the number of triples which are to be joined and thus also the overall costs.

Unlike in databases, both functionality and performance of distributed RDF systems are very context dependent. In order to be able to apply the optimization methods devised in the database field, the implicit context (determined by the application domain and other conditions) needs to be made explicit. Therefore, it is essential for the optimizer to undergo a so-called meta-optimization phase in which it is fine-tuned to a concrete context situation. Before the optimizer starts reordering joins and searching for an optimal query plan, there are some high level optimization decisions to be made which influence both the type and the behavior of the actual optimization algorithm as well as the notion of optimality and the size of the solution space. The implicit context is given by several factors amongst which the source capabilities, the identity notion, the length of the query, and the available distribution dependencies play a crucial role.

The downside of keeping only the schema information in our index, is that query answering without the index support at the instance level is much more computationally intensive. Moreover, in the context of Semantic Web portal applications, the queries are not human-entered anymore but rather generated by a portal's front-end (triggered by the user) and often exceed a size that can be easily computed by using brute force. Therefore query optimization becomes an important part of our distributed RDF query system. We try to avoid re-inventing the wheel and once again seek inspiration in the database field, making it applicable by relationizing the RDF model: Each single schema path p_i of length 1 (also called 1-path) can be perceived as a relation with two attributes: the source vertex $s(p_i)$ and the target vertex $t(p_i)$. A schema path of length more than 1 is modelled as a set of relations joined together by the identity of the adjacent vertices, essentially representing a chain query of joins. This allows us to directly adopt the results of comparison of different join ordering heuristics in [19]. In particular, a two-phase optimization consisting of the iterative improvement (II) algorithm followed by the simulated annealing (SA) algorithm performs very well on the class of chain join queries we are interested in.

2.3.4 Object Identity

The notion of identity in RDF is a complex issue albeit an important one. To determine whether two resources are identical is not only important for avoiding duplicates in the result set, but it is also an essential requirement for being able to compute the join of two paths and thus compute an answer to a distributed query.

With respect to the identity notion, we divide RDF models into two groups: (1) those where a URI comparison suffices for establishing identity and (2) those where the simple comparison does not work. In the following we focus on the second group, the more difficult one. In the case of document repositories, it might be the case that a certain book or report is only contained in one repository; authors, projects and organizations, however, will often occur in different sources. Therefore, we need mechanisms for deciding whether two resources describe the same real-world object. Under certain circumstances creating an explicit mapping between objects of a certain type in different sources can be an appropriate solution for this situation. If the number of potential objects in a class is relatively low, it is beneficial to use explicit mappings instead of recursively checking equality between objects.

The problem of object identity is also a special characteristic of RDF data that influences the applicability of existing query processing methods. In particular, it distinguishes RDF from relational databases where keys are often assumed to be unique. This difference also impacts the choice of the query processing strategy, because object comparison has to be taken into account. In the presence of this problem it is, for example, not possible to use efficient join operations based on hash tables, but the less efficient but more flexible ways of computing joins in chain queries are still available.

2.3.5 HMA Advantages and Limitations

Moving from isolated information sources to an integrated data access architecture has a number of advantages both at the conceptual and at the technical level.

At the conceptual level, it allows the data to reside at their original location where it is created and maintained. From the user point of view, the conceptual advantage is that the information can be accessed just like a single information source because the mediator takes care of locating relevant information and sending parts of the query to the respective source. At the technical level, the distributed architecture has the advantage of an integrated querying process that offers more potential for optimization than the isolated querying of different sources (see 2.4). First of all, it can make use of the parallelism of the information sources to carry out necessary selection operations in parallel. Further, the mediator is able to determine a near-optimal plan for the complete query. In the isolated setting the planning is less flexible because it is partially pre-determined by the sequential querying of the different sources.

The distribution architecture discussed so far has some serious limitations with respect to scalability and efficiency. The problem lies in the fact that the information sources only offer a very limited functionality and most of the operations are executed by the mediator. This centralization of the querying process is problematic because:

- the mediator constitutes a single point of failure;

- the communication cost for sending large result sets from individual information sources is a major performance penalty;
- the maintenance of a centralized index in the mediator creates an update problem if sources are frequently updated.

The extension to a hierarchical architecture where some of the sources can be mediators themselves reduces some of these problems. If the central mediator fails it is still possible to access data at the lower levels of the hierarchy through the subordinate mediators. From a performance point of view, the mediators at the lower levels take over parts of the processing. In particular, they process the sub-query sent to them thereby reducing the amount of data that is extracted from the underlying data sources. Further, as discussed above, these mediators can contribute to the creation and maintenace of the source index and thereby reduce the update problem.

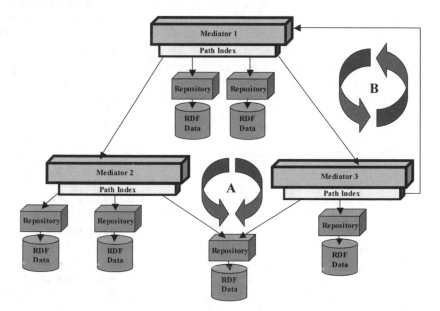

Fig. 2.5. Possible Problems in a Mediated System

The HMA architecture introduces some problems of its own as can be seen from Fig. 2.5. Care has to be taken when clustering information sources into a mediator hierarchy that a pure hierarchical structure results. When an information source is indexed and monitored by more than one mediator (Fig. 2.5 A), inefficiencies are introduced. A query that refers to the common source will be answered by the two mediators that index it, resulting in duplication of retrieval and communication effort. Another flaw in the construction of the hierarchy arises when a mediator will index one of its ancestors (Fig. 2.5 B).

A well-conceived mediator hierarchy has some advantages, but the problems mentioned above still remain and ask for more flexible architectures.

2.4 Cooperative Mediator Architecture

The architectures discussed above were all data centric in the sense that the communication between two related nodes in the system was strictly data driven with a simple protocol consisting of a request (query) followed by a response (RDF data). As a consequence, the processing of partial results had to be always performed on the upper node in the hierarchy. This in turn was the major cause of the disadvantages listed in the previous section.

In order to address these issues a more flexible architecture is needed. In such architecture, (some) mediators should agree to cooperate by offering processing capabilities, especially the join evaluation, to other nodes in the network. To facilitate this functionality, the software stack of the mediator has to be extended with a new communication layer. This layer allows for requests of type "join the attached data with the data obtained from your sources and deliver the result to mediator X."

Figure 2.6 depicts such cooperative mediator architecture (CMA). The solid directional lines indicate the usual data request/response channel (the direction pointed towards the source node), while the dotted lines represent the newly introduced processing channels which connect communication layers of the cooperating mediators. The CMA is a natural evolutionary step from approaches described in the previous sections since it still maintains the simple data request-response communication, but the evaluation of the partial results can be distributed over the cooperating mediators.

2.4.1 Paradigm Shift

While the distributed mediator architecture described in Sect. 2.3 is more of a client-server nature, the cooperative architecture moves us closer towards the P2P paradigm. A mediator which implements the communication layer can be considered as a peer that offers its processing capabilities to some of the other peers.

However, unlike in a typical P2P system where the number of peers is likely to be quite high, our target applications, like digital libraries or internet portals, do not typically reach millions of collaborating nodes. The growth of such network is usually much more controlled and also peers are less volatile than in a typical P2P system where peers join and leave the network in very dynamic fashion. Another difference is that broadcasting which causes the main bottleneck in P2P systems occurs in our system very seldom as the mediator keeps the index of its sources and knows exactly how to split the query and where to route the sub-queries. For this reasons, we do not impose any particular selforganizing network topology on the way cooperating peers are connected. The data channels however, still remain hierarchical. Should the application demand a very high number of cooperating peers, efficient network topologies such as [18] would have to be considered.

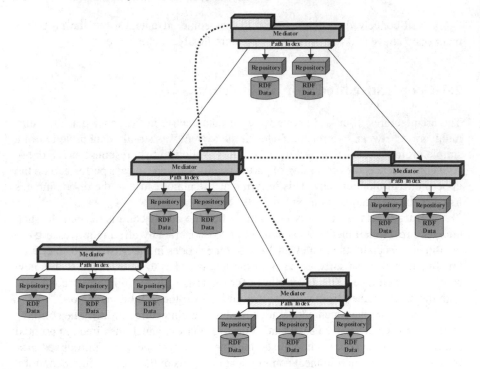

Fig. 2.6. Cooperative Mediator Architecture

From the user's point of view, our system offers a number of entry points to the underlying data sources. The user poses a query against one of the mediators and the peers in the system cooperate in order to deliver the answer faster. From this point of view it resembles the grid computing where several geographically distributed computers jointly cooperate on solving a given task.

2.4.2 Query Processing and Query Optimization

Like the HMA, the query processing in the CMA starts with the node that receives the initial query, the path index is consulted and the query is split into sub-queries and routed to the appropriate sources, among which can be local sources as well as other mediators some of which may have agreed to cooperate on query processing. The results from "simple" sources are transferred to the initiating mediator — this part of the query plan is identical to that in the HMA. The difference is in treating the co-operating nodes (mediators that implement the communication layer). The mediator with the initial query becomes a coordinator and orchestrates the other cooperating peers. It creates an extended query plan that takes into account the connection speed among different nodes, their processing capacity as well as available data statistics.[1] For the cooperating nodes, this query plan may consists of a sequence of the following query processing instructions:

- Gather data from the local sources (given a sub-query)
- Receive external data
- Join (a part of) the obtained data
- Ship (a part of) data to another node
- Provide local statistics (cardinalities, work-load, etc.)

Since the data sources are autonomous the statistics that are needed to make a good query plan are often not readily available. The mediator gathers these statistics about its subordinate sources in time with every new query. On top of that, there is a so-called calibration phase during the mediator setup, where several pre-compiled queries are fired; the system tries to assess some of the necessary parameters. All this is, however, not enough if the data in the underlying sources changes rapidly or if the load of the cooperating peers varies considerably. To tackle these conditions, it is sometimes necessary to intertwine the query processing with query planning. In ideal circumstances, the optimizer makes one plan at the beginning and this plan is executed during the query processing. In more volatile environments or in cases where no or very little statics are available, the mediator makes first a partial query plan and requests the up-to-date statistics from the cooperating peers; these are subsequently used by the optimizer to improve the initial plan.

As an example let us consider a case of a heterogenous cooperative network where two nodes $Mediator2$ and $Mediator3$ are connected via a high speed connection while their connection to $Mediator1$ is considerably slower. Figure 2.7 depicts a message sequence chart of processing a query issued against $Mediator1$. First, $Mediator1$ consults its index and splits the query into sub-queries. Then it consults the two cooperative peer mediators and requests statistics about their partial results. This information is then used by the optimizer, which makes a query plan for a two-way semi-join [6] in which $Mediator2$ and $Mediator3$ exchange their data (the set of URI's of resources, which is needed to make a join between the two sub-paths); each of the nodes filters out path instances that will not be present in the result, i.e. they perform a join on their local data with the joining attribute from each other. Subsequently both peers ship the filtered results to $Mediator1$ which performs the final join together with the data obtained locally. Due to the semi-join method, all data coming from the cooperative peers will appear in the result, the advantage being that the data transfer on the "expensive" lines (i.e., those that connect $Mediator2$ and $Mediator3$ with $Mediator1$) is kept minimal.

2.4.3 Making the Query Plan Robust

Extending the hierarchical mediator architecture towards a network of cooperative mediators has the potential to bring benefits both in terms of improved performance

---

[1] We assume a heterogenous network both in terms of network bandwidth, processing power, and (local) data amounts.

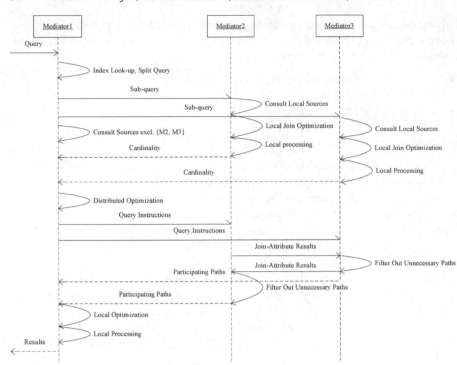

Fig. 2.7. Query processing and optimization message sequence in a cooperative setting

and flexibility. However, since the cooperating nodes are still autonomous, their agreement to cooperate does not guarantee exclusivity, i.e. they can accept requests from other nodes at the same time. Therefore it is desirable that the query optimization in such a distributed setting is resilient — at least to some extent — to sudden changes of workload (and therefore performance) which may occur in some of the cooperating nodes.

The idea of intertwining query planning with query processing is the first step to make the query answering more robust. By splitting the query plan into smaller pieces (which may change during the course of answering the query once the necessary statistics are present) the optimizer better reacts on the actual situation of the entire system. Every such split, however, introduces the overhead of statistics retrieval and re-optimizing the rest of the plan. Thus it is important to keep the number of planing preemptions minimal. The chosen (sub)plan should not turn from a reasonably good plan to a very bad plan if one or more sources do not perform as expected. There is an inherent tradeoff between how robust or safe the plan can be and how good it is, given that the initial assumptions hold.

The translation of the query optimization problem into a search problem, led us to identify the following main dimensions: the join ordering problem and the problem of distributing the work among the cooperating nodes. Our optimizer implements a heuristic algorithm that walks the problem space evaluating the cost function (the cost model). The idea of finding a robust query plan corresponds to finding a high plateau in hill-climbing terminology. In such a plan even if some of the parameters change the overall cost will not deteriorate much. On the other hand, even a very good solution which is found on the border of an abyss in our search space should be avoided since a small change in the underlying assumptions can cause a big cost penalty. In order to obtain a relatively stable solution, the optimizer explores the neighborhood of k top plans and picks the one which meets the "safety" requirements and offers a good performance tradeoff.

2.5 Summary and Discussion

In this chapter we discussed several architectures for querying RDF data sources. The most flexible and robust, but also most complex one, is the cooperating mediator architecture (CMA). This is a hybrid architecture. At the top level, it satisfies the pure P2P organizational model of full decentralization of services. This level shows the redundancy of service that is required to make it robust against server-failure[1]. The lower levels of the CMA display a master-slave or client-server like architecture. Note that the CMS architecture can achieve the same results as the hierarchical mediator architecture, but with only two layers. It is more flexible than the HMA, since every mediator node can act as root of a virtual HMA system. The CMA architecture resembles the two layer architecture of the Edutella system[16]. The Edutella upper layer consists of superpeers that are distinguished by their superior processing and storage capabilities. The superpeers constitute the stable, performant backbone of the Edutalla system and can collaborate with each other in answering queries. The lower layers consists of peers that have generally less resources and operate under the control of one superpeer.

In the CMA architecture, every top-level node can access the other top-level nodes directly on the basis of its indices, and each lower level node through the node above it. In P2P systems each node only knows its neighboring nodes. In some P2P systems, such as Gnutella [1], and Freenet [2], items, such as files, are located by using a generic routing strategy, hopping from one neighbor to the next until the item is found. In other P2P systems, such as P-Grid [4], and CAN [17], a much more efficient goal-directed search can be performed, which uses the distributed indexing structures that are built up in the construction process of the network. The degree of overview of the system has consequences for query optimization. Since each top-level node in a CMA knows the other top-level nodes and can cooperate with them, query plans can be made and optimized. In schema-aware P2P systems like Edutella [16] and Piazza (Chap. 12), each node only knows its peers. This means in Edutella, that queries are split up and passed on to other superpeers, that are likely to control

---

[1] Note that not all P2P systems possess this property. An early P2P system such as Napster [3], has a centralized search service where peers have to register and submit their requests for files. Only the file transfer itself is Peer-to-Peer.

relevant data and the answers, upon return, are combined at the originating peer. This is an iterative process. In Piazza, each node has semantic mappings of its own schema to the schemas of its neighbors, as well as a concordance table to match values. It is thus capable of reformulating a query into one that its neighbor can understand. Each node that is posed a query thus constructs an anwer based on its own data and the data that it obtains from its direct neighbors. Again, this is an iterative process. Since there is no global view in these systems, no advanced query planning can be performed. The important query optimization issue is to avoid to send a query to a peer which will not be able to give an answer (that is whose schema has no overlap with the query).

Peer-to-Peer systems, such as Napster and Gnutella, deal with rather coarse-grained items, such as files that have to be retrieved in their entirety. The files are distributed across the peers. To make these systems fault-tolerant items are repli-cated. Where a file is replicated to, depends on the copying behaviour of the peers. In the kind of RDF querying systems considered here, where the repositories are in principle independent and can add their own data, replication only arises when the same data is entered at different locations. These systems are rather characterized by fragmentation. Horizontally, for data with a similar schema but with instances of local interest (the collection of triples is then split up over different nodes), and ver-tically, when it represents a local specialization. The knowledge repositories, such as library catalogs, we have been considering are rather vertically fragmented. That is, when one wants to ask a path query the answering process usually will have to obtain the pieces of the path from several sources.

The schema in the CMA is global. Integration is done at the peer repositories. This situation resembles that of Edutella, where each superpeer has a global schema, covering the peers that it controls, and the schema of these peers is mapped to it. In Piazza, the integration is done by each peer that joins, by constructing the semantic mapping to its new neighbors.

In this chapter we focused on the architectural support for RDF query execution and planning. We did not cover issues such as the composition of the system, and the joining or leaving of peers. Theses are often important in P2P systems, however, the systems we consider have a rather stable composition. Another issue not touched upon is the interplay between extentional and intentional data, that is a part the RDF querying process and also plays a role in the optimization process.

References

[1] The annotated gnutella protocol specification v0.4, 2001. http://rfc-gnutella.sourceforge.net.
[2] The freenet website can be found at:. http://freenet.sourcefourge.net.
[3] The napster website can be found at:. http://www.napster.com.
[4] K. Aberer. P-grid: A self-organizing access structure for p2p information sys-tems. In *Sixth International Conference on Cooperative Information Systems*

(CoopIS 2001), volume 2172, pages 179 – 194, Trento, Italy, September 2001. Springer-Verlag.

[5] S. Alexaki, V. Christophides, G. Karvounarakis, D. Plexousakis, and K. Tolle. The rdfsuite: Managing voluminous rdf description bases, 2000.

[6] P.A. Bernstein and D.W. Chiu. Using semijoins to solve relational queries. *Journal of the ACM*, 28(1):25–40, 1981.

[7] D. Brickley, R. Guha, and A. Layman. Resource description framework (RDF) schema specification. Working draft, W3C, August 1998. http://www.w3c.org/TR/WD-rdf-schema.

[8] J. Broekstra, A. Kampman, and F. van Harmelen. Sesame: A generic architecture for storing and querying rdf and rdf schema. In *The Semantic Web - ISWC 2002*, volume 2342 of *LNCS*, pages 54–68. Springer, 2002.

[9] I. Brunkhorst, H. Dhraief, A. Kemper, W. Nejdl, and C. Wiesner. Distributed queries and query optimization in schema-based p2p-systems. In *International Workshop On Databases, Information Systems and Peer-to-Peer Computing*, Humboldt University, Berlin, Germany, September 2003.

[10] Stefan Decker, Sergey Melnik, Frank Van Harmelen, Dieter Fensel, Michel Klein, Jeen Broekstra, Michael Erdmann, and Ian Horrocks. The semantic web: The roles of XML and RDF. *IEEE Internet Computing*, 4(5):2–13, September 2000.

[11] Stefan Decker, Prasenjit Mitra, and Sergey Melnik. Framework for the semantic web: An RDF tutorial. *IEEE Internet Computing*, 4(6):68–73, November 2000.

[12] Lorcan Dempsey. The recombinant library: portals and people. *Journal of Library Administration*, 39(4):103–136, 2003.

[13] A. Halevy, Z. Ives, P. Mork, and I. Tatarinov. Piazza: Mediation and integration infrastructure for semantic web data, 2003.

[14] William Kilbride. From one context to another: Building a common information environment for archaeology. *CSA Newsletter*, 16(3), 2004.

[15] O. Lassila and R. Swick. Resource description framework (RDF). Proposed recommendation, W3C, January 1999. http://www.w3c.org/TR/WD-rdf-syntax.

[16] W. Nejdl, B. Wolf, C. Qu, S. Decker, M. Sintek, A. Naeve, M. Nilsson, M. Palmer, and R. Risch. Edutella: A p2p networking infrastructure based on rdf. In *WWW 11 Proceedings*, Hawaii, USA, May 2002.

[17] S. Ratnasamy and et al. A scalable content-adressable network. In *Proc. ACM SIGCOMM*, pages 161 – 172. ACM Press, 2001.

[18] M. Schlosser, M. Sintek, S. Decker, and W. Nejdl. Hypercup – hypercubes, ontologies and efficient search on p2p networks. In *Proceedings of the International Workshop on Agents and P2P Computing*, 2002.

[19] M. Steinbrunn, G. Moerkotte, and A. Kemper. Heuristic and randomized optimization for join ordering problem. *The VLDB Journal*, 6:191–208, 1997.

[20] H. Stuckenschmidt, R. Vdovjak, J. Broekstra, and G.-J. Houben. Data structures and algorithms for querying distributed rdf repositories. In *Proceedings of the International World Wide Web Conference WWW'04*, New York, USA, 2004.

[21] Gio Wiederhold. Mediators in the architecture of future information systems. *Computer*, 25(3):38–49, 1992.

[22] Z. Xie and J. Han. Join index hierarchies for supporting efficient navigations in object-oriented databases. In *Proceedings of the International Conference on Very Large Data Bases*, pages 522–533, 1994.

3

Query Processing in RDF/S-Based P2P Database Systems

George Kokkinidis, Lefteris Sidirourgos, Vassilis Christophides

Institute of Computer Science - FORTH, Heraklion, Greece and
Department of Computer Science, University of Crete, Heraklion, Greece
{kokkinid,lsidir,christop}@ics.forth.gr

Summary. In Peer-to-peer (P2P) systems a very large number of autonomous computing nodes (the peers) pool together their resources and rely on each other for data and services. More and more P2P data management systems rely nowadays on intensional (i.e., schema) information for integrating and querying peer bases. Such information can be easily captured by emerging Semantic Web languages such as RDF/S. In this chapter, we present the SQPeer middleware for processing RQL queries over peer RDF/S bases (materialized or virtual), which are advertised using adequate RVL views. The novelty of SQPeer lies on the interleaved execution of the query routing and planning phases using intensional advertisements of peer bases under the form of RDF/S schema fragments (i.e., views). More precisely, routing is responsible for discovering peer views relevant to a specific query based on appropriate subsumption techniques of RDF/S schema fragments. On the other hand, query planning relies on the obtained data localization information, as well as compile and run-time optimization techniques. The generated plans are then executed in a fully distributed way by the involved peers for obtaining as fast as possible the first results of a query available in peer bases. This can be achieved by initially considering the peer bases that answer the whole query and at each iteration round, to route and evaluate smaller query fragments. The interleaved execution not only favors intra-peer processing, which is less expensive that the inter-peer one, but additionally takes benefit of a parallel execution of the query routing, planning and execution in different peers. Peers can exchange query plans and results, as well as, revisit established plans using appropriate communication channels. We finally demonstrate through examples the execution of two main query processing phases for two different architectural alternatives, namely a hybrid and a structured RDF/S schema-based P2P system.

3.1 Introduction

Peer-to-peer (P2P) computing is currently attracting enormous attention, spurred by the popularity of file sharing systems such as Napster [29], Gnutella [14], Freenet [8], Morpheus [28] and Kazaa [23]. In P2P systems a very large number of autonomous computing nodes (the peers) pool together their resources and rely on each other for data and services. P2P computing introduces an interesting paradigm of decentralization going hand in hand with an increasing self-organization of highly autonomous peers. This new paradigm bears the potential to realize computing systems that scale to very large numbers of participating nodes while ensuring fault-tolerance.

However, existing P2P systems offer very limited data management facilities. In most of the cases, searching relies on simple selection conditions on attribute-value pairs or IR-style string pattern matching. These limitations are acceptable for file-sharing applications, but in order to support highly dynamic, ever-changing, autonomous social organizations (e.g., scientific or educational communities) we need richer facilities in exchanging, querying and integrating (semi-) structured data hosted by peers. To this end, we essentially need to adapt the P2P computing paradigm to a distributed data management setting. More precisely, we would like to support loosely coupled communities of peer bases, where each base can join and leave the network at free will, while groups of peers can collaboratively undertake the responsibility of query processing.

The importance of intensional (i.e., schema) information for integrating and querying peer bases has been highlighted by a number of recent projects [3, 32] (see also Chap. 12,13). A natural candidate for representing descriptive schemata of information resources (ranging from simple structured vocabularies to complex reference models [38]) is the Resource Description Framework/Schema Language (RDF/S). In particular, RDF/S (a) enables a *modular design* of descriptive schemata based on the mechanism of *namespaces*; (b) allows easy *reuse* or *refinement* of existing schemata through *subsumption* of both class and property definitions; (c) supports partial descriptions since *properties* associated with a resource are by default *optional and repeated* and (d) permits *super-imposed descriptions* in the sense that a resource may be multiply classified under several classes from one or several schemata. These modelling primitives are crucial for P2P data management systems where monolithic RDF/S schemata and resource descriptions cannot be constructed in advance and peers may have only partial descriptions about the available resources.

In this chapter, we present the ongoing SQPeer middleware for routing and planning declarative queries in peer RDF/S bases by exploiting the schema of peers. More precisely, we make the following contributions:

- In Sect. 3.2.1 we illustrate how peers can formulate complex (conjunctive) queries against an RDF/S schema using *RQL query patterns* [21].
- In Sect. 3.2.2 we detail how peers can advertise their base at a fine-grained level. In particular, we are employing *RVL view patterns* [27] for declaring the parts of an RDF/S schema which are actually (or can be) populated in a peer base.
- In Sect. 3.2.3 we introduce a semantic routing algorithm that matches a given RQL query against a set of RVL peer views in order to localize relevant peer bases. More precisely, this algorithm relies on the query/view subsumption techniques introduced in [7] to produce *query patterns annotated with localization information*.
- In Sect. 3.2.4 we describe how SQPeer *query plans* are generated by taking into account the involved data distribution (e.g., vertical, horizontal) in peer bases. To this end, we employ an object algebra for RQL queries introduced in [22].

- In Sect. 3.2.5 we discuss several *compile* and *run-time optimization opportunities* for SQPeer query plans.
- In Sect. 3.3 we sketch how the SQPeer query routing and planning phases can be actually used by groups of peers in order to deploy *hybrid* (i.e., super-peer) and *structured* P2P database systems.

Finally, Sect. 3.4 discusses related work and Section 3.5 summarizes our contributions.

3.2 The SQPeer Middleware

In order to design an effective query routing and planning middleware for peer RDF/S bases, we need to address the following issues:

1. How do peer nodes formulate queries?
2. How do peer nodes advertise their bases?
3. How do peer nodes route a query?
4. How do peer nodes process a query?
5. How are distributed query plans optimized?

In the following subsections, we will present the main design choices for SQPeer in response to the above issues.

Table 3.1. RQL class and property query patterns

Path Patterns	Interpretation
Class Path Patterns	
$C	$\{c \mid c$ is a schema class$\}$
$C\{X\}	$\{[c, x] \mid c$ a schema class, x in the interpretation of class $c\}$
$C\{X;$D\}	$\{[c, x, d] \mid c, d$ are schema classes, d is a subclass of c, x is in the interpretation of class $d\}$
Property Path Patterns	
@P	$\{p \mid p$ is a schema property$\}$
\{X\} @P \{Y\}	$\{[x, p, y] \mid p$ is a schema property, $[x, y]$ in the interpretation of property $p\}$
\{$C\} @P \{$D\}	$\{[c, p, d] \mid p$ is a schema property, c, d are schema classes, c is a subclass of p's domain, d is a subclass of p's range$\}$
\{X; $C\} @P \{Y; $D\}	$\{[x, c, p, y, d] \mid p$ is a schema property, c, d are schema classes, c is a subclass of p's domain, d is a subclass of p's range, x is in the interpretation of c, y is in the interpretation of d, $[x, y]$ is in the interpretation of $p\}$

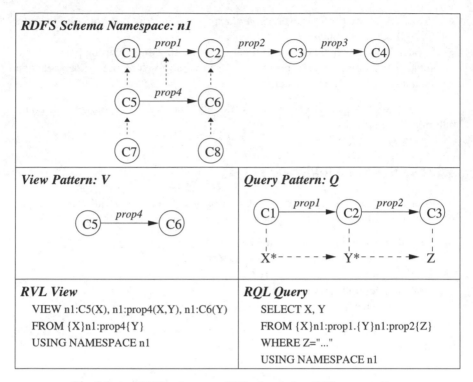

Fig. 3.1. An RDF/S schema, an RVL view and an RQL query pattern

3.2.1 RDF/S-based P2P databases and RQL Queries

In SQPeer we consider that each peer provides RDF/S descriptions about information resources available in the network that conform to a number of RDF/S schemata (e.g., for e-learning, e-science, etc.). Peers employing the same schema to create such descriptions in their local bases belong essentially to the same Semantic Overlay Network (SON) [9, 37]. In the upper part of Fig. 3.1, we can see an example of an RDF/S schema defining such a SON, which comprises four classes, C1, C2, C3 and C4, that are connected through three properties, prop1, prop2 and prop3. There are also two subsumed classes, C5 and C6, of C1 and C2 respectively, which are related with the subsumed property prop4 of prop1. Finally, classes C7 and C8 are subsumed by C5 and C6 respectively.

Queries in SQPeer are formulated by peers in RQL, according to the RDF/S schema (e.g., defined in a namespace n1) of the SON they belong using an appropriate GUI [1]. RQL queries allow us to retrieve the contents of any peer base, namely resources classified under classes or associated to other resources using properties defined in the RDF/S schema. It is worth noting that RQL queries incur both intensional (i.e., schema) and extensional (i.e., data) filtering conditions. Table 3.1 summarizes the basic *class* and *property path patterns*, which can be employed in order

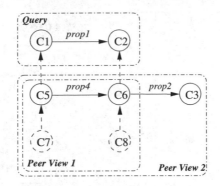

Fig. 3.2. Peer view advertisements and subsuming queries

to formulate complex RQL *query patterns*. These patterns are matched against the RDF/S schema or data graph of a peer base in order to bind graph nodes or edges to the variables introduced in the *from-clause*. The most commonly used RQL patterns essentially specify the fragment of the RDF/S schema graph (i.e., the intensional information), which is actually involved in the retrieval of resources hosted by a peer base.

For instance, in the bottom right part of Fig. 3.1 we can see an RQL query **Q** returning in the *select-clause* all the resources binded by the variables X and Y. The *from-clause* employs two property patterns (i.e., $\{X\}n1:prop1\{Y\}$ and $\{Y\}n1:prop2\{Z\}$), which imply a join on Y between the target resources of the property prop1 and the origin resources of the property prop2. Note that no restrictions are considered for the domain and range classes of the two properties, so the end-point classes C1, C2 and C3 of prop1 and prop2 are obtained from their corresponding schema definitions in the namespace n1. The *where-clause*, as usual, filters the binded resources according to the provided boolean conditions (e.g., on variable Z). The right middle part of Fig. 3.1 illustrates the pattern of query **Q**, where X and Y resource variables are marked with "*" to denote projections.

In the rest of this chapter, we are focusing on conjunctive queries formed only by RQL class and property patterns, as well as projected variables (filtering conditions are ignored). We should also note that SQPeer's query routing and planning algorithms can be also applied to less expressive RDF/S query languages [15].

3.2.2 RVL Advertisements of Peer Bases

Each peer should be able to advertise the content of its local base to others. Using these advertisements a peer becomes aware of the bases hosted by others in the system. Advertisements may provide descriptive information about the actual data values (extensional) or the actual schema (intensional) of a peer base. In order to reason on the intension of both the query requests and peer base contents, SQPeer relies on materialized or virtual RDF/S schema-based advertisements. In the former case, a peer RDF/S base actually holds resource descriptions created according to the

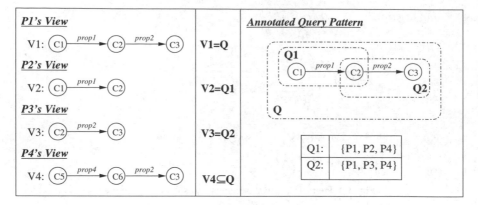

Fig. 3.3. An annotated RQL query pattern

employed schema(s), while in the latter, schema(s) can be populated on demand with data residing in a relational or an XML peer base. In both cases, the RDF/S schema defining a SON may contain numerous classes and properties not necessarily populated in a peer base. Therefore, we need a fine-grained definition of schema-based advertisements. We employ *RVL views* to specify the fragment of an RDF/S schema for which all classes and properties are (in the materialized scenario) or can be (in the virtual scenario) populated in a peer base. These views may be broadcasted to (or requested by) other peers, thus informing the rest of the P2P system of the information available in the peer bases. As we will see in Section 3.3, peer view propagation depends strongly on the underlying P2P system architecture.

The bottom left part of Fig. 3.1 illustrates the RVL statement employed to advertise a peer base according to the RDF/S schema identified by the namespace n1. This statement populates classes C5 and C6 and property prop4 (in the *view-clause*) with appropriate resources from the peer's base according to the bindings introduced in the *from-clause*. Given the query pattern used in the *from-clause*, C5 and C6 are populated with resources that are direct instances of C5 and C6 or any of their subsumed classes, i.e., C7 and C8. Actually, a peer advertising its base using this view is capable to answer query patterns involving not only the classes C5 and C6 (and prop4), but also any of the classes (or properties) that subsume them. For example, Fig. 3.2 illustrates a simple query involving classes C1, C2 and property prop1 subsuming the above peer view 1 (vertical subsumption). The second peer view illustrated in Fig. 3.2 extends the previous view with resource instances of class C3, which are reachable through prop2 with instances of C6. Peer view 2 can be employed to answer not only a query {X;C5}prop4{Y;C6}prop2{Z;C3} but also any of its fragments. As a matter of fact, the results of this query are contained in either {X;C5}prop4{Y;C6} or {Y;C6}prop2{Z;C3} (horizontal subsumption). Therefore peer view 2 can also contribute to the query {X;C1}prop1{Y;C2}.

Routing Algorithm:
`Input:` A query pattern QP.
`Output:` An annotated query pattern QP$'$.

1. QP$'$:= *construct an empty annotated query pattern for QP*
2. VP := *lookup(QP)*
3. for all *view patterns VP$_i$ ϵ VP, i=1 ... n do*
        if *isSubsumed(VP$_i$, QP) then*
            annotate QP$'$ with peer P responsible for VP$_i$
        end if
    end for
4. return QP$'$

Fig. 3.4. Query Routing Algorithm

It is worth noting that the class and property patterns appearing in the *from-clause* of an RVL statement are the same as those appearing in the corresponding clause of RQL, while the *view-clause* states explicitly the schema information related with the view results (see view pattern in the middle of Fig. 3.1). A more complex example is illustrated in the left part of Fig. 3.3, comprising the view patterns of four peers. Peer P1 contains resources related through properties `prop1` and `prop2`, while peer P4 contains resources related through properties `prop4` and `prop2`. Peer P2 contains resources related through `prop1`, while peer P3 contains resources related through `prop2`.

We can note the similarity in the intensional representation of peer base advertisements and query requests, respectively, as view and query patterns. This representation provides a uniform logical framework to route and plan queries through distributed peer bases using exclusively intensional information (i.e., schema/typing), while it exhibits significant performance advantages. First, the size of the indices, which can be constructed on the intensional peer base advertisements, is considerably smaller than on the extensional ones. Second, by representing in the same way what is queried by a peer and what is contained in a peer base, we can reuse the RQL query/RVL view (sound and complete) subsumption algorithms, proposed in the Semantic Web Integration Middleware (SWIM [7]). Finally, compared to global schema-based advertisements [32], we expect that the load of queries processed by each peer is smaller, since a peer receives queries that exactly match its base. This also affects the amount of network bandwidth consumed by the P2P system.

3.2.3 Query Routing and Fragmentation

Query routing in SQPeer is responsible for finding the relevant to a query peer views by taking into account data distribution (vertical, horizontal and mixed) of peer bases committing to an RDF/S schema.

The routing algorithm (outlined in Fig. 3.4) takes as input a query pattern and returns a query pattern annotated with information about the peers that can actually answer it. A lookup service (i.e., function *lookup*), which strongly depends on the underlying P2P topology, is employed to find peer views relevant to the input pattern. The query/view subsumption algorithms of [7] are employed to determine whether a query can be answered by a peer view. More precisely, function *isSubsumed* checks whether every class/property in the query is present or subsumes a class/property of the view (as previously illustrated in Fig. 3.2).

Prior to the execution of the routing algorithm, a *fragmentor* is employed to break a complex query pattern given as input into more simple ones, according to the number of joins (input parameter *#joins*) between the resulting fragments, which are required to answer the original pattern. Recall that a query pattern is always a fragment graph of the underlying RDF/S schema graph. The input parameter *#joins* is determined by the optimization techniques employed by the query processor. In the simplest case (i.e., *#joins* equals to the maximum number of joins in the input query), both query and view patterns are decomposed into their basic class and property patterns (see Table 3.1). For each query fragment pattern, the routing algorithm is executed and all the available views are checked for identifying those that can answer it.

Figure 3.3 illustrates an example of how SQPeer routing algorithm works given an RQL query **Q** composed by two property patterns, namely **Q1** and **Q2**, as well as the views of four peers. The middle part of the figure depicts how each pattern matches one of the four peer views. The variable *#joins* in this example is set to 1, so the two simple property patterns of query **Q** are checked. A more sophisticated fragmentation example will be presented in Section 3.3. P1's view consists of the property patterns **Q1** and **Q2**, so both patterns are annotated with P1. P2's view consists of pattern **Q1** and P3's view consists of **Q2**, so **Q1** and **Q2** are annotated with P2 and P3 respectively. Finally, P4's view is subsumed by patterns **Q1** and **Q2**, since `prop4` is a subproperty of `prop1`. Similarly to P1, **Q1** and **Q2** are annotated with P4. In the right part of Fig. 3.3 we can see the annotated query pattern returned by the SQPeer routing algorithm, when applied to the RQL query and RVL views of our example.

It should be also stressed that SQPeer is capable to reformulate queries expressed against a SON RDF/S schema in terms of heterogeneous descriptive schemata employed by remote peers. This functionality is supported by powerful mappings to RDF/S of both structured relational and semistructured XML peer bases offered by SWIM [7].

3.2.4 Query Planning and Execution

Query planning in SQPeer is responsible for generating a distributed query plan according to the localization information returned by the routing algorithm. The first step towards this end, is to provide an algebraic translation of the RQL query patterns annotated with data localization information.

The algebraic translation algorithm (see Fig. 3.5) relies on the object algebra of RQL [22] (see also Chap. 1,2). Initially, the annotated query pattern (i.e., a schema fragment) is traversed and for each subfragment considered by the fragmentation policy the annotations with relevant peers are extracted. If more than one peer can

Algebraic Translation Algorithm:
`Input:` An annotated query pattern AQ′ and current fragment
pattern PP (initially the root).
`Output:` A query plan QP corresponding to the annotated query
pattern AQ′.

```
1. QP := ∅
2. P := {P₁...Pₙ}, set of peers obtained by the annotation of
   PP in AQ
3. for all peers Pₓ ∈ P do
        QP := QP⋃PP@Pₓ  -Horizontal Distribution-
   end for
4. for all fragment patterns PPᵢ ∈ children(PP)
        TPᵢ := Algebraic Translation Algorithm(PPᵢ, AQ′)
   end for
   QP := ⋈Cp(QP, TP₁, ..., TPₘ)  -Vertical Distribution-
5. return QP
```

Fig. 3.5. Algebraic Translation Algorithm

answer the same pattern, the results from each such peer base are "unioned" (horizontal distribution). As the query pattern is traversed, the results obtained for different patterns that are connected at a specific domain or range class are "joined" (vertical distribution). The final query plan is created when all fragment patterns are translated.

Figure 3.6 illustrates how the RQL query **Q** introduced in Fig. 3.1 can be translated given the four peer views presented in Fig. 3.3. In this example, we assume that P1 has already executed the routing algorithm in order to generate the annotated query pattern depicted in Fig. 3.3. The algebraic translation algorithm, also running at P1, initially translates the root pattern, i.e., **Q1**, into the algebraic `Subplan 1` depicted in Fig. 3.6 (i.e., P1, P2 and P4 can effectively answer the subquery). The partial results obtained by these peers should be "unioned" (horizontal distribution). By checking all the children patterns of the root, we recursively traverse the input annotated query pattern and translate its constituent fragment plans. For instance, when **Q2** is visited as the first (and only) child of **Q1** the algebraic `Subplan 2` is created (i.e., P1, P3 and P4 can effectively answer the subquery). Then, the returned query plan concerning **Q2** is "joined" (vertical distribution) with `Subplan 1`, thus producing the final plan illustrated in the left part of Fig. 3.6 (i.e., no more fragments of the initial annotated query pattern **Q** need to be traversed). We can easily observe from our example that taking into account the vertical distribution ensures *correctness* of query results (i.e., produce a valid answer), while considering horizontal distribution in query plans favours *completeness* of query results (i.e., produce more and more valid answers).

In order to create the necessary foundation for executing distributed query (sub)plans among the involved peers, SQPeer relies on appropriate communication *channels*. Through channels, peers are able to route (sub)plans and exchange the in-

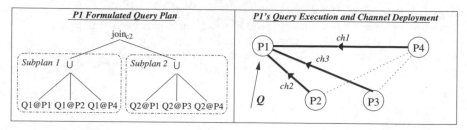

Fig. 3.6. Query plan generation and channel deployment in SQPeer

termediary results produced by their execution. It is worth noticing that channels allow each peer to further route and process autonomously the received (sub)plans, by contacting peers independently of the previous routing operations. Finally, channel deployment can be adapted during query execution in order to response to network failures or peer processing limitations. Each channel has a root and a destination node. The root node of a channel is responsible for the management of the channel by using its local unique id. Data packets are sent through each channel from the destination to the root node. Beside query results, these packets can also contain information about network or peer failures for possible plan modification or even statistics for query optimization purposes. The channel construct and operations of ubQL [33] are employed to implement the above functionality in the SQPeer middleware.

Once a query plan is created and a peer is assigned to its execution (see Sect. 3.2.5), this peer becomes responsible for the deployment of the necessary channels in the system (see right part of Fig. 3.6). A channel is created having as root the peer launching the execution of the plan and as destination one of the peers that need to be contacted each time according to the plan. Although each of these peers may contribute in the execution of the plan by answering to more than one fragment queries, only one channel is of course created. This is one of the objectives of the optimization techniques presented in the sequel.

3.2.5 Query Optimization

The query optimizer receives an algebraic query plan created and outputs an optimized execution plan. In SQPeer, we consider two possible optimization strategies of distributed query plans, namely *compile* and *run-time optimizations*.

Compile-time Optimization

Compile-time optimization relies on algebraic equivalences (e.g., distribution of joins and unions) and heuristics allowing us to push, as much as, possible query evaluation to the same peers. Additionally, cost-based optimization relies on statistics about the peer bases in order to reorder joins and choose between different execution policies (e.g., data versus query shipping).

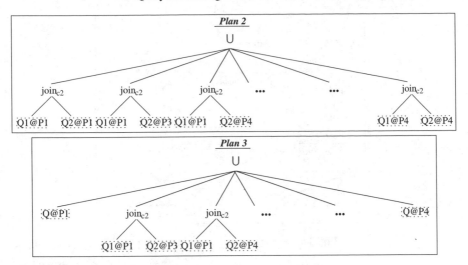

Fig. 3.7. Optimizing query plans by applying algebraic equivalences and heuristics

As we have seen in Fig. 3.6, the algebraic query plan produced contains unions only at the bottom of the plan tree. We can push unions to the top and consequently push joins closer to the leaves. This makes possible (a) to evaluate an entire join at a single peer (intra-peer processing) when its view is subsumed by the query fragment, and (b) to parallelize the execution of the union in several peers. The latter can be achieved by allowing for example each fragment plan (consisting of only joins) to be autonomously processed and executed by different peers. The former suggests applying the following algebraic equivalence as long as the number of inter-peer (i.e., between different peers) joins in the equivalent query plan is less than the intra-peer one. This heuristic comes in accordance to best effort query processing strategies for P2P systems introduced in [41]. Moreover, promoting intra-peer processing exploits the benefits of query shipping as discussed in [12].

Algebraic equivalence: Distribution of joins and unions

Given a subquery $\bowtie (\bigcup(Q_{11}, \ldots, Q_{1n}), \bigcup(Q_{21}, \ldots, Q_{2m}))$ *rewrite it into* $\bigcup(\bowtie$ $(Q_{11}, Q_{21}), \bowtie (Q_{11}, Q_{22}), \ldots, \bowtie (Q_{1n}, Q_{2m}))$.

According to the above algebraic equivalence, the algebraic query plan of Fig. 3.6 is transformed into the equivalent query execution `Plan 2` of Fig. 3.7. One can easily observe that query `Plan 2` does not take into account the fact that one peer (e.g., P4) can answer more than one successive patterns, unless more sophisticated fragmentation is considered (see Section 3.2.4). To this end, we apply the following two heuristics for identifying those subplans that can be answered by the same peer.

Heuristic 1:

Given a subquery $\bowtie (Q_1 @P_i, \ldots, Q_n @P_i)$ *rewrite it into* $Q @ P_i$, *where* $Q = Q_1 \bowtie \ldots \bowtie Q_n$.

Heuristic 2:

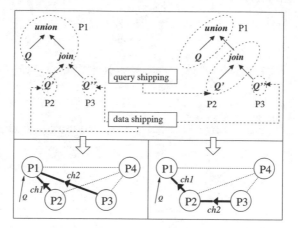

Fig. 3.8. Data and Query Shipping Example

Given a subquery $\bowtie (\bowtie (QP, Q_1@P_i), Q_2@P_i)$ rewrite it into $\bowtie (QP, Q@P_i)$, where $Q = Q_1 \bowtie Q_2$.

As we can see in Fig. 3.7, the produced `Plan 3` enables to execute the entire query pattern **Q** to the relevant peers, i.e., joins on properties `prop1` and `prop2` will be executed by peers P1 and P4 respectively.

Furthermore, statistics about the communication cost between peers (e.g., measured by the speed of their connection) and the size of expected intermediary query results (given by a cost-model) can be used to decide which peer and in what order will undertake the execution of each query operator and thus the concrete channel deployment. To this end, the processing load of the peers should also be taken into account, since a peer that processes fewer queries, even if its connection is slow, may offer a better execution time. This processing load can be measured by the existence of slots in each peer, which show the amount of queries that can be handled simultaneously.

Having these statistics in hand, a peer (e.g., P1) can decide at compile-time between *data, query* or *hybrid shipping* execution policies. In the left part of Fig. 3.8 we can see the data shipping alternative, since P1 sends queries **Q'** and **Q"** to peers P2 and P3 and joins their results locally. In the right part of Fig. 3.8 we can see the query shipping alternative, since P1 decides to forward the join operation down to P2, which in turn receives the results from P3 and executes the join locally before sending the full answer to P1 for further processing. At the bottom of the figure, we can see the deployment of the corresponding channels for each of these two alternative execution policies. In the case where the communication cost between peers P1 and P3 is greater than the cost between peers P2 and P3 or P2 intermediate results for subquery **Q'** are large, query-shipping is preferable, since it exploits the fastest peer connection. In the case where peer P2 has a heavy processing load, data-shipping should be chosen, since P1 will execute both the union and the join operators of the plan. In a situation where we have to choose between two or more of the above optimizations, SQPeer favors the execution of the intra-site query operators.

Run-time Optimization

On the other hand, run-time adaptability of query plans is an essential characteristic of query processing when peer bases join and leave the system at free will or more generally when system resources are exhausted. For example, the optimizer may alter a running query plan by observing the throughput of a certain channel. This throughput can be measured by the number of incoming or outgoing tuples (i.e., resources related through one or several properties). Changing query plans may alter an already installed channel, as well as the query plans of the root and destination peer of the channel. These changes include deciding at execution time on altering the data or query shipping decision or discovering alternative peers for answering a certain subplan. The root peer of each channel is responsible for identifying possible problems caused by environmental changes and for handling them accordingly. It should also inform all the involved peers that are affected by the alteration of the plan. Since the alteration is done on a subplan and not on the whole query plan, only the peers related to this subplan should be informed and possibly a few other peers that contain partial results from the execution of the failed plan. Finally, the root peer should create a new query plan by re-executing the routing and planning phases and not taking into consideration those peers that became obsolete.

We should keep in mind that switching to a different query plan in the middle of the query execution raises interesting problems. Previous results, which were already created by the execution of the query to possible multiple peers, have to be handled, since the new query plan will produce new results. There are two possible solutions to this issue. The ubQL approach [33] proposes to discard previous intermediate results and all on-going computations are terminated. Alternatively, [19] proposes a phased query execution, in which each time the query plan is changed, the system enters into a new phase. The final phase, which is called the cleanup phase, is responsible for combining the sub-results from the other phases in order to obtain a full answer. In SQPeer middleware, we have adopted the ubQL approach.

3.3 P2P Architectures and SQPeer

SQPeer can be used in different P2P architectural settings. Even though the specific P2P architecture affects peers' topology, the proposed algorithms can be applied to any particular architectural setting. Recall that the existence of SONs minimizes the broadcasting (flooding) activity in the P2P system, since a query is received and processed only by the relevant peers. In the sequel, we detail the possible roles that peers may play in each setting with respect to their corresponding computing capabilities.

On the one hand, we have *client-peers*, which may frequently join or leave the system. These peers have only the ability to pose RQL queries to the rest of the P2P system. Since these peers usually have limited computing capabilities and they are connected to the system for short period of time, they do not participate in the query routing and planning phases.

On the other hand, we may have *simple-peers* that also act autonomously by joining or leaving the system, maybe not so frequently as client-peers. Their corresponding bases can be shared by other peers during their connection to the P2P system. When they join the system, simple-peers can broadcast their views or alternatively request the RVL views of their known neighbors. Thus, a simple-peer identifies and connects physically with the SON(s) it belongs to and becomes aware of its new neighborhood. Simple-peers have also the ability to pose queries as client-peers, but with the extra functionality of executing these queries against their own local bases or coordinate the execution of fragment queries on remote peers.

Additionally, a small percentage of the peers may play the role of *super-peers*. Super-peers are usually highly-available nodes offering high computing capabilities and each one acts as a centralized server for a subset of simple-peers. Super-peers are mainly responsible for routing queries through the system and for managing the cluster of simple-peers that are responsible for. Furthermore, super-peers may play the role of a mediator in a scenario where a query expressed in terms of a globally known schema needs to be reformulated in terms of the schemata employed by the local bases of the simple-peers by using appropriate mapping rules.

In this context, we consider two architectural alternatives distinguished according to the topology of the peer network and the distribution of peer base advertisements. The first alternative corresponds to a *hybrid* P2P architecture based on the notion of *super-peers*, while the second one is closer to a *structured* P2P architecture based on *Distributed Hash Tables* (DHTs). In the structured architecture, SONs are created in a *self-adaptive way*, while in the super-peer architecture SONs are created in a more *static way*, since each super-peer is responsible for the creation and further management of SONs. It should be stressed that while in the structured architecture, peers handle both the query routing and planning load, super-peers are primarily responsible for routing and simple-peers for query planning in two distinct phases. Additionally, super-peers are aware of all simple-peer views in a SON, while in the structured alternative this knowledge is distributed and becomes available through an adequate lookup service.

3.3.1 Hybrid P2P SONs

In a hybrid P2P system [42, 32] (see also Chapt. 8) each peer is connected with at least one super-peer, who is responsible for collecting the views (materialized or virtual) of all its simple-peers. The peers, holding bases described according to the same RDF/S schema, are clustered under the same super-peer. Thus, each peer implicitly knows the views of all its semantic neighbors. In a more sophisticated scenario, super-peers are responsible only for a specific fragment of the RDF/S schema and thus a cluster of super-peers is responsible for the entire schema. Moreover, a hierarchical organization of super-peers can be adopted, where the classes and properties managed at each level are connected through semantic relationships (e.g., subsumption) with the class and properties of the upper and lower levels.

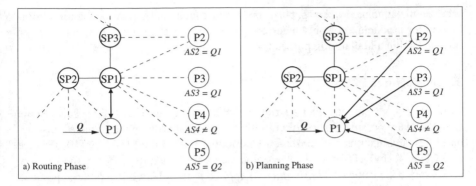

Fig. 3.9. SQPeer separated query routing and planning phases in a hybrid P2P system

When a peer connects to a super-peer, it forwards its corresponding view. All super-peers are aware of each other, in order to be able to answer queries expressed in terms of different RDF/S schemata (or fragments), while a simple-peer should be connected to several super-peers when its base commits to more than one schemata. The exact topology of the P2P system depends on the clustering policy with respect to the number of available super-peers providing the bandwidth and connectivity guarantees of the system.

A client-peer can connect to a simple-peer and issue a query request for further processing to the system. The simple-peer forwards the query to the appropriate super-peer according to the schema employed by the query (e.g., by examining the involved namespaces). If this schema is unknown to the simple-peer, it sends the query randomly to one of its known super-peers, which will consecutively discover the appropriate super-peer through the super-peer backbone. In this alternative, we distinguish two separate query evaluation phases: the first corresponds to *query routing* performed exclusively at the super-peers, while the second to *query planning and execution*, which is usually performed by the simple-peers.

For example, in Fig. 3.9, we consider a super-peer backbone containing three super-peers, SP1, SP2 and SP3, and a set of client-peers, P1 to P5. All the simple-peers are connected with at least SP1, since their bases commit to the schema that SP1 is responsible for. When P1 receives a query **Q**, it initially contacts SP1, which is the super-peer responsible for the SON on which the query is addressed (Fig. 3.9a). Since SP1 contains all related peer views, it can also decide on the appropriate fragmentation of the received query pattern according to the view patterns of its simple-peers. Then, SP1 creates an annotated query pattern containing the localization information that P2 and P3 can answer only the **Q1** pattern, while P5 can answer only the **Q2** pattern. SP1 sends this annotated pattern to P1 to generate the appropriate query plan. In our example, this plan implies the creation of three channels with P2, P3 and P5 for gathering the results (Fig. 3.9b). P2, P3 and P5 send their results back to P1, who joins them locally in order to produce the final answer. We should point out that since a super-peer contains all the peer views related to a specific RDF/S schema, the annotated query pattern for **Q** will contain sufficient localization information for producing not only a correct but also a complete query plan and thus no further routing and planning phases for **Q** are required.

3.3.2 Structured P2P SONs

Alternatively, we can consider a structured P2P architecture [5, 6, 36]. Peers in the same SON are organized according to the topology imposed by the underline structured P2P architecture, e.g., based on Distributed Hash Tables (DHTs) [40, 18] (see also Chap. 4). In DHT-based P2P systems, peers are logically placed in the network according to the value of a *hash function* applied to their IP, while a table of pointers to a predefined number of neighbor peers is maintained. Each information resource (e.g., a document or a tuple) is uniquely identified within the system by a key. In order to locate the peers hosting a specific resource, we need to match the hash value of a given key with the hash value of a peer and forward the lookup request to other peers by taking into account the hash table maintained by each contacted peer. In our context, unique keys are assigned to each view pattern and hence peers, whose hash values match those keys, are aware of the peer bases that are populated with data answering a specific schema fragment. An appropriate key assignment and hash function should be used in order neighbor peers to hold successive view patterns with respect to the class/property hierarchy defined in the employed RDF/S schema. This is necessary for optimizing query routing, since successive view patterns are likely to be subsumed by the same query pattern.

Unlike super-peers, in this alternative there is no peer with a global knowledge of all peer views in the SON. The localization information about remote peer views is acquired by the lookup service supported by the system. Specifically, we are interested in identifying peer views that can actually answer an entire (sub)query pattern given as input. This implies an *interleaved execution of query routing and planning phases* in several iteration rounds leading to the creation and execution of multiple query plans that when "unioned" offer completeness in the results. Note that the generated plans at each round can be actually executed (in contrast to bottom-up dynamic programming algorithms) by the involved peers in order to obtain the first parts of the final query answer. Starting with the initial query pattern, at each round, smaller fragments are considered in order to find the relevant peer bases (routing phase) that can actually answer them (planning phase). In this context, the interleaved query processing terminates when the initial query is decomposed into its basic class and property patterns. It should be also stressed that SQPeer interleaved query routing and planning favors intra-site joins, since each query fragment is looked up as a whole and only peers that can fully answer it are contacted.

For example, in Fig. 3.10 we consider that peers P1 to P8 are connected in a structured P2P system. When P1 receives the query **Q**, it launches the interleaved query routing and planning. At round 1, P1 issues a lookup request for the entire query pattern **Q**, and annotates **Q** with peers P2 and P4. In this initial round, plan `Plan 1` $= Q@P2 \bigcup Q@P4$ is created and executed. At round 2, the fragmentor is called with *#joins* equal to 1. The two possible fragmentations of query **Q** are depicted in

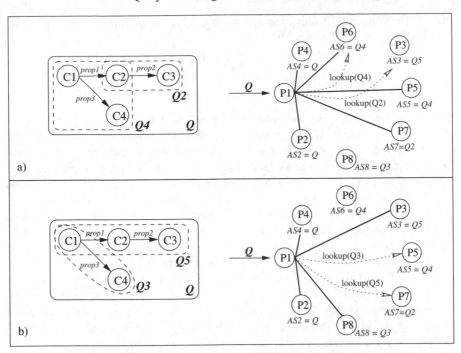

Fig. 3.10. SQPeer interleaved query routing and planning mechanism in a structured P2P system for a fragmentation round with *#joins*=1

Fig. 3.10a and b. First, peers P6 and P3 are contacted through the lookup service, since they contain the list of peer bases answering query fragment patterns **Q4** and **Q2** respectively (seen in the left part of Fig. 3.10a). P6 returns the list of peers P2, P4, P5 and P6, while P3 returns peers P2, P3, P4 and P7. For this fragmentation, the query plan Plan 2 = $\bigcup (\bowtie (Q4@P2, Q2@P3), \bowtie (Q4@P2, Q2@P4), \ldots, \bowtie (Q4@P6, Q2@P4), \bowtie (Q4@P6, Q2@P7))$ is created and executed by deploying the necessary channels between the involved peers (see right part of Fig. 3.10a). It is worth noticing that the generated plans at each round do not include redundant computations already considered in a previous round. For example Plan 2 produced in round 2 excludes the query fragment plan $\bowtie (Q4@P2, Q2@P2)$ generated in round 1. Next, peers P5 and P7 are contacted through the lookup service, since they contain the list of peer bases answering query patterns **Q3** and **Q5** respectively (seen in the left part of Fig. 3.10b). P5 returns the list of peers P2, P4, P5, P6 and P8, while P7 returns peers P2, P3 and P4 and the query plan Plan 3 = $\bigcup (\bowtie (Q3@P2, Q4@P3), \bowtie (Q3@P2, Q4@P4), \ldots, \bowtie (Q3@P8, Q4@P3), \bowtie (Q3@P8, Q4@P4))$ is created and executed (see right part of Fig. 3.10b). Again, Plan 3 is disjoint with the plans already generated. At the last round (*#joins* equals to 2), we consider all basic property and class patterns of query **Q** and run one more time the routing and planning algorithms to produce query plans returning the remaining parts of the final answer.

3.4 Related Work

Several projects address query planning issues in P2P database systems. Query Flow [24] is a system offering dynamic and distributed query processing using the notion of HyperQueries. HyperQueries are essentially subplans that exist in each peer and guide routing and processing of a query through the network. Furthermore, ubQL [33] provides a suite of process manipulation primitives that can be added on top of any declarative query language to support distributed query optimization. ubQL distinguishes the deployment from the execution phase of a query and supports adaptability of query plans during the execution phase. Compared to these projects, SQPeer does not require an a priori knowledge of the relevant to a query peers.

Mutant Query Plans (MQPs) [39] are logical query plans, where leaf nodes may consist of URN/URL references, or of materialized XML data. The references to resource locations (URLs) point to peers where the actual data reside, while the abstract resource names (URNs) can be seen as the thematic topics of the requested data in a SON. MQPs are themselves serialized as XML elements and are exchanged among the peers. When a peer N receives a MQP M, N can resolve the URN references and/or materialize the URL references, thus offering its local localization information. Furthermore, S can evaluate and re-optimize MQP fragment plans by adding XML fragments to the leafs. Finally, it can just route M to another peer. When a MQP is fully evaluated, i.e., reduced to a concreate XML document, the result is returned to the *target* peer, which has initiated the query. The efficient routing of MQPs is preserved by information derived from multi-hierarchic topic namespaces (e.g., for educational material on computer science or for geographical information) organized by assigning different roles to specific peers. This approach is similar to a super-peer architecture, with the difference that a distributed query routing phase is introduced involving more than one peers. Unlike SQPeer, MQP reduces the optimization opportunities by simply migrating possibly big XML fragments of query plans along with partial results of query fragments. In addition, it is not clear how subtopics can be exploited during query routing.

AmbientDB [5] addresses P2P data management issues in a digital environment, i.e., audio players exchanging music collections. AmbientDB provides full relational database functionality and assumes the existence of a common global schema, although peers may dispose their own schemata (mappings are used in this case). In AmbientDB, apart from the local tables stored at each peer, horizontal data distribution is considered, since fragments of a table, called distributed tables, may be stored at different peers. The query processing mechanism is based on a three-level translation of an "abstract global algebra" into stream based query plans, distributed over an ad-hoc and self-organizing P2P network. Initially, a query is translated into standard relational operators for selection, join, aggregation and sort over "abstract table types." Then, this abstract query plan becomes concrete by instantiating the abstract table types with concrete ones, i.e., the local or distributed tables that exist in the peer bases. Finally at the execution level, the concrete query plan is executed by selecting between different query execution strategies. The AmbientDB P2P protocol is responsible for query routing and relies on temporary (logical) routing trees, which are created on-the-fly as subgraphs of the Chord network. Chord is also used to implement clustered indices of distributed tables in AmbientDB. Each AmbientDB peer contains the index table partition that corresponds to it after hashing the key-values of all tuples in the distributed table. The user decides for the use of such DHTs, thus accelerating relevant lookup queries. Compared to AmbientDB, SQPeer provides a richer data framework, as well as exhibits a run-time adaptability of generated query plans. More importantly, DHT in SQPeer is based not on data values but on peer views, thus providing efficient intensional indexing and routing capabilities.

Other projects address mainly query routing issues in SONs. In [13] indices are used to identify peers that can handle containment queries (e.g., in XML). For each keyword in the query, a peer searches its indices and returns a set of peers that can answer it. According to the operators used to connect these keywords, the peer decides whether to union or intersect the sets of relevant peers. In this approach, queries are directly sent to the set of peers returned by the routing phase with no further details on how a set of semantically related peers can actually execute a complex query involving both vertical and horizontal data distribution.

RDFPeers [6] is a scalable distributed RDF/S repository based on an extension of Chord, namely MAAN (Multi-Attribute Addressable Network), which efficiently answers multi-attribute and range queries. Peers are organized into a Chord-like ring. In MAAN, each RDF triple is hashed and stored for each of its subject, predicate or object values in corresponding positions of the ring. Furthermore, for numerical attributes MAAN uses order preserving hash functions for placing close values to neighboring peers in the ring, thus optimizing the evaluation of range queries. Routing is performed as in Chord by searching for each value of the query and combining the results at the peer launching the initial query. This approach ignores RDF/S schema information during query routing, while distributed query planning and execution policies are not addressed.

In [34], a super-peer like P2P architecture is introduced, which relies on the extension of an existing RDF/S store. Authors propose an index structure for all the path patterns that can be extracted given an RDF/S schema. The paths in the index are organized hierarchically according to their length (simple properties appear as leaves of the tree). For each path in the tree, the index maintains information about the peers that can answer it, as well as the size of path instantiations. A query processing algorithm determines all possible combinations of the subpaths of a given query pattern, as well as, the peers that can answer it. The proposed index structure, which is considered to be controlled by a mediator, is difficult to be updated and handled in a situation where peers frequently enter or leave the system. The localization information concerning different query fragments is held in a centralized way. Although schema information is used for indexing, RDF/S class and property subsumption is not considered as in SQPeer. Finally, optimization (based on a cost model) is focused only on join re-orderings, which is a subset of the optimizations considered in SQPeer.

The Edutella project [32] explores the design and implementation of a schema-based P2P infrastructure for the Semantic Web. In Edutella, peer content is described by different and extensible RDF/S schemata. Super-peers are responsible for message routing and integration/mediation of peer bases. The routing mechanism is based on appropriate indices to route a query initially within the super-peer backbone and then between super-peers and their respective simple peers. A query processing mechanism in such a schema-based P2P system is presented in [4]. Query evaluation plans (QEPs) containing selection predicates, aggregation functions, joins, etc., are pushed from clients to simple or super-peers where they are executed. Super-peers dispose an optimizer for generating plans determining which fragments of the original query will be sent to the next (super-)peers and which operators will be locally executed. This approach involves rather simple query/view rewriting techniques (i.e., exact matching of basic class and property patterns) which ignores subsumption. In addition, a query is fragmented in its simple class and property patterns, thus not allowing the handling of more complex fragment graphs of the employed RDF/S schema.

To conclude, although the use of indices and super-peer topologies facilitate query routing, the cost of maintaining (XML or RDF) extensional indices of entire peer bases is important compared to the cost of maintaining intensional peer views, as in the case of SQPeer. In addition, SQPeer's interleaved execution of the routing and planning phases enables to obtain quickly the first results of the query (and probably the most relevant ones) while planning is still running. This is an original feature of the SQPeer query processing, taking into account that the search space of plans required to obtain a complete result in P2P systems is exponential. Last but not least, SQPeer can be used to deploy both hybrid and structured P2P systems.

3.5 Summary

In this chapter, we have presented the design of the ICS-FORTH SQPeer middleware offering sophisticated query routing and planning services for P2P database systems. We presented how declarative RQL queries and RVL views expressed against an RDF/S schema can be represented as schema-based patterns. We sketched a semantic routing algorithm, which relies on query/view subsumption techniques to annotate query patterns with peer localization information. We also presented how SQPeer query plans are created and executed by taking into account the data distribution in peer bases. Finally, we have discussed several compile and run-time optimization opportunities for SQPeer query plans, as well as possible architectural alternatives for static or self-adaptive RDF/S-based P2P database systems.

Several issues remain open with respect to the effective and efficient processing of distributed queries in SQPeer. The number of plans that need to be considered by our dynamic programming planner can be fairly large especially when we generate all fragmentation alternatives of a large query pattern given as input. To this end, we intend to investigate to what extend heuristic pruning techniques (e.g., iterative dynamic programming [26]) can be employed to prune subplans as soon as possible [10]. Furthermore, we plan to study the tradeoff between result completeness and response time of queries using appropriate information quality metrics (e.g., coverage of schema classes and properties [11, 31, 30, 16]) enabling to obtain quickly the Top-K answers [25, 35]. Finally, we plan to consider adaptive implementations of algebraic operators borrowing ideas from [2, 17, 20].

References

[1]   Athanasis N, Christophides V, Kotzinos D (2004), Generating On the Fly Queries for the Semantic Web: The ICS-FORTH Graphical RQL Interface (GRQL). In Proceedings of the 3rd International Semantic Web Conference (ISWC'04), Hiroshima, Japan
[2]   Avnur R, Hellerstein JM (2000) Eddies: Continuously Adaptive Query Processing. ACM SIGMOD, pp.261–272, Dallas, TX
[3]   Bernstein PA, Giunchiglia F, Kementsietsidis A, Mylopoulos J, Serafini L, Zaihrayeu I (2002) Data management for peer-to-peer computing: A vision. In Proceedings of the 5th International Workshop on the Web and Databases (WebDB), Madison, Wisconsin
[4]   Brunkhorst I, Dhraief H, Kemper A, Nejdl W, Wiesner C (2003) Distributed Queries and Query Optimization in Schema-Based P2P-Systems. In Proceedings of the International Workshop on Databases, Information Systems and Peer-to-Peer Computing (DBISP2P), Berlin, Germany
[5]   Boncz P, Treijtel C (2003) AmbientDB: relational query processing in a P2P network. In Proceedings of the International Workshop on Databases, Information Systems and Peer-to-Peer Computing (DBISP2P), LNCS 2788, Springer, Berlin Heidelberg New York
[6]   Cai M, Frank M (2004) RDFPeers: A Scalable Distributed RDF Repository based on A Structured Peer-to-Peer Network. In Proceedings of the 13th International World Wide Web Conference (WWW), New York
[7]   Christophides V, Karvounarakis G, Koffina I, Kokkinidis G, Magkanaraki A, Plexousakis D, Serfiotis G, Tannen V (2003) The ICS-FORTH SWIM: A Powerful Semantic Web Integration Middleware. In Proceedings of the 1st International Workshop on Semantic Web and Databases (SWDB), Co-located with VLDB 2003, Humboldt-Universitat, Berlin, Germany
[8]   Clarke I, Sandberg O, Wiley B, Hong TW (2001) Freenet: A Distributed Anonymous Information Storage and Retrieval System. In Proceedings of the International Workshop on Design Issues in Anonymity and Unobservability, Volume 2009 of LNCS, Springer-Verlag
[9]   Crespo A, Garcia-Molina H (2003) Semantic Overlay Networks for P2P Systems. Stanford Technical Report

[10] Deshpande A, Hellerstein JM, (2002) Decoupled Query Optimization for Federated Database Systems. In Proceedings of the 18th International Conference on Data Engineering (ICDE'02), San Jose, California

[11] Doan A, Halevy A (2002) Efficiently Ordering Query Plans for Data Integration. In Proceedings of the 18th IEEE Conference on Data Engineering (ICDE)

[12] Franklin MJ, Jonsson BT, Kossmann D (1996) Performance Tradeoffs for Client-Server Query Processing. In Proceedings of the ACM SIGMOD Conference, pp.149–160, Montreal, Canada

[13] Galanis L, Wang Y, Jeffery SR, DeWitt DJ (2003) Processing Queries in a Large P2P System. In Proceedings of the 15th International Conference on Advanced Information Systems Engineering (CAiSE)

[14] The Gnutella file-sharing protocol. Available at : http://gnutella.wego.com

[15] Haase P, Broekstra J, Eberhart A, Volz R (2004) A Comparison of RDF Query Languages. In Proceedings of the 3rd International Semantic Web Conference, Hiroshima, Japan

[16] Heese R, Herschel S, Naumann F, Roth A (2005) Self-Extending Peer Data Management. In GI-Fachtagung fur Datenbanksysteme in Business, Technologie und Web (BTW 2005), Karlsruhe, Germany

[17] Huebsch R, Jeffery SR (2004) FREddies: DHT-based Adaptive Query Processing via FedeRated Eddies. Technical report, Computer Science Division, University of Berkeley

[18] Stoica I, Morris R, Karger D, Kaashoek MF, Balakrishnan H (2001) Chord: A Scalable Peer-to-peer Lookup Service for Internet Applications, ACM SIG-COMM 2001, pp.149–160, San Diego, CA

[19] Ives ZG (2002) Efficient Query Processing for Data Integration. phD Thesis, University of Washington

[20] Ives ZG, Levy AY, Weld DS, Florescu D, Friedman M (2000) Adaptive Query Processing for Internet Applications. IEEE Data Engineering Bulletin 23:19–26

[21] Karvounarakis G, Alexaki S, Christophides V, Plexousakis D, Scholl M (2002) RQL: A Declarative Query Language for RDF. In Proceedings of the 11th International World Wide Web Conference (WWW), Honolulu, Hawaii, USA

[22] Karvounarakis G, Christophides V, Plexousakis D, Alexaki S (2001) Querying RDF Descriptions for Community Web Portals. 17ie'mes Journees Bases de Donnees Avancees (BDA'01), Agadir, Maroc

[23] The Kazaa file-sharing system. Available at : http://www.kazaa.com

[24] Kemper A, Wiesner C (2001) HyperQueries: Dynamic Distributed Query Processing on the Internet. In Proceedings of the International Conference on Very Large Data Bases (VLDB), Rome, Italy

[25] Kossmann D (2000) The State of the Art in Distributed Query Processing. ACM Computer Surveys 32:422–469

[26] Kossmann D, Stocker K (2000) Iterative Dynamic Programming: A new class of query optimization algorithms, ACM Transactions on Database Systems, volume 25, number 1

[27] Magkanaraki A, Tannen V, Christophides V, Plexousakis D (2003) Viewing the Semantic Web Through RVL Lenses. In Proceedings of the 2nd International Semantic Web Conference (ISWC)

[28] The Morpheus file-sharing system. Available at: http://www.musiccity.com

[29] The Napster file-sharing system. Available at : http://www.napster.com

[30] Naumann F, Leser U, Freytag JC (1999) Quality-driven Integration of Heterogeneous Information Systems. In Proceeedings of the 25th International Conference on Very Large Data Bases (VLDB), Edinburgh, UK

[31] Nie Z, Kambhampati S (2001) Joint Optimization of Cost and Coverage of Query Plans in Data Integration. In Proccedings of the 10th International Conference on Information and Knowledge Management, Atlanta, Georgia, USA

[32] Nejdl W, Wolpers M, Siberski W, Schmitz C, Schlosser M, Brunkhorst I, Loser A (2003) Super-Peer-Based Routing and Clustering Strategies for RDF-Based P2P Networks. In Proceedings of the 12th International World Wide Web Conference (WWW), Budapest, Hungary

[33] Sahuguet A (2002) ubQL: A Distributed Query Language to Program Distributed Query Systems. phD Thesis, University of Pennsylvania

[34] Stuckenschmidt H, Vdovjak R, Houben G, Broekstra J (2004) Index Structures and Algorithms for Querying Distributed RDF Repositories. In Proceedings of the International World Wide Web Conference (WWW), New York, USA

[35] Thaden U, Siberski W, Balke WT, Nedjl W (2004) Top-k Query Evaluation for Schema-Based Peer-to-Peer Networks. In Proceedings of the International Semantic Web Conference (ISWC2004), Hiroshima, Japan

[36] Triantafillou P, Pitoura T (2003) Towards a Unifying Framework for Complex Query Processing over Structured Peer-to-Peer Data Networks. In Proceedings of the Workshop on Databases, Information Systems, and Peer-to-Peer Computing (DBISP2P), Collocated with VLDB '03

[37] Triantafillou P, Xiruhaki C, Koubarakis M, Ntarmos N (2003) Towards High Performance Peer-to-Peer Content and Resource Sharing Systems. In Proceedings of the Conference on Innovative Data Systems Research (CIDR)

[38] Magkanaraki A, Alexaki S, Christophides V, Plexousakis D (2002) Benchmarking RDF Schemas for the Semantic Web. In Proceedings of the 1st International Semantic Web Conference (ISWC'02)

[39] Papadimos V, Maier D, Tufte K (2003) Distributed Query Processing and Catalogs for P2P Systems. In Proceedings of the 2003 CIDR Conference

[40] Ratnasamy S, Francis P, Handley M, Karp R, Shenker S (2001) A Scalable Content-Addressable Network. ACM SIGCOMM 2001, San Diego, CA

[41] Rosch P, Sattler K, Weth C, Buchmann E (2005) Best Effort Query Processing in DHT-based P2P Systems. ICDE Workshop NetDB 2005, Tokyo

[42] Yang B, Garcia-Molina H (2003) Designing a Super-Peer Network. In Proceedings of the 19th International Conference Data Engineering (ICDE), IEEE Computer Society Press, Los Alamitos, CA

Part II

Querying the Network

Overview: Querying the Network

Steffen Staab

The basic idea behind a Peer-to-Peer-based system for information sharing and knowledge management is that one adds resources to the network and queries the network in a completely transparent manner. In the first place, this means that we as a user might not care about how information is found and where it is found. The peer network is supposed to self-organize itself.

Let us perform a small experiment to demonstrate some typical requirements for such a task, let us query for all the publications of my late granduncle Karl Staab. This query is not answered in a satisfactory way by either Google^{TM} or Google^{TM} Scholar. The reason is that my granduncle wrote about the New Testament in German in the middle of the 20th century. His books are out of print by now and, because of the topic, also leave fewer traces on the Web than what we are used to in the Computer Science domain. Querying specific databases, e.g. the database of the library of University Koblenz-Landau, which actually constitutes a batch integration of resources from several places spread over the local state, improves precision a lot, but it actually still leaves much to be desired because of its low recall. Much better, KVK Karlsruhe virtual catalogue (http://www.ubka.uni-karlsruhe.de/hylib/en/kvk.html) allows the sending of queries ad hoc to dozens of different resources across Germany, Switzerland and Austria yielding several dozens of answers most of which are relevant and, hence, give a good impression about the work of my granduncle.

What helped to fulfill the information need in the small experiment described above was that we have *focused querying* by selecting the kind of information resources we would query. Naturally, databases about books in German academic institutions would yield more relevant hits for German literature. At the same time, we went from a centralized model to a model of *distributed querying* in which some information resources would hold no relevant information at all, while others would contain many relevant results. Overall, this resulted in a high precision and high recall for our information need.

Likewise, Semantic Web and Peer-to-Peer are set out to do both, i.e. focusing queries by explicit semantics and distributing queries by the Peer-to-Peer network. However, KVK Karlsruhe virtual catalogue is a carefully built service that forwards queries to a set of other carefully selected and carefully engineered information services. In the Peer-to-Peer network we must be able to let the user compose meaningful queries for information without much advance selection and engineering. This objective is approached by the contributions presented in this chapter.

The contribution by Qu, Nejdl and Kriesell (Chap. 4) shows how self-organizing properties of various versions of distributed hash-tables (DHTs; a common infrastructure for structured networks) may be mapped onto the common framework of Cayley DHTs, allowing for deep insight into the crucial properties, such as connectivity, fault tolerance, or load balancing. Interestingly, the Cayley DHTs may also be applied to ontology-based Peer-to-Peer networks, e.g. HyperCup.

The contributions by Tempich and Staab (Chap. 5) as well as by Siebes, Haase, and van Harmelen go into a different direction, as they investigate the use of unstructured networks. In unstructured networks, one does not enforce properties like connectivity; instead, one pursues an information architecture that more closely reflects the social structure of the network and the ownership of individual resources. In such a model, either one pursues a query forwarding strategy that targets all peers (which is possible in small networks with at most a few dozens of peers) or one needs some effective heuristics that restricts query forwarding to promising subparts of the network. Such heuristic means may be quite effective, especially when they are geared towards organizational needs. The two contributions here approach the problem by different means. In the model by Siebes et al. peers publish advertisements of their capabilities into the network and thereby construct a semantic topology that resembles the ontology structures. In the model by Tempich & Staab, peers adopt a lazy approach, observing their local environment in order to find out about the semantic capabilities of their peers and of parts of the network. The two approaches exhibit complementary capabilities. Initial experiments indicate that such capabilities should be integrated to arrive at maximal benefits — but this integration is not yet mature enough to be presented here.

Beyond traditional information search, information resources on the Web, e.g. online book shops, offer further capabilities to arrive at personalized descriptions of information needs. Thus, common online book shops provide recommendation capabilities and let users define topics into which they are interested such that if a new item arrives users are notified about their potential interest.

Similar functionality should also be provided in a Peer-to-Peer environment. However, basic assumptions that appear to be trivial for a centralized information resource may not hold anymore. For instance, between subscribing to a topic in a Peer-to-Peer environment and receiving the answer, the network topology may change completely at the physical layer, the underlying information communication layer and at the logical communication layer. The two contributions by Haase, Ehrig, Hotho & Schnizler (Chap. 7) and Chirita, Idreos, Koubarakis, & Nejdl (Chap. 8) address such issues.

In summary, this part addresses the problem of querying the network in a transparent manner. Allowing for concept-based search in the Peer-to-Peer network, the three contributions in Chapters 5 to 6 provide capabilities for *focused querying* and *distributed querying in a self-organizing network*. By personalizing query capabilities through recommendations and publish/subscribe techniques that work in a distributed system of peers, Chap. 7 and 8 further fulfill users' needs for staying informed about information in the network.

Cayley DHTs — A Group-Theoretic Framework for Analyzing DHTs Based on Cayley Graphs

Changtao Qu[1], Wolfgang Nejdl[1], Matthias Kriesell[2]

[1] L3S and University of Hannover, Hannover, Germany
   {qu,nejdl}@l3s.de
[2] Institute of Mathematics (A), University of Hannover, Germany
   kriesell@math.uni-hannover.de

Summary. Static DHT topologies influence important features of DHT systems such as their scalability, communication load balancing properties, routing efficiency and their fault tolerance. While obviously dynamic DHT algorithms which have to approximate these topologies for dynamically changing sets of peers play a very important role for DHT networks, important insights can be gained by clearly focussing on the static DHT topology as well. In this paper we analyze and classify current DHTs in terms of their static topologies based on the Cayley graph group-theoretic model and show that most DHT proposals use Cayley graphs as static DHT topologies, thus taking advantage of several important Cayley graph properties such as symmetry, decomposability and optimal fault tolerance. Using these insights, Cayley DHT design can directly leverage algebraic design methods to generate high-performance DHTs adopting Cayley graph based static DHT topologies, extended with suitable dynamic DHT algorithms.

4.1 DHTs and Static DHT Topologies

An important class of Peer-to-Peer-Systems is formed by a variety of *Distributed Hash Table Architectures*, briefly, *DHT systems* or *DHTs*. The object is to partition a large key space into a smaller number of key blocks by assigning a hash value to every key; those keys which receive the same hash value form a key block. One employs a P2P system to operate queries, say, for keys, by giving the responsibility for one key block to one peer. The classical design goal of a *balanced* hash function has its counterpart in the goal of providing a highly symmetric P2P network topology. It turns out here that, therefore, *Cayley graphs* are the appropriate objects to discuss DHT systems systematically.

Two important characteristics of DHTs are network degree and network diameter. As DHTs are maintained through dynamic DHT algorithms, high network degree means that joining, leaving and failing nodes affect more other nodes. Based on network degree, we group classes of static DHT topologies into two types: *non–constant degree DHT topologies*, where the degree of the members of the class under consideration increases (usually logarithmically) with the number of their nodes, and *constant (average) degree DHT topologies*, where the degree is constant for all class members. Consequently, (classes of) DHTs can be classified into *non-constant degree DHTs* such as HyperCup(hypercubes), Chord (ring graphs), Pastry/Tapestry (Plaxton trees), etc., and *constant degree DHTs* such as Viceroy (butterfly), Cycloid (cube connected cycles), and CAN (tori).

Though this classification is certainly useful, the listed DHT topologies seem to have nothing more in common. Each topology exhibits specific graph properties resulting in specific DHT system features. Consequently, DHTs have so far been analyzed comparing individual systems, without a unified analytical framework which allows further insight into DHT system features and DHT system design.

The unified analytical framework discussed in this paper – *Cayley DHTs* – allows us to compare DHT topologies on a more abstract level and characterizes common features of current DHT designs. In a nutshell, we show that most current static DHT topologies such as hypercubes, ring graphs, butterflies, cube-connected cycles, and d-dimensional tori fall into a generic group-theoretic model, Cayley graphs, and can be analyzed as one class. These Cayley graph based DHTs (hereafter *Cayley DHTs*), including both non-constant degree DHTs and constant degree DHTs, intentionally or unintentionally take advantage of several important Cayley graph properties such as vertex/edge symmetry, decomposability, good connectivity and hamiltonicity to achieve DHT design goals such as scalability, communication load balancing, optimal fault tolerance, and routing efficiency. Several non-Cayley DHTs also utilize techniques in their dynamic DHT algorithms that try to imitate desirable Cayley graph properties, again showing the close relationship between Cayley graph properties and desirable DHT system features.

4.2 Cayley DHTs — A Group-Theoretic Model for Analyzing DHTs

We start the discussion by presenting the two central definitions of groups and Cayley graphs. Though rather abstract in the beginning, this allows us to describe the particular network topologies coming up later in the paper in a very condensed form, thus illustrating one of the advantages of our point of view.

4.2.1 Groups and Cayley Graphs

Cayley graphs were proposed as a generic group-theoretic model for analyzing symmetric interconnection networks [2]. The most notable feature of Cayley graphs is their universality. Cayley graphs embody almost all symmetric interconnection networks, as every vertex transitive interconnection network can be represented as the quotient of two Cayley graphs [21]. They represent a class of high performance interconnection networks with small degree and diameter, good connectivity, and simple routing algorithms. While reading the following definition of a group, it could be useful for some readers to check that the axioms are satisfied for, say, the nonzero real numbers with · being ordinary multiplication.

Definition 1. *A* group *is a pair* $\Gamma := (V, \cdot)$ *such that V is a (nonempty) set and* $\cdot : V \times V \longrightarrow V$ *maps each pair* (a, b) *of elements of V to an element $a \cdot b$ of V such that $a \cdot (b \cdot c) = (a \cdot b) \cdot c$ for all $a, b, c \in V$, and such that there exists an element $1 \in V$ with the following properties:*

(i) $1 \cdot a = a$ *for all $a \in V$ and*
(ii) for every $a \in V$, there exists some $b \in V$ with $b \cdot a = 1$.

1 is the unique element having properties (i) and (ii). It is called the *neutral element* of Γ, and $a \cdot 1 = a$ holds for all $a \in V$. b as in (ii) is uniquely determined by a and is called the *inverse* of a, written as $b = a^{-1}$. It is the unique element b for which $a \cdot b = 1$ holds. If $a \cdot b = b \cdot a$ holds for all $a, b \in V$ then Γ is called an *abelian* group. This is usually expressed by *additive notation*, i. e. by writing $\Gamma = (V, +)$, 0 for the neutral element, and $-a$ for the inverse of a. For example, $\{0, 1\}$ with $+$ defined by $0 + 0 = 1 + 1 = 0, 0 + 1 = 1 + 0 = 1$ forms a group with neutral element 0, where $-0 = 0$ and $-1 = 1$. Groups are fundamental objects of mathematics, and the foundation for Cayley graphs.

Definition 2. *Let $\Gamma := (V, \cdot)$ be a finite group, 1 its neutral element, and let $S \subseteq V - \{1\}$ be closed under inversion (i. e. $x^{-1} \in S$ for all $x \in S$). The* Cayley graph $G(\Gamma, S) = (V, E)$ *of $(V, \cdot)$ and S is the graph on the vertex set V where x, y form a member of the edge set E if and only if $x \cdot y^{-1} \in S$.*

Note that an edge connecting x and y is usually denoted by xy. The context will always prevent the reader from getting into a conflict with the widely accepted group theory convention of writing xy for $x \cdot y$. We can also define *directed versions* of this concept, which are obtained by omitting the symmetry condition $S^{-1} = S$ to S. The condition $1 \notin S$ keeps Cayley graphs *loopless*. Cayley graph are sometimes called *group graphs*.

4.2.2 Non-constant Degree Cayley DHTs

HyperCup [22]

Though HyperCup itself is not a DHT system, it is a topology for structured P2P networks which could also be used for DHT design, and which represents an important type of Cayley graphs, hypercubes. So far there are no DHTs which use pure hypercubes as static DHT topologies, even though some authors (i.e. [23, 11]) argue that Pastry/Tapestry and Chord emulate approximate hypercubes when taking into account the dynamic DHT algorithm design. However, differentiating cleanly between static DHT topologies and dynamic DHT algorithms, it is more appropriate to describe their static topologies as Plaxton trees and ring graphs, respectively.

Hypercubes are typical Cayley graphs. For a natural number m, let $(\mathcal{Z}_m, +)$ denote the group of residuals modulo m. Consider the group $\Gamma := (\mathcal{Z}_2^d, +)$, where $\mathcal{Z}_2^d$ denotes the set of all 0, 1-words of length d and $+$ is the componentwise addition modulo 2. We want to make a, b adjacent whenever they differ in exactly one digit, i.e. whenever $a - b$ is a word containing precisely one letter 1. So if S is the set of these d words then S is closed under inversion, and $H_2^d := G(\Gamma, S)$ is called the *d-dimensional (binary) hypercube*.

In Fig. 4.1, a 5-dimensional hypercube is shown.

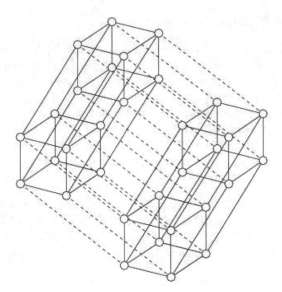

Fig. 4.1. The 5-dimensional hypercube

It is also possible to give a *hierarchical description* of H_2^d by means of the following recursion. Set $H_2^1 = (\{0, 1\}, \{01\})$, and for $d > 1$ define H_2^d recursively by

$$V(H_2^d) := \{xv : x \in \{0, 1\}, v \in V(H_2^{d-1})\} \text{ and}$$
$$E(H_2^d) := \{xvyw : xv, yw \in V(H_2^d) \text{ and:}$$
$$(x = y \wedge vw \in E(H_2^{d-1})) \text{ or}$$
$$(x \neq y \wedge v = w)\}.$$

Roughly, in every step, we take two disjoint copies of the previously constructed graph and add edges between pairs of corresponding vertices.

This concept can be generalized by looking at *cartesian products* of graphs: For graphs G, H, let their *product* $G \times H$ be defined by

$$V(G \times H) := V(G) \times V(H) \text{ and}$$
$$E(G \times H) := \{(x, v)(y, w) :$$
$$(x = y \in V(G) \wedge vw \in E(H)) \text{ or}$$
$$(v = w \in V(H) \wedge xy \in E(G))\}.$$

Clearly, $G \times H$ and $H \times G$ are isomorphic (take $(w, x) \mapsto (x, w)$ as an isomorphism). Defining $K_2 := (\{0, 1\}, \{01\})$ to be the complete graph on two vertices, we see that H_2^1 is isomorphic to K_2 and H_2^d is isomorphic to $H_2^{d-1} \times K_2$ for $d > 1$, which is in turn isomorphic to $K_2 \times \cdots \times K_2$ (d factors K_2).

As every finite group is isomorphic to some group of permutations, it is possible to unify the Cayley graph notion once more. Without loss of generality, we can assume that the generating group Γ is a permutation group. This is certainly useful when describing algorithms on general Cayley graphs. For the presentation here, it is, however, more convenient to involve other groups as well.

Chord [24]

Chord uses a 1-dimensional circular key space. The nodes have identifiers within that key space, and the node responsible for some key is the node whose identifier most closely follows the key in the circular numeric order (the key's *successor*). All nodes in Chord are arranged into a *ring graph*. In a m-bit Chord key space, each Chord node maintains two sets of neighbors: a successor list of k nodes that immediately follow it in the key space, and a finger list of $O(\log N)$ nodes spaced exponentially around the key space. The ith entry of the finger list of a node indexed by a points to the successor node of $a + 2^i$.

The graphs approximated here are special *circulant graphs*, i. e. Cayley graphs obtained from the cyclic group $(\mathcal{Z}_n, +)$ and an arbitrary (inversion–closed) generator set. The most prominent example is the *cycle*

$$C_n := G(\mathcal{Z}_n, \{\pm 1\}) = (\mathcal{Z}_n, \{01, 12, 23, \ldots, (n-1)n, n0\})$$

of length n. For the topology of the ideal d-bit Chord key space, we simply take the Cayley graph $G((\mathcal{Z}_{2^d}, +), \{\pm 2^k : k \in \{0, \ldots, d-1\}\})$. As an example, Fig. 4.2 displays the case $d = 4$.

4.2.3 Constant Degree Cayley DHTs

Cycloid [23]

Cycloid is a constant degree DHT emulating a cube connected cycle as its static DHT topology. In Cycloid, each node is specified by a pair of cyclic and cube indices. In order to dynamically maintain connectivity of the DHT topology, the dynamic DHT algorithm of Cycloid forces each node to keep a routing table consisting of 7 entries. Among them, several entries (so-called leaf sets) only make sense for the dynamic DHT algorithm to deal with network connectivity in sparsely populated identifier spaces. A d-*dimensional cube connected cycle graph* is obtained from the d-dimensional cube by replacing each vertex with a cycle of d nodes in a certain manner (see below). It contains $d \cdot 2^d$ nodes of degree d each. Each node is represented by a pair of indices (k, v), where $k \in \mathcal{Z}_d$ is a cyclic index and $v \in \mathcal{Z}_2^d$ is a cube index. A cube connected cycle graph can be viewed as a specific case of Cayley Graph Connected Cycles (CGCC) [18], defined as:

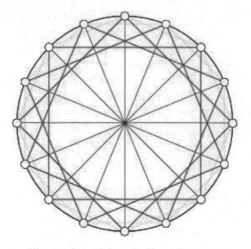

Fig. 4.2. The ideal 4-bit Chord Topology

Let $\Gamma = (V, \cdot)$ be a group and $S := \{s_0, \ldots, s_{d-1}\} \subseteq V - \{1\}$ closed under inversion with $d \geq 3$. The Cayley graph connected cycles network $CGCC(\Gamma, S) = (V', E')$ is the graph defined by

$$V' := \mathcal{Z}_d \times V \text{ and}$$
$$E' := \{(i, x)(j, y) : (x = y \wedge i = j \pm 1) \text{ or } (i = j \wedge x = s_i \cdot y)\}.$$

$CGCC(\Gamma, S)$ is obtained by replacing each vertex of the Cayley graph $G(\Gamma, S)$ with a cycle of length d and replacing each edge of $G(\Gamma, S)$ with an edge connecting two members of a cycle in a certain way. The edges $(i, x)(j, y)$ with $i = j$ form *cycle connections*, the others form *cayley graph connections*. [12] proves that these graphs are Cayley graphs. Following the definition of CGCC, the n-dimensional cube connected cycle is a graph built from a n-cube replacing each node with a cycle of length n. Figure 4.3 shows the 3-dimensional CDCC.

Viceroy [15]

Viceroy is a constant degree DHT emulating an approximate butterfly graph as its static DHT topology. The dynamic DHT algorithm of Viceroy is rather involved. It works based on a rough estimate of the network size and forces each node to keep a routing table containing five to seven entries [15]. Like Cycloids, part of the entries only make sense for the dynamic DHT algorithm to deal with a sparsely populated identifier space (i.e. ring links [15]).

The *d-dimensional (binary, unwrapped) butterfly* $\mathbf{B}_2^d$ is a graph with vertices $V = V(\mathbf{B}_2^d) = \mathcal{Z}_{d-1} \times \mathcal{Z}_2^d$ such that there is an edge from $a = (i, v_1 \cdot v_d) \in V$ to $b = (j, w_1 \cdot w_d) \in V$ if and only if $i \in \{0, \ldots, d-1\}$, $j = i+1$ and $v_k = w_k$ for all $k \in \{0, \ldots, d-1\} - \{i\}$. One can think of i, j as of the *levels* of a and b, respectively, and some level i vertex (i, v) has precisely two neighbors $(i+1, v)$ and

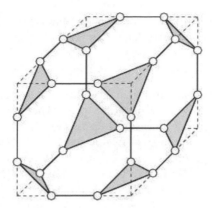

Fig. 4.3. The 3-dimensional CGCC

$(i + 1, v')$, where v' is obtained from v by adding 1 (modulo 2)in the ith component of v. The *d-dimensional (binary) wrapped butterfly* B_2^d is the underlying graph of the digraph $\mathbf{B}_2^d$, where there is a (single) edge ab whenever there is an edge (a, b) or an edge (b, a) in $\mathbf{B}_2^d$. As we can see, B_2^d is 4-regular for $d \geq 3$. Fig. 4.4 shows the 4-dimensional butterfly.

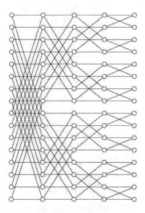

Fig. 4.4. The 4-dimensional Butterfly

The advantage of taking the wrapped rather than the unwrapped version of the butterfly is that B_2^d is a Cayley graph, whereas unwrapped ones are not even regular, since for $d \geq 3$ the vertices on the border levels have degree 2 and the others have degree 4. We represent B_2^d as a Cayley graph of the *wreath product* of the groups $(\mathcal{Z}_d, +)$ and $(\mathcal{Z}_2^d, +)$. For (i, v) and (j, w) in V, we define $(i, v) \bullet (j, w)$ $:= (i + j, (v_0 + w_{-\ell}, v_1 + w_{-\ell+1}, \ldots, v_{d-1} + w_{-\ell+d-1}))$. Note that $i + j$ and the indices at the components of v and w are to be taken modulo d. This operation constitutes a *group* $\Gamma = (V, \bullet)$, with neutral element $(0, 0)$. By taking $S =$

$\{(1,0),(1,(1,0,\ldots,00\cdots0))\} \subseteq V$ we obtain the representation $B_2^d = G(\Gamma, S)$ of B_2^d as a Cayley graph (for more details see [12]).

CAN [19]

CAN is an (adjustable) constant degree DHT using a virtual d-dimensional Cartesian coordinate space to store $(key, value)$–pairs. The topology under this Cartesian coordinate space is a d-dimensional torus. Let $T_{m,n} := C_m \times C_n$ of length m and n be the Cartesian product of two cycles C_m, C_n. The componentwise addition $+$ establishes a group $\Gamma(\mathcal{Z}_m \times \mathcal{Z}_n, +)$ on its vertices, and clearly $T_{m,n} = G(\Gamma, \{(0, \pm 1), (\pm 1, 0)\})$. Hence the torus is a Cayley graph as well. Figure 4.5 shows a non–canonical drawing of $T_{5,5}$, which reflects nicely its cyclic symmetries.

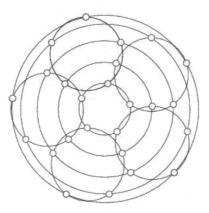

Fig. 4.5. A toroidal quadrangulation

One could consider such a toroidal graph as a rectangular grid, where the points on opposite borders are identified. We can extend this definition easily to higher dimensions: Let $n_1, \ldots, n_d$ be numbers ≥ 2. Componentwise addition $+$ of elements in $V := \mathcal{Z}_{n_1} \times \cdots \times \mathcal{Z}_{n_d}$ establishes a group $\Gamma(V, +)$, and by taking S to be the set $\{(z_1, \ldots, z_d) \in V$: there is an $i \in \{1, \ldots, d\}$ such that $z_i = \pm 1$ and $z_j = 0$ for all $j \neq i$ in $\{1, \ldots, d\}\}$ and we obtain a d-*dimensional torus* $T_{n_1, \ldots, n_d} = G(\Gamma, S)$. Explicitly, $T_{n_1, \ldots, n_d}$ is a graph on the vertex set V, where $(v_1, \ldots, v_d)$ and $(w_1, \ldots, w_d)$ are adjacent if and only if they differ in exactly one component and the difference in this component is either $+1$ or -1. As the presence of i's with $n_i = 2$ stretches formal arguments slightly (for example, when considering degrees), some authors force $n_i \geq 3$ for all $i \in \{1, \ldots, d\}$. They lose then, however, the possibility to consider the d-dimensional hypercube as a special torus, namely as $T_{2,\ldots,2}$ (d indices 2).

4.2.4 Non-Cayley DHTs

P-Grid [1]

Among non-Cayley DHTs, to the best of our knowledge, only P-Grid [1] still retains most of the advantages of Cayley networks. P-Grid uses prefix based routing, and can be considered as a randomized approximation of hypercube. The routing network has a binary tree abstraction, with peers residing only at the leaf nodes. Each peer is thus responsible for all data items with the prefix corresponding to the peer's path in the tree. For routing, peers need to maintain routing information for the complimentary prefix for each of the intermediate nodes in its path. However, routing choice can be made for any peer belonging to the complimentary paths, and P-Grid exploits these options in order to randomly choose routing peer(s), which in turn provides query-forwarding load-balancing and — by choosing more than one routing option — resilience. Additionally, the choices can be made based on proximity considerations, and though routing is randomized, since it is to complimentary key-space partitions, P-Grid routes have the added flexibility to be either bidirectional or unidirectional.

Pastry/Tapestry [20] [26]

The static DHT topology emulated by Pastry/ Tapestry are Plaxton trees. However, when taking the dynamic DHT algorithms of Pastry/Tapestry into account, we find that the static DHT topology of Pastry/Tapestry behaves quite similar to an approximation of hypercubes. As analyzed in [11], in the Pastry/Tapestry identifier space, each node on the Plaxton tree differs from its ith neighbor on only the ith bit, dynamic routing is done by correcting a single bit at a time in the left-to-right order. This turns out to be the same routing mechanism adopted by DHTs using hypercubes as static DHT topologies, even though hypercube based DHTs allow bits to be corrected in any order.

4.3 Cayley Graph Properties and DHTs

Cayley graphs have a specific set of properties which can be closely associated with important DHT system features. The following paragraphs include a discussion of these Cayley DHT properties and provide a good insight into Cayley DHT design.

4.3.1 Symmetry and Load Balancing

The most useful properties of Cayley graphs are *symmetry properties*. Recall that an *automorphism* of some graph G is a bijection $\varphi : V(G) \longrightarrow V(G)$ with $\varphi(x)\varphi(y) \in E(G)$ if and only if $xy \in E(G)$.

Definition 3. *A graph G is called* vertex symmetric *or* vertex transitive *if for arbitrary $x, y \in V(G)$ there exists an automorphism φ of G such that $\varphi(x) = y$.*

As the automorphism $z \mapsto z \cdot x^{-1} \cdot y$ maps x to y, we obtain the following classical observation.

Theorem 1. *Every Cayley graph is vertex transitive.*

This property results in an important feature of Cayley graphs — routing between two arbitrary vertices can be reduced to the routing from an arbitrary vertex to a special vertex [2]. This feature is significant for Cayley DHTs because it enables an algebraic design approach for the routing algorithm. Suppose that $\Gamma = (V, \circ)$ is a group of permutations, let $S \subseteq V - \{id_V\}$ be closed under inversion and consider the Cayley graph $G = G(\Gamma, S)$. For a path $P = x_0, \dots, x_\ell$ from x_0 to x_ℓ set $s_i :=$ $x_{i-1}x_i^{-1}$ for $i \in \{1, \dots, \ell\}$. Then the sequence $s_1, \dots, s_\ell$ in S *represents* the path P, and it also represents the path from $x_0 x^{-1}$ to id_V. Consequently, the routing problem G is equivalent to a certain sorting problem [2]. Taking V to be the set of all permutations of some set and $S \subseteq V$ to be the set of all transpositions will produce a *bubble sort graph* (see [12]).

We can leverage this property to implement optimized routing algorithms for Cayley DHTs through purely algebraic approaches supported by sets of mature algebraic methods. Furthermore, vertex transitivity provides a unified method to evaluate communication load on DHT nodes. In Cayley DHTs, the communication load is uniformly distributed on all vertices without any point of congestion once the routing algorithm under consideration is symmetric in the sense that every vertex is on the same number of routing paths. In contrast, non-Cayley DHTs exhibit congestion points. As communication load balancing is one of the principal design concerns of DHTs, this points out major drawback of non-Cayley DHTs.

In addition to vertex transitivity, Cayley graphs may also have another important property, edge transitivity.

A graph G is *edge symmetric* or *edge transitive* if for arbitrary edges wx, yz there exists an automorphism φ such that $\varphi(w)\varphi(x) = yz$.

For a discussion of the problem of determining the edge transitive Cayley graphs we refer to [2] and [12].

Among Cayley DHTs, HyperCup (hypercubes), CAN (d-dimensional tori), and Viceroy (butterflies) are edge transitive, whereas Chord (ring graphs) and Cycloid (cube connected cycles) are not. Non–Cayley DHTs are not edge transitive. Edge transitivity results in a unified method to evaluate communication load on edges, again under the assumption that the routing algorithm is symmetric in the sense that every edge is on the same number of routing paths. In this case, communication load is uniformly distributed on all edges. For constant degree Cayley DHTs such as Cycloid, the loss of edge transitivity can be seen as a reasonable tradeoff against the constant degree property. For non-constant degree Cayley DHTs such as Chord, the loss of edge transitivity is disadvantageous, and has to be compensated through the design of the routing algorithm.

4.3.2 Hierarchy, Fault Tolerance, and Proximity

Let us denote by $< S >_\Gamma$ the subgroup of $\Gamma = (V, \cdot)$ *generated* by $S \subseteq V$ i. e. the smallest subgroup of Γ which contains S.

Let $\Gamma = (V, S)$ be a group and $S \subseteq V(G) - \{1\}$ such that $S^{-1} = S$. The Cayley graph $G(\Gamma, S)$ is *strongly hierarchical* if S is a *minimal generator* for G, i. e. if $< S >_G = G$ but $< S - \{s, s^{-1}\} >_G$ is a proper subgroup of G for every $s \in S$.

Among Cayley DHTs, HyperCup (hypercubes) and Chord (ring graphs) can be proven to be hierarchical [12]. Hierarchical Cayley graphs "often allow inductive proofs by decomposing (stripping) the graph into smaller members of the same family, thus are scalable in the sense that they recursively consist of copies of smaller Cayley graphs of the same variety" [12]. In DHT design, hierarchy can strongly affect the node organization and aggregation, which is closely associated with two important DHT system features: fault tolerance (i.e. network resilience, to be described formally in the next section) and proximity (i.e. network latency). Most hierarchical Cayley DHTs, except for a very particular family, are optimally fault tolerant as their connectivity is equal to their degree [3]. Furthermore, in hierarchical Cayley DHTs, there are usually support easy solutions to dynamically organize nodes (or node aggregations) to ensure proximity of DHTs. Hierarchical Cayley graphs have not yet been intensively investigated for DHT design. Two promising hierarchical Cayley graphs not yet utilized in DHT design are star graphs and pancake networks [4], which have smaller network diameter than hypercubes of the same degree.

4.3.3 Connectivity and Fault Tolerance

A graph G is *disconnected* if it contains two vertices x, y such that there is no x, y-path in G. The *connectivity* $\kappa(G)$ of a finite (nonempty) graph is the minimum cardinality of a set X of vertices such that $G - X$ is disconnected or has less than two vertices. A graph is called *d-regular* if every vertex has degree d. For example, every vertex transitive graph is regular. Clearly, d is an upper bound for the connectivity of a d-regular graph. Let us call a d-regular graph G *optimally fault tolerant* if its connectivity equals d. That is, if it is as highly connected as it is possible by means of its degree. (In many cases, the only separators in G which realize the connectivity are the neighborhoods of single vertices, and the neighborhoods of "large" connected subgraphs in G will be much larger than d unless their complement in G is "small".) — For example, complete graphs are optimally fault tolerant, so are hypercubes (as one can prove by induction on the dimension, using the recursive characterizations). For edge transitive graphs, we have the following:

Theorem 2. *[14, 13, 25] (cf. [6]) Every connected edge transitive graph is optimally fault tolerant.*

In general, connected Cayley graphs are not optimally fault tolerant; the smallest example showing this is the 5-regular circulant graph $G := G(\mathcal{Z}_8, \{\pm 1, \pm 3, 4\})$, as $G - \{0, 2, 4, 6\}$ is disconnected; see Fig. 4.6.

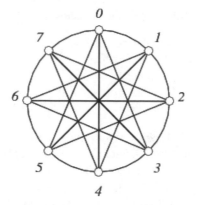

Fig. 4.6. A Cayley Graph which is not optimally fault tolerant

However, the following theorem on connected vertex transitive graphs shows that connectivity and degree cannot differ too much.

Theorem 3. *[14, 13, 25] (cf. [6]) The connectivity of a connected vertex transitive d-regular graph is at most d and at least $\frac{2}{3}(d+1)$.*

In particular, for $d \in \{2, 3, 4\}$, every d-regular connected vertex transitive graph is d-connected, i.e. optimally fault tolerant. For $d = 5$, this statement is wrong even for Cayley graphs as seen in the previous example, but for $d = 6$ it's true "again". Every 6-regular vertex transitive graph is 6-connected. This follows easily from the main result in [14] which implies that *every triangle free connected vertex transitive graph is optimally fault tolerant*. More generally, every vertex transitive graph without four pairwise adjacent vertices is optimally fault tolerant [13]. This gives alternative proofs of the optimal fault tolerance of hypercubes and of d-dimensional tori $T_{n_1,\ldots,n_d}$ with $n_i \geq 4$ for all $i \in \{1, \ldots, d\}$. The graph $G(\mathcal{Z}_8, \{\pm 1, \pm 3, 4\})$ indicates that it might be already a problem to characterize the optimally fault tolerant circulants (solved in [5]).

Edge connectivity is less interesting from the point of view of optimal fault tolerance, as every d-regular vertex transitive graph has edge connectivity equal to d [13, 25] (cf. [6]). Hierarchical Cayley graphs as defined above and in [12] or [3] are also known to be optimally fault tolerant unless they belong to a particular family of graphs whose d-regular members still have connectivity $d - 1$. For the technical details, we refer the reader to [12] or [3].

Among Cayley DHTs, HyperCup (hierarchical Cayley graphs), Chord (hierarchical Cayley graphs), Cycloid (3-regular Cayley graphs) and Viceroy (4-regular Cayley graphs) are optimally fault tolerant based on their static DHT topology perspective. CAN can also be proven optimally fault tolerant based on its dynamic DHT algorithm features such as multiple realities and multiple dimensions [19]. For non-DHTs it is much harder to prove optimal fault tolerance. However, as fault tolerance is one of the principal design concerns of DHTs, most non–Cayley DHTs have included various techniques in their dynamic DHT algorithms to pursue possibly higher fault tolerance, although optimality cannot guaranteed. One possible such technique is to force each node to maintain a successor list in dynamic DHT algorithms.

For DHTs whose static DHT topologies are optimal fault tolerant, it is much easier to also ensure this in the dynamic algorithm design for sparsely populated DHT identifier spaces, or frequently leaving/failing nodes. Possible techniques include the successor list in Chord [24] or the state-machine approach based replication in Viceroy [15].

4.3.4 Hamiltonicity and Cyclic Routing

A path or cycle which visits every vertex in a graph G exactly once is called a *hamiltonian path* or *hamiltonian cycle*, respectively.

Hamiltonicity has been received much attention of theorists in this context, as it is still open whether every 2-connected Cayley graph has a hamiltonian path.

The question of *hamiltonian cycles and paths* in Cayley graphs has a long history [8]. All aforementioned topologies of Cayley DHTs such as hypercubes, ring graphs, butterfly, cube-connected cycles, and d-dimensional tori have been proven to be hamiltonian.

Hamiltonicity is important for DHT design because it enables DHTs to embed a ring structure so as to implement ring based routing in dynamic DHT algorithms. Ring based routing, characterized by the particular organization of the DHT identifier space and ensuring the DHT fault tolerance in a dynamic P2P environment by means of maintaining successor/predecessor relationships between nodes, is used by almost all DHT proposals. Gummadi et al. [11] observe that the ring structure "allows the greatest flexibility and hence achieves the best resilience and proximity performance of DHTs". Although in terms of our analytical framework, we do not fully agree with Gummadi et al. on the conclusion that ring graphs are the best static DHT topologies, we agree that an hamiltonian cycle should exist in static DHT topologies in order to ease the dynamic DHT algorithm design. From the static DHT topology perspective, all aforementioned DHTs are hamiltonian except for Pastry/Tapestry (Plaxton trees), which, however, maintain a ring structure through their dynamic DHT algorithm.

4.4 Discussion and Related Work

Some desirable DHT system features are inconsistent with each other, which means that tradeoffs must be considered when deciding on a static DHT topology. As a general conclusion, we have shown that Cayley DHTs have clear advantages over non–Cayley DHT designs, naturally supporting desirable DHT features such as communication load balancing and fault tolerance.

Cayley DHTs cover both non-constant degree DHTs and constant degree ones, so in each case we can start from Cayley graphs as underlying topology for DHT design. Constant-degree Cayley graphs have the main advantage that their "maintainability" (regarding leaving / failing nodes) is independent of the size of the network. In a dynamic P2P environment, maintainability of nodes might be preferrable to other desirable DHT system features such as communication load balancing and fault tolerance, since the loss of other DHT system features can often be compensated through some additional techniques in the dynamic DHT algorithm design, whereas maintainability is almost uniquely determined by the static DHT topology.

When designing constant degree Cayley DHTs, cube connected cycles are an especially promising family of static DHT topologies in terms of our analytical framework, taking into account the simplicity they enable for dynamic DHT algorithm design in comparison to for example butterfly graphs. This conclusion can be extended to a generalized type of constant degree Cayley graphs: Cayley Graph Connected Cycles (CGCC), as we have discussed in the paragraph on the Constant Degree DHT system Cycloid. We therefore expect that different variants of CGCC will heavily influence the design mainstream for future constant degree Cayley DHTs.

Looking at non-constant degree Cayley DHTs, the most promising family are hypercubes, as they achieve all desirable DHT system features except for the constant degree property. This conclusion can be extended to k-ary n-cube, which can be regarded as a generalization of the d-dimensional hypercube by taking $k = 2$. Formally, the k-ary d-cubes can be defined as in [9].

Consider the group $\Gamma := (\mathcal{Z}_k^d, +)$, where $V := \mathcal{Z}_k^d$ denotes the set of all words of length d over the alphabet $\mathcal{Z}_k$ and where $+$ is the componentwise addition modulo k. Let S be the set of all $(k-1) \cdot d$ words in V which have exactly one entry ± 1 and all other entries being 0. The graph $H_k^d := G((\mathcal{Z}_k^d, +), S)$ is the k-ary d-cube.

By definition, k-ary n-cubes are Cayley graphs. They can be defined recursively as well: Denoting by C_k the cycle of length k, we see that H_k^1 is isomorphic to C_k and H_k^d is isomorphic to $H_k^{d-1} \times C_k$ for $d > 1$, which is in turn isomorphic to $C_k \times \cdots \times C_k$ (d factors). Note that a k-ary n-cube is a special torus.

Most current Cayley DHTs such as HyperCup, CAN, and Chord use static DHT topologies that are either k-ary d-cubes or isomorphic to k-ary d-cubes such as ring graphs, tori, direct or undirected d-cubes [9]. Even for constant degree Cayley DHTs or non-Cayley DHTs, the static DHT topologies of Cycloid (cube-connected cycles) and Pastry/Tapestry (Plaxton trees) are closely associated with k-ary d-cubes. As we have mentioned, Plaxton trees can be viewed as approximate hypercubes, whereas cube-connected cycles can be viewed as cycle expansions of hypercubes.

Gummadi et al. [11] investigate some commonly used static DHT topologies and explore how these topologies affect static resilience and proximity routing by analyzing the flexibility of different DHTs, i.e. the algorithmic freedom left after the static topologies has been chosen. Manku's [16] analysis starts from static DHT topologies, but then heavily involves dynamic DHT algorithms. His classification for DHT systems (deterministic and randomized) are certainly of value, but cannot serve as an analytical framework for comparing static DHT topologies. Datar [10] provides an in-depth investigation to butterfly graphs and further proposes a new DHT system using multi-butterfles as the static DHT topology. Castro et al. [7] make a comparative study of Pastry, taking Chord and CAN as reference systems.

4.5 Conclusions

We have discussed DHT topologies in the framework of Cayley Graphs, which is one of the most important group-theoretic models for the design of parallel interconnection networks. Associating Cayley graphs with DHTs enables us to directly leverage the research results for interconnection networks for the DHT design without the need of starting from scratch. Cayley graphs explicitly support an algebraic design approach, which allows us to start with an arbitrary finite group and construct symmetric DHTs using that group as the algebraic model, concisely specifying a DHT topology by providing the appropriate group plus a set of generators. This algebraic design approach also enables us to build new types of structured P2P networks in which data and nodes do not necessarily need to be hashed in order to build content delivery overlay networks, as discussed in [22, 17] for hypercube topologies. Such non-hashed, structured P2P networks allow us to apply semantic Web and database technologies for data organization and query processing and implement expressive distributed information infrastructures which are not implemented easily based on pure DHT designs.

Our analytical framework and its notion of Cayley DHTs provides a unified view of DHTs, which gives us excellent insight for designing and comparing DHT designs. Identifying a DHT design as Cayley DHTs immediately allows us to infer all generic properties for this design, and, through the correspondence of Cayley graph properties to DHT system features, allows us to directly infer the generic DHT features implemented by this design. Furthermore, we can investigate the various tradeoffs between different DHT designs features and use them to guide the design of future DHTs.

Casting and understanding static DHT topologies in a common framework is but the first important step towards principled DHT design. In order to cover all features of a particular design, we also have to explore the general design of dynamic DHT algorithms which can in principle be used to emulate any Cayley graph based static DHT topologies. Such dynamic DHT algorithms need not necessarily be bound to any individual Cayley graph, instead they could be universally applicable to any Cayley graphs, leveraging algebraic design methods in order to build arbitrary Cayley DHTs. Some of these methods and design issues are currently investigated in more detail in our group.

References

[1] K. Aberer, A. Datta, and M. Hauswirth. *P-Grid: Dynamics of self-organization in structured P2P systems*, chapter 21, "Peer-to-Peer-Systems and Applications". Springer LNCS, In Press, 2004.

[2] Sheldon B. Akers and Balakrishnan Krishnamurthy. A group-theoretic model for symmetric interconnection networks. *IEEE Trans. Comput.*, 38(4):555–566, 1989.

104   Changtao Qu, Wolfgang Nejdl, Matthias Kriesell

[3]   Brian Alspach. Cayley graphs with optimal fault tolerance. *IEEE Trans. Comput.*, 41(10):1337–1339, 1992.
[4]   P. Berthomé, A. Ferreira, and S. Perennes. Optimal information dissemination in star and pancake networks. *IEEE Tran. on Parallel and Distrubuted Systems*, 7(12), 1996.
[5]   F. Boesch and R. Tindell. Circulants and their connectivities. *J. Graph Theory*, 8(4):487–499, 1984.
[6]   F. Boesch and R. Tindell. Connectivity and symmetry in graphs. In *Graphs and applications (Boulder, Colo., 1982)*, Wiley-Intersci. Publ., pages 53–67. Wiley, New York, 1985.
[7]   M. Castro, P. Druschel, Y. C. Hu, and A. Rowstron. Exploiting network proximity in distributed hash tables. In *International Workshop on Future Directions in Distributed Computing (FuDiCo)*, Bertinoro, Italy, June 2002.
[8]   Stephen J. Curran and Joseph A. Gallian. Hamiltonian cycles and paths in Cayley graphs and digraphs—a survey. *Discrete Math.*, 156(1-3):1–18, 1996.
[9]   W. J. Dally. *A VLSI Architecture for Concurrent Data Structures*. Hingham, MA: Kluwer, 1987.
[10] M. Datar. Butterflies and peer-to-peer networks. In *10th Annual European Symposium*, Lecture Notes in Computer Science, Rome, Italy, September 2002. Springer.
[11] K. Gummadi, R. Gummadi, S. Gribble, S. Ratnasamy, S. Shenker, and I. Stoica. The impact of dht routing geometry on resilience and proximity. In *ACM Annual Conference of the Special Interest Group on Data Communication (SIGCOMM)*, Karlsruhe, Germany, August 2003.
[12] M. C. Heydemann and B. Ducourthial. Cayley graphs and interconnection networks. *Graph Symmetry, Algebraic Methods and Applications,"NATO ASI C"*, 497:167–226, 1997.
[13] W. Mader. Über den Zusammenhang symmetrischer Graphen. *Arch. Math. (Basel)*, 21:331–336, 1970.
[14] W. Mader. Eine Eigenschaft der Atome endlicher Graphen. *Arch. Math. (Basel)*, 22:333–336, 1971.
[15] D. Malkhi, M. Naor, and D. Ratajczak. Viceroy: A scalable and dynamic emulation of the butterfly. In *21st ACM Symposium on Principles of Distributed Computing (PODC 2002)*, Monterey, California, USA, July 2002.
[16] G. S. Manku. Routing networks for distributed hash tables. In *22nd ACM Symposium on Principles of Distributed Computing (PODC 2003)*, Boston, USA, July 2003.
[17] W. Nejdl, M. Wolpers, W. Siberski, C. Schmitz, M. Schlosser, I. Brunkhorst, and A. Löser. Super-peer-based routing and clustering strategies for rdf-based peer-to-peer networks. In *12th Intl. World Wide Web Conference*, Budapest, Hungary, May 2003.
[18] S. R. Oehring, F. Sarkar, S. K. Das, and D. H. Hohndel. Cayley graph connected cycles : A new class of fixed-degree interconnection networks. In *28th Annual Hawaii International Conference on System Sciences*, Hawaii, USA, May 1995.

[19] S. Ratnasamy, P. Francis, M. Handley, R. Karp, and S. Shenker. A scalable content-addressable network. In *Annual Conference of the ACM Special Interest Group on Data Communications (ACM SIGCOMM 2001)*, San Diego, CA, USA, August 2001.

[20] A. Rowstron and P. Druschel. Pastry: Scalable, distributed object location and routing for large-scale peer-to-peer systems. In *IFIP/ACM International Conference on Distributed Systems Platforms (Middleware)*, Heidelberg, Germany, November 2001.

[21] Gert Sabidussi. Vertex–transitive graphs. *Monatsh. Math.*, 68:426–438, 1964.

[22] M. Schlosser, M. Sintek, S. Decker, and W. Nejdl. Hypercup - hypercubes, ontologies and efficient search on p2p networks. In *International Workshop on Agents and Peer-to-Peer Computing*, Bologna, Italy, July 2002.

[23] H. Shen, C. Xu, and G. Chen. Cycloid: A constant-degree and lookup-efficient p2p overlay network. In *International Parallel and Distributed Processing Symposium (IPDPS2004)*, Santa Fe, New Mexico, April 2004.

[24] I. Stoica, R. Morris, D. Karger, M. F. Kaashoek, and H. Balakrishnan. Chord: A scalable peer-to-peer lookup service for internet applications. In *Annual Conference of the ACM Special Interest Group on Data Communications (ACM SIGCOMM 2001)*, San Diego, CA, USA, August 2001.

[25] Mark E. Watkins. Connectivity of transitive graphs. *J. Combinatorial Theory*, 8:23–29, 1970.

[26] B. Y. Zhao, L. Huang, J. Stribling, S. C. Rhea, A. D. Joseph, and J. D. Kubiatowicz. Tapestry: A resilient global-scale overlay for service deployment. *IEEE Journal on Selected Areas in Communications*, 22(1), 2004.

5

Semantic Query Routing in Unstructured Networks Using Social Metaphors

Christoph Tempich[1], Steffen Staab[2]

[1] AIFB, University of Karlsruhe, Germany
    tempich@aifb.uni-karlsruhe.de
[2] ISWeb, University of Koblenz-Landau, Koblenz, Germany
    staab@uni-koblenz.de

Summary. In Peer-to-Peer networks, finding the appropriate answer for an information request, such as the answer to a query for RDF(S) data, depends on selecting the right peer in the network. We here investigate how social metaphors can be exploited effectively and efficiently to solve this task. To this end, we define a method for query routing, REMINDIN', that lets *(i)* peers observe which queries are successfully answered by other peers, *(ii)* memorizes this observation, and, *(iii)* subsequently uses this information in order to select peers to forward requests to.

REMINDIN' has been implemented for the SWAP Peer-to-Peer platform as well as for a simulation environment. We have used the simulation environment in order to investigate how successful variations of REMINDIN' are and how they compare to baseline strategies in terms of number of messages forwarded in the network and statements appropriately retrieved.

5.1 Introduction

In spite of the success of distributed systems like the World Wide Web, a large share of today's information available on computers is not made available to the outside, but it remains secluded on personal computers stored in files, emails and databases — information that we will call *PC data* in the following. In theory, Peer-to-Peer networks are ideally suited to facilitate PC data exchange between peers. In practice, however, there remain unsurmountable obstacles:

1. PC data constitutes an *open domain*. Though one can define some core schema, e.g., as has been done for learning object metadata (LOM[1]; [11]), the core schema needs to be extended frequently.
2. Peers do not know *where* to find information.
3. Deciding *what* information about other peers to maintain is difficult, because relevance of data is hard to assess and possibilities for replication are limited.

---

[1] http://kmr.nada.kth.se/el/ims/md-lomrdf.html

For some of these individual problems solutions have been found: For instance, Haystack has shown that PC data can be nicely managed via RDF as it supports a flexible semi-structured data model [16]. Current search engines show how to find information. Current applications, such as TAP [10] show how to handle text as well as semi-structured data. Then, full text search indices can be maintained via centralized indices or through Peer-to-Peer exchange of indices [6]. Also, for fixed schemata algorithms exist that allow the finding of relevant information with only local knowledge [18].

Together, however, the requirements given above overstretch the possibilities that current Peer-to-Peer systems offer. This has been recognized only recently e.g. in [5, 19]. We have proposed an innovative solution for the SWAP platform in [22] that easily accommodates various semantic descriptions, that organizes itself in a way such that local knowledge is sufficient to localize data sources and that maintains its knowledge in a non-obtrusive manner based on what is observed as answers by other peers.

In brief, what we have conceived is a query routing capability that mimics what a person is doing in a social network:

- She retains meta-information about what other peers know;
- She might not even ask the others about their knowledge, but observe it from communication;
- She does not have a fixed schema, but easily builds up new schematic or taxonomic knowledge structure;
- She then decides to ask one or a few peers based on how she estimates their coverage and reliability of information about particular topics.

Based on the **SWAP platform** we have developed an original algorithm, **RE-MINDIN' (Routing Enabled by Memorizing INformation about Distributed INformation)**, that

1. Selects (at most) two peers from a set of known peers based on a given triple query, hence avoids network flooding;
2. Forwards the query; and
3. Assesses and retains knowledge about which peer has answered which queries successfully.

In contrast to, e.g. [2, 14], this is a lazy learning approach [3] that does not advertise peer capabilities upfront, but that estimates it from observation — the main advantage being that a dynamic semantic topology is made possible by adapting to user queries. This semantic topology corresponds to a semantic overlay network on top of the physical network and is similar to the ideas presented in [7].

We evaluate the algorithm on a simulation platform with a structure that is aligned to the structure of the original system. Thereby, we evaluate the hypotheses that

1. REMINDIN' is advantageous for effective query routing to estimate capabilities from observation of queries. In particular, this effect is achieved as meta-information is accumulated over time;

2. REMINDIN' can accommodate for changes when the typical information being available and queried changes;
3. REMINDIN's use of background knowledge further improves effectiveness.
4. REMINDIN' is in particular powerful in combination with the advertisement based peer selection algorithm presented in Chap. 6.

We conclude with a survey of related work and an embedding of our work into some overall objectives for self-organizing information systems.

5.2 SWAP Platform

The routing algorithm presented in this chapter is based on the general SWAP platform described in more detail in Chap. 18 and uses the SWAP meta data model. Therefore, we summarize here only the features needed for the algorithm and refer the reader to the related articles for more detailed information.

5.2.1 Meta-information

The SWAP storage model[1] provides meta-information about the content stored in the local repository in order to memorize where the statement came from and how much resource-specific confidence and overall confidence is put into these statements and peers, respectively. The SWAP model for meta-information consists of two RDFS classes, namely **Swabbi** and **Peer**. For these classes, several properties are defined to provide the basis for the social metaphors outlined above and specified further below. Their corresponding data structures are summarized in Table 5.1.

Swabbi (MO)**:** Swabbi objects are used to capture meta-information about statements and resources. They comprise the following properties:

- **hasPeer** ($MO.peer$): This property is used to track which peer this **Swabbi** object is associated with.
- **Resource-specific Confidence** ($MO.RC$): This confidence value indicates how knowledgeable a peer is about a specific resource on a scale from 0 to 1. High confidence is expressed by values near 1 and low or no confidence is expressed by values near or equaling 0.

Peer (P)**:** For each statement we have to memorize which peer it originated from. Information about a peer, e.g. its name, is specified by instances of the class **Peer**. The **Swabbi** links via **hasPeer** to **Peer**. In particular, each peer also memorizes and updates how much he confides overall into the other one:

- **Overall Confidence** ($P.OC$): Some peers may be more knowledgeable than others. This peer attribute is used to measure the overall confidence on a scale from 0 to 1, with 1 indicating that the remote peer is knowledgeable and 0 indicating the opposite. Knowledgeable peers are the ones that provide a lot of information in general.

---

[1] http://swap.semanticweb.org/2003/01/swap-peer#

Table 5.1. Data structures and parameters

Data structures	
O	Local node repository (ontology)
Q	Query
MO	Meta data object for a specific peer and resource
Configuration Parameter	
$p_{max} \in \mathbb{N}^+$	The maximum number of peers selected for query forwarding
$h_{max} \in \mathbb{N}^+$	The maximum number of hops a query is allowed to travel (the horizon of the query)
$NoPeers_{max} \in \mathbb{N}^+$	The maximum number of remote peers a local peer stores a reference to
$randomContribution \in \{0..1\}$	A proportion of peers which are selected randomly instead of by the algorithm
Parameters observed during runtime	
$P.OC$	Overall confidence into a peer
$MO.RC$	Confidence into knowledge of a specific peer about a specific resource
$selectedPeers_Q$	A set of peers to forward query Q to

5.2.2 Querying for Data

We here consider two querying modes of the SWAP platform. First, we have a general query language, SeRQL (cf. Chap. 1). Second, to reduce complexity of the simulation and get a better experimental grip at what peers do ask in the simulation environment, we have restricted the general SeRQL queries to the parts that it consists of, viz. queries for triples. Comparably to TAP [10], we query by

$$getData(s,p,o) \qquad (5.1)$$

With s, p, o being either concrete URIs or (for o only) literals. In addition, s, p, o may be a wildcard '*' with the intuitive meaning that any URI or literal would match here. For instance, $getData(*, uri2, *)$ would match triples like $(uri - bill, uri2, uri - hillary)$ and $(uri - ronald, uri2, uri - nancy)$.

This is a reasonable simplification, as all SeRQL queries are eventually compiled to sets of such triple queries and since even such a simple querying mechanism allows comprehensive information requests.

5.3 Algorithm

5.3.1 The Social Metaphors

Peer-to-Peer systems are computer networks. The decentralized governing principles of Peer-to-Peer networks resemble social networks to a large extent. As mentioned before, a core task in such a network is finding the right peer among the multitude of possible addressees such that this peer returns a good answer to a given question. To do this effectively and efficiently, REMINDIN' builds on social metaphors of how such a human network works: We observe that a human who searches for answers to a question may exploit the following assumptions[1]:

1. A question is asked to the person who one expects best answers the question.[2]
2. One perceives a person as knowledgeable in a certain domain if he/she knew answers to our previous questions.
3. A general assumption is that if a person is well informed about a specific domain, he/she will probably be well informed about a similar, e.g. the next more general, topic, too.
4. To quite some extent, people are more or less knowledgeable independently of the domain.
5. The profoundness of knowledge that one perceives in other persons is not measured on an absolute scale. Rather, it is often considered to be relative to one's own knowledge.

REMINDIN' builds on the metaphors of Peer-to-Peer networks being like a human social network and adopts the above mentioned assumptions in an algorithmic manner.

REMINDIN' consists of three major phases realizing these assumptions. *Peer selection* of REMINDIN' is based on assumptions (1) and (2). *Query relaxation* of REMINDIN' weakens the conditions that must be met such that we select a peer (assumption 3). *Statement evaluation* modifies our estimation of the general profoundness of a peer's knowledge (4) as well as its topic specific profoundness (5). These phases are embedded in the following into the overall, high level network protocol.

5.3.2 Protocol Scenario

REMINDIN' consists of several steps executed *locally* and *across the network* when *forwarding* as well as *answering queries* and when *receiving responses*. Assuming the user of a peer issues a query to the peer network, the query is evaluated:

Locally against the local node repository. Its answers are presented.

Across the network: Forwarding. Simultaneously, *peer selection* is invoked to select a set of peers which appear more promising than the others to answer the given query. If it cannot select any peers for the given query, the *query relaxation* will be used to broaden the query until either all peers can be selected or eventually all known peers are returned. The original query is then sent to a subset of the selected peers according to their *strength*. The message containing the query has a unique id and stores the ids of visited peers (message path) to avoid cycles.

---

[1] We do not claim that these observations of social networks are in any way exhaustive or without exceptions.

[2] "Best" in our current terms only means that he has the most knowledge. In future versions one may consider properties like latency, costs, etc.

Across the network: Answering Queries. When a peer receives a query, it will try to answer it and it will store an instance of the class Peer in its local repository referencing the querying peer and its unique peer identifier. A meta object is created for each resource the query was about. If the number of remote peers stored in the local repository increases above $NoPeers_{max}$ the peer deletion algorithm is invoked. The answer is returned directly to the querying peer. We return an answer if it is not empty. However, for the peers selected by the querying peer the peer rating algorithm is invoked even if they have no answers. If the number of maximum hops is not reached yet, the query will be forwarded to a selected set of peers — using the same peer selection described before.

Receiving Responses. On the arrival of answers at the querying peer, relevant answers are selected with the *statement selection* algorithm and included into the repository. The answering peer and the included statements are rated according to the *statement evaluation* algorithm. Again, if the number of stored peers in the local repository exceeds its foreseen levels references to peers are deleted.

5.3.3 Peer selection algorithm

We here survey the just mentioned algorithms in a descriptive manner, and refer the reader to [22] for a more algorithmic description.

Peer selection: As discussed in Sect. 5.3.1, peer selection is based on observations of remote peers' knowledge. Statements from the local node repository that match the query constitute the basis yielding meta-information about where they came from. Thus, these statements help to identify the set of most knowledgeable peers.

Often, this procedure alone does not result in a sufficient number of peers to forward the query to. Then, the query relaxation algorithm is applied to the query. Based on the resulting set of statements and peers, we combine the $P.OC$ value into each peer as well as the $MO.RC$ values, which may vary for each statement and peer, in order to derive a ranking. This results in an ordered set of peers to forward a query to.

Query relaxation: As just outlined, a query to the local node repository may not directly match any of its statements. Following observation (3), REMINDIN' relaxes the given query subsequently targeting peers with similar knowledge. We relax the queries based on the triple structure of RDF.

Statement selection: Often the answer of a query contains more information than one wants to retain in the local node repository. Then, the user must either manually determine which information to store or the system must provide an automatic mechanism. Currently SWAP supports only manual statement selection. For evaluation of REMINDIN'in our simulation, we have not retained any statement of any answer at all in order to test REMINDIN'with the worst-case assumption.

Update overall ($P.OC$) and resource-specific ($MO.RC$) confidence values : The $P.OC$ and $MO.RC$ values a peer assigns to remote peers and its associated statements are updated separately on the basis of the received answers. The number of statements returned is measured against the statements matching the original query already known by the querying peer. This measure is combined with the existing ratings in order to adjust the $P.OC$ and $MO.RC$ values. The size of the modifications depend in particular on the size of the result set as compared to the local result.

An interesting special case happens when a remote peer has been asked directly by the local peer, but when it has not returned an answer.[1] REMINDIN' then assumes after a certain time that the queried peer has no answer at all and correspondingly, the $P.OC$ and $MO.RC$ values are downgraded. Thus, even if the remote peer is very knowledgeable, but unwilling to answer or overfreight with queries, the remote peer will be considered as a less worthy candidate for querying — hence, a simple form of load balancing will be achieved, too.

Delete Peers As stated above we store references to remote peers each time the local peer is queried or it receives an answer. Hence, in small networks a local peer acquires quickly references to almost all remote peers in the network. This strategy does obviously not scale to larger Peer-to-Peer systems. Hence, we define an index size ($NoPeers_{max}$) for the number of remote peers visible to the local peer. If the number of **Peer** objects exceeds the predefined levels we use a peer selection strategy to determine, which peer objects we want to delete from the local repository. We rank all peers according to their $P.OC$ values, and delete the peers with the lowest one and all corresponding meta information.

5.4 Evaluation Setting

Though the SWAP bibliography case study involved on some days the participation of up to 50 researchers (cf. Chap. 18), even this number was too small to actually evaluate REMINDIN'. In addition, it would have been difficult to investigate crucial parameters of REMINDIN' without jeopardizing the running of the overall network. Hence, we opted for evaluating REMINDIN' by simulating a Peer-to-Peer network with plausible datasets of statements and query routing by REMINDIN'.

5.4.1 Data Source and Peer setup

We chose DMOZ, the open directory project[2], as an input to set up the local node repositories of the individual peers. DMOZ manually categorises Web pages of general interest into a topic hierarchy. For each topic one or several editors are responsible to define subtopics or related topics and to contribute links to outside Web pages to the topic pages of DMOZ. In our simulations an editor corresponds to a single peer. Hence, the local node repository of one peer contains the topic hierarchy and links to outside Web pages of the topics he is responsible for. Consequently, in the

---

[1] This is not observed if the remote peer has been asked indirectly.

[2] http://www.dmoz.org/

simulation, an editor asks for links to outside Web pages which belong to a certain topic. For a detailed description of the peer setup we refer to [22], and report here only the major statistical parameters of the simulated network in Table 5.2.

Table 5.2. Major statistical parameters

Property	Mean	Standard deviation
No. of topics / editor	4	5,4
No. of links / topic	27	35,2
No. of links / editor	53	69,1
No. of queries	1657	
No. of peers	1024	
Expected no. of answers / query / peer	13	23,1

5.4.2 Generation of queries in experiment

Queries are generated in the experiments by instantiating the blueprint $(*, < rdf : type >, topic)$, with $topics$ arbitrarily chosen from the set of topics that had at least one instance. Thus, generated queries retrieved all instances of a topic — considering also the transitivity of the subclassOf-relationship to subtopics. That is, we generated 1657 different queries.

To evaluate the effectiveness of REMINDIN'we partitioned the set of 1657 queries into two sets of equal size. There were two phases. First, there was a "learning phase" where the peer network was confronted with the first set 828 queries. Then, there was an explicit "test phase", in which one could observe how the peer network would re-adjust to the second set of queries.

5.4.3 Initial configuration of the Peer-to-Peer network simulation

The simulation is initialized with a network topology which resembles the small world properties of file sharing networks [1]. Initially each peer was connected to five remote peers. We simulated 1024 peers, during the simulation any peer can become visible to any other peer in the network, by creating a Swabbi object with its unique identifer[2]. In the simulation, peers were chosen randomly and they were given a randomly selected query to question the remote peers in the network. The peers decide on the basis of their local node repository which remote peers to send the query to. Each peer uses REMINDIN' to select up to $p_{max} = 2$ peers to send the query to. A peer that has received a query tries to answer it. In each query message we store the

---

[1] We used the Colt library $http : //nicewww.cern.ch/ hoschek/colt/$, with a clustering coefficient of 2.1.

[2] In our setting "being visible," "being known" and "being a possible direct addressee of a query" a synonymous to each other

path that it is forwarded along and if a peer had appeared in this path, it was deselected. In some evaluation scenarios, we have integrated a *randomContribution*. The *randomContribution* percentage of selected peers were randomly exchanged again randomly selected ones known by the querying peer. Each query was forwarded until the maximal number of hops $hmax = 6$ is reached. In our experiments, we have not considered the leaving or joining of nodes, so far.

As a baseline we compare REMINDIN' with the interest based locality strategy of Sripanidkulchai [19], the advertisement based strategy (Chap. 6) and the naive algorithm, which are briefly described here:

Naive Algorithm works similar to the flooding strategy of Gnutella. Each query is tagged with a maximum number of hops, to bound the number of hops it can travel. In addition Gnutella employs a duplicate detection mechanism, so that peers do not forward queries that they have already previously forwarded. A query is forwarded to randomly picked neighbors. Note that the Gnutella protocol does no foresee to remember references to peers which have answered a query.

Kunwadee Sripanidkulchai et al. exploit interest-based locality to employ interest-based shortcuts. These shortcuts are generated after each successful query and are used to further requests, hence they are comparable to creating a Swabbi object for a peer. However, their search strategy differs from ours, since they only follow a shortcut if it exactly matches a query, else they use a flooding approach. They further do not create short cuts when remote peers query the local one.

Advertisement based selection lite Additionally, we compare REMINDIN' with the advertisement based approach presented in Chap. 6. We chose a simplified version of the algorithm to account for the different data sets. Peers advertise their expertise only to remote peers which they know in the initial topology. They do not discard advertisements, if the similarity to the local knowledge is below a threshold as proposed in the original version. We also simulated the combination of the two algorithms. In this case local peers treat the advertisements, like answers to queries. Hence, Swabbi objects are created for the received statements. Than REMINDIN' is used to select peers.

5.4.4 Evaluation measures

There are many criteria to evaluate algorithms for Peer-to-Peer systems. In [8] we summarize some of them. For our evaluation we rely on two major measures.

Recall is a standard measure in information retrieval. In our setting, it describes the proportion between all relevant documents in peer network and the retrieved ones. We use recall to assess the effectiveness of REMINDIN', i.e. to measure to which extent one may retrieve statements from the Peer-to-Peer network based only on local knowledge about possibly relevant peers.

Messages represent the required search costs per query that can be used to indirectly justify the system scalability.

5.5 Results

Our simulations show that REMINDIN' reaches a significant higher recall than the naive baseline and other algorithms using local information only. In particular, peer selection is improved by query relaxation and some random selection of peers. Before we present the final evaluation results, we summarize here the major hypotheses we wanted to investigate.

5.5.1 Hypotheses

1. The proposed algorithm provides better results in terms of recall than the naive algorithm and other comparable algorithms.
2. The network load needed to reach a specific recall decreases over time, such as measured in terms of messages per query.
3. Using our query relaxation mechanism is better than considering just the original query to select peers.
4. Some randomness contributing to peer selection helps to escape over-fitting.
5. The index size $NoPeers_{max}$ – the number of remote peers which can become visible to a local peer – has no significant effect on REMINDIN's performance.
6. The combination of the advertisement based approach with REMINDIN' is particulary powerful.

5.5.2 Evaluation

Table 5.3. Standard parameter in evaluation

Parameter	Value
p_{max}	2
h_{max}	6
$randomContribution$	0.0
$NoPeers_{max}$	∞
$Peers$	1024

In Table 5.1 we define the different parameters of the algorithm. In case we did not state otherwise, they were set to the values given in Table 5.3. In the naive approach the peer has used the same parameters as REMINDIN' — except that all the peers were chosen randomly. Points in all the graphs represent averages for 1000 queries. Originating peer and query for a query message are selected randomly in our simulations. Hence, different simulations with the same parameters provide varying result. All experiments were thus repeated five times. We calculated the standard error for each experiments and the 95% confidence interval for our observations. In Fig. 5.3 we visualize our observation and the range of expected results. We observe that differences of less than 5% are statistically not significant.

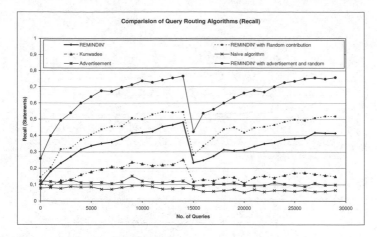

Fig. 5.1. 1024 Peers, 6 Hops, Top k=2, Recall per Query

Hypothesis 1: Figure 5.1 summarizes the comparison between REMINDIN', RE-MINDIN' with random contribution, the naive approach, the Sripanidkulchai et al. strategy, the advertisement based approach, and the combination of REMINDIN' and the advertisement based approach. In this scenario the peers send 30,000 query messages. During the first 15,000 query messages 50% of the available queries were used and than changed to the remaining queries. The naive approach has a constant recall of approximately 7%, the advertisement based approach reaches in our experiments 11%, while the Sripanidkulchai et al. approach learns over time and reaches its highest recall with 25%. The recall of REMINDIN' without random contribution increases steadily over time and reaches a recall of 45%.[1] After the introduction of new queries the recall decreases, but the algorithm adapts to the new requirements and reaches almost the same recall as before, after 15,000 queries. Note that 15,000 queries in total result in just about 15 queries per peer, a fairly low number. RE-MINDIN' with a little random contribution (15%) to the peer selection produces even better results. After 15,000 queries it reaches a recall of almost 55%.

Hypothesis 2: Figure 5.2 illustrates the same simulation run as before but focuses on the number of messages per query. The number of messages used by the different algorithms is always lower than the theoretically maximum number of messages $(126 + 13 = 139^2)$, since the query messages are forwarded to the same remote peer through different routes and not processed further. We observe that REMIND-IN' uses in average significantly less messages than the naive approach. In the case

---

[1] Note that the results presented here can be different in other evaluations, due to different initial configurations, different network sizes, different data sets, different data distributions and other factors. However, changing these factors in experiments not reported here does change the actual results, but not the general observation.

[2] The number of hops is set to six, and two peers are selected each time. Thus the query can reach $2 + 4 + 8 + 16 + 32 + 64 = 126$ peers. On average 13 peers can provide a partial answer to a query.

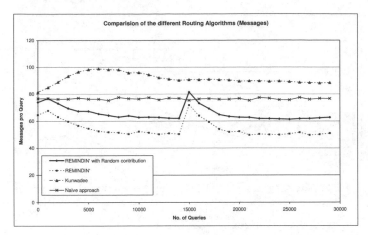

Fig. 5.2. 1024 Peers, 6 Hops, Top k=2, Messages per Query

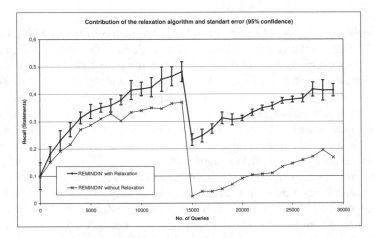

Fig. 5.3. 1024 Peers, 6 Hops, Top k=2, Contribution of the Relaxation

of new queries the number of messages increases. The decision to whom to send a query to can initially be made only on the basis of the overall confidence value of a peer instead of the more precise resource-specific confidence value. The Sripanidkulchai et al. strategy uses still more query messages per query. Initially, the number of messages goes up, since the local peer learns shortcuts to remote peers and can thus select from more. The number of messages decreases when redundant information is built up.

Hypothesis 3: Figure 5.3 nicely exemplifies the effect of the query relaxation algorithm. In the beginning the peer selection without relaxation works almost as good as with relaxation. When new queries arise, REMINDIN' with relaxation performs significantly better than without.

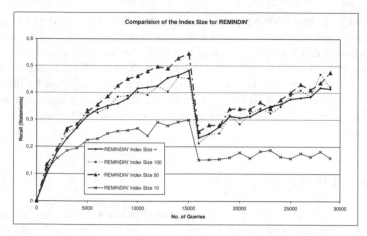

Fig. 5.4. 1024 Peers, 6 Hops, Top k=2, Different Index Sizes

Hypothesis 4: Most of our hypotheses were supported with most strength when we combined our algorithm with a proportion of randomly selected peers. Let us recall an observation from human interaction. It happens sometimes that we meet a previously unknown person and she provides us with a yet new view on the world or on a certain topics. Figure 5.2 analyzes the observation. We put side by side the average recall with and without random contribution (15%). It is obvious that the achievable recall of REMINDIN' without random contribution reaches a certain level and does not increase further. With the introduction of randomness, the algorithm adapts more quickly to new requirements and reaches an overall better recall. However, with the introduction of randomness the the number of messages per query also increases.

Hypothesis 5: In Fig. 5.4 we plot the results of our simulations with the index size $NoPeers_{max}$ set to 10, 50, 100 and ∞(1024). We observe that within a certain range the limit to the number of remote peers visible to the local one does not affect the results in terms of recall. Intriguingly, the recall increases slightly with a lower $NoPeers_{max}$ before it collapses when to few remote peers are referenced. Applying the Student's t-Test to the results, using a 95% confidence interval, reveals that the differences in recall are not statistically significant. We could explain the increase, though, since the number of messages send per query increases significantly to constantly 110 ($NoPeers_{max} = 10$) and 99 ($NoPeers_{max} = 50$). There is no difference between $NoPeers_{max} = 100$ and $NoPeers_{max} = \infty$ regarding the number of query messages per query.[1] The number of query messages increases, because peers build up less redundant information, and the probability that the local peer's selection decision is based on overall trust rather than resource specific is higher. We also notice that the recall does not recover in a advantageous way. The further reduction of messages and a better recovery after the introduction of new messages is left for future work.

---

[1] Not visualized

Hypothesis 6: In the SWAP project we have conceived two different routing algorithms, targeted at different scenarios. As we can observe in Fig. 5.1 the advertisement based selection lite approach does result in a lower recall than REMINDIN'. This is due to the learning mechanisms applied in REMINDIN'. However, the advertisement based approach, has the advantage that it is not effected by the change of queries. The combination of the both approaches has the advantage, that the algorithm learns faster and is less affected by new requirements and reaches generally a higher recall.

5.6 Related Work

The usage of results of past queries for peer selection has been investigated recently. These approaches deal with search performance improvements which hold independently of any semantic structure, either in the document collections or in the successive searches made by individual nodes. This semantic structure can be used in several ways. In [7] Crespo and Garcia-Molina explicitly identified distinct semantic groups of documents, and built corresponding, possibly overlapping, overlay networks for each group.

Sripanidkulchai et al. [19] take an alternative approach, attempting to cluster nodes sharing similar interests, rather than similar documents. Nejdl et al. presented in [4] a similar approach that uses an exact match between content provider shortcuts and queries.

[5] uses the concept of Infobeacons which is similar to our content provider shortcuts. Their ranking is based on the product of the expected number of results for a query from peers that contain a particular word of the query. Their similarity message is based on term frequencies.

General research in Peer-to-Peer system concentrates either on efficient topologies for these networks or on distribution of documents. The *small-world-effect* (cf. [2]) is one example how those topologies can be exploited to establish a connection between two nodes efficiently. In contrast to our work the content of a node is advertised to all neighbors, and thus needs updates when a nodes content changes. The algorithm ensures that a given query is forwarded to a node with the most neighbors. There are a number of other Peer-to-Peer research systems which are related to the question of how to allocate documents within a Peer-to-Peer network. They mostly require equally shaped keys for nodes and their contents [17] [21], thus once a key for the searched content has been created, the address and thus the root to the target peer can be easily found. One problem with this system is that it generates a substantial overhead when nodes join and leave the network.

EDUTELLA [13] is a Peer-to-Peer system based on the JXTA platform, which offers very similar base functionality as the SWAP system. In [14] they propose a query routing mechanism based on super peers. Peers which have topics in common are arranged in a hypercube topology. This topology guarantees that each node is queried exactly once for each query.

5.7 Conclusion

The principle of self-organization has been discussed for a long time as a paradigm for introducing order into complex systems without centralized control. In recent years one could see that this principle has found its entry into different types of engineering applications (cf., e.g., [20]) — in particular ones that involve the Web, such as identification of communities for better harvesting and classification of information [9] or ones that use self-organization in Peer-to-Peer networks [1]. In theory, the possibilities of self-organizing appear to be open-ended with ideas ranging up to social systems of human and machine agents that form networks with enormously effective communication structures — as one knows, e.g., from Milgram's experiment on six degrees of separation in 1967 [12]. Though the idea of transferring such communication principles from the original social networks to comparable technical networks like Peer-to-Peer networks has been ventilated for some time (cf. [15]), corresponding research has not taken a serious stance to it.[1] To this end, we have devised the REMINDIN' algorithm to find peers in a semantic Peer-to-Peer network based on social metaphors. The algorithm comprises a peer selection algorithm based on confidence ratings, query relaxation and observation of useful responses given by other peers. The algorithm provides significantly better results than its naive counterpart and other related approaches. Our experiments with REMINDIN' have shown interesting results: *(1)* some randomness in peer selection helps escape overfitting and improves effectiveness of REMINDIN', *(2)* self-organized learning by the network reduces the network load over time, and, *(3)* parameter settings play a role, but the behavior of REMINDIN'is rather elastic to changing boundary conditions.

References

[1]   Karl Aberer, Philippe Cudré-Mauroux, Anwitaman Datta, Zoran Despotovic, Manfred Hauswirth, Magdalena Punceva, and Roman Schmidt. P-Grid: a self-organizing structured p2p system. *ACM SIGMOD Record*, 32(3):29–33, 2003.

[2]   Lada A. Adamic, Rajan M. Lukose, Amit R. Puniyani, and Bernardo A. Huberman. Search in power-law networks. *Physical Review E*, 64(46135), 2001.

[3]   David W. Aha, editor. *Lazy Learning*. Kluwer, Dordrecht, 1997.

[4]   Wolf-Tilo Balke, Wolfgang Nejdl, Wolf Siberski, and Uwe Thaden. Progressive distributed top-k retrieval in Peer-to-Peer networks. In *21st International Conference on Data Engineering (ICDE)*, Tokyo, Japan, 2005.

[5]   Brian Cooper. Guiding queries to information sources with infobeacons. In *ACM/IFIP/USENIX 5th International Middleware Conference*, Toronto, 2004.

[6]   A. Crespo and H. Garcia-Molina. Routing indices for Peer-to-Peer systems. In *Proceedings of the 22nd International Conference on Distributed Computing Systems*, pages 23–32. IEEE Press, 2002.

---

[1] We have discussed some very few noteworthy exceptions in Sect. 5.6.

[7] Arturo Crespo and Hector Garcia-Molina. Semantic Overlay Networks for P2P Systems. Submitted for publication `http://www-db.stanford.edu/~crespo/publications/op2p.pdf`, 2002.

[8] M. Ehrig et al. Towards evaluation of Peer-to-Peer-based distributed knowledge management systems. In Ludger van Elst, Virginia Dignum, and Andreas Abecker, editors, *"Agent-Mediated Knowledge Management International Symposium AMKM 2003" Stanford, CA, USA*, Lecture Notes in Artificial Intelligence (LNAI) 2926, pages 73–88. Springer, Berlin, 2003.

[9] G. W. Flake, S. Lawrence, C. L. Giles, and F. M. Coetzee. Self-organization and identification of web communities. *IEEE Computer*, 35(3):66–70, March 2002.

[10] R. Guha and R. McCool. TAP: a Semantic Web platform. *Computer Networks*, 42(5):557–577, August 2003.

[11] A. Löser et al. Efficient data store discovery in a scientific P2P network. In N. Ashish and C. Goble, editors, *Proc. of the WS on Semantic Web Technologies for Searching and Retrieving Scientific Data*, CEUR WS 83, 2003. Colocated with the 2. ISWC-03 `http://sunsite.informatik.rwth-aachen.de/Publications/CEUR-WS/Vol-83/`.

[12] Stanlay Milgram. The small world problem. *Psychology Today*, 67(1), 1967.

[13] W. Nejdl et al. EDUTELLA: A P2P networking infrastructure based on RDF. In *Proc. of the 2002 WWW Conference*, pages 604–615, Hawaii, USA, May 2002.

[14] W. Nejdl et al. Super-peer-based routing and clustering strategies for rdf-based Peer-to-Peer networks. In *Proc. of the 12th World Wide Web Conference*, Budapest, Hungary, 20-24 May 2003. ACM.

[15] Andy Oram, editor. *Peer-to-Peer. Harnessing the Power of Disruptive Technologies*. O'Reilly, 2001.

[16] Dennis Quan, David Huynh, and David R. Karger. Haystack: A platform for authoring end user semantic web applications. In *The SemanticWeb — ISWC 2003*, LNCS 2870, pages 738–753, Heidelberg, 2003. Springer-Verlag.

[17] A. Rowstron and P. Druschel. Pastry: Scalable, distributed object location and routing for large-scale Peer-to-Peer systems. In *Proc. of the Int. Conference on Distributed Systems Platforms (Middleware)*, pages 329–350, 2001.

[18] M. Schlosser et al. A scalable and ontology-based P2P infrastructure for Semantic Web Services. In *P2P-2002 — Proceedings of the 2nd Int. Conf. on Peer-to-Peer Computing*, pages 104–111. IEEE Press, 2002.

[19] Kunwadee Sripanidkulchai, Bruc Maggs, and Hui Zhang. Efficient content location using interest based locality in Peer-to-Peer system. In *Infocom*. IEEE, 2003.

[20] S. Staab, F. Heylighen, C. Gershenson, G. W. Flake, D. M. Pennock, D. C. Fain, D. De Roure, K. Aberer, W.-M. Shen, O. Dousse, and P. Thiran. Neurons, viscose fluids, freshwater polyp hydra — and self-organizing information systems. *IEEE Intelligent Systems*, 18(4):72–86, July-Aug. 2003.

[21] I. Stoica et al. Chord: A scalable Peer-To-Peer lookup service for internet applications. In *Proc. of the 2001 ACM SIGCOMM Conference*, pages 149–160, 2001.

[22] C. Tempich, S. Staab, and A. Wranik. REMINDIN': Semantic query routing in Peer-to-Peer networks based on social metaphors. In *Proc. of the 13th World Wide Web Conference*, New York, USA, May 17-22 2004. ACM.

6

Expertise-Based Peer Selection

Ronny Siebes[1], Peter Haase[2], Frank van Harmelen[1]

[1] Vrije Universiteit Amsterdam, The Netherlands
{ronny,frankh}@cs.vu.nl
[2] Institute AIFB, University of Karlsruhe, Germany
haase@aifb.uni-karlsruhe.de

Summary. Peer-to-Peer systems have proven to be an effective way of sharing data. Finding the data in an efficient and robust manner still is a challenging problem. We propose a model in which peers advertise their expertise in the Peer-to-Peer network. The knowledge about the expertise of other peers forms a semantic overlay network (SON). Based on the semantic similarity between the subject of a query and the expertise of other peers, a peer can select appropriate peers to forward queries to, instead of broadcasting the query or sending it to a random set of peers. We evaluate the model in a bibliographic scenario, where peers share bibliographic descriptions of publications among each other. In simulation experiments complemented with a real-world field experiment we show how expertise based peer selection improves the performance of a Peer-to-Peer system with respect to precision, recall and the number of messages.

6.1 Introduction

Peer-to-Peer systems are distributed systems without centralized control or hierarchical organization, in which each node runs software with equivalent functionality. A review of the features of recent Peer-to-Peer applications yields a long list: redundant storage, permanence, selection of nearby servers, anonymity, search, authentication, and hierarchical naming. Despite this rich set of features, scalability is a significant challenge: Peer-to-Peer networks that broadcast the queries to all peers do not scale – intelligent query routing and network topologies are required to be able to route queries to a relevant subset of peers. In this chapter we give an overview and an evaluation of the model of expertise based peer selection as proposed in [4] and how it is used in the Bibster system 18. In this model, peers use a shared ontology to advertise semantic descriptions of their expertise in the Peer-to-Peer network. The knowledge about the expertise of other peers forms a semantic overlay network, independent of the underlying network topology. If the peer receives a query, it can decide to forward it to peers about which it knows that their expertise is similar to the subject of the query. The advantage of this approach is that queries will not be forwarded to all or a random set of known peers, but only to the ones that have a good chance of answering it.

The organization of the sections in this chapter is as follows: In the next section, we give a small overview of related work in the domain of Semantic Overlay Networks. In Section 3 we provide our generic model on expertise-based peer selection. In Section 4, we instantiate the generic model with the Bibster case-study. In section 5, we show simulation experiments and their results on the selection method. Section 6 shows the results of an evaluation study on the Bibster application which was installed on different machines of interested people. Section 7 shows a comparison between the simulation results and the results obtained from the field study. Section 8 concludes our work.

6.2 Related Work on Semantic Overlay Networks

Peers that keep pointers to other peers that have similar content to themselves form a Semantic Overlay Network (SON). Edutella [6] is a schema based network where peers describe their functionality (i.e. services) and share these descriptions with other peers. In this way, peers know about the capabilities of other peers and only route a query to those peers that are probably able to handle it. Although Edutella provides complex query facilities, it has still no sophisticated means for semantic clustering of peers, and their broadcasting does not scale well. Gridvine [3] uses the semantic overlay for managing and mapping data and metadata schemas, on top of a physical layer consisting of a structured Peer-to-Peer overlay network, namely P-Grid, for efficient routing of messages. In essence, the good efficiency of the search algorithm is caused not clustering of semantically related peers based on the semantic overlay, but by efficient term storage and retrieval characteristics of the underlying DHT approach for mapping terms to peers.

Another SON approach is to classify the content of a peer into a shared topic vector where each element in the vector contains the relevance for that given peer for the respective topic. pSearch [8] is such an example where documents in the network are organized around their vector representations (based on modern document ranking algorithms) such that the search space for a given query is organized around related documents, achieving both efficiency and accuracy. In pSearch each peer has the responsibility for a range for each element in the topic vector, e.g. ($[0.2 - 0.4], [0.1 - 0.3]$). Now all expertise vectors that fall in that range are routed to that peer, meaning that, following the example vector, the expertise vector $[0.23, 0.19]$ would be routed to this peer and $[0.13, 0.19]$ not because 0.13 does not fall in between 0.2 and 0.4. Besides the responsibility for a vector range, a peer also knows the list of neighbors which are responsible to vector ranges close to itself. The characteristic of pSearch is that the way that peers know about close neighbors is very efficient. A disadvantage of pSearch is that all documents have to be mapped into the same (low dimensional) semantic search space and that the dimensionality on the overlay is strongly dependent of the dimensionality of the vector, with the result that each peer has to know many neighbors when the vectors have high a dimension.

Another approach is based on random walk clustering [9], where peers with similar content are going to know each other. The assumption is that queries posted by peers are semantically closely related to the content of the peer itself. This results in a high probability that the neighbors of the peer (the peers in the cluster of that peer) have answers to the query. The problem of this approach, in the domain of full-text searches, is to select which information a peer has to tell to another peer so that they are able to determine if they are related or not. When there is no shared data-structure (like a fixed set of terms) in which they can describe their content, the whole content has to be shared. This results in that much data has to be shared between peers for determining closeness.

In contrast to the previous approach, the last SON approach that we discuss here lets peers describe their content in a shared set of terms. Usually these terms are organized in a topic network or hierarchy, making it able to determine the semantic similarity between terms. Each peer is characterized by a set of topics that describe its expertise. A peer knows about the expertise topics from other peers by analyzing advertisement messages [4] or answers (Chap. 5). In this way peers form clusters of semantically related expertise descriptions. Given a query, a shared distance metric allows the forwarding of queries (described by a shared set of terms) to neighbors of which their expertise description is semantically closely related to the query. The advantages of this approach are threefold:

- *Peer autonomy* Each peer can, in principle, have its own distance measure, peer selection mechanism and clustering strategy. This allows peers, for example, to keep their neighbor list or similarity metric secret. Also, peers can decide at any time to change their visibility on the network by sending advertisement messages.
- *Automatic load balancing* When some content is provided by many peers also the semantic cluster on that content will contain many peers. In this way, load balancing is an emergent property of this approach.
- *Robustness/fault tolerance* When peers leave the network or do not respond to a query, the only consequence is that they probably will not be asked a next time until they send new advertisement messages or are recommended by other peers. In contrast, most DHT approaches have to move routing tables to other peers in order to restore the overlay.

However, there is also a disadvantage: terms that are not shared cannot be found. For example, imagine that a peer has some documents containing the word "abstract", but the shared data-structure only contains the term "summary", then two things can be done (1) extend the shared data-structure with the word "abstract" so that peers are able to query and describe their expertise with that term or (2) the functions that extracts the expertise description and abstract the queries should be intelligent enough to see that "summary" is a good replacement for "abstract". Note that in this case the original query still contains "summary", but the routing mechanism uses the shared term "abstract" to route it to the peer that registered itself on that term. Both solutions have their own problems, the first one will lead eventually to very large data-structures, the second one depends very heavily on the quality of the extraction and abstraction algorithms.

6.3 A Model for Expertise Based Peer Selection

In the model that we propose, peers advertise their expertise in the network. The peer selection is based on matching the subject of a query and the expertise according to their semantic similarity. Figure 6.1 below shows the idea of the model in one picture.

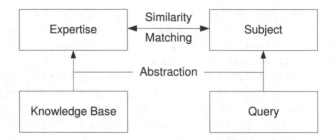

Fig. 6.1. Expertise Based Matching

In this section we first introduce a model to semantically describe the expertise of peers and how peers promote their expertise as advertisement messages in the network. Second, we describe how the received advertisements allow a peer to select other remote peers for a given query based on a semantic matching of query subjects against expertise descriptions. The third part describes how a *semantic overlay network* can be formed by advertising expertise.

6.3.1 Semantic Description of Expertise

Peers

The Peer-to-Peer network consists of a set of peers P. Every peer $p \in P$ has a knowledge base that contains the knowledge that it wants to share.

Shared Ontology

The peers share an ontology O, which provides a shared conceptualization of their domain. The ontology is used for describing the expertise of peers and the subject of queries.

Expertise

An expertise description $e \in E$ is a abstract, semantic description of the knowledge base of a peer based on the shared ontology O. This expertise can either be extracted from the knowledge base automatically or specified in some other manner.

Advertisements

Advertisements $A \subseteq P \times E$ are used to promote descriptions of the expertise of peers in the network. An advertisement $a \in A$ associates a peer p with a an expertise e. Peers decide autonomously, without central control, whom to promote advertisements to and which advertisements to accept. This decision can be based on the semantic similarity between expertise descriptions.

6.3.2 Matching and Peer Selection

Queries

Queries $q \in Q$ are posed by a user and are evaluated against the knowledge bases of the peers. First a peer evaluates the query against its local knowledge base and then decides which peers the query should be forwarded to. Query results are returned to the peer that originally initiated the query.

Subjects

A subject $s \in S$ is an abstraction of a given query q expressed in terms of the shared ontology. The subject can be seen a complement to an expertise description, as it specifies the required expertise to answer the query. We do not make any assumptions about the abstraction process, which preferably is done automatically. For example, a string matching approach could determine which parts of the ontology match with strings in the query.

Similarity Function

The similarity function $SF : S \times E \mapsto [0, 1]$ yields the semantic similarity between a subject $s \in S$ and an expertise description $e \in E$. An high value indicates high similarity. If the value is 0, s and e are not similar at all, if the value is 1, they match exactly. SF is used for determining to which peers a query should be forwarded. Analogously, a same kind of similarity function $E \times E \mapsto [0, 1]$ can be defined to determine the similarity between the expertise of two peers.

Peer Selection Algorithm

The peer selection algorithm (c.f. Algorithm 1) returns a ranked set of peers. The rank value is equal to the similarity value provided by the similarity function.

From this set of ranked peers one can, for example, select the best n peers.

6.3.3 Semantic Overlay

The knowledge of the peers about the expertise of other remote peers is the basis for the Semantic Overlay Network (SON). Here it is important to state that this SON is independent of the underlying network topology. At this point, we do not make any assumptions about the properties of the topology on the network layer.

The SON can be described by the following relation:

Algorithm 1 Peer Selection

let A be the advertisements that are available on the peer
let γ be a system parameter that indicates the minimal required similarity between the expertise of a peer and the topics of the query.
$subject := ExtractSubject(query)$
$rankedPeers := \emptyset$
for all $ad \in A$ **do**
   $peer := Peer(ad)$
   $rank := SF(Expertise(ad), subject)$
   if $rank > \gamma$ **then**
      $rankedPeers := (peer, rank) \cup rankedPeers$
   end if
end for
return $rankedPeers$

$Knows \subseteq P \times P$, where $Knows(p_1, p_2)$ means that p_1 knows about the expertise of p_2.

The relation $Knows$ is established by the selection of which peers a peer sends its advertisements to. Furthermore, peers can decide to accept an advertisement, e.g. to include it in their registries, or to discard the advertisement. The SON in combination with the expertise based peer selection is the basis for intelligent query routing.

6.4 Expertise Based Peer Selection in Bibster

We now describe the bibliographic scenario using the general model presented in the previous section. This scenario is identical to Bibster, which is described in Chap. 18.

Peers

A researcher is represented by a peer $p \in P$. Each peer has an RDF knowledge base, which consists of a set of bibliographic metadata items that are classified according to the ACM topic hierarchy [1] The following example shows a fragment of a sample bibliographic item based on the Semantic Web Research Community Ontology (SWRC)[2]:

```
<rdf:RDF xmlns=
 "http://www.semanticweb.org/ontologies/swrc-onto.daml#"
  xmlns:rdf ="http://www.w3.org/1999/02/22-rdf-syntax-ns#"
  xmlns:acm ="http://daml.umbc.edu/ontologies/topic-ont#">
<Publication rdf:about="dblp:persons/Codd81">
 <title>The Capabilities of
        Relational Database Management Systems.</title>
 <acm:topic rdf:resource=
   "http://daml.umbc.edu/ontologies/classification#
   ACMTopic/Information_Systems/Database_Management"/>
 <!-- ... -->
</Publication> </rdf:RDF>
```

Shared Ontology

The ontology O that is shared by all the peers is the ACM topic hierarchy. The topic hierarchy contains a set, T, of 1287 topics in the computer science domain and relations $(T \times T)$ between them: *SubTopic* and *seeAlso*.

Expertise

The ACM topic hierarchy is the basis for our expertise model. Expertise E is defined as $E \subseteq 2^T$, where each $e \in E$ denotes a set of ACM topics, for which a peer provides classified instances.

Advertisements

Advertisements associate peers with their expertise: $A \subseteq P \times E$. A single advertisement therefore consists of a set of ACM topics [1] for which the peer is an expert.

Queries

We use the RDF query language SeRQL (Chap. 1) to express queries against the RDF knowledge base of a peer. The following sample query asks for publications with their title about the ACM topic *Information Systems / Database Management*:

```
CONSTRUCT {pub} <swrc:title> {title} FROM {Subject} <rdf:type>
{<swrc:Publication>};
  <swrc:title> {title};
  <acm:topic>
  {<topic:ACMTopic/Information_Systems/Database_Management>}
USING NAMESPACE
swrc=<!http://www.semanticweb.org/ontologies/swrc-onto.daml#>, rdf
=<!http://www.w3.org/1999/02/22-rdf-syntax-ns#>, acm
=<!http://daml.umbc.edu/ontologies/topic-ont#>,
topic=<!http://daml.umbc.edu/ontologies/classification#>
```

Subjects

Analogously to the expertise, a subject $s \in S$ is an abstraction of a query q. In our scenario, each s is a set of ACM topics, thus $s \subseteq T$. For example, the extracted subject of the query above would be *Information Systems/Database Management*.

Similarity Function

In this scenario, the similarity function SF is based on the idea that topics which are close according to their positions in the topic hierarchy are more similar than topics that have a larger distance. For example, an expert on ACM topic *Information Systems/Information Storage and Retrieval* has a higher chance of giving a correct answer on a query about *Information Systems/Database Management* than an expert on a less similar topic like *Hardware/Memory Structures*.

To be able to define the similarity of a peer's expertise and a query subject, which are both represented as a set of topics, we first define the similarity for individual topics. [5] have compared different similarity measures and have shown that for measuring the similarity between concepts in a hierarchically structured semantic network, like the ACM topic hierarchy, the following similarity measure yields the best results:

$$S(t_1, t_2) = \begin{cases} e^{-\alpha l} \cdot \frac{e^{\beta h} - e^{-\beta h}}{e^{\beta h} + e^{-\beta h}} & \text{if } t_1 \neq t_2, \\ 1 & \text{otherwise} \end{cases} \tag{6.1}$$

Here l is the length of the shortest path between topic t_1 and t_2 in the graph spanned by the *SubTopic* relation. h is the level in the tree of the direct common subsumer from t_1 and t_2.

$\alpha \geq 0$ and $\beta \geq 0$ are parameters scaling the contribution of shortest path length l and depth h, respectively. Based on their benchmark data set, the optimal values are: $\alpha = 0.2$, $\beta = 0.6$. Using the shortest path between two topics is a measure for similarity because Rada et al. [7] have proven that the minimum number of edges separating topics t_1 and t_2 is a metric for measuring the conceptual distance of t_1 and t_2. The intuition behind using the depth of the direct common subsumer in the calculation is that topics at upper layers of hierarchical semantic nets are more general and are semantically less similar than topics at lower levels.

Now that we have a function for calculating the similarity between two individual topics, we define SF as:

$$SF(s, e) = \frac{1}{|s|} \sum_{t_i \in s} \max_{t_j \in e} S(t_i, t_j) \tag{6.2}$$

With this function we iterate over all topics of the subject and average their similarities with the most similar topic of the expertise.

Peer Selection Algorithm

The peer selection algorithm ranks the known peers according to the similarity function described above. Therefore, peers that have an expertise more similar to that of the subject of the query will have a higher rank. From the set of ranked peers, we now only consider a selection algorithm that selects the best n peers.

6.5 Results of Simulation Experiments

In this section we describe the simulation of the scenario presented in Sect. 6.4. With the experiments we try to validate the following hypotheses:

- **H1 - Expertise based selection:** The proposed approach of expertise based peer selection yields better results than a naive approach based on random selection. The higher precision of the expertise based selection results in a higher recall of peers and documents, while reducing the number of messages per query.

- **H2 - Ontology based matching:** Using a shared ontology with a metric for semantic similarity improves the recall rate of the system compared with an approach that relies on exact matches, such as a simple keyword based approach.
- **H3 - Semantic Overlay:** The performance of the system can be improved further, if the SON is built according to the semantic similarity of the expertise descriptions of the peers. This can be realized, for example, by accepting advertisements that are semantically similar to the own expertise.
- **H4 - The "Perfect" SON:** Perfect results in terms of precision and recall can be achieved, if the SON coincides with a distribution of the documents according to the expertise model.

Data Set

To obtain a critical mass of bibliographic data, we used the DBLP data set, which consists of metadata for 380440 publications in the computer science domain.

We have classified the publications of the DBLP data set according to the ACM topic hierarchy using a simple classification scheme based on lexical analysis: A publication is said to be about a topic, if the label of the topic occurs in the title of the publication. For example, a publication with the title "The Capabilities of Relational Database Management Systems." is classified into the topic *Database Management*. Topics with labels that are not unique (e.g. *General* is a subtopic of both *General Literature* and *Hardware*) have been excluded from the classification, because typically these labels are too general and would result in publications classified into multiple, distant topics in the hierarchy. Obviously, this method of classification is not as precise as a sophisticated or manual classification. However, a high precision of the classification is not required for the purpose of our simulations. As a result of the classification, about one third of the DBLP publications (126247 out of 380440) have been classified, where 553 out of the 1287 ACM topics actually have classified publications. The classified DBLP subset has been used for our simulations.

Document Distribution

We have simulated and evaluated the scenario with two different distributions, which we describe in the following. Note that for the simulation of the scenario we disregard the actual documents and only distribute the bibliographic metadata of the publications.

Topic Distribution: In the first distribution, the bibliographic metadata are distributed according to their topic classification. There is one dedicated peer for each of the 1287 ACM topics. The distribution is directly correlated with the expertise model, each peer is an expert on exactly one ACM topic and contains all the corresponding publications. This also implies that there are peers that do not contain publications, because not all topics have classified instances.

Proceedings Distribution: In the second distribution, the bibliographic metadata are distributed according to conference proceedings and journals in which the according publications were published. For each of the conference proceedings and journals covered in DBLP there is a dedicated peer that contains all the associated publication descriptions (in the case of the 328 journals) or inproceedings (in the case of the 2006 conference proceedings). Publications that are published neither in a journal nor in conference proceedings are contained by one separate peer. The total number of peers therefore is 2335 (=328+2006+1). With this distribution one peer can be an expert on multiple topics, as a journal or conference typically covers mutliple ACM topics. Note that there is still a correlation between the distribution and the expertise, as a conference or journal typically covers a coherent set of topics.

Simulation Environment

To simulate the scenario we have developed and used a controlled, configurable Peer-to-Peer simulation environment. A single simulation experiment consists of the following sequence of operations:

1. *Setup network topology:* In the first step we create the peers with their knowledge bases according to the document distribution and arrange them in a random network topology, where every peer knows 10 random peers. We do not make any further assumptions about the network topology.
2. *Advertising Knowledge:* In the second step, the SON is created. Every peer sends an advertisement of its expertise to all other remote peers it knows based on the network topology. When a peer receives an advertisement, it may decide to store all or selected advertisements, e.g. if the advertised expertise is semantically similar to its own expertise. After this step the SON is static and will not change anymore.
3. *Query Processing:* The peers randomly initiate queries from a set of randomly created 12870 queries, 10 for each of the 1287 ACM topic. The peers first evaluate the queries against their local knowledge base and then propagate the query according to their peer selection algorithms described below.

Experimental Settings

In our experiments we have systematically simulated various settings with different values of input variables. In the following we will describe an interesting selected subset of the settings to prove the validity of our hypotheses.

Setting 1

In the first setting we use a naive peer selection algorithm, which selects *n random* peers from the set of peers that are known from advertisements received, but disregarding the content of the advertisement. In the experiments, we have used *n=2* in every setting, as a rather arbitrary choice.

Setting 2

In the second setting we apply the expertise based selection algorithm. The *best n* *(n=2)* peers are selected for query forwarding. Here the peer selection algorithm only considers *exact* matches of topics.

Setting 3

In the third setting we modify the peer selection algorithm to use the ontology based similarity measure, instead of only exact matches. The peer selection only selects peers whose expertise is equally or more similar to the subject of the query than the expertise of the forwarding peer.

Setting 4

In the fourth setting we modify the peer to only accept advertisements that are semantically similar to its own expertise. The threshold for accepting advertisements was set to accept on average half of the incoming advertisements.

Setting 5

In this setting we assume global knowledge to impose a perfect topology on the peer network. In this perfect topology the *knows* relation conincides with the ACM topic hierarchy: Every peer knows exactly those peers that are experts on the neighboring topics of its own expertise. This setting is only applicable for the distribution of the publications according to their topics, as this model assumes exactly one expert per topic.

Table 6.1 summarizes the instantiations of the input variables for the described settings:

Table 6.1. Instantiations of the input variables

Setting #	Peer Selection	Advertisements	Topology
Setting 1	random	accept all	random
Setting 2	exact match	accept all	random
Setting 3	ontology based match	accept all	random
Setting 4	ontology based match	accept similar	random
Setting 5	ontology based match	accept similar	perfect

Simulation Results

Figures 6.2 through 6.5 show the results for the different settings and distributions. The simulations have been run with a varying number of allowed hops. In the results we show the performance for a maximum of up to eight hops. Zero hops means that the query is processed locally and not forwarded. Please note that the diagrams for the number of messages per query and recall (i.e. Fig. 6.5, 6.3, 6.4) present cumulative values, i.e. they include the sum of the results for *up to* n hops. The diagram for the precision (Fig. 6.2) of the peer selection displays the precision for a particular number of hops.

In the following, we will interpret the results of the experiments for the various settings described above with respect to our hypotheses H1 through H4.

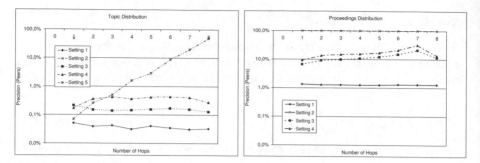

Fig. 6.2. $Precision_{Peers}$

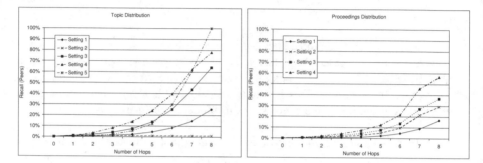

Fig. 6.3. $Recall_{Peers}$

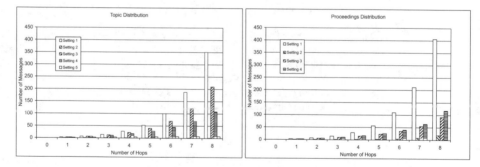

Fig. 6.4. $Number_{Messages}$

R1 - Expertise based selection

The results of Fig. 6.2, Setting 1, show that the naive approach of random peer selection gives a constant low precision of 0.03% for the topic distribution and 1.3% for the proceedings distribution. This results in a fairly low recall of peers and documents despite a high number of messages, as shown in Fig. 6.3, 6.5, 6.4, respectively. With the expertise based selection, either exact or similarity based matching, the precision can be improved considerably by about one order of magnitude. For example, with the expertise based selection in Setting 3, the precision of the peer selection (Fig.

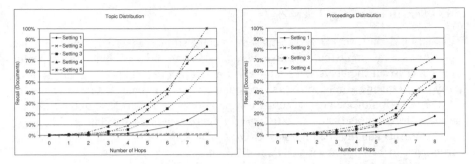

Fig. 6.5. $Recall_{Documents}$

6.2) can be improved from 0.03% to 0.15% for the topic distribution and from 1.3% to 15% for the proceedings distribution. With the precision, the recall of peers and documents also rises (Fig. 6.3, 6.5). At the same time, the number of messages per query can be reduced. The number of messages sent is influenced by two effects. The first effect is message redundancy: The more precise the peer selection, the higher is the chance of a peer receiving a query multiple times on different routes. This redundancy is detected by the receiving peer, which will forward the query only once, thus resulting in a decreasing number of queries sent across the network. The other effect is caused by the selectivity of the peer selection: It only forwards the query to peers whose expertise is semantically more or equally similar to the query than that of the own expertise. With an increasing number of hops, as the semantic similarity of the expertise of the peer and the query increases, the chance of knowing a qualifying peer decreases, which results in a decrease of messages.

R2 - Ontology based matching

The result of Fig. 6.2, Setting 2, shows that the exact match approach results in a maximum precision already after one hop, which is obvious because it only selects peers that match exactly with the query's subject. However, Figure 6.3 shows that the recall in this case is very low in the case of the topic distribution. This can be explained as follows: For every query subject, there is only one peer that exactly matches in the entire network. In a sparse topology, the chance of knowing that relevant peer is very low. Thus the query cannot spread effectively across the network, resulting in a document recall of only 1%. In contrary, Setting 3 shows that when semantically similar peers are selected, it is possible to improve the recall of peers and documents, to 62% after eight hops. Also in the case of the proceedings distribution, where multiple exact matches are possible, we see an improvement from 49% in the case of exact matches (Setting 2), to 54% in the case of ontology based matches (Setting 3). Naturally, this approach requires to send more messages per query and also results in a lower precision.

R3 - Semantic Overlay Network

In Setting 4 the peers only accept semantically similar advertisements. This has proven to be a simple, but effective, way for creating the SON that correlates with the expertise of the peers. This allows to forward queries along the gradient of increasing semantic similarity. When we compare this approach with that of Setting 3, the precision of the peer selection can be improved from 0.15% to 0.4% for the topic distribution and from 14% to 20% for the proceedings distribution. The recall of documents can thus be improved from 62% to 83% for the topic distribution and from 54% to 72% for the proceedings distribution.

It is also interesting to note that the precision of the peer selection for the similarity based matching decreases slightly after seven hops (Fig. 6.2). The reason is that after seven hops the majority of the relevant peers has already been reached. Thus the chance of finding relevant peers decreases, resulting in a lower precision of the peer selection.

R4 - The "Perfect" SON

The results for Setting 5 show how one could obtain the maximum recall and precision, if it were possible to impose an ideal SON. All relevant peers and thus all bibliographic descriptions can be found in a deterministic manner, as the query is simply routed along the route that corresponds to the shortest path in the ACM topic hierarchy. At each hop the query is forwarded to exactly one peer until the relevant peer is reached. The number of messages required per query is therefore the length of the shortest path from the topic of expertise of the originating peer to that of the topic of the query subject. The precision of the peer selection increases to the maximum when arriving at the eight hop, which is the maximum possible length of a shortest path in the ACM topic hierarchy. Accordingly, the maximum number of messages (Fig. 6.4) required is also eight.

6.6 Results of Field Study

In the Bibster system (cf. Chap. 18) we implemented two different query forwarding strategies that ran at the same time, namely our expertise-based method and a random query forwarding algorithm. In this way we are able to see how our approach performs in real life. The Bibster system was made publicly available and advertised to researchers in the Computer Science domain. The evaluation was based on the analysis of system activity that was automatically logged to log files on the individual Bibster clients. We have analyzed the results for a period of three months (June to August 2004). With respect to query routing and the use of the expertise based peer selection, we were able to reduce the number of query messages by more than 50 percent, while retaining the same recall of documents compared with a naive broadcasting approach. Figure 6.6 shows the precision of the peer selection (the percentage of the reached peers that actually provided answers to a given query): While the expertise based peer selection results in an almost constant high precision of 28%, the naive algorithm results in a lower precision decreasing from 22% after 1 hop to 14% after 4 hops[1].

Figure 6.7 shows the number of forwarded query messages sent per query. It can be seen that with an increasing number of hops, the number of messages sent with the expertise based peer selection is considerably lower than with the naive algorithm. Although we have shown an improvement in the performance, the results also show that with a network of the size as in the field experiment, a naive approach is also acceptable. On the other hand, with a growing number of peers, query routing and peer selection becomes critical. In the previous discussed simulation experiments, networks with thousands of peers improve in the order of one magnitude in terms of recall of documents and relevant peers.

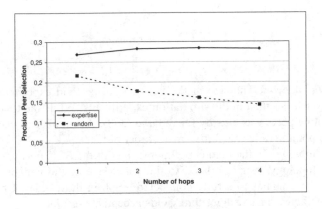

Fig. 6.6. $Precision_{Peers}$

6.7 Comparison with Results from Simulation Experiments

Overall, the results of the simulation experiments have been validated: We were able to improve the precision of the peer selection and thus reduce the number of sent messages. However, the performance gain by using the expertise based peer selection was not as significant as in the simulation experiments[2].

This is mainly due to the following reasons:

---

[1] The decrease is due the redundancy of relevant peers found on different message paths: Only distinct relevant peers are considered.

[2] In terms of recall, there were no improvements at all, as even the naive algorithm generally was able to reach all relevant peers.

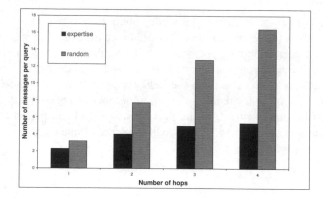

Fig. 6.7. $Number_{Messages}$

- *Size of the network* The size of the network in the field experiment was con-siderably *smaller* than in the simulation experiments. While the total number of participating peers was already fairly large (398), the number of peers online at a certain point in time was fairly small (order of tens).
- *Network topology* In the field experiment we built the SON on-top of the JXTA network topology. Again, related to the small size of the network, the JXTA topology degenerates to a fully connected graph in most cases. Obviously, for these topologies, a naive algorithm yields acceptable results.
- *Distribution of the content* In the simulation experiments, we distributed the shared content according to certain assumptions (based on topics, conferences, journals). In real world experiments, the distribution is much more heteroge-neous, both in terms of the expertise of the peers and the amount of shared con-tent.

6.8 Conclusion

In this paper we have presented a model for expertise-based peer selection, in which a SON among the peers is created by advertising the expertise of the peers. We have shown how the model can be applied in a bibliographic scenario. Simulation experiments that we performed with this bibliographic scenario show the following results:

- Using expertise-based peer selection can increase the performance of the peer selection by an order of magnitude (result R1).

- However, if expertise-based peer selection uses simple exact matching, the recall drops to unacceptable levels. It is necessary to use an ontology-based similarity measure as the basis for expertise-based matching (result R2).
- An advertising strategy where peers only accept advertisements that are semantically close to their own profile (i.e. that are in their semantic neighborhood) is a simple and effective way of creating a SON. This semantic topology allows to forward queries along the gradient of increasing semantic similarity (result R3).
- The above results depend on how closely the SON mirrors the structure of the ontology. All relevant performance measure reach their optimal value when the network is organized exactly according to the structure of the ontology (result R4). Although this situation is idealized and in will in practice not be achievable, the experiment serves to confirm our intuitions on this.

Also, the field experiment showed that we were able to improve the precision of the peer selection and thus reduce the number of sent messages. However, the performance gained by using the expertise based peer selection was not as significant as in the simulation experiments. Summarizing, in both the simulation experiments and the field experiments, we have shown that expertise-based peer selection combined with ontology-based matching outperforms both random peer selection and selection based on exact matches, and that this performance increase grows when the SON more closely mirrors the domain ontology.

References

[1] The ACM Topic Hierarchy.
     http://www.acm.org/class/1998/.
[2] The Semantic Web Research Community Ontology.
     http://ontobroker.semanticweb.org/ontos/swrc.html.
[3] K. Aberer, P. Cudré-Mauroux, M. Hauswirth, and T. Van Pelt. Gridvine: Building internet-scale semantic overlay networks. In *3rd International Semantic Web Conference (ISWC2004)*, pages 107–121, Hiroshima, Japan, 7-11 November 2004.
[4] P. Haase, R. Siebes, and F. van Harmelen. Peer selection in peer-to-peer networks with semantic topologies. In Mokrane Bouzeghoub, editor, *Proceedings of the International Conference on Semantics in a Networked World (IC-NSW'04)*, volume 3226 of *LNCS*, pages 108–125, Paris, June 2004. Springer Verlag.
[5] Y. Li, Z. A. Bandar, and D. McLean. An approach for measuring semantic similarity between words using multiple information sources. *Transactions on Knowledge and Data Engineering*, 15(4):871–882, July/August 2003.
[6] W. Nejdl, B. Wolf, C. Qu, S. Decker, M. Sintek, A. Naeve, M. Nilsson, M. Palmer, and T. Risch. Edutella: A p2p networking infrastructure based on rdf. In*Proceedings of the 11th International World Wide Web Conference*, May 2002. schema based searching Presentation: http://www2002.org/presentations/nejdl.pdf.

[7] R. Rada, H. Mili, E. Bicknell, and M. Blettner. Development and application of a metric on semantic nets. *IEEE Transactions on Systems, Man, and Cybernetics*, 19(1):17–30, 1989.

[8] C. Tang, Z. Xu, and S. Dwarkadas. Peer-to-peer information retrieval using self-organizing semantic overlay networks. Technical report, HP Labs, November 2002.

[9] S. Voulgaris, A.-M. Kermarrec, L. Massoulie, and M. van Steen. Exploiting semantic proximity in peer-to-peer content searching. In *10th International Workshop on Future Trends in Distributed Computing Systems (FTDCS)*, Suzhou, China, May 2004.

Personalized Information Access in a Bibliographic Peer-to-Peer System

Peter Haase[1], Marc Ehrig[1], Andreas Hotho[1], Björn Schnizler[2]

[1] Institute AIFB, University of Karlsruhe, Germany
   {pha,meh,aho}@aifb.uni-karlsruhe.de
[2] Information Management and Systems, University of Karlsruhe, Germany
   schnizler@iw.uka.de

Summary. The Bibster system is an application of the use of semantics in Peer-to-Peer systems, which is aimed at researchers that share bibliographic metadata. In this paper we describe the design and implementation of recommender functionality in the Bibster system which allows personalized access to the bibliographic metadata available in the Peer-to-Peer network. These functions are based on a semantic user profile which is created from content and usage information as well as a similarity function. Furthermore, these functions make use of the semantic topology of the Peer-to-Peer system.

7.1 Introduction

The Bibster system[1] is an application of the use of semantics in Peer-to-Peer systems [5] (cf. Chap. 18 for a comprehensive description). Bibster is aimed at researchers that share bibliographic metadata. Currently, many researchers in computer science keep lists of bibliographic metadata in BibTeX format, that they must laboriously maintain manually, for which they do not have an easy overview, and that has greatly varying quality. Many researchers own hundreds of kilobytes of bibliographic information, in dozens of BibTeX files. At the same time, many researchers are willing to share these resources, provided they do not have to invest work in doing so.

Bibster enables the management of bibliographic metadata in a Peer-to-Peer fashion: it allows to import bibliographic metadata, e.g. from BibTeX files, into a local knowledge repository, to share and search the knowledge in the Peer-to-Peer system, as well as to edit and export the bibliographic metadata.

In this chapter we describe the design and implementation of recommender functionality in the Bibster system which allows personalized access to the bibliographic metadata available in the Peer-to-Peer network according to the particular needs of the users.

These recommender functions build upon two main features of the Bibster system:

---

[1] http://bibster.semanticweb.org/

- *Semantic representation of metadata*: When bibliographic entries are made available for use in Bibster, they are structured and classified according to two bibliographic ontologies, the SWRC[1] ontology and the ACM[2] topic hierarchy. This ontological structure is then exploited to help the user formulate semantic queries. Query results again are represented according to the ontology. These semantic representations of the knowledge available on the peers, the user queries and relevant results allow us to directly create a semantic user profile and rich semantic similarity functions as a basis for recommending information that may potentially be interesting to the user.

- *Peer-to-Peer infrastructure with a semantic topology*: The Peer-to-Peer infrastructure reflects the distributed, decentralized and dynamic nature of creation of bibliographic metadata in a research community. The decentralized Peer-to-Peer architecture can immediately be exploited for recommending newly created data as soon as it becomes available in the network.

  Using semantic descriptions of the knowledge available on the peers, we are able to create semantic topologies that reflect the social networks of research communities: Peers with similar interests and expertise are clustered, such that the semantic neighborhood of a peer automatically covers a set of peers that contain relevant information for the specific community of interest. Furthermore, to address the cold start problem that recommender systems typically have to face [14], we can make use of the of the peer's semantic neighbors to create an initial user profile.

7.1.1 Example Scenarios

We will now illustrate the advantages of Bibster as a semantics-based, Peer-to-Peer recommender system with three typical usage scenarios, which we will use as a running example throughout the paper.

In the first scenario, suppose a researcher who is an expert on the topic of "Intelligent Agents" is searching for bibliographic metadata of new books about the topic "Artificial Intelligence" using the regular search functionality of the Bibster system. The corresponding query is routed in the semantic topology of the Peer-to-Peer network to the peers that may potentially return relevant answers. Among the results there may be an entry of the book "Handbook on Ontologies". Suppose the researcher considers this book relevant and saves the corresponding metadata into his local knowledge base. Now, the researcher might be interested in *similar publications*, which address similar topics or were written by a similar author constellation. Therefor the researcher could use the recommender function of Bibster to find similar entries – according to his definition of similarity – in the semantic neighborhood of the peer, again exploiting the semantic topology. The system might find the article "Knowledge Processes and Ontologies," which is about a subtopic of "Artificial Intelligence" and was written by a similar author constellation.

---

[1] http://www.semanticweb.org/ontologies/swrc-onto-2001-12-11.daml

[2] http://www.acm.org/class/1988/

In the second scenario, the researcher might also want the system to proactively *recommend relevant publications* when they are available in the network. He could thus avoid searching the network manually in regular intervals. For example, the peer may have a semantic link to a special conference peer which provides the bibliographic metadata of conferences covering a certain set of topics, say a dedicated AAAI peer for the topic of "Artificial Intelligence." Without performing explicit queries, the researcher would be proactively provided with information about the new publications of his interest which were published at the relevant conferences. The recommender function can here exploit the area of expertise of the researcher, the queries he performed recently and the results that he considered relevant.

In a final scenario, the researcher may want to explore the semantic topology, e.g. to find *similar peers*. On the one hand, this information would make it possible to query a specific peer, e.g. with a query for all journal items shared by this peer. On the other hand, the researcher could establish a personal contact to researchers interested in similar topics.

For the remainder of this chapter we assume the design of the Bibster system as described in Chap. 18. We will present a model of ontology-based similarity for the bibliographic domain and the user profile, which are the basis for the recommender functions presented in the subsequent section. We will conclude after a discussion of related work.

7.2 Ontology Based Similarity

In this section we will first describe the bibliographic ontologies employed in the Bibster system. Subsequently, we will define a semantic similarity function for this bibliographic ontology, which serves as the basis for the recommender functions presented in a following section.

7.2.1 The Bibliographic Ontologies

In our bibliographic scenario we make use of two common ontologies:

The first ontology is the Semantic Web Research Community Ontology (SWRC), which models, among others, a research community, its researchers, topics, publications, and properties between them [6]. The SWRC ontology defines a shared and common domain theory which helps users and machines to communicate concisely and supports exchange of semantics.

The second ontology is the ACM topic hierarchy. It describes specific categories of literature for the Computer Science domain, covering 1287 topics. Figure 7.1 shows a small fragment of the hierarchy relevant for our example scenarios. In addition to the sub- and super-topic relations, the hierarchy also provides information

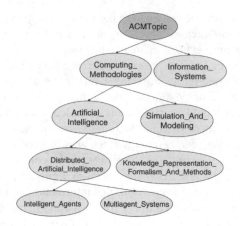

Fig. 7.1. Fragment of the ACM Topic Hierarchy

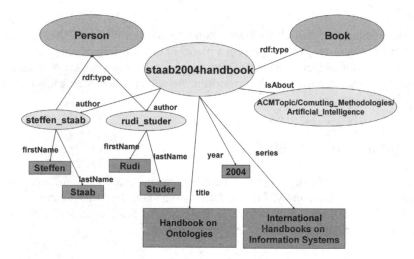

Fig. 7.2. RDF graph for Example 1

about related topics. The topic hierarchy therefore provides a quick content reference and assists users in searching for related publications. In the context of a recommender system this classification is crucial for identifying similarities.

Bibliographic entries that a user made available to Bibster are described using these two ontologies. The classification according to the ACM ontology is initially done automatically using lexical matching of the topic labels against the titles of the publications. Additionally, it is possible to reclassify the entries manually in the user interface of Bibster.

The ontologies and the specific bibliographic instance data are represented in RDF.

Figure 7.2 shows a sample bibliographic item as an RDF graph.

Authors and editors are represented as instances of the `Person` class. The publication itself is instantiated as a `Book`, which is a subclass of `Publication`. The ACM topics corresponding to the publications are represented with the `isAbout` properties. In this example the associated topic is `Artificial Intelligence`.

7.2.2 Semantic Similarity

We will now first describe our notion of similarity we use in our recommender system. Then we will present individual similarity functions and show how to combine these. Some of the measures are generic similarity functions independent of a specific domain ontology. However, using background knowledge about the bibliography domain allows to define more specific similarity functions.

Similarity Function

A similarity function for RDF resources R of a knowledge base is a function

$$sim : R \times R \rightarrow [0..1],$$

with the properties as presented in [2]. This function is based on different features of the respective resources. Individual functions for each feature are combined using an aggregation function to compute an overall similarity result.

Features

Each resource type is compared based on specific features. For persons and organizations we rely solely on the their names, whereas for publications we use a wide range of features: title, publication type, authors and editors, publisher, institute and university, booktitle or journal with the series number and address, page numbers, publication year, and the ACM topic the publication was classified to.

Individual Similarity Functions

For these individual features we use specific functions, which do not only determine the similarity on the syntactic level, but also consider the semantics of the ontological structures. The individual functions take the following characteristics of the ontology into account:

- *Data Value Layer*, where we consider the atomic data values of the attributes of the instances, which in RDF are represented as typed literals,
- *Graph Layer*, where we consider relations between the RDF resources,
- *Ontology Layer*, where we consider ontological information, such as the class hierarchy,

- *Domain Specific Knowledge*, where we use domain specific features with corresponding heuristics.

We will now present the specific methods used for the bibliographic ontology:

Data Value Layer: To determine the similarity of data values d_1, d_2 of type string (e.g. to compare the titles of publications) we use the syntactic similarity sim_{syn} of [8]. It relies on the edit distance (ed) of [7], which basically determines how many atomic actions as character addition or deletion are required to transform one string into the other one:

$$sim_{syn}(d_1, d_2) = max(0, \frac{min(|d_1|, |d_2|) - ed(d_1, d_2)}{min(|d_1|, |d_2|)}).$$

Graph Structure Layer: A publication resource is structurally linked with person resources, e.g. authors. Thus we can compare two publications on the basis of the similarity of the sets of authors. To compare the similarity of two sets of resources E and F, we average over the similarities of the resources of the one set with the most similar resource of the respective other set:

$$sim_{set}(E, F) = \frac{\sum_{e \in E} \max_{f \in F} sim(e, f) + \sum_{f \in F} \max_{e \in E} sim(f, e)}{|E| + |F|}.$$

Ontology Layer: One possible generic function to determine the semantic similarity of concepts in a concept hierarchy (such as topics in the ACM topic hierarchy) has been presented by [13]:

$$sim_{taxonomic}(c_1, c_2) = \begin{cases} e^{-\alpha l} \cdot \frac{e^{\beta h} - e^{-\beta h}}{e^{\beta h} + e^{-\beta h}}, & \text{if } c_1 \neq c_2, \\ 1, & \text{otherwise} \end{cases}$$

$\alpha \geq 0$ and $\beta \geq 0$ are parameters scaling the contribution of shortest path length l and depth h in the concept hierarchy, respectively. The shortest path length is a metric for measuring the conceptual distance of c_1 and c_2. The intuition behind using the depth of the direct common subsumer in the calculation is that concepts at upper layers of the concept hierarchy are more general and are semantically less similar than concepts at lower layers. Complying with [13], for the comparison of ACM topics the parameters are set to $\alpha = 0.2$, $\beta = 0.6$.

Domain Specific Knowledge: In the SWRC domain ontology there are many subconcepts of publications: articles, books, and technical reports to just name a few. We know that if the type of a publication is not known, it is often provided as "Misc" (e.g. in Citeseer[1]).

Instead of using a generic similarity function, we can thus define:

$$sim_{type}(c_1, c_2) = \begin{cases} 1, & \text{if } c_1 = c_2, \\ 0.75, & \text{if } (c_1 = \text{Misc} \vee c_2 = \text{Misc}) \\ 0, & \text{otherwise} \end{cases}$$

---

[1] http://citeseer.nj.nec.com/

Experiments with sample data have shown that a similarity value of 0.75 yields meaningful results if one of the publications is of type Misc.

Another domain specific function is used for the similarity between years. The closer the years of the publications are, the higher their similarity:

$$sim_{year}(year_1, year_2) = \frac{1}{1 + |year_1 - year_2|}$$

Aggregated Similarity Function

Based on the individual similarity functions, an overall value can be obtained for example using a weighted average function

$$Sim_W(i_1, i_2) = \frac{1}{\sum_{k=1}^{n} w_k} \sum_{k=1}^{n} w_k sim_k(i_1, i_2),$$

with w_k being the weight for a specific function sim_k. Because of the semi-structured nature of bibliographic metadata, some attributes may not be provided such that some individual measures may not apply. Therefore, for non-mandatory attributes, the weight w_k will be adjusted to 0 if either one of the compared resources does not provide the attribute.

Example 1. We now present a complete example of a combined similarity function for the bibliographic scenario, in which we compute the semantic similarity of the publication p_1 from example 7.2 with the publication p_2 as shown in Fig. 7.3. When comparing the two example publications applying the similarity functions from above we obtain:

$sim_1(p_1, p_2) = sim_{type}(Book, Article) = 0$
$sim_2(p_1, p_2) = sim_{syn}(\text{"Handbook on Ontologies"},$
    "Knowledge Processes and Ontologies"$) = 0.14$
$sim_3(p_1, p_2) = sim_{taxonomic}(Artificial\_Intelligence,$
    $Knowledge\_Representation\_Formalisms\_And\_Methods) = 0.98$
$sim_4(p_1, p_2) = sim_{set}(\ (steffen\_staab, rudi\_studer),$
    $(steffen\_staab, rudi\_studer, hans\_schnurr, york\_sure)\ ) = 0.67$
$sim_5(p_1, p_2) = sim_{year}(2004, 2001) = 0.25$

In our example, we use a weight-vector of $W = (2, 2, 9, 9, 2)$, which prefers the topic and the author attributes over the rest of the attributes:

$$Sim_W(p_1, p_2) = \frac{1}{\sum_{k=1}^{n} w_k} \sum_{k=1}^{n} w_k sim_k(p_1, p_2) = 0.65$$

The similarity value indicates the similarity of the resources and can be used directly as a rank value. With an assumed threshold for similarity of 0.5, the publication p_2 would be considered similar to p_1.

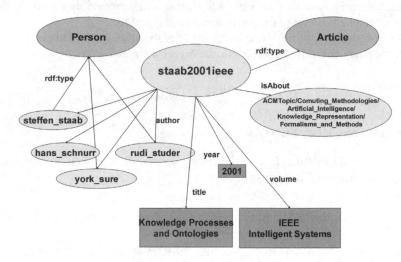

Fig. 7.3. RDF graph for Example 2

7.3 Semantic User Profile

The user profile is built on the basis of the semantic representation of the shared knowledge (content) and usage information. Conforming with the model presented in [12], we will now describe the user profile representation, the initial user profile and profile adaptation.

7.3.1 User Profile Representation

Definition 1. *A* user profile *is a structure* $PR := (e, Q, R, W, t)$ *consisting of*

- *the expertise description* e,
- *a set of recent queries Q,*
- *a set of recent relevant instances R,*
- *a structure W which defines the weights for the similarity function, and*
- *a threshold* $t \in [0, 1]$.

We will now describe the roles of the elements of a user profile.

Expertise e**:** The expertise e is a set of topics about which the user is knowledgeable about. It is built on the assumption that if a user has a knowledge base with bibliographic items about certain topics, he is a researcher with a certain expertise and interests in these topics. Consequently, he might be interested in other bibliographic items about these topics that are not available in his local knowledge base. The expertise model is constructed directly from the knowledge base of the peer: It comprises all topics for which the knowledge base contains classified instances. In this sense, the expertise model can be seen as an abstraction or index structure of the knowledge base.

The expertise model can easily be extended to not only cover topics, but also, for example, certain conferences, authors, etc.

Recent queries Q: The queries are an important part of the interaction of the user with the system that reflect the information need and interest of the user. To exploit this knowledge about the interest, we store a set of recent queries as part of the user profile. However, during the transformation of the information need into a query, information may get lost. In this sense, the user might be interested in instances that may not exactly match the query, but are semantically similar. Another reason to remember recent queries is the following: It may be possible that at the time of querying no entries match a given query, either because matching entries do not exists or the relevant peer is currently offline. However, at a later point in time, matching entries could possibly be found.

In our sample scenario, the user is searching for books about the topic of Artificial Intelligence. The user specifies his search request through the user interface as shown in the previous section. Internally, this request is formulated as a SeRQL query that looks as follows:

Example 2.
```
construct distinct
  {s} prop {val}
from
  {s} <rdf:type> {<swrc:Book>};
      <swrc:isAbout>
          {<acm:ACMTopic/Computing_Methodologies/Artificial_Intelligence>}
```

Instead of storing the SeRQL query itself, for each query $q \in Q$ we store the corresponding attribute value pairs that the user specified as an RDF resource.

This set of attribute value pairs is thus represented in the same way as the specification of a publication itself. We can therefore apply the semantic similarity measures defined before to calculate how close a bibliographic instance matches a query.

When considering the set of recent queries, we may be able to recommend items that may not have matched any of the queries exactly, but are semantically very close to the information need of the user.

Recent Relevant Results R: The recent relevant results are a set of bibliographic instances obtained from previous searches. Here a bibliographic instance is considered relevant if it has been included into the local knowledge base by the user. We thus do not store all results that match the user query, instead we only store those instances that were subjectively relevant to the user. The recent relevant results therefore better reflect the information need of the user.

Weights W: Just as relevance, also similarity is a very subjective measure. We therefore allow to adjust the weights of the similarity function presented in the previous section as part of the user profile. By adjusting these weights, the user can specify which attributes of a the bibliographic metadata are more important for determining the relevance of similar items. For example, when the user requests the system to recommend publications similar to an existing one, he might indicate that he does not care about similarity of the title, but is interested in a similar constellation of co-authors. Another option might be that the user is interested in publications at similar conferences in the same or close year.

Threshold t**:** With the threshold t the user can specify how closely a resource must match the profile to considered relevant by the recommender functions. The threshold is used to filter the ranked results of the similarity functions. An increasing threshold will result in a more selective matching. The user can thus use the threshold to influence the result size: Depending on the amount of data available, the threshold may be increased or decreased to obtain a useful result size.

7.3.2 Initial User Profile and Profile Adaptation

We will now describe how the initial user profile is created and adapted. It is important to note how the cold start problem is addressed: We use a combination of content and usage based information in the user profile. In typical recommender systems, the cold start problem is caused by the initially unavailable usage information. In our system, we make use of the properties of the Peer-to-Peer network: Instead of starting with an empty profile, we reuse the profiles of similar peers in the semantic neighborhood.

Expertise: The initial expertise description e will be, as defined, the set of topics for which classified instances exist in the knowledge base KB of the peer. The expertise profile of the user is adapted whenever the knowledge base of the peer is updated. This means that whenever publications covering certain topics are added or removed from the knowledge base, the expertise description is updated accordingly.

Recent queries: To avoid to start with an empty set of recent queries, we start out with a sample of queries that were recently performed by the peers in the neighborhood (given by the semantic topology) of the peer.

When the user performs a query, it is added to the set of recent queries. As only n recent queries are stored, old queries are gradually forgotten. This could be done by always remembering the last n queries (FIFO), however, by temporary changes in the query behavior, the previous profile may get lost. Therefore, the items to be removed from the set of recent queries are selected randomly.

Recent Relevant Results: As for the recent queries, for the initial set of relevant results we also rely on the profile of the peers in the semantic neighborhood and use a sample of results that were recently considered relevant by other peers. Whenever the user decides to store a bibliographic item to its local knowledge base, it is added to the list of recent relevant results. With the recent relevant results we realize an implicit relevance feedback: The recommended entries that were considered relevant by the user are immediately added to the user profile. For the gradual forgetting of results, the same mechanisms are applied as described above for the recent queries.

Weights: As initial weights W for the similarity function, default values are used. For the Bibster system, useful default values have been determined heuristically with experiments.

The weights of the similarity function can be adapted manually by the user. Using the relevance feedback mechanisms described above, the weights could also be adjusted automatically by the system.

Threshold: The threshold is initially set to 0.5, which is a more or less arbitrary choice. The threshold can be increased or decreased by the user to affect the amount of recommended information. Alternatively, the threshold could be adjusted automatically by the system such that the amount of recommended data is kept manageable.

7.4 Recommender Functions

In this section we will explain how the three scenarios described in the introduction of this paper are realized in Bibster. The recommendation functions are realized using the similarity functions and user profiles previously presented.

7.4.1 Recommending Similar Items

The first recommender function provides the user with bibliographic entries that are semantically similar to relevant results from previous searches. In a typical browsing scenario the user may start out with a vague idea of his search criteria. The information need may not have been transformed into the correct query. Thus the available relevant content may not necessarily match the specified search. By recommending entries that are similar to the results that the user has considered as relevant, the quality of the search can be improved. As previously discussed, similar may mean various things depending on the user context. Therefore, the weights of similarity function as part of the user profile are taken into account.

The set of relevant results, R, and the weights of the similarity function, W, are routed in the Peer-to-Peer network as a special request to the potentially relevant peers. The remote peers evaluate the request against their local knowledge base KB using the recommendation function defined as follows:

$$Rec_1(KB, R, W, t) := \{i \in KB | \exists r \in R : Sim_W(i, r) \geq t\}$$

The function thus returns the set of bibliographic items from the instance set of the knowledge base whose semantic similarity with one of the relevant results is greater than the defined threshold t, determined by the specified weights W. The set of similar entries is then sent back and presented to the user.

Example 3. In our scenario, the user has performed the query for books on the topic of "Artifical Intelligence", as shown in example 2. He may have selected the "Handbook on Ontologies" from the example in Fig. 7.2 as a relevant result. The peer selection algorithm may have routed the request for similar publications to a remote peer because of its expertise in "Knowledge Representation Formalisms And Methods." This peer's knowledge base KB contains the entry "Knowledge Processes and Ontologies" from Fig. 7.3, which would be recommended to the originating peer based on the calculation shown in example 1.

7.4.2 Recommending Potentially Relevant Items

Unlike the previous function, which required a set of relevant results to be identified by the user, this function proactively recommends potentially relevant items based solely on the user profile.

Analogously to the previous function, the Profile, $PR := (e, Q, R, W, t)$, is propagated as a special request in the Peer-to-Peer network, and the function Rec_2 is evaluated against the knowledge base KB of the remote peer:

$$Rec_2(KB, PR) = \{i \in KB | \exists q \in Q, \exists r \in R :$$
$$\mathcal{A}(Sim_{Topics}(E, Topics(i)), Sim_W(i, q), Sim_W(i, r)) \geq t\}$$

The recommender function Rec_2 computes a combined relevance of bibliographic items based on the individual elements of the user profile, i.e. expertise, recent queries and recent relevant results. It uses an aggregation function $\mathcal{A}$ that determines the overall similarity as a composition of the individual similarity measures. In the easiest case, the aggregation function $\mathcal{A}$ is again simply a weighted average.

The following individual similarity measures are used: For the expertise we determine the similarity of the set of expertise topics with the set of topics for which the instances i of the knowledge base are classified for (determined by the $Topic(i)$ function) using the function Sim_{Topics} (based on $sim_{taxonomic}$ presented above). We then compute the weighted similarity of the recent queries using the instances of the knowledge base. Here the queries are treated as instances, as described above. Similarly, the similarity of the recent relevant results with the instances of the knowledge base is determined.

The relevant results are returned to the querying peer.

Example 4. Continuing with our scenario, the user profile now consists of the following: The user's expertise is the topic of "Intelligent Agents," the user recently performed the query from Example 2 and considered the result "Handbook on Ontologies" as relevant. Suppose the user's peer is connected in the semantic topology to a peer that covers publications published at AAAI conferences and associated workshops. Among these publications is for example "Towards Evaluation of Peer-to-Peer-based Distributed Knowledge Management Systems" [4], which was co-authored by one of the authors of the recently relevant "Handbook on Ontologies" and is classified to be about "Multiagent Systems", a topic similar to "Intelligent Agents". This publication would therefore match the user profile and would be recommended as relevant. For space constraints we omit the complete calculations of the recommender function.

7.4.3 Recommending Similar Peers

This last recommender function allows to find peers in the network with a similar expertise e. Unlike the two previous functions, Rec_3 can be evaluated on the local peer, as from the advertisements (cf. Chap. 6) the peers' P expertise are already known to the local peer :

$$Rec_3(p_1) := \{p_2 \in P | (p_1, p_2) \in Knows\}$$

The function is implicitly realized by the semantic topology of the Peer-to-Peer network: The similar peers are all those peers that have a link in the semantic topology, which was created because their expertise is semantically similar, determined by a threshold t:

$$Knows(p_1, p_2) \implies Sim_{Topics}(Expertise(p_1), Expertise(p_2)) \geq t$$

(Here $Expertise(p)$ returns the set of topics that the peer has advertised.)

The semantic topology thus is not only used for efficient peer selection and query routing, but also enables the user to find similar peers in the Peer-to-Peer network. The user can then, for example, address queries directly to relevant peers.

Example 5. The user from our scenario may now be interested in exploring the semantic topology to find peers with a similar expertise. As stated in the previous example, among these peers may be the dedicated AAAI peer, because of the similarity of the topics covered by AAAI and the expertise of the user. Knowing of the existence of this special peer, the user could now direct specific queries directly to the peer, for example to retrieve the complete proceedings of the workshop from the previous example.

7.5 Related Work

As the field of related work in semantics-based Peer-to-Peer systems has already been covered in previous chapters, we focus here on the research done in the field of ontology based recommender systems and their application to personalized information access.

Following the taxonomy of recommender systems in [12] our system contains a semantics based profile, without profile learning techniques, using implicit relevance feedback. The profile adaptation takes place through adding new items and a gradual forgetting function. The most relevant part in the field of recommender systems are content based, especially ontology based, recommender systems, as our knowledge base represents the content of a peer.

[11] describe the improvement of classical recommender systems with ontologies. They use the ontology to enhance the user interface, to reduce the staring effort [10] and to improve the recommendation accuracy [9]. The approaches were tested on two user groups where the recommender system recommends research paper. Theses works shows the benefits of ontologies for recommender systems. Our approach is also based in ontologies, but we use a Peer-to-Peer and not a central server system.

[1] discuss the relevance of user profiles to model the information need of users and to personalize the access. Bibster captures the information for one peer in a

similar way as it also derives a profile for every peer. [15] describes how the user interaction of a semantic portal can be improved by utilizing personal knowledge bases, which express semantic properties. This utilization is similar to the exploitation of the expertise obtained from the user's knowledge base in our user profile. [3] present a rule-based approach to personalization in adaptive educational hypermedia systems, where the user's current knowledge state is used as the user profile and relevant content is determined using FOL rules. Bibster can be compared with adaptive hypermedia systems in the sense that relevant RDF-subgraphs are presented to the user using semantic similarity measures.

7.6 Conclusion

In this paper, we have described the design and implementation of recommender functionality in Bibster, a semantics-based Peer-to-Peer system for the exchange of bibliographic metadata between researchers.

We have presented a semantic similarity function for a bibliographic ontology, based on which we are able to match the bibliographic metadata against user profiles. These user profiles are built from content and usage information. We have shown how three specific recommendation functions are realized to recommend similar bibliographic entries, to proactively provide potentially relevant entries and to find similar peers in the Peer-to-Peer network. Further, we have shown how the semantic topology of the Peer-to-Peer network is used to route requests and efficiently find the relevant content as well as to address the cold start problem.

In Chap. 18 we present evaluation results of a case study with the Bibster system. An evaluation of the recommender functionality is currently outstanding, but it will follow the same methodology for evaluation, based on (1) automated data collecting for recording and analyzing user and system activity by means of log files, and (2) user questionnaires to evaluate the user satisfaction of the recommendations of our system.

References

[1]   Giuseppe Amato and Umberto Straccia. User profile modeling and applications to digital libraries. In S. Abiteboul and A.-M. Vercoustre, editors, *Proc. 3rd European Conf. Research and Advanced Technology for Digital Libraries, ECDL*, pages 184–197. Springer-Verlag, 1999.

[2]   G. Bisson. Why and how to define a similarity measure for object based representation systems. *Towards Very Large Knowledge Bases*, pages 236–246, 1995.

[3]   Peter Dolog, Nicola Henzen, Wolfgang Nejdl, and Michael Sintek. Towards the adaptive semantic web. In *1st Workshop on Principles and Practice of Semantic Web Reasoning (PPSWR'03)*, 2003.

[4] Marc Ehrig, Christoph Schmitz, Steffen Staab, Julien Tane, and Christoph Tempich. Towards evaluation of peer-to-peer-based distributed knowledge management systems. In *Proceedings of the AAAI Spring Symposium "Agent-Mediated Knowledge Management (AMKM-2003)"*, 2003.

[5] Peter Haase, Jeen Broekstra, Marc Ehrig, Maarten Menken, Peter Mika, Michal Plechawski, Pawel Pyszlak, Björn Schnizler, Ronny Siebes, Steffen Staab, and Christoph Tempich. Bibster - a semantics-based bibliographic peer-to-peer system. In *Proceedings of the Third International Semantic Web Conference, Hiroshima, Japan, 2004*, NOV 2004.

[6] S. Handschuh, S. Staab, and A. Maedche. Cream - creating relational metadata with a component-based, ontology-driven annotation framework. In *Proceedings of the First International Conference on Knowledge Capture K-CAP 2001*, 2001.

[7] I. V. Levenshtein. Binary codes capable of correcting deletions, insertions, and reversals. *Cybernetics and Control Theory*, 1966.

[8] Alexander Maedche. Comparing ontologies - similarity measures and a comparison study. Technical report, Forschungszentrum Informatik, Karlsruhe, Germany, 2001.

[9] S.E. Middleton, D.C. De Roure, and N.R.Shadbolt. Capturing knowledge of user preferences: ontologies on recommender systems. In *In Proceedings of the First International Conference on Knowledge Capture (K-CAP 2001)*, Victoria, B.C. Canada, October 2001.

[10] Stuart E. Middleton, Harith Alani, Nigel Shadbolt, and David De Roure. Exploiting synergy between ontologies and recommender systems. In Martin Frank, Natasha Noy, and Steffen Staab, editors, *Proceedings of the WWW2002 International Workshop on the Semantic Web, Hawaii, May 7, 2002*, volume 55 of *CEUR Workshop Proceedings*, 2002.

[11] Stuart E. Middleton, David De Roure, and Nigel R. Shadbolt. Ontology-based recommender systems. In Steffen Staab and Rudi Studer, editors, *Handbook on Ontologies*. Springer, 2003.

[12] Miquel Montaner, Beatriz Lopez, and Josep Lluis De La Rosa. A taxonomy of recommender agents on the internet. *Artif. Intell. Rev.*, 19(4):285–330, 2003.

[13] R. Rada, H. Mili, E. Bicknell, and M. Blettner. Development and application of a metric on semantic nets. In *IEEE Transactions on Systems, Man and Cybernetics*, pages 17–30, 1989.

[14] A. Schein, A. Popescul, L. Ungar, and D. Pennock. Methods and metrics for cold-start recommendations. In *Proceedings of the 25th Annual International ACM SIGIR Conference on Research and Development in Information Retrieval*, 2002.

[15] Eric Schwarzkopf. Enhancing the interaction with information portals. In *Intelligent User Interfaces 2004*, pages 322–324, 2004.

8

Designing Semantic Publish/Subscribe Networks Using Super-Peers

Paul-Alexandru Chirita[1], Stratos Idreos[2], Manolis Koubarakis[2], Wolfgang Nejdl[1]

[1] L3S and University of Hannover, Hannover, Germany
{chirita,nejdl}@learninglab.de
[2] Department of Electronic and Computer Engineering, Technical University of Crete, Greece
{sidraios,manolis}@intelligence.tuc.gr

Summary. Publish/subscribe systems are an alternative to query-based systems in cases where the same information is asked for over and over, and where clients want to get updated answers for the same query over a period of time. Recent publish/subscribe systems such as P2P-DIET have introduced this paradigm in the P2P context. In this chapter we build on the experience gained with P2P-DIET and the Edutella super-peer infrastructure and present a semantic publish/subscribe system supporting metadata and a query language based on RDF. We define formally the basic concepts of our system and present detailed protocols for its operation.

8.1 Introduction

Consider a P2P network which manages metadata about publications, and a user of this network, Bob, who is interested in the *new* publications of some specific authors, e.g., Koubarakis and Nejdl. With conventional P2P file sharing networks like Gnutella or Kazaa, this is very difficult, because sending out queries which either include "Koubarakis" or "Nejdl" in the search string will return all publications from these authors, and Bob has to filter out the new publications each time. With an RDF-based P2P network like Edutella [29], this is a bit easier, because Bob can formulate a query, which includes a disjunction for the attribute dc:creator (i.e., dc:creator includes "Nejdl" or dc:creator includes "Koubarakis"), as well as a constraint on the date attribute (i.e., dc:date > 2003), which includes all necessary constraints in one query and will only return answers containing publications from 2004 on. Still, this is not quite what Bob wants, because whenever he uses this query, he will get all 2004 publications including the ones he has already seen.

What Bob really needs from his P2P file sharing network are *publish/subscribe* capabilities [11]:

1. *Advertising*: Peers send information about the content they will publish, for example a Hannover peer announces that it will make available all L3S publica-

tions, including publications from Nejdl, a Crete peer announces that it would do the same for Koubarakis' group.

2. *Subscribing*: Peers send subscriptions to the network, defining the kind of documents they want to retrieve. Bob's profile would then express his subscription for Nejdl and Koubarakis papers. The network might store these subscriptions near the peers which will provide these resources, in our case near the Hannover and the Crete peer.

3. *Notifying*: Peers notify the network whenever new resources become available. These resources should be forwarded to all peers whose subscription profiles match them, so Bob should regularily receive all new publications from Nejdl and Koubarakis.

In this chapter we will describe how to provide publish/subscribe capabilities in an RDF-based P2P system, which manages arbitrary digital resources, identified by their URI and described by a set of RDF metadata. This functionality is useful in many application scenarios including distributed educational content repositories in the context of the EU/IST project ELENA [36, 1] whose participants include e-learning and e-training companies, learning technology providers, universities and research institutes. A second application scenario that interests us is information alert in distributed digital library environments [23].

The organization of this chapter is as follows. The next section specifies the formal framework for RDF-based pub/sub systems, including the languages used to express publications and subscriptions in our network. Section 8.3 presents our super-peer architecture and compares it briefly with other alternatives. Section 8.4 discusses the most important design aspects and optimizations necessary to handle large numbers of subscriptions and notifications, building upon the super-peer architecture and HyperCuP protocol implemented in the Edutella system [29], as well as on index optimizations recently explored in P2P-DIET [24]. Section 8.5 includes a short discussion of other important features of our system, and Sect. 8.6 includes a survey of related work. Section 8.7 concludes the chapter.

8.2 A Formalism for Pub/Sub Systems Based on RDF

In this section we formalize the basic concepts of pub/sub systems based on RDF: advertisements, subscriptions, and notifications. We will need a *typed first-order language* $\mathcal{L}$. $\mathcal{L}$ is equivalent to a subset of the Query Exchange Language (QEL) but has a slightly different syntax that makes our presentation more formal. QEL is a Datalog-inspired RDF query language that is used in the Edutella P2P network [28].

The logical symbols of $\mathcal{L}$ include parentheses, a countably infinite set of variables (denoted by capital letters), the equality symbol ($=$) and the standard sentential connectives. The parameter (or non-logical) symbols of $\mathcal{L}$ include types, constants and predicates. $\mathcal{L}$ has four types: $\mathcal{U}$ (for *RDF resource identifiers* i.e., *URI references* or *URIrefs*), $\mathcal{S}$ (for RDF literals that are *strings*), $\mathcal{Z}$ (for RDF literals that are *integers*), and $\mathcal{UL}$ (for the union of RDF resource identifiers and RDF literals that are strings or integers). The predicates of our language are $<$ of type $(\mathcal{Z}, \mathcal{Z})$, $\sqsupseteq$ of type $(\mathcal{S}, \mathcal{S})$, and t of type $(\mathcal{U}, \mathcal{U}, \mathcal{UL})$. Predicate $<$ will be used to compare integers, predicate $\sqsupseteq$ (read "contains") will be used to compare strings and t (read "triple") will be used to represent *RDF triples*. Following the RDF jargon, in an expression $t(s, p, o)$, s will be called the *subject*, p the *predicate* and o the *object* of the triple.

The well-formed formulas of $\mathcal{L}$ (atomic or complex) can now be defined as usual. We can also define a semantics for $\mathcal{L}$ in the usual way. Due to space considerations, we omit the technical details.

The following definitions give the syntax of our subscription language.

Definition 1. *An* atomic *constraint is a formula of $\mathcal{L}$ in one of the following three forms: (a) $X = c$ where X is a variable and c is a constant of type $\mathcal{U}$, (b) $X \; r \; c$ where X is a variable of type $\mathcal{Z}$, c is a constant of type $\mathcal{Z}$ and r is one of the binary operators $=, <, \leq, >, \geq$, and (c) $X \sqsupseteq c$ where X is a variable and c is a constant, both of type $\mathcal{S}$. A* constraint *is a disjunction of conjunctions of atomic constraints (i.e., it is in DNF form).*

We can now define the notion of a *satisfiable* constraint as it is standard.

Definition 2. *A* query (subscription) *is a formula of the form*

$$X_1, \ldots, X_n : t(S, p_1, O_1) \wedge t(S, p_2, O_2) \wedge \cdots \wedge t(S, p_m, O_m) \wedge \phi$$

where S is a variable of type $\mathcal{U}$, $p_1, \ldots, p_m$ are constants of type $\mathcal{U}$, $O_1, \ldots, O_m$ are distinct *variables of type $\mathcal{UL}$, $\{X_1, \ldots, X_n\} \subseteq \{S, O_1, \ldots, O_m\}$, and ϕ is a constraint involving a subset of the variables $S, O_1, \ldots, O_m$.*

The above definition denotes the class of *single-resource multi-predicate* queries in QEL. This class of queries can be implemented efficiently (as we will show in Sect. 8.4) and contains many interesting queries for P2P file sharing systems based on RDF. It is easy to see that only *join* on variable S is allowed by the above class of queries (i.e., S is a subject *common to all* triples appearing in the subscription).

As it is standard in RDF literature, the triple notation utilizes *qualified names or QNames* to avoid having to write long formulas. A QName contains a prefix that has been assigned to a namespace URI, followed by a colon, and then a *local name*. In this chapter, we will use the following prefixes in QNames:

```
@prefix dc: <http://purl.org/dc/elements/1.1/>
@prefix rdf: <http://www.w3.org/1999/02/22-rdf-syntax-ns#>
@prefix isl: <http://www.intelligence.tuc.gr/publications/>
```

Example 1. The subscription "I am interested in articles authored by Nejdl or Koubarakis in 2004" can be expressed by the following subscription:[1]

---

[1] Sometimes we will abuse Definition 2 and write a constant o_i in the place of variable O_i to avoid an extra equality $O_i = o_i$ in ϕ.

```
X: t(X,<rdf:type>, <dc:article>) ∧ t(X,<dc:creator>,Y) ∧
   t(X,<dc:date>,D) ∧(Y ⊒ "Nejdl" ∨ Y ⊒ "Koubarakis") ∧
   D=2004
```

Let q be a query. We will use the functions $schemas(q)$ and $properties(q)$ to refer to the sets of schemas (namespaces) and properties that appear in q. For instance, if q is the query of Example 1 then $schemas(q) = \{dc\}$ and $properties(q) = \{<dc : article >, < dc : creator >, < dc : date >\}$.

Queries (subscriptions) are evaluated over sets of RDF triples. If T is a set of RDF triples, then $ans(q, T)$ will denote the answer set of q when it is evaluated over T. This concept can be formally defined as for relational queries with constraints.

We can now define the concept of subscription subsumption that is heavily exploited in the architecture of Sect. 8.4.

Definition 3. *Let q_1, q_2 be subscriptions. We will say that q_1 subsumes q_2 iff for all sets of RDF triples T, $ans(q_2, T) \subseteq ans(q_1, T)$.*

We now define the concept of *notification*: the meta-data clients send to super-peers whenever they make available new content. Notifications and subscriptions are matched at super-peers and appropriate subscribers are notified.

Definition 4. *A notification n is a pair (T, I) where T is a set of ground (i.e., with no variables) atomic formulas of $\mathcal{L}$ of the form $t(s, p, o)$ with the same constant s (i.e., a set of RDF triples with the same subject-URIref) and I is a client identifier. A notification $n = (T, I)$ matches a subscription q if $ans(q, T) \neq \emptyset$.*

Notice that because URIrefs are assumed to be *unique*, and subscriptions and notifications obey Definitions 2 and 4, notification matching in the architecture of Section 3.2.3 takes place *locally* at each super-peer.

Example 2. The notification

```
({t(<isl:esws04.pdf>, <rdf:type>, <dc:article>),
  t(<isl:esws04.pdf>, <dc:creator>, "Koubarakis"),
  t(<isl:esws04.pdf>, <dc:date>, 2004)}, C3)
```
matches the subscription of Example 1.

We now define three progressively more comprehensive kinds of advertisement. Advertisements formalize the notion of what clients or super-peers send to other nodes of the network to describe their content in a *high-level intentional* manner. Super-peers will match client subscriptions with advertisements to determine the routes that subscriptions will follow in the architecture of Sect. 8.4. This is formalized by the notion of "covers" below.

Definition 5. *A schema advertisement d is a pair (S, I) where S is a set of schemas (constants of type $\mathcal{U}$ i.e., URIrefs) and I is a super-peer id. If $d = (S, I)$ then the expression $schemas(d)$ will also be used to denote S. A schema advertisement d covers a subscription q if $schemas(q) \subseteq schemas(d)$.*

Example 3. The schema advertisement (`{dc, lom}`, SP_1) covers the subscription of Example 1.

Definition 6. *A* property advertisement *d is a pair* (P, I) *where P is a set of properties (constants of type* $\mathcal{U}$ *i.e., URIrefs) and I is a super-peer identifier. If* $d = (P, I)$ *then the expression* $properties(d)$ *will also be used to denote P. A property advertisement d covers a subscription q if* $properties(q) \subseteq properties(d)$.

Example 4. The property advertisement (`{<dc:article>, <dc:creator>, <dc:date>, <dc:subject>, <lom:context>}`, SP_6) covers the subscription of Example 1.

Definition 7. *A* property/value advertisement *d is a pair* $((P_1, V_1), \ldots, (P_k, V_k)), I)$ *where* $P_1, \ldots, P_k$ *are distinct properties (constants of type* $\mathcal{U}$ *i.e., URIrefs),* $V_1, \ldots, V_k$ *are sets of values for* $P_1, \ldots, P_k$ *(constants of type* $\mathcal{UL}$*) and I is a super-peer identifier.*

Definition 8. *Let q be a subscription of the form of Definition 2 and d be a property/value advertisement of the form of Definition 7. Let* $Y_1, \ldots, Y_k$ *(*$1 \leq k \leq m$*) be the variables among the objects* $o_1, \ldots, o_m$ *of the triples of q that correspond to the properties* $P_1, \ldots, P_k$ *of d. We will say that d covers a subscription q if there exist values* $v_1 \in V_1, \ldots, v_k \in V_k$ *such that the constraint* $\phi[Y_1 \leftarrow v_1, \ldots, Y_k \leftarrow v_k]$ *resulting from substituting variables* $Y_1, \ldots, Y_k$ *with constants* $v_1, \ldots, v_k$ *in* ϕ *is satisfiable.*

Example 5. The property/value advertisement

```
( (<dc:creator>, { W. Nejdl, P. Chirita}),
    (<dc:title>, {"Algorithms", "Data Structures"}),
    (<dc:year>, [2002, ∞]), SP₁ )
```

covers the subscription of Example 1.

8.3 The Super-Peer Architecture

The algorithms that we present in this chapter are designed for super-peer systems [45]. Thus, we assume two types of nodes: *super-peers* and *peers*. A peer is a typical network node that wants to advertise and publish its data and/or subscribe to data owned by others. A super-peer is a node with more capabilities than a peer (e.g., more cpu power and bandwidth). Staying on-line for long periods of time is another desirable property for super-peers. In our architecture, super-peers are organized in a separate network which we call the *super-peer backbone* and are responsible for processing notifications, advertisements and subscriptions. Peers connect to super-peers in a star-like fashion, providing content and content metadata. Each peer is connected to a single super-peer which is its *access point* to the rest of the network and its services. Once connected, a peer can disconnect, reconnect or even migrate to a different super-peer. A high level view of this architecture is shown in Fig. 8.1.

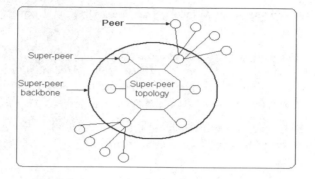

Fig. 8.1. An example of a super-peer architecture

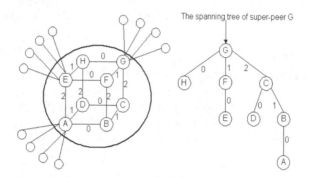

Fig. 8.2. The HyperCuP topology and an example of a spanning tree

Our super-peers are arranged in the HyperCuP topology. This is the solution adopted in the Edutella infrastructure [28] because of its special characteristics regarding broadcasts and network partitioning. An example of this architecture is shown in Fig. 8.2. The HyperCuP algorithm, described in [27], is capable of organizing the super-peers of a P2P network into a binary hypercube, a member of the family of Cayley graphs. Super-peers join the network by contacting any of the already integrated super-peers, which then carries out the super-peer integration protocol. No central maintenance is necessary. HyperCuP enables efficient and non-redundant broadcasts. For broadcasts, each node can be seen as the root of a specific spanning tree through the super-peer backbone, as shown in Fig. 8.2. The topology allows for $log_2 N$ path length between any two peers and $log_2 N$ number of neighbors for each peer, where N is the total number of nodes in the network (i.e., the number of super-peers in this case).

Super-peer architectures are usually based on a two-phase routing protocol, which routes messages first in the super-peer backbone and then distributes them to the peers connected to the super-peers. Super-peer based routing can be based on different kinds of indexing and routing tables, as discussed in [14, 29]. In the following sections we present indexing and routing mechanisms appropriate for publish/subscribe services.

In this chapter we do not deal with the question of "Who becomes a super-peer?" As an example, super-peers can be centrally managed by a company that owns and runs the overlay to offer a service (e.g., a content provider such as Akamai). A more challenging design is that super-peers are normal peers that either volunteer to play the role of a super-peer for a time window (i.e., because they will get a number of privileges as a return) or the system forces all peers to become super-peers periodically in order to be able to use the services of the overlay. This is an area where some interesting research has been carried out recently e.g., [26, 31]. The authors of [31] introduce the concept of altruistic peers, namely peers with the following characteristics, (a) they stay on line for long periods and (b) they are willing to offer a significant portion of their resources to speedup the performance of the network. Although [31] does not uses the term super-peer directly, the concepts of super-peers and altruistic peers are related: one can view altruistic peers as one kind of super-peers in a P2P network.

Alternatives to this topology are possible, provided that they guarantee the spanning tree characteristic of the super-peer backbone, which we exploit for maintaining our index structures. For example, the super-peers may form an unstructured overlay like in P2P-DIET [21]. P2P-DIET does not force any kind of structure between super-peers. Instead it lets super-peers choose their neighbour peers. An example is shown in Fig. 8.3(b). A minimum weight spanning tree is formed for each super-peer based on the algorithm presented in [7]. Brodcasting in the super-peer backbone then takes place according to a well-known and widely used solution, *reverse path forwarding* [46]. This is a very simple technique with minimum storage requirements for the nodes of the network. According to reverse path forwarding, a node that receives a message will accept it only if the sender is part of the shortest path that connects this node with the node that generated and broadcasted the original message (the root of the message). Then it will forward the message to all its neighbors except the sender.

A crucial difference between an unstructured and a structured super-peer topology is the depth of the spanning tree which is unbounded for the structured topologies but bounded for unstructured ones. The HyperCuP protocol can limit this depth to $logN$ by forcing the HyperCuP structure as super-peers join or leave (see Fig. 8.3(a)). Of course, this brings an extra cost to the join and leave operation for the super-peers, but it is a cost that we are willing to pay given our wish for efficient query processing. The main advantage of limiting the depth of the spanning tree is the low latency achieved for broadcast operations. For example, consider the extreme case of an unstructured super-peer backbone where the super-peers form a chain. In this case, if a super-peer at the one end of the chain decides to broadcast a message, then the super-peer at the other end will see the message only after all other peers have received it (i.e., after $N - 1$ steps). The advantage of HyperCup is that it limits the path between any two super-peers to $log_2 N$ which is much better than the $N - 1$ path length of the unstructured design of the previous example.

Another architectural choice for the super-peer backbone is to organize the super-peers according to a distributed hash table based protocol like Chord [37] as shown in Fig. 8.3(c). An interesting approach is that even the peers attached to a super-peer

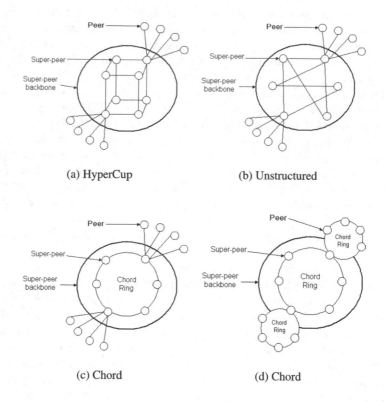

(a) HyperCup   (b) Unstructured

(c) Chord   (d) Chord

Fig. 8.3. Various super-peer architectures

can be organized according to a DHT based protocol. An example is shown in Fig. 8.3(d). A good discussion of such possible architectural choices can be found in [31].

8.4 Processing Advertisements, Subscriptions and Notifications

In this section we present protocols for processing advertisements, subscriptions and notifications in a super-peer based network. In addition, we discuss the data structures and indices that a super-peer uses.

8.4.1 Processing Advertisements

Once a peer connects to the network, it is *mandatory* to advertise the kind of resources it will offer in the future. For example, an advertisement can include information on the schema that a peer supports. As we have already discussed, each peer is attached to one super-peer, which is its access point to the rest of the network. Thus, a peer constructs an *advertisement* and sends it to its access point. A peer will send an advertisement again if its information needs to be updated.

A super-peer receives advertisements from all peers that are attached to it. A super-peer uses these advertisements to construct *advertisement routing indices* that are utilized when processing subscriptions. There are three levels of indexing: the schema level, the property (attribute) level, and the property/value level. Each time an advertisement arrives from one of the peers, the super-peer updates those three indices. In the following paragraphs we give a description of each index.

Schema Index. The first level of indexing contains information on the schema that peers support. We assume that different peers will support different RDF schemas and that these schemas can be uniquely identified (e.g., by a URI). The schema index contains zero or more schema identifiers. Each schema identifier points to one or more peers that support this schema. As an example of the use of this index, we can say that subscriptions are forwarded only to peers which support the schemas used in the subscription. We discuss this in more detail in the next section.

Property Index. The second level of indexing is the property index. This index is useful in cases where a peer might choose to use only part of one or more schemas, i.e., certain properties/attributes, to describe its content. While this is unusual in conventional database systems, it is more often used for data stores that use semi-structured data, and very common for RDF-based systems. In such a case, the schema index cannot be used and indexing is done at the property level. Thus, the property index contains properties, uniquely identified by name space/schema ID plus property name. Each property points to one or more peers that support them.

Property/Value Index. Finally, the third index is the property/value index. For many properties it will be advantageous to create a value index to reduce network traffic. This case is identical to a classical database index with the exception that the index entries do not refer to the resource, but the peer providing it.

We use two kinds of indices, namely the super-peer/super-peer indices (*SP/SP indices*) that handle communication in the super-peer backbone and the super-peer/peer indices (*SP/P indices*) that handle communication between a super-peer and all peers connected to it. These indices draw upon our previous work for query routing, as discussed in [29], as well as further extensions and modifications necessary for publish/subscribe services based on [24, 21]. Except for the functionality they employ, both indices use the same data structures, have the same update process, etc. Figure 8.4 shows an example of super-peer/super-peer indices.

Let us now discuss how a super-peer reacts upon receiving an advertisement. Assume a super-peer SP_i that receives a new advertisement d from a peer p which is one of the peers that are directly connected to SP_i. First the new advertisement has to be inserted in the local indices as follows. An advertisement contains one or more elements. Each element is either a property value pair, for example, {<dc:year>, 1900}, or a property, for example, <dc:year> or a schema identifier, for example, <dc>. For each element e, SP_i does the following.

1. If e is a property value pair, then e is inserted in the property/value index.
2. If e is just a property, then it is inserted in the property index.
3. If e is just a schema identifier, then it is inserted in the schema index.

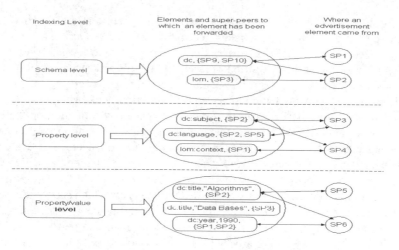

Fig. 8.4. An example of SP/SP advertisement routing indices

After having updated the local indices, the advertisement is *selectively broad-casted* from SP_i to reach other super-peers. This is necessary so that subscriptions of peers that are attached to other access points are able to reach SP_i and the peer that advertised d. Thus, for each super-peer SP_x that is a child of SP_i in the spanning tree of SP_i, SP_i does the following. For each element e of d, SP_i checks if it has already forwarded an identical element of e to SP_x, i.e., because of an advertisement of another peer. If this is not true then e is forwarded to SP_x.

When another super-peer, say SP_y, receives a forwarded element e, it inserts it into its local indices as described above. Then for each super-peer SP_x that is a child of SP_y in the spanning tree of SP_i (that originally initiated the selective broadcast procedure), SP_y checks if it has already forwarded an identical element of e to SP_x. If not, the element is forwarded to SP_x.

Updating Advertisement Indices. Index updates as discussed above are triggered when (a) a new peer connects, (b) a peer leaves the system permanently, (c) a peer migrates to another access point, or (d) the metadata information of a registered peer changes.

In the case of a peer joining the network, its respective metadata/schema information are matched against the SP/P entries of the respective super-peer. If the SP/P advertisement indices of the super-peer already contain the peers' metadata, only a reference to the peer is stored in them. Otherwise, the respective metadata with references to the peer are added to SP/P indices and then are selectively broadcasted to the rest of the super-peer backbone. If a peer leaves from a super-peer AP permanently, then all references to this peer have to be removed from the SP/P indices of AP. If no other peer attached to AP supports the same metadata/schema information, then AP has to selectively broadcast a remove message to the rest of the super-peers so believes that AP supports this schema anymore. This is done in the same way as selectively broadcasting advertisements with the difference that now advertisements

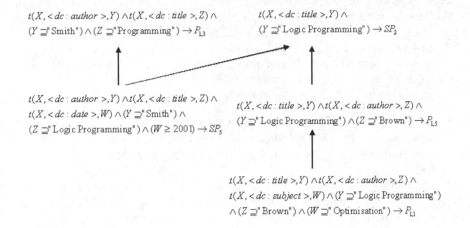

$t(X,<dc:author>,Y) \wedge t(X,<dc:title>,Z) \wedge$
$(Y \sqsupseteq "Smith") \wedge (Z \sqsupseteq "Programming") \rightarrow P_{13}$

$t(X,<dc:title>,Y) \wedge$
$(Y \sqsupseteq "Logic Programming") \rightarrow SP_2$

$t(X,<dc:author>,Y) \wedge t(X,<dc:title>,Z) \wedge$
$t(X,<dc:date>,W) \wedge (Y \sqsupseteq "Smith") \wedge$
$(Z \sqsupseteq "Logic Programming") \wedge (W \geq 2001) \rightarrow SP_5$

$t(X,<dc:title>,Y) \wedge t(X,<dc:author>,Z) \wedge$
$(Y \sqsupseteq "Logic Programming") \wedge (Z \sqsupseteq "Brown") \rightarrow P_{15}$

$t(X,<dc:title>,Y) \wedge t(X,<dc:author>,Z) \wedge$
$t(X,<dc:subject>,W) \wedge (Y \sqsupseteq "Logic Programming")$
$\wedge (Z \sqsupseteq "Brown") \wedge (W \sqsupseteq "Optimisation") \rightarrow P_{11}$

Fig. 8.5. An example of a poset

are removed from the SP/SP indices. In the case that a peer x migrates from an access point $AP1$ to an access point $AP2$, then $AP1$ acts as if x left permanently while $AP2$ acts as if x just joined the network.

8.4.2 Processing Subscriptions

Until now we have described how a super-peer reacts upon receiving an advertisement either from a peer or from a super-peer. In this section we present the protocol used by a peer for inserting a subscription in the network. Remember that the purpose of the subscription is that the subscriber peer will receive all future matching notifications from all peers of the network.

A peer always sends a new subscription to its access point. When a super-peer receives a subscription, it inserts it into the *local subscription poset*. A subscription poset is a partially ordered set (a hierarchical structure of subscriptions), and captures the notion of subscription subsumption defined in Sect. 8.2. Figure 8.5 shows an example of a poset. Each super-peer adds to its local subscription poset information about where the subscription came from (either from one of the peers connected to it or from another super-peer). The addition of super-peer information in the poset reduces the overall network traffic and is therefore very important. The use of subscription posets in publish/subscribe systems was originally proposed in SIENA [11].

Like SIENA, our system utilizes the subscription poset to minimize network traffic, i.e., super-peers do not forward subscriptions which are subsumed by previously forwarded subscriptions. In this way, when a super-peer receives a subscription, it inserts it into the local poset and decides whether to further forward it in the super-peer backbone or not. If this super-peer has already forwarded a subscription that subsumes the new one, then no forwarding takes place. If not, then the subscription has to be forwarded to all neighbour super-peers (according to the spanning tree of the super-peer that broadcasted the subscription) that may have peers that will create matching notifications. Once a super-peer has decided to send the subscription further, it will initiate a selective broadcast procedure. This procedure depends on the advertisement routing indices of the super-peer in the following way.

Assume a super-peer SP_i that receives a new subscription q from one of the peers that are directly connected to it. Then for each super-peer SP_x that is a child of SP_i in the spanning tree of SP_i, SP_i performs the following steps.

1. If the local index at the property/value level contains SP_x and one or more of its advertisements cover the subscription q, i.e., the values of the properties in an advertisement are consistent with the constraints of q, then q is forwarded to SP_x.
2. If the above is not true and the indices in the schema or property level contain SP_x and one or more of its advertisements cover the targeted schema (or properties) used in the subscription q, then q is forwarded to SP_x.

When another super-peer, say SP_y, receives a forwarded subscription q, it inserts it into its local subscription poset. Then, for each super-peer SP_x that is a child of SP_y in the spanning tree of SP_i (that originally initiated the selective broadcast procedure), SP_y checks if it has already forwarded a subscription q' to SP_x that subsumes q. If not, q is forwarded to SP_x.

Forwarding subscriptions when advertisement indices are updated. As we have already discussed, when a super-peer receives a subscription q, it forwards q to a portion of its neighbor super-peers or it does not forward it at all, according to the local subscription poset and advertisement indices. However, advertisement indices may change in the future so the following process takes place each time a new advertisement arrives to a super-peer AP from another super-peer $AP1$: AP has to check if there are one or more subscriptions in its local subscription poset that (a) cover the new advertisement and (b) have not been forwarded towards $AP1$. Any found subscriptions are sent to $AP1$. This is necessary to happen in order not to ignore future matching notifications that are generated by $AP1$ or by other super-peers that forward those notifications through $AP1$.

8.4.3 Processing Notifications

Let us now discuss how subscriptions are triggered by notifications. A peer creates a notification for a new resource that it wants to make available to other peers, and publishes the notification to the network. The goal is that all appropriate subscriptions are triggered and their subscribers receive the notification.

A peer always forwards a new notification to its access point. A notification is a message that contains metadata about the new item and additional information on the peer that makes it available, i.e., its IP address and its identifier. The schema that is used to create a notification has to agree with the schema that this peer has previously advertised, otherwise the protocols cannot guarantee that all relevant subscribers will receive the notification.

When a new notification n arrives at a super-peer with a database db of local subscriptions, the super-peer has to find all subscriptions $q \in db$ that satisfy n. This can be done as follows using ideas from SIENA [11]. The new notification is first matched against the root subscriptions of a super-peer's local subscription poset. In case of a match with the subscription stored in a root node R, the notification is further matched against the children of R, which contain subscriptions refining the subscription from R. For each match, the notification is sent to a group of peers/super-peers (those where the subscription came from), thus following backwards the exact path of the subscription. It is also possible to use more sophisticated filtering algorithms like those in P2P-DIET [42] and those in [6, 12, 16, 19].

8.5 Dynamics of P2P Pub/Sub Networks

As peers dynamically join and leave the network, they may be off-line when new resources arrive for them. These are lost if no special precautions are taken. In the following paragraphs, we discuss which measures are necessary to enable peers to receive notifications that are generated when those peers are off-line.

8.5.1 Offline Notifications and Rendezvous at Super-Peers

Whenever a peer A disconnects from the network, its access point AP *keeps* the peer's identification information and subscriptions for a specified period of time, and its indices will not reflect that A has left the network. This means that notifications for A will still arrive at AP, which has to store these and deliver them to A after it reconnects. A peer may request a resource at the time that it receives a notification n, or later on, using a saved notification n on his local *notifications directory*.

Let us now consider the case when a peer A requests a resource r, but the resource owner peer B is not on-line. Peer A requests the address of B directly from $AP2$ (the access point of B). This is feasible since the address of $AP2$ is included in r. In such a case, peer A may request a *rendezvous* with resource r from $AP2$ with a message that contains the identifier of A, the identifier of B, the address of AP and the location of r. When peer B reconnects, $AP2$ informs B that it must upload resource r to AP as a *rendezvous file* for peer A. Then B uploads r. AP checks if A is on-line and if it is, AP forwards r to A or else r is stored in the *rendezvous directory* of AP and when A reconnects, it receives a rendezvous notification from AP.

The features of off-line notifications and rendezvous take place even if peers migrate to different access points. For example, let us assume that peer A has migrated to $AP3$. The peer program understands that it is connected to a different access point $AP3$, so it requests from AP any rendezvous or off-line notifications and informs AP that it is connected to a different access point. A receives the rendezvous and off-line notifications and updates the variable's *previous access point* with the address of $AP3$. Then, AP updates its SP/P and SP/SP indices. Finally, A sends to $AP3$ its subscriptions and $AP3$ updates its SP/P and SP/SP indices. A complete example is shown in Fig. 8.6.

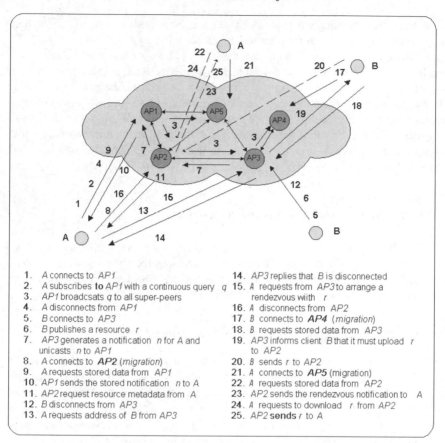

1. A connects to *AP1*
2. A subscribes to *AP1* with a continuous query *q*
3. *AP1* broadcsats *q* to all super-peers
4. A disconnects from *AP1*
5. B connects to *AP3*
6. B publishes a resource *r*
7. *AP3* generates a notification *n* for A and unicasts *n* to *AP1*
8. A connects to ***AP2*** (*migration*)
9. A requests stored data from *AP1*
10. *AP1* sends the stored notification *n* to A
11. *AP2* request resource metadata from A
12. B disconnects from *AP3*
13. A requests address of B from *AP3*
14. *AP3* replies that B is disconnected
15. A requests from *AP3* to arrange a rendezvous wiith *r*
16. A disconnects from *AP2*
17. B connects to ***AP4*** (*migration*)
18. B requests stored data from *AP3*
19. *AP3* informs client B that it must upload *r* to *AP2*
20. B sends *r* to *AP2*
21. A connects to ***AP5*** (migration)
22. A requests stored data from *AP2*
23. *AP2* sends the rendezvous notification to A
24. A requests to download *r* from *AP2*
25. *AP2* **sends** *r* to A

Fig. 8.6. An off-line notification, rendezvous and migration example

8.5.2 Peer Authentication

Typically, authentication of peers in a P2P network is not crucial, and peers connecting to the network identify themselves by simply using their IP-addresses. In a pub/sub environment, however, where we have to connect peers with their subscriptions and want to send them all notifications relevant for them, this leads to two problems:

- IP addresses of peers may change. Therefore, the network will not be able to deliver any notifications, which might have been stored for a peer during its absence, after it reconnects with another IP address. Furthermore, all subscriptions stored in the network for this peer lose their relationship to this peer.
- Malicious peers can masquerade as other peers by using the IP address of a peer currently offline. They get all notifications for this peer, which are then lost to the original peer. Moreover, they can change the original peer's subscriptions maliciously.

We therefore have to use suitable cryptography algorithms to provide unique identifiers for the peers in our network (see also the discussion in [4]).

When a new peer x wants to register to the network, it generates a pair of keys (E_x, D_x) where E_x is the *public key* of x (or the *encryption key*) and D_x is the *private key* of x (or the *decryption key*) as in [34]. We assume that the peer x has already found the IP address and public key of one of the super-peers s, through some secure means e.g., a secure web site. Then, x securely identifies the super-peer s and if this succeeds, it sends an encrypted message to s (secure identification and encryption are explained below). The message contains the public key, the IP address and port of x. The super-peer s decrypts the message and creates a *private unique identifier* and a *public unique identifier* for x by applying the cryptographically secure hash function SHA-1 to the concatenated values of current date and time, the IP address of s, the current IP address of x and a very large random number. The properties of the cryptographically secure hash function now guarantee that it is highly unlikely that a peer with exactly the same identifiers will enter the network. Then, s sends the identifiers to x with an encrypted message. From there on the private identifier is included to all messages from x to its access-point and in this way a super-peer knows who sends a message. The private identifier of a peer is never included in messages that other peers will receive; instead the public identifier is used. To clarify the reason why we need both public and private identifiers we give the following example. When a peer x receives a notification n, n contains the public identifier of the resource owner $x1$. When x is ready to download the resource, it communicates with the access-point of $x1$ and uses this public identifier to request the address of $x1$. If a peer knows the private identifier of x then it can authenticate itself as x, but if it knows the public identifier of x then it can only use it to request the address of x or set up a rendezvous with a resource owned by x. All the messages that a peer x sends to a super-peer and contain the private identifier of x are encrypted. In this way, no other peer can read such a message and acquire the private identifier of x.

Secure identification of peers is carried out as in [4]. A peer A can securely identify another peer B by generating a random number r and send $E_B(r)$ to B. Peer B sends a reply message that contains the number $D_B(E_B(r))$. Then, peer A checks if $D_B(E_B(r)) = r$ in which case peer B is correctly identified. For example, in our system super-peers securely identify peers as described above before delivering a notification. In this case, the super-peer starts a communication session with a peer so it cannot be sure that the peer listens on the specific IP address.

When a peer disconnects, its access point does not erase the public key or identifiers of; it only erases the private identifier from the active peer list. Later on, when the peer reconnects, it will identify itself using its private identifier and it will send to its access point, its new IP address. In case that the peer migrates to a different access point, it will notify the previous one, so that it erases all information about the peer. Then, the peer securely identifies the new access point and sends a message to it that contains the public key, the public and the private identifiers and the new IP address of the peer. All the above messages are encrypted since they contain the private identifier of the peer.

8.6 Related Work

In this section we review related research on pub/sub systems in the areas of distributed systems, networks and databases.

Most of the work on pub/sub in the database literature has its origins in the paper [17] by Franklin and Zdonik who coined the term *selective dissemination of information (SDI)*. Their preliminary work on the system DBIS appears in [6]. Another influential system is SIFT [43, 44] where publications are documents in free text form and queries are conjunctions of keywords. SIFT was the first system to emphasize query indexing as a means to achieve scalability in pub/sub systems [43]. Later on, similar work concentrated on pub/sub systems with data models based on attribute-value pairs and query languages based on attributes with comparison operators (e.g., Le Subscribe [16], the monitoring subsystem of Xyleme [30] and others). [10] is also notable because it considers a data model based on attribute-value pairs but goes beyond conjunctive queries – the standard class of queries considered by other systems [16]. More recent work has concentrated on publications that are XML documents and queries that are subsets of XPath or XQuery (e.g., XFilter [25], YFilter [15], Xtrie [12] and $xmltk$ [19]). All these papers discuss sophisticated filtering algorithms based on indexing queries.

In the area of distributed systems and networks various pub/sub systems have been developed over the years. Researchers have utilized various data models here based on channels, topics and attribute-value pairs (exactly like the models of the database papers discussed above) [11]. The latter systems are usually called *content-based* because attribute-value data models are flexible enough to express the content of messages in various applications. Work in this area has concentrated not only on filtering algorithms as in the database papers surveyed above, but also on distributed pub/sub architectures [5, 11]. SIENA [11] is probably the most well-known example of system to be developed in this area. SIENA uses a data model and language based on attribute-value pairs and demonstrates how to express notifications, subscriptions and advertisements in this language. From the point of view of this paper, a very important contribution of SIENA is the adoption of a *P2P* model of interaction among servers (super-peers in our terminology) and the exploitation of traditional network algorithms based on shortest paths and minimum-weight spanning trees for routing messages. SIENA servers additionally utilize partially ordered sets encoding subscription and advertisement subsumption to minimize network traffic. The core ideas of SIENA have recently been used in the pub/sub systems DIAS [23] and P2P-DIET [2, 24, 21] but now the data models utilized were inspired from Information Retrieval. DIAS and P2P-DIET have also emphasized the use of sophisticated subscription indexing at each server to facilitate efficient forwarding of notifications [42]. In some sense, the approach of DIAS and P2P-DIET puts together the best ideas from the database and distributed systems tradition in a single unifying framework. Another important contribution of P2P-DIET is that it demonstrates how to support, by very similar protocols, the traditional *ad-hoc* or *one-time* query scenarios of standard super-peer systems [45] and the pub/sub features of SIENA [11].

With the advent of distributed hash-tables (DHTs) such as CAN [33], CHORD [37] and Pastry [3], a new wave of pub/sub systems based on DHTs has appeared. Scribe [35] is a topic-based publish/subscribe system based on Pastry [3]. Hermes [32] is similar to Scribe because it uses the same underlying DHT (Pastry) but it allows more expressive subscriptions by supporting the notion of an event type with attributes. Each event type in Hermes is managed by an event broker which is a rendezvous node for subscriptions and publications related to this event. Related ideas appear in [38] and [39]. PeerCQ [18] is another notable pub/sub system implemented on top of a DHT infrastructure. The most important contribution of PeerCQ is that it takes into account peer heterogeneity and extends consistent hashing [22] with simple load balancing techniques based on appropriate assignment of peer identifiers to network nodes.

Meghdoot [20] is a very recent pub/sub system implemented on top of a CAN-like DHT [33]. Meghdoot supports an attribute-value data model and offers new ideas for the processing of subscriptions with range predicates (e.g., the price is between 20 and 40 euro) and load balancing. A P2P system with a similar attribute-value data model that has been utilized in the implementation of a publish-subscribe system for network games is Mercury [8]. Two other recent proposals on publish/subscribe using DHTs is DHTrie [41] and LibraRing [40]. These works use the same data models with P2P-DIET and concentrate on publish/subscribe functionality for information retrieval and digital library applications.

In the area of RDF-based P2P systems, Min Cai et al. have also recently studied publish/subscribe systems for RDF [9] using essentially the same query language as this chapter and our original paper [13]. The approach of [9] is complementary to ours since their design builds on Chord. It would be interesting to compare experimentally the algorithms of this paper and the algorithms of [9] in more detail.

8.7 Conclusions

Publish/subscribe capabilities are a necessary extension of the usual query answering capabilities of P2P networks, and enable us to efficiently receive answers to long-standing queries over a given period of time, even if peers connect to and disconnect from the network during this period.

In this chapter we have discussed how to incorporate publish/subscribe capabilities in an RDF-based P2P network, specified a formal framework for this integration, including appropriate subscription and advertisement languages, and described how to optimize the processing of subscriptions and notifications handling in this network.

Further work will include the full integration of these capabilities into our existing P2P prototypes Edutella and P2P-DIET, as well as further investigations for extending the query language in this chapter with more expressive relational algebra and IR operators, while still maintaining efficient subscription/notification processing.

8.8 Acknowledgements

The work of Stratos Idreos and Manolis Koubarakis is supported by projects Ever-grow http://www.evergrow.org/ and OntoGrid http://www.ontogrid.net/ funded by the European Commission under the 6th Framework Programme.

References

[1]   Elena project home page. http://www.elena-project.org/.
[2]   P2P-DIET home page. http://www.intelligence.tuc.gr/p2pdiet/.
[3]   A. Rowstron and P. Druschel. Pastry: Scalable, distributed object location and routing for large-scale- peer-to-peer storage utility. In *Proceedings of the 18th IFIP/ACM International Conference on Distributed Systems Paltforms (Middleware 2001)*, November 2001.
[4]   K. Aberer, A. Datta, and M. Hauswirth. Efficient, self-contained handling of identity in Peer-to-Peer systems. *IEEE Transactions on Knowledge and Data Engineering*, 16(7), May 2004.
[5]   M. K. Aguilera, R. E. Strom, D.C. Sturman, M. Astley, and T.D. Chandra. Matching Events in a Content-based Subscription System. In *Proceedings of the Eighteenth Annual ACM Symposium on Principles of Distributed Computing (PODC '99)*, pages 53–62, New York, May 1999. Association for Computing Machinery.
[6]   M. Altinel, D. Aksoy, T. Baby, M. Franklin, W. Shapiro, and S. Zdonik. DBIS-toolkit: Adaptable Middleware for Large-scale Data Delivery. In *Proceedings of the 1999 ACM SIGMOD International Conference on Management of Data, Philadelphia, USA*, 1999.
[7]   D. Bertsekas and R. Gallager. *Data Networks*. Prentice-Hall, 1987.
[8]   A. Bharambe, S. Rao, and S. Seshan. Mercury: A Scalable Publish-Subscribe System for Internet Games. In *Proceedings of the First International Workshop on Network and System Support for Games (Netgames)*, Braunchweig, Germany, 2002.
[9]   M. Cai, M. Frank, B. Yan, and R.MacGregor. A Subscribable Peer-to-Peer RDF Repository for Distributed Metadata Management. *Journal of Web Semantics: Science, Services and Agents on the World Wide Web*, 2(2), 2005.
[10]   A. Campialla, S. Chaki, E. Clarke, S. Jha, and H. Veith. Efficient Filtering in Publish Subscribe Systems Using Binary Decision Diagrams. In *Proceedings of the 23rd International Conference on Software Engeneering (ICSE-01)*, pages 443–452, Los Alamitos, California, May12–19 2001. IEEE Computer Society.
[11]   A. Carzaniga, D.-S. Rosenblum, and A.L Wolf. Design and evaluation of a wide-area event notification service. *ACM Transactions on Computer Systems*, 19(3):332–383, August 2001.
[12]   C.-Y. Chan, P. Felber, M. Garofalakis, and R. Rastogi. Efficient Filtering of XML Documents with XPath Expressions. In *Proceedings of the 18th International Conference on Data Engineering*, pages 235–244, February 2002.

[13] P.-A. Chirita, S. Idreos, M. Koubarakis, and W. Nejdl. Publish/Subscribe for RDF-based P2P Networks. In *Proceedings of the 1st European Semantic Web Symposium (ESWS 2004)*, volume 3053 of *Lecture Notes in Computer Science*, pages 182–197, May 10-12, 2004.

[14] A. Crespo and H. Garcia-Molina. Routing Indices for Peer-to-peer Systems. In *Proceedings of the 22nd International Conference on Distributed Computing Systems (ICDCS '02)*, pages 23–34, Vienna, Austria, July 2002. IEEE.

[15] Y. Diao, M. Altinel, M.J. Franklin, H. Zhang, and P. Fischer. Path Sharing and Predicate Evaluation for High-performance XML Filtering. *ACM Transactions on Database Systems*, 28(4):467–516, December 2003.

[16] F. Fabret, H. A. Jacobsen, F. Llirbat, J. Pereira, K. A. Ross, and D. Shasha. Filtering algorithms and implementation for very fast publish/subscribe systems. In *Proceedings of ACM SIGMOD-2001*, 2001.

[17] M. Franklin and S. Zdonik. "Data in Your Face": Push Technology in Perspective. *SIGMOD Record (ACM Special Interest Group on Management of Data)*, 27(2):516–519, June 1998.

[18] B. Gedik and L. Liu. PeerCQ:A Decentralized and Self-Configuring Peer-to-Peer Information Monitoring System. In *Proceedings of the the 23rd International Conference on Distributed Computing Systems*, May 2003.

[19] T. J. Green, G. Miklau, M. Onizuka, and D. Suciu. Processing XML Streams with Deterministic Automata. In *Proceedings of the 9th International Conference on Database Theory (ICDT)*, pages 173–189, Siena, Italy, January 2003.

[20] A. Gupta, O. D. Sahin, D. Agrawal, and A. E. Abbadi. Meghdoot: Content-Based Publish/Subscribe over P2P Networks. In *Proceedings of ACM/IFIP/USENIX 5th International Middleware Conference*, Toronto, Ontario, Canada, October 18-22, 2004.

[21] S. Idreos, C. Tryfonopoulos, M. Koubarakis, and Y. Drougas. Query Processing in Super-Peer Networks with Languages Based on Information Retrieval: the P2P-DIET Approach. In *Proceedings of the 1st International Workshop on Peer-to-Peer Computing and DataBases (P2P&DB 2004)*, volume 3268 of *Lecture Notes in Computer Science*, pages 496–505, March 2004.

[22] D. Karger, E. Lehman, T. Leighton, M. Levine, D. Lewin, and R. Panigrahy. Consistent Hashing and Random Trees: Distributed Caching Protocols for Relieving Hot Spots on the World Wide Web. In *Proceedings of the Twenty-Ninth Annual ACM Symposium on Theory of Computing*, pages 654–663, El Paso, Texas, May 4-6, 1997.

[23] M. Koubarakis, T. Koutris, C. Tryfonopoulos, and P. Raftopoulou. Information Alert in Distributed Digital Libraries: The Models, Languages and Architecture of DIAS. In *Proceedings of the 6th European Conference on Digital Libraries (ECDL2002)*, volume 2458 of *Lecture Notes in Computer Science*, pages 527–542, September 2002.

[24] M. Koubarakis, C. Tryfonopoulos, S. Idreos, and Y. Drougas. Selective Information Dissemination in P2P Networks: Problems and Solutions. *ACM SIGMOD Record, Special issue on Peer-to-Peer Data Management, K. Aberer (editor)*, 32(3):71–76, September 2003.

[25] M. Altinel and M.J. Franklin. Efficient Filtering of XML Documents for Selective Dissemination of Information. In *Proceedings of the 26th VLDB Conference*, 2000.

[26] A. Montresor. A Robust Protocol for Building Superpeer Overlay Topologies. In *Proceedings of the 4th International Conference on Peer-to-Peer Computing*, Zurich, Switzerland, August 2004.

[27] M.Schlosser, M. Sintek, S. Decker, and W. Nejdl. HyperCuP – Hypercubes, Ontologies and Efficient Search on Peer-to-peer Networks. In *Proceedings of the 1st Workshop on Agents and P2P Computing, Bologna*, 2002.

[28] W. Nejdl, B. Wolf, Ch. Qu, S.Decker, M. Sintek, A.Naeve, M. Nilsson, M. Palmer, and T.Risch. EDUTELLA: A P2P Networking Infrastructure Based on RDF. In *Proceedings of the 11th International World Wide Web Conference*, 2002.

[29] W. Nejdl, M. Wolpers, W. Siberski, C. Schmitz, M. Schlosser, I. Brunkhorst, and A. Loser. Super-peer Based Routing and Clustering Strategies for RDF-based Peer-to-peer Networks. In *Proceedings of the 12th International World Wide Web Conference*, 2003.

[30] B. Nguyen, S. Abiteboul, G.Cobena, and M. Preda. Monitoring XML Data on the Web. In *Proceedings of the ACM SIGMOD Conference 2001*, Santa Barbara, CA, USA, 2001.

[31] N. Ntarmos and P. Triantafillou. AESOP: Altruism-Endowed Self Organizing Peers. In *Proceedings of the 2nd International Workshop on Databases, Information Systems and Peer-to-Peer Computing*, August 2004.

[32] P.R. Pietzuch and J.M. Bacon. Hermes: A distributed event-based middleware architecture. In *Proceedings of the 1st International Workshop on Distributed Event-Based Systems (DEBS'02)*, July 2002.

[33] S. Ratnasamy, P. Francis, M. Handley, R. Karp, and S. Shenker. A Scalable Content-addressable Network. In *Proceedings of the ACM SIGCOMM '01 Conference*, San Diego, California, August 2001.

[34] R.L. Rivest, A. Shamir, and L.M. Adleman. A Method for Obtaining Digital Signatures and Public-Key Cryptosystems. *CACM*, 21(2):120–126, February 1978.

[35] A. Rowstron, A.-M. Kermarrec, M. Castro, and P. Druschel. Scribe: The Design of a Large-scale Event Notification Infrastructure. In J. Crowcroft and M. Hofmann, editors, *3rd International COST264 Workshop*, 2001.

[36] B. Simon, Z. Miklós, W. Nejdl, M. Sintek, and J. Salvachua. Smart Space for Learning: A Mediation Infrastructure for Learning Services. In *Proceedings of the Twelfth International Conference on World Wide Web*, Budapest, Hungary, May 2003.

[37] I. Stoica, R. Morris, D. Karger, M.F. Kaashoek, and H. Balakrishnan. Chord: A Scalable Peer-to-peer Lookup Service for Internet Applications. In *Proceedings of the ACM SIGCOMM '01 Conference*, San Diego, California, August 2001.

[38] D. Tam, R. Azimi, and H.-Arno Jacobsen. Building Content-Based Publish/Subscribe Systems with Distributed Hash Tables. In *Proceedings of the*

1st International Workshop On Databases, Information Systems and Peer-to-Peer Computing, September 2003.

[39] W.W. Terpstra, S. Behnel, L. Fiege, A. Zeidler, and A.P. Buchmann. A Peer-to-Peer Approach to Content-Based Publish/Subscribe. In *Proceedings of the 2nd International Workshop on Distributed Event-Based Systems (DEBS'03)*, June 2003.

[40] C. Tryfonopoulos, S. Idreos, and M. Koubarakis. LibraRing: An Architecture for Distributed Digital Libraries Based on DHTs. In *Proceedings of the 9th European Conference on Research and Advanced Technology for Digital Libraries (ECDL)*, Vienna, Austria, September 18-23, 2005.

[41] C. Tryfonopoulos, S. Idreos, and M. Koubarakis. Publish/Subscribe Functionality in IR Environments using Structured Overlay Networks. In *Proceedings of the 28th Annual ACM SIGIR Conference*, Salvador, Brazil, August 15-19, 2005.

[42] C. Tryfonopoulos, M. Koubarakis, and Y. Drougas. Filtering Algorithms for Information Retrieval Models with Named Attributes and Proximity Operators. In *Proceedings of the 27th Annual ACM SIGIR Conference*, Sheffield, United Kingdom, July 25-July 29, 2004.

[43] T.W. Yan and H. Garcia-Molina. Index Structures for Selective Dissemination of Information Under the Boolean Model. *ACM Transactions on Database Systems*, 19(2):332–364, 1994.

[44] T.W. Yan and H. Garcia-Molina. The SIFT Information Dissemination System. *ACM Transactions on Database Systems*, 24(4):529–565, 1999.

[45] B. Yang and H. Garcia-Molina. Designing a Super-peer Network. In *Proceedings of the 19th International Conference on Data Engineering (ICDE 2003)*, March 5–8, 2003.

[46] Y.K. Dalal and R.M. Metcalfe. Reverse Path Forwarding of Broadcast Packets. *Communications of the ACM*, 21(12):1040–1048, December 1978.

Part III

Semantic Integration

Overview: Semantic Integration

Heiner Stuckenschmidt

The problem of heterogeneity is well known in the area of databases and information systems. Different systems tend to represent the same information in different ways using different syntactic and conceptual structures and often also using different terminologies or different interpretations of the same terminology. This problem, of course, also appears in P2P systems where a potentially large number of independent peers provide and request information about a certain domain. Dealing with heterogeneity in a P2P setting is much harder than in more centralized systems. The lack of a central control element leads to the problem that a peer will often not even know if other peers in the system use the same or a different way of modelling information because only the direct system neighborhood is known to him. This means that semantic mismatches will often only be discovered during query processing. Further, providing solution for the heterogeneity problem often involves an great manual effort for identifying semantically equivalent information in different sources. In P2P systems this effort can often not be justified because of the high number of potential integration problems (in the worst case quadratic to the number of peers) and because P2P systems are often highly dynamic, which means that peers can leave the network at any point. In this case the effort for integrating the information of this peer with others is wasted.

On the technical level traditional solution to the problem of heterogeneity is the use of a global schema for representing information. The structures used in different information sources to organize information are linked to this global schema in terms of views that define elements of the local sources in terms of the global schema. These views can then be used to translate queries posted to the global schema into queries to the local sources. In a decentralized setting this approach does not work because there is no central point of access that could host the global schema and it is not realistic to assume that all peers agree to use the same global schema in addition to their locally defined ones. Chapter 12 presents an approach that extends the idea of view-based information integration to cope with the special requirements of semantics-based P2P systems where views do not not connect sources to a global schema, but directly to each other. While traditional approaches mostly consider information to be represented in the relational data model, the approach in Chap. 12

builds on top of XML and provides mechanisms for defining views over different XML schemas. This makes the approach applicable to the XML serialization of Semantic Web data as well.

While being suited for P2P architectures in general, the approach described in Chap. 12 still requires substantial manual work in terms of identifying and encoding of mappings between different information structures. In order to avoid this effort, recent approaches address the problem of automatically detecting semantic relationships between conceptual structures. Corresponding approaches are presented in Chap. 9 to 11. Based on the nature of the conceptual information to be integrated, methods for automatically detecting mappings have to implement different strategies. The approach of Chap. 9 focusses on the use classification hierarchies to organize documents according to their topics. These kinds of structures are often found in P2P document sharing solutions. The integration task here is to identify classes in different hierarchies that contain documents on the same topic. The approach presented is based on the use of linguistic background knowledge to disambiguate the meaning of class names and for the explication of semantic relations between terms occurring in the names. In Chapter 10 this approach is extended for situations in which artificial class names are used (eg. descriptions of musical genres) that cannot easily be linked to linguistic background knowledge. In order to cope with this situation, the requirements for regarding two classes as describing the same topic are relaxed to compensate for errors that occur due to the inability of disambiguating terms. Chapter 11 finally presents an approaching for matching richer conceptual structures that include at least relations between classes. It is shown how these structures can be used as a basis for heuristic rules that determine related classes.

It is well known that the results of automatic methods for detecting mappings are not always correct. In order to avoid unexpected behavior of the system, these errors have to be detected and corrected. At the moment, there is no formal theory of correctness and consistency of mappings that could be used to check mappings independently of their use. Chapter 13 presents an interesting approach for checking mapping consistency. The approach makes use of the special characteristics of P2P systems. In particular it builds on the idea that in large systems cyclic mapping relations will appear that provide feedback on whether the equality of a class to itself is actually preserved in the cyclic relationship. The authors show that this kind of feedback can be used to improve the mapping accuracy in large systems.

In summary, this part addresses the problem of dealing with heterogeneous information in P2P systems. We present an extension of well known database methods for schema integration XML-based P2P systems based on manually created mappings. We further present a number of approaches for automatically identifying mappings between conceptual models as well as an approach for validating and improving mappings in large systems.

9

Semantic Coordination of Heterogeneous Classifications Schemas

Paolo Bouquet[1], Luciano Serafini[2], Stefano Zanobini[1]

[1] University of Trento, Italy, {bouquet,zanobini}@dit.unitn.it
[2] IRST, Trento, Italy, serafini@itc.it

Summary. A large amount of data, organized in heterogeneous schemas, is now available through the web. The problem of matching such schemas in order to allow global access to information has been recognized as one of the main challenges of the Semantic Web. In this paper, we propose a method for discovering mappings across schemas based on a new approach. This shifts the problem of schema matching from the process of computing linguistic or structural similarities between schema elements (what most other proposed approaches do) to the problem of deducing relations between sets of logical formulas representing the meaning of schema elements. We then show how to apply the approach to an interesting family of schemas, namely hierarchical classifications.

9.1 Introduction

One of the key challenges in the development of open distributed systems is enabling the exchange of meaningful information across applications which (i) may use autonomously developed schemas for organizing locally available data, and (ii) need to discover relations between schemas to achieve their users' goals. Typical examples are databases using different schemas, and document repositories using different classification structures.

In restricted environments, like a small corporate Intranet, this problem is typically addressed by introducing shared models (e.g., ontologies) throughout the entire organization[1]. The idea is that once local schemas are mapped onto a shared ontology, the required relations between them is completely defined. However, in open environments (like the Web), this approach cannot work for several reasons, including the difficulty of "negotiating" a shared model of data that suits the needs of all parties involved, and the practical impossibility of maintaining such a shared model in a highly dynamic environment. In this kind of scenario, a more dynamic and flexible method is needed, where no shared model can be assumed to exist, and

---

[1] But see [3] for a discussion of the drawbacks of this approach from the standpoint of Knowledge Management applications.

semantic relations between concepts belonging to different schemas must be discovered on-the-fly. In other words, we need a sort of Peer-to-Peer form of semantic coordination, in which two or more *semantic peers* (i.e. agents with autonomously developed schemas and possibly heterogeneous ontologies) discover relations across their schemas and use them to provide the required services.

In this chapter, we propose a general approach to the problem of discovering mappings across the schemas of two or more semantic peers. The method we propose is *intrinsically semantic*, as the mappings it discovers between nodes of different schemas are computed as a logical consequence of (1) the explicit representation of the meaning of each node in the schemas, and (2) additional background knowledge (if available). The method is illustrated and tested on a significant instance of the problem, namely the problem of matching hierarchical classifications (HCs). The main technical contribution of this part is an algorithm, called CTXMATCH, which takes in input two HCs H and H' and, for each pair of concepts $k \in H$ and $k' \in H'$, returns their semantic relation (called a mapping).

With respect to other methods proposed in the literature (often under different "headings", such as schema matching, ontology mapping, semantic integration), the main innovation of our approach is that mappings across elements belonging to different schemas are deduced via logical reasoning, rather then derived through (more or less) complex heuristic techniques, and thus can be assigned a clearly defined model–theoretic semantics. This shifts the problem of semantic coordination from the problem of computing linguistic or structural similarities between schemas to the problem of deducing relations between formulas that represent the meaning of each concept in a schema. This explains, for example, why our approach performs much better than most heuristic-based methods when two nodes intuitively represent equivalent concetps, but occur in classification schemas which are structurally very different.

The chapter is organized as follows. In Sect. 9.2 we introduce the main conceptual assumptions of the new approach we propose to semantic coordination. In Sect. 9.3, we present the main features of CTXMATCH, the proposed algorithm for coordinating HCs. Finally, we compare our approach with other proposed approaches for matching schemas (Sect. 9.4).

9.2 Our Approach

The method we propose assumes that we deal with a network of *semantic peers*, namely physically connected entities which can autonomously decide how to organize locally available data (in this sense, each peer is a semantically autonomous agent). Each peer can organize data using one or more schemas (e.g., database schemas, directory trees in a file system, classification schemas, taxonomies, and so on). Different peers may use different schemas to organize the same collection of data, and conversely the same schema can be used to organize different collections of data.

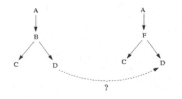

Fig. 9.1. Mapping abstract structures

We also assume that semantic peers need to exchange data (e.g. documents classified under different classification schemas) to perform complex tasks. To do this, each semantic peer needs to compute mappings between its local schema and other peers' schemas. Intuitively, a mapping can be viewed as a set of pairwise relations between elements of two distinct schemas.

The first idea behind our approach is that mappings must be semantic relations, namely relations with a well-defined model-theoretic interpretation. This is an important difference with respect to approaches based on matching techniques, where a mapping is a measure of (linguistic, structural, etc.) similarity between schemas (e.g., a real number between 0 and 1). The main problem with the latter techniques is that the interpretation of their results is an open problem. For example, how should we interpret a 0.9 similarity? Does it mean that one concept is slightly more general than the other one? Or maybe slightly less general? Or that their meaning 90% overlaps (whatever that means)? Instead, our method returns semantic relations, e.g. that the two concepts are (logically) equivalent, or that one is (logically) more/less general, or that they are mutually exclusive. As we will argue, this gives us many advantages essentially related to the consequences we can infer from the discovery of such a relation.

The second idea is that to discover semantic relations, one must make explicit the meaning implicit in each element of a schema. The claim is that this is the only way of computing semantic relations between elements of distinct schemas, and that this can be done only for schemas in which meaningful labels are used. If this is true, then addressing the problem of discovering semantic relations as a problem of matching abstract graphs is conceptually wrong. To illustrate this point, consider the difference between the problem of mapping abstract schemas (like those in Fig. 9.1) and the problem of mapping schemas with meaningful labels (like those in Fig. 9.2). Nodes in abstract schemas do not have an implicit meaning, and therefore, whatever technique we use to map them, we will find that there is some relation between the two nodes D in the two schemas, and this relation depends on the abstract form of the two schemas. The situation is completely different for schemas with meaningful labels, as we can make explicit a lot of information that we have about the terms which appear in the graph, and their relations (e.g., that Tuscany is part of Italy, that Florence is in Tuscany, and so on). It is only this information which allows us to understand why the semantic relation between the two nodes MOUNTAIN and the two nodes FLORENCE is different, despite the fact that the two pairs of schemas are structurally equivalent between them, and both are structurally isomorphic with the

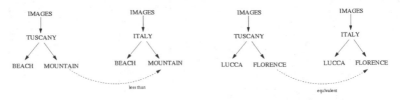

Fig. 9.2. Mapping schemas with meaningful labels

pair of abstract schemas in Fig. 9.1. Indeed, for the first pair of nodes, the set of documents we would classify under the node MOUNTAIN on the left hand side is a subset of the documents we would classify under the node MOUNTAIN on the right; whereas the set of documents which we would classify under the node FLORENCE in the left schema is exactly the same as the set of documents we would classify under the node FLORENCE on the right hand side.

As a consequence, our method is mainly applied to schemas with labels which are meaningful for the community of their users. This gives us the chance of exploiting the complex degree of semantic coordination implicit in the way a community uses the language from which the labels are taken. Notice that the status of this linguistic coordination at a given time is already "codified" in artifacts (e.g., dictionaries, but today also ontologies and other formalized models), which provide senses for words and more complex expressions, relations between senses, and other important knowledge about them. Our aim is to exploit these artifacts as an essential source of constraints on possible/acceptable mappings across structures. The method is based on the elicitation of the meaning associated to each node in a schema[1]. The semantic elicitation process may require the use if three different levels of knowledge:

Lexical knowledge: knowledge about the words used in the labels. For example, the fact that the word "Florence" can be used to indicate "a city in Italy" or "a city in the South Carolina" (homonymy), or the fact that "bachelor" and "unmarried man" can mean the same thing (synonymy).

World Knowledge: knowledge about the relations between the concepts expressed by words. For example, the fact that Tuscany is part of Italy, or that Florence is in Italy.

Structural knowledge: knowledge which derives from how labeled nodes are arranged in a given schema. For example, the fact that the node labeled MOUNTAIN

---

[1] Even though a discussion on the difference between schemas and ontologies is beyond the scope of this paper, notice that schemas – such as the two classifications in Fig. 9.2 – cannot be viewed as straight ontologies (not even *lightweight* ontologies), as the information they convey is mostly implicit in their labels, and in a body of knowledge associated with labels. Indeed, we can say that a classification schema, as many other types of schemas, is a very concise way of referring to complex concepts (like "images of Tuscan montains"), but the identification of the concept corresponding to each element in a schema may require a lot of semantic and world knowledge, which can only be made available to computer programs via explicit semantic models (ontologies). See the rest of the paper for a practical illustration of this point

is below a node IMAGES tells us that it classifies images of mountains, and not, say, books about mountains.

As an example of how the three levels are used, consider again the mapping between the two nodes MOUNTAIN of Fig. 9.2. Lexical knowledge is used to determine what concepts can be expressed by each label, e.g. that the word "Images" can denote the concept "a visual representation produced on a surface". World knowledge tells us, among other things, that Tuscany is part of Italy. Finally, structural knowledge tells us that the intended meanings of the two nodes MOUNTAIN is "images of Tuscan mountains" on the left hand side, and "images of Italian mountains" on the right hand side. Using this information, human reasoners (i) elicit the meaning expressed by the left hand node, ("images of Tuscan mountains", denoted by P), (ii) elicit the meaning expressed by the right hand node ("images of Italian mountains", denoted by P'), and finally (iii) derive the semantic relation between the meaning of the two nodes, namely that $P \sqsubseteq P'$ (intuitively, subsumption between the concepts corresponding to the two schema elements).

These three levels of knowledge are used to produce a new, richer representation of the schema, where the meaning of each node is made explicit and encoded as a logical formula and a set of axioms. This formula is an approximation of the meaning of the node when it occurs in that schema. The problem of discovering the semantic relation between two nodes can now be stated not as a matching problem, but as a relatively simple problem of logical deduction. Intuitively, as we will say in a more technical form in the rest of the paper, determining whether there is an equivalence relation between the meaning of two nodes can be encoded as a problem of testing whether the first implies the second and vice versa (given a suitable collection of axioms, which acts as a sort of background theory); and determining whether one is less general than the other one amounts to testing if the first implies the second. As we will say, in the current version of the algorithm we encode this reasoning problem as a problem of logical satisfiability, and then compute mappings by feeding the problem to a standard SAT solver.

9.3 The Algorithm: CTXMATCH

In this section we show how to apply the general approach described in the previous section to the problem of coordinating *Hierarchical Classifications* (hereafter HCs), namely concept hierarchies [5] used for grouping/organizing/classifying data (such as documents, goods, activities, services) in categories. Some well-known examples of HCs are web directories (see e.g. the Google[TM] Directory or the Yahoo![TM]Directory), file systems, document databases, ...

In our approach, we assume the presence of a network of semantic peers, where each peer is defined as follows:

Definition 1. *A semantic peer is a triple $\langle \mathcal{D}, \mathcal{S}, \langle L, O \rangle \rangle$, where:*

- $\mathcal{D}$ *is a set of documents;*

- S represents the set of schemas used by the peer for organizing its data;
- $\langle L, O \rangle$ is a pair composed by a lexicon L and some representation O of world knowledge.

The structure of the semantic peer reflects the three levels of knowledge we showed before: S represents structural knowledge, L contains lexical knowledge, and O is world knowledge. Formally, L is a repository of pairs $\langle w, C \rangle$, where w is a word and C is a set of concepts. Each pair $\langle w, C \rangle$ represents the set of concepts C denoted by a word w. For example, a possible entry for a lexicon should express that the word "fish" can denote at least two concepts: "an aquatic vertebrate" and "the twelfth sign of zodiac". An important example of this kind of repository is represented by WORDNET [9]. A knowledge base O expresses the set of relations holding between different concepts. For example, a knowledge base O should express that the concept "an aquatic vertebrate" denoted by the word "fish" stays in a *IsA* relation with the concept of "animal" ("fish are animals") and that the concept "the twelfth sign of zodiac" denoted by the same word "fish" stays in a *IsA* relations with a geometrical shape ("fish is a geometrical shape"). Formally, knowledge base is a logical theory written is a specific language, like OWL, Prolog clauses, DAML/OIL, RDFS.

Our method is designed for scenarios in which an agent A (called the *seeker*) needs to find new documents relative to some category in its local HC S_A. Imagine that another agent B (called the *provider*) owns a collection of potentially relevant documents, but they are classified using a different HC S_B. Our problem is to discover semantic relations between A's original category in S_A and the categories in S_B, and – based on the discovered relations – return the relevant documents. A and B are called semantic peers because, as we will say, each of them has equivalent capabilities and responsibilities in assigning meaning to the classification schemas used to organize local documents, and in assigning documents to categories.

A collection of point-to-point relations between categories of two distinct HCs is called a mapping:

Definition 2. *A mapping $\mathcal{M}$ between two schemas S and S' is a set of mapping elements $\langle m, n, R \rangle$ where m is a node in S, n is anode in S' and R is a semantic relation between m and n.*

In this version of the algorithm, five relations are allowed between the concepts corresponding to two nodes belonging to different HCs: $m \sqsupseteq n$ (m is *more general than n*); $m \sqsubseteq n$ (m is *less general than n*); $m \equiv n$ (m is *equivalent* to n); $m \sqcap n$ is consistent (i.e. it has an interpretation which is not empty and thus m is *compatible* with n); $m \sqcap n \sqsubseteq \bot$ (m is *disjoint* from n).

The algorithm CTXMATCH takes as **inputs** the seeker's and the provider's classification schemas S and S', and the provider's lexicon L and knowledge base O^1. As it will become clear in what follows, this means that the resulting mapping is *directional*, as it represents the provider's point of view on the relation between S and

---

[1] In the version of the algorithm presented here, we use WORDNET both as a source of lexical and world knowledge. However, WORDNET can be replaced by any other combination of a lexical and a world knowledge source.

S' (because it is based on the provider's lexicon and knowledge base, and thus on the provider's understanding of the two schemas). As the seeker in principle may use different lexical and background knowledge, a different mapping between the same schemas S and S' might be computed. The reason why we privilege the provider's perspective here is that it reflects the scenario in which an agent asks for information from one or more agents, whose answers are necessarily based on their understanding of the question.

The **output** of the algorithm is a mapping $\mathcal{M}$.

Algorithm 2 CTXMATCH(S, S', L, O)

   ▷ *Hierarchical classifications S, S'*

   ▷ *Lexicon L*

   ▷ *knowledge base O*

   VarDeclarations

      contextualized concept $\langle \phi, \Theta \rangle, \langle \psi, \Upsilon \rangle$

      relation R

      mapping $\mathcal{M}$

1   **for** each pair of nodes $m \in S$ and $n \in S'$ **do**

2      $\langle \phi, \Theta \rangle \leftarrow$ SEMANTIC–ELICITATION(m, S, L, O);

3      $\langle \psi, \Upsilon \rangle \leftarrow$ SEMANTIC–ELICITATION(n, S', L, O);

4      $R \leftarrow$ SEMANTIC–COMPARISON($\langle \phi, \Theta \rangle, \langle \psi, \Upsilon \rangle, O$);

5      $\mathcal{M} \leftarrow \mathcal{M} \cup \langle m, n, R \rangle$;

6   **Return** M;

The algorithm has essentially the following two main macro steps.

Steps 2–3: in this phase, called *semantic elicitation*, the algorithm tries to interpret pair of nodes m, n in the respective HCs S and S' by means of the lexicon L and the knowledge base O. The idea is trying to generate a formula approximating the meaning expressed by a node in a structure (ϕ), and a set of axioms formalizing relevant knowledge about it (Θ). Consider, for example, the node FLORENCE in left lower HC of Fig. 9.2: steps 2–3 will generate a formula approximating the statement "Images of Florence in Tuscany" (ϕ) and an axiom approximating the statement "Florence is in Tuscany" (Θ). In our framework, the pair $\langle \phi, \Theta \rangle$, called *contextualized concept*, expresses the meaning of a node in a structure.

Step 4: in this phase, called *Semantic comparison*, the problem of finding the semantic relation between two nodes m and n is encoded as the problem of finding the semantic relation holding between two contextualized concepts, $\langle \phi, \Theta \rangle$ and $\langle \psi, \Upsilon \rangle$.

Finally, Step 5 generates the mapping simply by reiteration of the same process over all the possible pair of nodes $m \in S\ n \in S'$ and Step 6 returns the mapping.

The two following sections describe in detail these two top-level operations, implemented by the functions SEMANTIC–ELICITATION and SEMANTIC–COMPARISON.

9.3.1 Semantic Elicitation

In this phase we make explicit in a logical formula[1] the meaning of a node n in a HC S.

Algorithm 3 SEMANTIC–ELICITATION(t, S, L, O)
  ▷ t *is a node in* S
  ▷ *structure* S
  ▷ *lexicon* L
  ▷ *knowledge base* O

VarDeclarations
    single concept $con[]$
    set of formulas Σ
    formula δ

1 **for** each node n in S **do**
2      $con[n] \leftarrow$ EXTRACT–CANDIDATE–CONCEPTS(n, L);
3   $\Sigma \leftarrow$ EXTRACT–LOCAL-AXIOMS$(t, S, con[], O)$;
4   $con[] \leftarrow$ FILTER–CONCEPTS$(S, \Sigma, con[])$;
5   $\delta \leftarrow$ BUILD–COMPLEX–CONCEPT$(t, S, con[])$;
6   **Return** $\langle \delta, \Sigma \rangle$;

In Step 1 and Step 2, the function EXTRACT–CANDIDATE–CONCEPTS uses lexical knowledge to associate to each word occurring in the nodes of an HC all concepts possibly denoted by the word itself. Consider the lower left structure of Fig. 9.2. The label "Florence" is associated with two concepts, provided by the lexicon (WORDNET), corresponding to "a city in central Italy on the Arno" (florence#1) or a "a town in northeast South Carolina" (florence#2). In order to maximize the possibility of finding an entry into the Lexicon, we use both a postagger and a lemmatizator over the labels[2].

In Step 3, the function EXTRACT–LOCAL–AXIOMS tries to define the ontological relations existing between the concepts in a structure. Consider again the left lower structure of Fig. 9.2. Imagine that the concept "a region in central Italy" (tuscany#1) has been associated to the node TUSCANY. The function EXTRACT–LOCAL–AXIOMS has the aim to discover if it exists some kind of relation be-

---

[1] The choice of the formal language depends on how expressive one wants to be in the approximation of the meaning of nodes, and on the complexity of the NLP techniques used to process labels. In this implementation we adopt the propositional fragment of Description logics, where each propositional letter corresponds to a concept (synset) provided by WORDNET. However, in [18], a richer encoding is described which uses also the DL roles. As an example, the node MOUNTAIN of the left hand schema of Fig. 9.2, now interpreted as (image#1⊔...⊔image#8)⊓tuscany#1⊓mountain#1, is encoded as (image#1⊔...⊔image#8)⊓∃about#3.(mountain#1⊓∃locatedIn#2.tuscany#1), namely "images about mountains that are located in Tuscany".

[2] Although in this paper we present very simple examples, the NLP techniques exploited in this phase allow us to handle labels containing complex expressions, as conjunctions, commas, prepositions, expressions denoting exclusion, like "except" or "but not", multiwords and so on.

tween the concepts tuscany#1, florence#1 and florence#2 (associated to node FLORENCE). Exploiting world knowledge, we can discover, for example, that "florence#1 PartOf tuscany#1", i.e. that there exists a "part of" relation between the first sense of "Florence" and the first sense of "Tuscany". World knowledge relations extracted from WORDNET are translated into logical axioms according to Table 9.1. So, the relation "florence#1 PartOf tuscany#1" is encoded as "florence#1 ⊑ tuscany#1"[1].

Table 9.1. WORDNET relations and corresponding axioms.

WORDNET World knowledge relations	axiom
s#k synonym t#h	s#k ≡ t#h
s#k { hyponym | PartOf } t#h	s#k ⊑ t#h
s#k { hypernym | HasPart } t#h	t#h ⊑ s#k
s#k antonym t#h	(t#k ⊓ s#h) ⊑ ⊥

Step 4 has the goal of filtering out unlikely senses associated to a node's label. Going back to the previous example, we tentatively discard one of the senses associated to the node FLORENCE ("a town in northeast South Carolina", florence#2), based on the fact that we found the local axiom "florence#1 PartOf tuscany#1" which links the other sens of "Florence" to a sense of "Tuscany". This fact is used to make the conjecture that the contextually relevant sense of Florence is the city in Tuscany, and not the city in the USA. When ambiguity persists (because there are axioms related to different senses, or no axioms at all), all possible senses are kept and encoded as a disjunction.

Step 5 has the objective of building a complex concept (i.e., the meaning of a node label when it occurs in a specific position in a schema) for nodes in HCs. As described in [4], node labels are first processed one by one to build a preliminary interpretation, called *simple concept*, which does not take into account the position of the node in the structure. For example, the simple concept associated to the node FLORENCE of the left hand structure of Fig. 9.2 is the atom florence#1 (i.e. one of the two senses provided by WORDNET and not discarded by filtering). Then, these results are combined for generating a formula approximating the meaning expressed by a node *in a schema*. In this version of the algorithm, we choose to express the meaning of a node n as the conjunction of the simple concepts associated to the nodes lying in the path from the root node to n. So, the formula approximating the meaning expressed by the node FLORENCE in that HC is (image#1 ⊔ ... ⊔ image#8) ⊓ tuscany#1 ⊓ florence#1.

Step 6 returns the formula expressing the meaning of the node and the set of local axioms found in Step 3. This formula represents what we call a contextualized concept, namely a complex concept associated to a node in a schema, given L and O.

---

[1] For heuristical reasons – see [4] – we consider only relations between concepts on the same path of a HC and their siblings.

This explains why the set of contextualized concepts extracted from a HC can be viewed as a *context* in the sense of [11, 1], namely a partial and approximate representation of the world from an individual's perspective. Indeed, it reflects a semantic peer's perspective on a collection of documents. As we already pointed out, the same schema can be transformed into a different context by different semantic peers, as they might use a different lexicon L' or different world knowledge O'. This explains why the mappings between the same pair of schemas computed by different peers are not identical.

9.3.2 Semantic Comparison

The goal of this phase is to find the semantic relation which holds between two contextualized concepts (associated to two nodes in different HCs).

In Step 1, the function EXTRACT–RELATIONAL–AXIOMS tries to find axioms which connect concepts belonging to different HCs. This function is similar to EXTRACT–LOCAL–AXIOMS in the semantic elicitation part. Consider, for example, the senses `italy#1` and `tuscany#1` associated respectively to nodes ITALY and TUSCANY of Fig. 9.2: the relational axioms express the fact that, for example, "Tuscany PartOf Italy" (`tuscany#1` $\sqsubseteq$ `italy#1`).

Algorithm 4 SEM–COMP($\langle \phi, \Theta \rangle, \langle \psi, \Upsilon \rangle, O$)
   ▷ *contextualized concept* $\langle \phi, \Theta \rangle$, $\langle \psi, \Upsilon \rangle$
   ▷ *world knowledge O*

   VarDeclarations
      set of formulas Γ
      semantic relation R

1   $\Gamma \leftarrow$ EXTRACT–RELATIONAL–AXIOMS(ϕ, ψ, O);
2   **if** $\Theta, \Upsilon, \Gamma \models (\phi \sqcap \psi) \sqsubseteq \bot$ **then** $R \leftarrow disjoint$;
3   **else if** $\Theta, \Upsilon, \Gamma \models (\phi \equiv \psi)$ **then** $R \leftarrow equivalent$;
4   **else if** $\Theta, \Upsilon, \Gamma \models (\phi \sqsubseteq \psi)$ **then** $R \leftarrow less\ general\ than$;
5   **else if** $\Theta, \Upsilon, \Gamma \models (\psi \sqsubseteq \phi)$ **then** $R \leftarrow more\ general\ than$;
6   **else** $R \leftarrow compatible$;
7   **Return** R;

In steps 2–6, the problem of finding the semantic relation between two nodes n and m (line 2) is encoded into a satisfiability problem involving both the contextualized concepts associated to the nodes and the relational axioms extracted in the previous phases. So, to prove whether the two nodes labeled FLORENCE in Fig. 9.2 are equivalent, we check the logical equivalence between the formulas approximating the meaning of the two nodes, given the local and the relational axioms. Formally, we have the satisfiability problem as stated in Table 9.2.

It is simple to see that the returned relation is "*equivalent*". Note the satisfiability problem for finding the semantic relation between the nodes MOUNTAIN of Fig. 9.2 as stated in Table 9.3.

The returned relation is "*less general than*".

Table 9.2. Satisfiability Problem for FLORENCE

Θ	florence#1 $\sqsubseteq$ tuscany#1
ϕ	(image#1 $\sqcup$ ... $\sqcup$ image#8) $\sqcap$ tuscany#1 $\sqcap$ florence#1
Δ	florence#1 $\sqsubseteq$ italy#1
ψ	(image#1 $\sqcup$ ... $\sqcup$ image#8) $\sqcap$ italy#1 $\sqcap$ florence#1
Γ	tuscany#1 $\sqsubseteq$ italy#1

Table 9.3. Satisfiability Problem for MOUNTAIN

Θ	$\emptyset$
ϕ	(image#1 $\sqcup$ ... $\sqcup$ image#8) $\sqcap$ tuscany#1 $\sqcap$ mountain#1
Δ	$\emptyset$
ψ	(image#1 $\sqcup$ ... $\sqcup$ image#8) $\sqcap$ italy#1 $\sqcap$ mountain#1
Γ	tuscany#1 $\sqsubseteq$ italy#1

Following on the idea that a semantically elicited schema is a context, a mapping between two contextualized concepts belonging to different contexts can be formally represented as a *compatibility relation* [10], namely a constraint on the local models of the two contexts. In this sense, the algorithm we present is a first attempt to discover (rather than assume) relations over local models of two or more contexts (which, from a proof–theoretical point of view, corresponds to discover bridge rules [12] across contexts).

9.4 Related Work

Recently, many methods have been proposed for matching heterogeneous schemas (see [17] for a well-known survey of the area). However, our method shifts the problem of semantic coordination from the problem of matching (in a more or less sophisticated way) schemas to the problem of inferring semantic relations between the meaning of schema elements. Under this respect, to the best of our knowledge, our approach is still original; an alternative (and partially extended) implementation, called S-Match, was proposed in [8] as a rationalization of CTXMATCH. Therefore, a straightforward comparison with other methods is not easy.

However, it is important to see how CTXMATCH compares with the performance of techniques based on different approaches to semantic coordination. There are four other families of approaches that we will consider: graph matching, automatic schema matching, semi-automatic schema matching, and instance based matching. For each of them, we will discuss the proposal that, in our opinion, is more significant. The comparison is based on the following five dimensions: (1) if and how structural knowledge is used; (2) if and how lexical knowledge is used; (3) if and how knowledge base is used; (4) if instances are considered; (5) the type of result returned. The general results of our comparison are reported in Table 9.4.

Table 9.4. Comparing CTXMATCH with other methods

	graph matching	CUPID	MOMIS	GLUE	CTXMATCH
Structural knowledge	•	•	•		•
Lexical knowledge		•	•	•	•
Knowledge base				•	•
Instance-based knowledge				•	
Type of result	Pairs of nodes	Similarity measure $\in$ [0..1] between pairs of nodes	Similarity measure $\in$ [0..1] between pairs of nodes	Similarity measure $\in$ [0..1] between pairs of nodes	Semantic relations between pairs of nodes

In graph matching techniques, a concept hierarchy is viewed as a tree of labelled nodes, but the semantic information associated to labels is substantially ignored. In this approach, matching two graphs G_1 and G_2 means finding a sub-graph of G_2 that is isomorphic to G_2 and reports as a result the mapping of nodes of G_1 into the nodes of G_2. These approaches consider only structural knowledge and completely ignore lexical knowledge and knowledge base. Some examples of this approach are described in [20, 19, 16, 15, 6].

CUPID [13] is a completely automatic algorithm for schema matching. Lexical knowledge is exploited for discovering linguistic similarity between labels (e.g., using synonyms), while the schema structure is used as a matching constraint. That is, the more the structure of the subtree of a node s is similar to the structure of a subtree of a node t, the more s is similar to t. For this reason CUPID is more effective in matching concept hierarchies that represent data types rather than hierarchical classifications. With hierarchical classifications, there are cases of equivalent concepts occurring in completely different structures, and completely independent concepts that belong to isomorphic structures. Two simple examples are depicted in Fig. 9.3. In case (a), CUPID does not match the two nodes labelled with ITALY; in case (b) CUPID finds a match between the node labelled with FRANCE and ENGLAND. The reason is that CUPID combines in an additive way lexical and structural information, so when structural similarity is very strong (for example, all neighbor nodes do match), then a relation between nodes is inferred without considering labels. So, for example, FRANCE and ENGLAND match because the structural similarity of the neighbor nodes is so strong that labels are ignored.

MOMIS (Mediator envirOnment for Multiple Information Sources) [2] is a set of tools for information integration of (semi-)structured data sources, whose main objective is to define a global schema that allows a uniform and transparent access to the data stored in a set of semantically heterogeneous sources. One of the key steps of MOMIS is the discovery of overlappings (relations) between the different source schemas. This is done by exploiting knowledge in a Common Thesaurus together with a combination of clustering techniques and Description Logics. The approach is very similar to CUPID and presents the same drawbacks in matching hierarchical

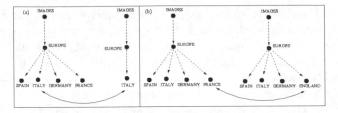

Fig. 9.3. Example of right and wrong mapping

classifications. Furthermore, MOMIS includes an interactive process as a step of the integration procedure, and thus, unlike CTXMATCH, it does not support a fully automatic and run-time generation of mappings.

GLUE [7] is a taxonomy matcher that builds mappings taking advantage of information contained in instances, using machine learning techniques and domain-dependent constraints, manually provided by domain experts. GLUE represents an approach complementary to CTXMATCH. GLUE is more effective when a large amount of data is available, while CTXMATCH is more performant when less data are available, or the application requires a quick, on-the-fly mapping between structures. So, for instance, in case of product classification such as UNSPSC or Eclss (which are pure hierarchies of concepts with no data attached), GLUE cannot be applied. Combining the two approaches is a challenging research topic, which can probably lead to a more precise and effective methodology for semantic coordination.

9.5 Conclusions

In this paper we presented a new approach to semantic coordination in open and distributed environments, and an algorithm (called CTXMATCH) that implements this method for hierarchical classifications. CTXMATCH has been successfully tested on real HCs (i.e., pre-existing classifications used in real applications) and the results are described in [14].

An important lesson we learned from this work is that methods for semantic coordinations should not be grouped together on the basis of the type of abstract structure they deal with (e.g., DAGs, concept hierarchies), but on the basis of the intended use of the structures under consideration. In this paper, we addressed the problem of semantic coordination for hierarchical classifications, and the elicitation method we proposed heavily relies on this assumption. However, there are other possible uses for "similar" structures, e.g. specifying the conceptualization of some domain (ontologies), describing web services (finite automata), describing data types (schemas). This "pragmatic" level (i.e., the use of a schema) is essential to provide the correct interpretation of a structure, and thus to discover the correct mappings with other structures.

The importance we assign to the fact that HCs are labelled with meaningful expressions does not mean that we see the problem of semantic coordination as a problem of natural language processing (NLP). On the contrary, the solution we provided is mostly based on knowledge representation and automated reasoning techniques. However, the problem of semantic coordination is a fertile field for collaboration between researchers in knowledge representation and in NLP. Indeed, if in describing the general approach one can assume that some linguistic analysis on labels is available and ready to use, real applications require a massive use of techniques and tools from NLP, as a reliable, automatic analysis of labels from a linguistic point of view is a necessary precondition for the quality of the algorithm's results.

The work we presented is only the first step of a very ambitious scientific challenge, namely to investigate what is the minimal common ground needed to enable communication between autonomous entities that cannot look into each others heads, and thus can achieve some degree of semantic coordination only through other means, like exchanging messages, passing examples, pointing to things, remembering past interactions, generalizing from past communications, and so on. To this end, a lot of work remains to be done. In particular, we stress that CTXMATCH is a one-shot method for discovering relations across static schemas; however, much more interesting is the problem of dynamically adapting the schemas (or their interpretation) as a result of the interaction between two (or more) semantic peers. This much more general task is what we call meaning negotiation (as opposed to meaning coordination), where peers may try to find an agreement on the meaning of schemas, or even update/change their lexical/background knowledge to achieve a more satisfactory mapping with other peers. This project seems quite exciting and challenging, as it requires to go beyond pure meaning, and take into account other dimensions like a cost/benefit analysis of changing a schema, updating/changing a body of lexical and/or background knowledge, redefining mappings across schemas. This *economics of meaning* is a completely new field, whose crucial relevance for large-scale projects (like the Semantic Web) and semantic-based applications have been recognized only recently, and where new models and tools need to be developed from scratch.

References

[1]   M. Benerecetti, P. Bouquet, and C. Ghidini. Contextual Reasoning Distilled. *Journal of Theoretical and Experimental Artificial Intelligence*, 12(3):279–305, 2000.

[2]   S. Bergamaschi, S. Castano, and M. Vincini. Semantic integration of semistructured and structured data sources. *SIGMOD Record*, 28(1):54–59, 1999.

[3]   M. Bonifacio, P. Bouquet, and P. Traverso. Enabling distributed knowledge management. managerial and technological implications. *Novatica and Informatik/Informatique*, III(1), 2002.

[4]   P. Bouquet, L. Serafini, and S. Zanobini. Semantic coordination: a new approach and an application. In K. Sycara, editor, *Second International Seman-*

tic Web Conference (ISWC-03), Lecture Notes in Computer Science (LNCS), Sanibel Island (Florida, USA), October 2003.

[5] A. Büchner, M. Ranta, J. Hughes, and M. Mäntylä. Semantic information mediation among multiple product ontologies. In *Proc. 4th World Conference on Integrated Design & Process Technology*, 1999.

[6] Jeremy Carroll and Hewlett-Packard. Matching rdf graphs. In *Proc. in the first International Semantic Web Conference - ISWC 2002*, pages 5–15, 2002.

[7] A. Doan, J. Madhavan, P. Domingos, and A. Halevy. Learning to map between ontologies on the semantic web. In *Proceedings of WWW-2002, 11th International WWW Conference, Hawaii*, 2002.

[8] F. Giunchiglia, P. Shvaiko, M. Yatskevich. S-Match: an Algorithm and an Implementation of Semantic Matching. In *Proceedings of the first European Semantic Web Symposium* (ESWC-2004), Springer, LNCS 3053, pp. 61-75.

[9] Christiane Fellbaum, editor. *WordNet: An Electronic Lexical Database*. The MIT Press, Cambridge, US, 1998.

[10] C. Ghidini and F. Giunchiglia. Local Models Semantics, or Contextual Reasoning = Locality + Compatibility. *Artificial Intelligence*, 127(2):221–259, 2001.

[11] F. Giunchiglia. Contextual reasoning. *Epistemologia, special issue on I Linguaggi e le Macchine*, XVI:345–364, 1993. Short version in Proceedings IJCAI'93 Workshop on Using Knowledge in its Context, Chambery, France, 1993, pp. 39–49. Also IRST-Technical Report 9211-20, IRST, Trento, Italy.

[12] F. Giunchiglia and L. Serafini. Multilanguage hierarchical logics or: how we can do without modal logics. *Artificial Intelligence*, 65(1):29–70, 1994. Also IRST-Technical Report 9110-07, IRST, Trento, Italy.

[13] Jayant Madhavan, Philip A. Bernstein, and Erhard Rahm. Generic schema matching with cupid. In *The VLDB Journal*, pages 49–58, 2001.

[14] B. M. Magnini, L. Serafini, A. Doná, L. Gatti, C. Girardi, , and M. Speranza. Large–scale evaluation of context matching. Technical Report 0301–07, ITC–IRST, Trento, Italy, 2003.

[15] Tova Milo and Sagit Zohar. Using schema matching to simplify heterogeneous data translation. In *Proc. 24th Int. Conf. Very Large Data Bases, VLDB*, pages 122–133, 24–27 1998.

[16] Marcello Pelillo, Kaleem Siddiqi, and Steven W. Zucker. Matching hierarchical structures using association graphs. Springer, LNCS 1407, 1998.

[17] E. Rahm, P.A. Bernstein. A survey of approaches to automatic schema matching. *VLDB Journal*, 10(4), 2001.

[18] S. Sceffer, L. Serafini, S. Zanobini. Semantic coordination of hierarchical classifications with attributes. Technical Report 706, University of Trento, Italy, December 2004. http://eprints.biblio.unitn.it/archive/00000706/

[19] Jason Tsong-Li Wang, Kaizhong Zhang, Karpjoo Jeong, and Dennis Shasha. A system for approximate tree matching. *Knowledge and Data Engineering*, 6(4):559–571, 1994.

[20] K. Zhang, J. T. L. Wang, and D. Shasha. On the editing distance between undirected acyclic graphs and related problems. In Z. Galil and E. Ukkonen, editors, *Proceedings of the 6th Annual Symposium on Combinatorial Pattern Matching*, volume 937, pages 395–407, Espoo, Finland, 1995. Springer.

10

Semantic Mapping by Approximation

Zharko Aleksovski[1,2], Warner ten Kate[2]

[1] Vrije Universiteit Amsterdam, The Netherlands, zharko@few.vu.nl
[2] Philips Research Eindhoven, The Netherlands

Summary. We address the problem of semantic coordination, namely finding an agreement between the meanings of heterogeneous semantic models. We propose a new approximation method to discover and assess the "strength" (preciseness) of semantic mappings between different concept hierarchies. We apply this method in the music domain. We present the results of tests on mapping two music concept hierarchies from actual sites on the Internet.

10.1 Introduction

The progress of information technology has made it possible to store and access large amounts of data. However, since people think in different ways and use different terminologies to store information, it becomes hard to search each other's data stores. With the advent of the Internet, which has enabled the integrated access of an ever-increasing number of such data stores, the problem becomes even more serious. The music domain is no exception. The variety and size of offered content makes it difficult to find music of interest. It is often cumbersome to retrieve even a known piece of music.

One way to improve this Internet music search is by using semantics in the retrieval process. It is in particular conveyed in the Semantic Web. In this context we study the problem of semantic integration over different music metadata schemas. More specific, the problem is to find pairs of concepts (e.g., genres, styles, classes) from different metadata schemas that relate to each other (e.g., have equivalent meaning, is more general than). It is not sufficient to use the concept labels only, since, for example, the positions of the concepts in the schemas influence their meaning as well. Figure 10.1 illustrates an example taken from existing music schemas. Although the labels are equivalent ("Experimental") they represent different classes of music entities.

The problem of finding the music that fits the preferences of a user is similar to the problem of matching the metadata schemas of two different music providers. In the latter case we need to find pairs of concepts that have an equivalent meaning. In

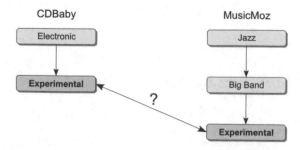

Fig. 10.1. Two music genres. Although the labels are equivalent they represent different classes.

the former case, we can treat the user's preferences as concepts themselves, and the problem is to match the preferred concept with those in the provider's terminology.

Being able to search for matches at the concept level (without using instances) is important. The search may use instances (artists, releases, tracks), but when it comes to the user preferences we cannot rely on instances solely, unlike the recommender systems [2]. Then users will be expected to provide example pieces of musics they like. Furthermore, the size of music offered by content providers may range from several thousands up to several millions of items. Solutions using instance data to discover matchings will also be very demanding on processing power. On the other hand, semantic based approaches would deal with the music classifications rather than the instances. Since these usually range in the several hundreds of classes, it would make this approach less demanding on processing power. In addition, semantic based approaches can deal with the ambiguity and vagueness in the music domain easier than the approaches using instance data.

The semantic approach offers the discovery of implicit matchings where the connection is not obvious. These matchings can be discovered using sources of domain knowledge. For example, the style of music called *Death metal* can be discovered to be form of *Rock* using the Free Encyclopedia[1].

In this chapter we address the problem of matching between two different metadata schemas. There already exists several techniques to solve this problem [4], [5]. We stress the importance of approximation when dealing with real-life data. The approach described here makes use of the method proposed by Bouquet et al. (Chap. 9).

In Chap. 9, the goal is to find mappings between the concepts of two so-called Concept Hierarchies. For the current discussion a Concept Hierarchy can be thought of as a rooted tree where each node has a label. The nodes represent the concepts. It has the explicit purpose to provide a classification. Next to the label of the nodes, the matching method accounts for the position of the nodes in the hierarchy. The method works in three main phases: In the first phase, *linguistic interpretation*, the senses that

---

[1] http://thefreeencyclopedia.com

Wordnet[1] returns on the node's label are combined as propositional terms in a logical formula. The formula represents all the possible linguistic interpretations of the label. In the second phase, *contextualization*, the position of the nodes in the hierarchy is encoded in the logical formula. Both steps are performed on the source and target hierarchy. In the final phase, *semantic comparison*, the so-obtained formulas from both hierarchies are evaluated for relationships. This is done by pair-wise encoding of the formulas in the relationship to be tested, and testing the satisfiability of the resulting formula. Five relationships are considered: (i) they are equivalent, (ii) they are disjoint, (iii) they are not in a subclass relation but have a non empty intersection, (iv) the first is a subclass of the second and (v) the second is a subclass of the first.

The main contributions of this chapter are:

- We describe a method for discovering approximate mappings between concepts from two different Concept Hierarchies. Given two concepts from different Concept Hierarchies, the method checks whether the first concept is a subconcept of the second. When this does not hold, the method calculates "how strongly" the first concept is a subconcept of the second. It calculates a value (we call it *sloppiness*) between 0.0 and 1.0 for each pair of concepts. The sloppiness indicates the error in the subsumption relation between the two concepts. Closer to 0.0 means that most of the (semantic) content of the first concept is also present in the second concept, while values closer to 1.0 indicate that there is no subsumption relation.
- We present results from an experiment using real-world metadata schemas from music sites on the Internet. These metadata schemas were extracted as the underlying navigation paths at the provider sites. We applied the approximation method on those schemas, and the results were tested against the matches based on the instances (music artists) we found in the classes. We discuss the problems that we encountered when applying the method, and the level of correspondence observed between the concept-based and instance-based matches.

The remainder of the chapter is structured as follows: Sect. 10.2 discusses the role and importance of the semantic integration problem in the real-life Peer-to-Peer applications. Sect. 10.3 presents the current situation of music metadata schemas available on the Internet. Sect. 10.4 introduces and explains our idea of approximate matching. Sect. 10.5 presents experimental results from applying our approximation method. Sect. 10.6 identifies possible improvements for future work. Sect. 10.7 concludes the work presented in this chapter.

10.2 Application in Peer-to-Peer

The success of systems like Napster and Kazaa made clear the new competition that traditional systems for distributing music are facing. Some reacted to this trend and are now offering P2P services for the legal exchange of electronic music via the

---

[1] http://wordnet.princeton.edu

Internet. It is not unlikely that others will follow. A drawback of this approach to exchanging digital music is the limitation of keyword based search. This means, that people can only find music they already know by name, making it hard to discover unknown artists. Also, portals that want to promote new songs need a generic search paradigm. The obvious solution is to classify music according to their genres (e.g., jazz). There has been various attempts to create such genre terminologies – [8]. They allow users to search for music of a genre rather than a certain song.

This approach of using genre classification of music, however, requires an agreement on the organization of genres and the assignment of artists and songs to these genres. In a portal solution, this agreement is enforced by the provider in charge of organizing information. In a P2P setting where each user is more or less free to choose his or her own organization of genres and songs, such an agreement has to be reached first. The idea is that different communities will evolve around different genres and negotiate an agreement on the organization of music. As we can expect that members of the community have some knowledge about the characteristics of that genre, an accurate organization is more likely to evolve than in an uncontrolled setting.

Exchanging music between peers in a Peer-to-Peer network requires establishment of mappings between the content offered by different peers. Discovering these mappings is a difficult task. Doing it manually is very time consuming, and it will require the user to have knowledge about the domain in advance. An automatic solution will ease a wider acceptance, as long as the results are of an acceptable quality. Also, users should not be required to perform extra work. Even more, they should be protected from the complexity of knowledge representation mechanisms used by the system. In an realistic system, however, the discovery of the mappings will be realized semi-automatically. The user will be given proposals for mappings with the other peers, and possibly with the opportunity to change them and define new ones.

A very important aspect of this automatic integration is the ability to give an advice for the mapping, in case where an exact mapping does not exist or the system can not discover it. When a class from one peer does not match any existing class from another peer, the system should try to identify the "closest" class. Such solution will be more robust to erroneous data, like typing mistakes. It is a well known fact that real-world data is noisy. If only exact mappings are allowed, the recall will drop, still leaving the user with a lot of manual work. Consequently, using methods to discover approximate mappings is expected to boost the performance of the system.

In Peer-to-Peer systems, the users are also providers at the same time. In order to examine the possibility of integrating music content, we have performed experiments to integrate music metadata schemas from Internet portals. The problem there is the same as the integration problem in the Peer-to-Peer setting. In the following section we give an overview of the music domain on the Internet portals and the data used for testing.

10.3 Internet Music Schemas

On the Internet, a visitor can interactively navigate through different pages that list the music offered. Since music metadata schemas are not always offered, we consider this structure of navigation paths together with the labeling on the links and pages as the metadata schema of that provider.

After considering several music provision sites, we selected seven of them and extracted the schema (navigation path): CDNow (Amazon.com)[1], MusicMoz (MM)[2], CDBaby[3], Artist Direct Network (ADN)[4], AllMusic (AMG)[5], LAUNCH cast on Yahoo (Yahoo)[6], and ArtistGigs.com[7]. There exists classes whose meaning lies outside the music style domain (e.g., "Music Accessories"). Most of the schemas have some peculiarities that are typical or unique for that schema. After the extraction we applied some simplifying modifications to the data. In the first place, we normalized the labels in order to make the data more suitable for our experiments. This included the correction of typing mistakes and the removal of abbreviations and similar peculiarities. Figure 10.2 presents a general overview of the data extracted. In the sequel we call the extracted schemas as the ontologies to be matched.

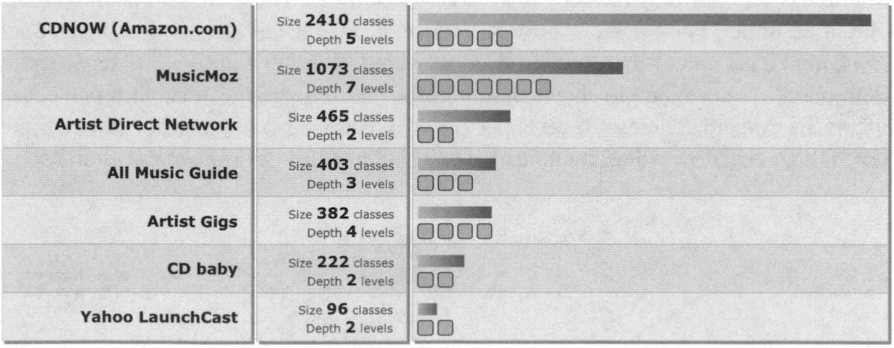

CDNOW (Amazon.com)	Size **2410** classes Depth **5** levels	
MusicMoz	Size **1073** classes Depth **7** levels	
Artist Direct Network	Size **465** classes Depth **2** levels	
All Music Guide	Size **403** classes Depth **3** levels	
Artist Gigs	Size **382** classes Depth **4** levels	
CD baby	Size **222** classes Depth **2** levels	
Yahoo LaunchCast	Size **96** classes Depth **2** levels	

Fig. 10.2. The extracted schemas.

Most of the labels in the ontologies appear to be one of the following kinds: style of music (the genre of the music), geographic region with music style (region where the music originates from), and time or historical period when the music was created (e.g., decades like "90's", named periods like "baroque"). All of the schemas

---

[1] http://www.cdnow.com

[2] http://musicmoz.org

[3] http://www.cdbaby.com

[4] http://artistdirect.com

[5] http://www.allmusic.com

[6] http://launch.yahoo.com

[7] http://www.artistgigs.com

are concept hierarchies that only use the subclass relationship. Sibling subclasses are often overlapping (i.e., they are not disjoint).

The nodes are often named with more then one word. These words either denote the intersection of the terms they express (e.g., "Chicago Blues"), or they constitute a single term (e.g., in "New Zealand Rock", "New Zealand" is one term and should not be considered as separate words). The first case occurs more frequently.

There is a considerable fuzziness in music classification. There are no objective criteria that sharply define music classes. Genre is not precisely defined. Even humans disagree on the classification of music. As a result, different providers often classify the same music entities (e.g., artists, albums, songs) differently. Common terms like "Pop" and "Rock" do not denote the same sets of artists at different portals. That is also the case for even more specific styles of music like *Speed Metal*.

In the experiments, when testing with instances, we restricted to the artists shared by MusicMoz and Artist Direct Network, i.e., artists that are present and classified in both portals. In the remainder we refer to them as MM and ADN, respectively. As shown in Fig. 10.3, under the class named *Rock* (including its subclasses), in MM there are 471-shared classified artists, i.e. artists who are also classified in ADN, but not necessarily in *Rock*. In ADN there are 245 of them. There are 196-shared artists classified under *Rock* in both portals. Hence, from all the artists classified under *Rock* in at least one of the two portals, only about 38% are classified under Rock in both portals. This example shows that there is a high degree of fuzziness present in the music domain. Therefore, we expect approximate reasoning methods to be more useful than exact reasoning methods for creating matchings in the music domain.

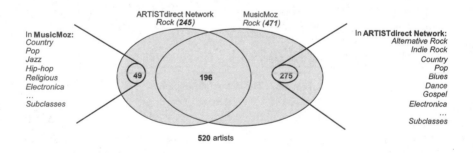

Fig. 10.3. Rock musical genre in ADN and MM.

10.4 Approximate Matching

We follow the approach of semantic coordination described in Chap. 9, to find relations between music classes. As explained above, this approach works as follows:

first the classes are transformed into logic formulas that capture the meaning of the classes by using Natural Language Processing techniques and relations between the classes, and subsequently relations between classes are discovered by determining the relations between the corresponding formulas. In Chap. 9 propositional logic is used to present the logic formulas, and the problem of discovering the relations between the formulas is reduced to the SAT (satisfiability) problem.

In the sequel of this section we explain how we extend the approach with a form of approximation to handle the impreciseness occurring in actual data. First, the (propositional) formulas representing the classes in the Concept Hierarchies are rewritten in normal forms.

We want to check whether a left-hand formula is a subclass of a right-hand formula. The left-hand formula is transformed into *disjunctive normal form* and the right-hand side into *conjunctive normal form*. In this way, the subclass check can be split into a set of subproblems, each checking if one (left) disjunct is a subclass of a (right) conjunct. If all the subproblems are satisfied, the original problem is satisfied. In our approximation, we allow a few of the subproblems to be unsatisfiable, while still declaring the original problem satisfiable. The (relative) number of satisfiable subproblems is a measure of *how strongly* the subclass relation between the two given formulas hold.

Below, we explain the approach more formally. In our notation we interpret formulas as sets and use the operators union, intersection, and subset instead of the logical operators disjunction, conjunction, and implication, respectively.

10.4.1 Normal Forms

Given two propositional logic formulas A and B, the problem is to check whether the relation $A \subseteq B$ holds. We transform A into disjunctive normal form and B into conjunctive normal form.

The Disjunctive Normal Form (DNF) has the following form:

$$A = (A_1^1 \cap A_1^2 \cap \cdots \cap A_1^{n_1}) \cup (A_2^1 \cap A_2^2 \cap \cdots \cap A_2^{n_2}) \cup \cdots \cup (A_I^1 \cap A_I^2 \cap \cdots \cap A_I^{n_I}),$$

where each A_i^n is an atomic concept. Shortly it can be written as $A = A_1 \cup A_2 \cup \cdots \cup A_I$ where $A_i = (A_i^1 \cap A_i^2 \cap \cdots \cap A_i^{n_i})$ for $i = 1, \ldots, I$. Each A_i is called a *disjunct*.

The Conjunctive Normal Form (CNF) has the following form:

$$B = (B_1^1 \cup B_1^2 \cup \cdots \cup B_1^{m_1}) \cap (B_2^1 \cup B_2^2 \cup \cdots \cup B_2^{m_2}) \cap \cdots \cap (B_J^1 \cup B_J^2 \cup \cdots \cup B_J^{m_J}),$$

where each B_j^m is an atomic concept. Shortly it can be written as $B = B_1 \cap B_2 \cap \cdots \cap B_J$ where $B_j = (B_j^1 \cup B_j^2 \cup \cdots \cup B_j^{m_j})$ for $j = 1, \ldots, J$. Each B_j is called a *conjunct*.

Now, the problem to check whether $A \subseteq B$ can be written as

$$A_1 \cup A_2 \cup \cdots \cup A_I \subseteq B_1 \cap B_2 \cap \cdots \cap B_J.$$

This relation holds if and only if (iff) anything that belongs to some of the disjuncts A_i on the left-hand side also belongs to all of the conjuncts B_j on the right-hand side. Written formally:

$$A_1 \cup A_2 \cup \cdots \cup A_I \subseteq B_1 \cap B_2 \cap \cdots \cap B_J \Leftrightarrow (\forall i = 1, \ldots, I, \forall j = 1, \ldots, J)(A_i \subseteq B_j).$$

Hence, the problem whether $A \subseteq B$ is transformed into $I \cdot J$ number of subproblems of the following form:

$$(\forall i, j)(A_i \subseteq B_j). \tag{10.1}$$

One such check will be referred to as a disjunct-conjunct pair.

Now we introduce the **idea of approximation**: the relation $A \subseteq B$ holds iff for all disjunct-conjunct pairs the subclass relation (10.1) holds. If most of the disjunct-conjunct pairs (10.1) hold we say that the relation $A \subseteq B$ **almost holds**. Even more, we can express the strength at which the relation $A \subseteq B$ holds as the ratio between the number of disjunct-conjunct pairs that satisfy the subclass relations and the total number of pairs. We call this ratio the sloppiness and use the letter s to denote its value:

$$s(A \subseteq B) = \frac{|\{(i,j) \mid A_i \not\subseteq B_j\}|}{I \cdot J}.$$

Here $|\{(i,j) \mid A_i \not\subseteq B_j\}|$ denotes the number of disjunct-conjunct pairs that do not satisfy the subclass relation, I is the number of disjuncts in the DNF of A, and J is the number of conjuncts in the CNF of B.

Note that this method works on the concept level and can be applied when no information about the instances is available.

10.5 Experiment with Approximate Matching

In this section we summarize the results of experiments that we conducted using the approximate matching method. We used the metadata schemas extracted from ArtistDirectNetwork and MusicMoz.

The linguistic interpretation (i.e., the formulas build from the labels of the nodes) were obtained using simple techniques. For example, "Alternative Rock" was transformed into the following formula:

$$(Alternative \cap Rock) \cup Alternative\_Rock.$$

Special characters "&" and "/" were treated as logical union. For example, "Pop & Rock" was transformed into the formula $Pop \cup Rock$. No background knowledge was used. When background knowledge is used, each atomic concept (e.g., *Alternative, Rock, Alternative_Rock*) should be replaced with the union of the different senses for that concept.

We made the assumption that concepts with the same label have the same meaning. When comparing the disjunct-conjunct relations we made a simplification: a disjunct A_i is considered to be a subclass of a conjunct B_j when some literal in the disjunct (which is an intersection of literals) is present in the conjunct (which is an union of literals). So, given a disjunct-conjunct pair:

$$A_i = (A_i^1 \cap A_i^2 \cap \cdots \cap A_i^{n_i}), B_j = (B_j^1 \cup B_j^2 \cup \cdots \cup B_j^{m_j}),$$

we say that $A_i \subseteq B_j$ if $A_i^n = B_j^m$ for some n and m. If no such pair is found, the disjunct A_i is not considered to be a subclass of the conjunct B_j. This simplification may lead to some incorrect rejections of subclass relations.

10.5.1 Example of an Approximate Matching

Now we explain the process of approximate inferring an equivalence relation in detail. For the sake of the explanation we have chosen an example that produces simple formulas, however, in practice these formulas can grow bigger and be more complex.

In our example, consider the relation between two styles from ADN and MM that are named "Glam Rock" on both portals (Fig. 10.4).

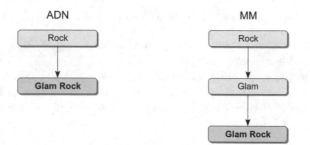

Fig. 10.4. Glam Rock style from the schemas of ADN and MM.

The first step is to transform the concepts into formulas. We first transform the "Glam Rock" style from ADN. Note that "Glam Rock" is a substyle of "Rock" as shown in Fig. 10.4. Also note that "Glam Rock" consists of two words. For the formula, we therefore have to take into account the separate meanings of those words (i.e., the intersection of their meanings), as well as those words constituting a single term (as is the case in "New Zealand"). Therefore the formula representing the meaning of "Glam Rock" from ADN is the following:

$$Glam\_Rock\_A = Rock \cap ((Glam \cap Rock) \cup Glam\_Rock).$$

This leads to the following normal forms:

$$Glam\_Rock\_DNF\_A = (Glam \cap Rock) \cup (Glam\_Rock \cap Rock), \text{ (10.2)}$$
$$Glam\_Rock\_CNF\_A = (Rock) \cap (Glam \cup Glam\_Rock). \qquad \text{(10.3)}$$

Analogously, the "Glam Rock" style from MM is transformed into the formula:

$$Glam\_Rock\_B = Rock \cap Glam \cap ((Glam \cap Rock) \cup Glam\_Rock)$$
$$= Rock \cap Glam.$$

The literal Glam_Rock in the formula is discarded because of the absorption rule [6]. This leads to the following normal forms:

$$Glam\_Rock\_DNF\_B = (Glam \cap Rock), \tag{10.4}$$

$$Glam\_Rock\_CNF\_B = (Rock) \cap (Glam). \tag{10.5}$$

The normal forms can be used to test the equivalence relation between the concepts $Glam\_Rock\_A$ and $Glam\_Rock\_B$. We therefore have to check the subclass relation for those two concepts in both directions.

In order to check the subsumption $Glam\_Rock\_B \subseteq Glam\_Rock\_A$ the normal forms (10.3) and (10.4) are needed. $Glam\_Rock\_B$ consists of only one disjunct, and $Glam\_Rock\_A$ consists of two conjuncts. We therefore have to check two disjunct-conjunct pairs:

$(Glam \cap Rock) \subseteq (Rock)$ – true (Rock is on both sides),
$(Glam \cap Rock) \subseteq (Glam \cup Glam\_Rock)$ – true (Glam is on both sides).

Both disjunct-conjunct pairs satisfy the relation, so $Glam\_Rock\_B \subseteq Glam\_Rock\_A$ holds with a sloppiness of 0%.

In order to check the subsumption $Glam\_Rock\_A \subseteq Glam\_Rock\_B$ the normal forms (10.2) and (10.5) are needed. $Glam\_Rock\_A$ consists of two disjuncts, and $Glam\_Rock\_B$ consists of two conjuncts. We therefore have to check four disjunct-conjunct pairs:

$(Glam \cap Rock) \subseteq (Rock)$ – true (Rock is on both sides),
$(Glam \cap Rock) \subseteq (Glam)$ – true (Glam is on both sides),
$(Glam\_Rock \cap Rock) \subseteq (Rock)$ – true (Rock is on both sides),
$(Glam\_Rock \cap Rock) \subseteq (Glam)$ – false.

Three out of four disjunct-conjunct pairs satisfy the relation, however, one disjunct-conjunct pair does not. Hence, 25% of the disjunct-conjunct pairs do not satisfy the subsumption relation, and the relation $Glam\_Rock\_A \subseteq Glam\_Rock\_B$ therefore holds with a sloppiness of 25%.

When assessing the sloppiness in the equivalence relation between $Glam\_Rock\_A$ and $Glam\_Rock\_B$, we take the maximum of the sloppiness values calculated in the two subsumptions. The equivalence relation between $Glam\_Rock\_A$ and $Glam\_Rock\_B$ therefore holds with a sloppiness of 25%.

10.5.2 Comparison with Instance Data

For our experiments we extracted real data from the Internet (Sect. 10.3). In the following, the results are presented that were obtained using the data sets MM and ADN (Fig. 10.5).

Name	Number of classes	Number of artists	Number of classified artists	Number of shared classified artists
Artist Direct Network	465	16072	16072	1183
MusicMoz	1073	6415	2356	

Fig. 10.5. Size of the data in ArtistDirectNetwork and MusicMoz.

Most of the shared classified artists are classified under "Rock"-related classes (e.g., Alternative Rock, Glam Rock, Heavy Metal). A significant limitation of our dataset is that the number of instances is of the same order as the number of classes.

The tests were performed to discover the equivalence matchings between the classes in both hierarchies, i.e., whether each is a subclass of the other. Different values for the sloppiness measure were used in the tests. In order to assess the success of the matching we introduce a value called significance, which we define as the cardinality ratio between the intersection and the union of the two classes. Formally:

$$significance(A \Leftrightarrow B) = \frac{|A \cap B|}{|A \cup B|}.$$

The significance is close to 0 when the two classes have no overlap, i.e., a relatively small amount of instances belong to their intersection. When the value is close to 1 (or 100%) then the two classes denote almost the same set of instances.

Sloppiness	Average significance	Equivalence matches
0%	28.290%	18
0% - 30%	29.055%	51
30% - 45%	26.778%	140
45% - 55%	11.439%	900
55% - 100%	< 6.7%	> 6,000

Fig. 10.6. Equivalence testing between ADN and MM.

The results presented in Fig. 10.6 are only from the equivalences where both of the classes had at least 10 instances. The equivalence relations inferred with a sloppiness of 30% or less, are almost always "true" matches, i.e., matches that the experts would accept as correct matches. However, it appears that most of them remain undiscovered when the sloppiness is set to 0% (i.e., when using exact matching). For example, the equivalence relation between the "Glam Rock" concepts in Fig. 10.4 can only be inferred with a sloppiness of 25% or more.

The relatively low value of the average significance revealed in the performed tests, is a notification that people do not agree on the meaning of the music style names. It is stated in [1] that the music domain constantly evolves, and there is no centralized authority that can assign styles to the artists. They are classified in different ways, although the same name is given from the music providers.

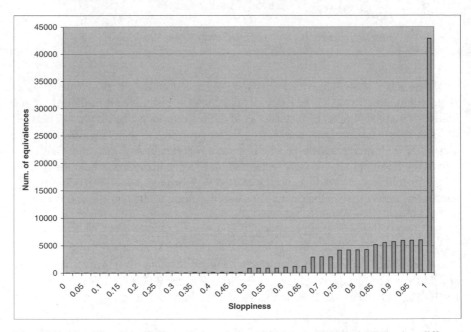

Fig. 10.7. Number of equivalent relations inferred between ADN and MM using different sloppiness parameter.

Figure 10.7 shows the number of equivalence relations inferred given some value for the sloppiness parameter. The number of inferences increases when the sloppiness is increased. At the beginning, the number of inferences increase slowly. This is reasonable since a relatively small amount of pairs of classes from different sources should be considered to be equivalent or approximately equivalent. In general, most of the pairs of classes are not related at all, and adding sloppiness should not change this. From 50% toward the end, the number of inferences increase more rapidly. At 100% there is a "cliff," because all classes are considered to be equivalent with a sloppiness of 100%. The results shown in Fig. 10.7 gives confidence in the approximation method.

10.6 Future Work

This general scheme of approximation can be improved in several directions. For example, instance data can be used, as in the work of [3] or [4]. Also, the formalism used to describe formulas is limited to the propositional logic, while in real world data there is an identified need of considering the attributes differently in the formulas. Next, we will shortly discuss two directions for major improvements: improving the accuracy in the approximation, and sources which can be used as background knowledge.

10.6.1 Improvements of Approximation Accuracy

For example, the contribution of all disjunct-conjunct pairs in the tested formulas is not equal. Disjuncts and conjuncts can have a different size, i.e., the number of literals they consist of. Also, literals represent sets of instances that themselves are of different size. Accounting for these differences may result in a more accurate sloppiness measure.

It is natural that a disjunct of bigger size should have less impact on the result. The intuition is that a disjunct (consisting of a number of intersections) having more literals, constitutes a subclass of smaller scope. Hence, its contribution to the total class (disjunction) is smaller. A similar intuition holds for conjuncts: more literals in the conjunct constitutes a larger subclass and its contribution to the total class (conjunction) is therefore larger.

A final heuristic is to assign more weight to "rare" classes. The intuition is that the more general concept names have wider use, and therefore matching them only provides general confidence. When matching "Rock" between two classes, or when matching "Cajun," a stronger relation is expected in the second case.

10.6.2 Sources of Background Knowledge

Background knowledge plays a crucial role in the matching process. That is the lift from the syntactic to the semantic level. It gives the opportunity to discover matches which are impossible to discover at the syntactic level. Work that uses background knowledge extensively has been done in the medical domain - [7], [9] where the interoperability problem exists as well. Matching imprecisely defined classes as in the case of music domain, requires more careful considering of the background knowledge. Chapter 9 used Wordnet to discard the senses of certain concepts that have no semantic relation with the concepts of the ancestor class.

Another problem is the availability of the background knowledge. We are not aware of such an ontology existing in the music domain. One approach is to create one through knowledge discovery mechanisms. We conducted some preliminary experiments in which we considered two ways to extract relations between terms from the music domain. For the first we used The Free Dictionary[1] as a source, and in the second we used Google[2]. In The Free Dictionary we used as strength measure of the relation between the terms, the level co-occurrence of words between the pages that describe the terms. In the Google case, we assumed that related terms occur on

---

[1] http://www.thefreedictionary.com/
[2] http://www.google.com/

the same pages, and then the number of Google hits relative to the number of hits for each term separately, was used as strength measure for the term relation. The experiments produced useful results and we plan to continue in this direction in the future.

10.7 Conclusion

We have presented a method to do approximate matching between concept hierarchies. We discussed an interesting application domain – music. The situation and the present problems in the music artist classifications on the Internet identifies the need of integration. Fuzziness is highly present and the approximate matching method that we proposed may help to deal with this problem. The results from applying the approximate matching method in the music domain were presented and showed promising results.

Acknowledgements

We are grateful to Heiner Stuckenschmidt for the useful feedback and fruitful discussions. We wish to thank Aleksandar Pechkov for his feedback about the relation extraction from the Internet. We also like to thank Perry Groot for his feedback and the translation into LaTeX.

References

[1] Jean-Julien Aucouturier and Francois Pachet. Representing musical genre: A state of the art. *Journal of New Music Research 2003, Vol. 32, No. 1, pp. 83-93*, 2003.

[2] Conor Hayes and Padraig Cunningham. Context boosting collaborative recommendations. Technical Report TCD-CS-2003-26, Trinity College Dublin, Computer Science Department, 2003.

[3] Ryutaro Ichise, Hiedeaki Takeda, and Shinichi Honiden. Integrating multiple internet directories by instance-based learning. In *Proc. 18th Int. Joint Conf. on Artificial Intelligence (IJCAI), Acapulco, Mexico*, pages 22–28, 2003.

[4] Jayant Madhavan, Philip A. Bernstein, and Erhard Rahm. Generic schema matching with cupid. In *Proc. 27th Int. Conf. on Very Large Data Bases (VLDB-01), Roma, Italy*, pages 49–58, 2001.

[5] Diana Maynard, Giorgos Stamou, Heiner Stuckenschmidt, Ilya Zaihrayeu, Jesus Barrasa, Jerome Euzenat, Manfred Hauswirth, Marc Ehrig, Mustafa Jarrar, Paolo Bouquet, Pavel Shvaiko, Rose Dieng-Kuntz, Ruben Lara Hernandez, Sergio Tessaris, Sven Van Acker, and Thanh-Le Bach. State of the art on ontology alignment. Knowledge Web Deliverable D2.2.3, INRIA, Saint Ismier, 2004.

[6] E. Mendelson. *Introduction to Mathematical Logic*. Chapman & Hall, 1997.

[7] Peter Mork and Philip A. Bernstein. Adapting a generic match algorithm to align ontologies of human anatomy. In *20th Int. Conf. on Data Engineering (ICDE), Boston, USA*, pages 787 – 790, March 2004.

[8] Francois Pachet and Daniel Cazaly. A taxonomy of musical genres. In *Proc. Content-Based Multimedia Information Access (RIAO), Paris, France*, pages 1238–1245, 2000.

[9] Songmao Zhang and Olivier Bodenreider. Comparing associative relationships among equivalent concepts across ontologies. In *Proc. Medinfo 2004, San Francisco, California, USA*, pages 459–463, Sep. 2004.

11

Satisficing Ontology Mapping

Marc Ehrig[1], Steffen Staab[2]

[1] Institute AIFB, University of Karlsruhe, Germany
ehrig@aifb.uni-karlsruhe.de
[2] ISWeb, University of Koblenz-Landau, Germany
staab@uni-koblenz.de

Summary. (Semi-)automatic mapping — also called (semi-)automatic alignment — of ontologies is a core task to achieve interoperability when two agents or services use different ontologies. In the existing literature, the focus has so far been on improving the quality of mapping results. In Peer-to-Peer systems, however, we frequently encounter the situation where large ontological structures must be mapped onto each other in a few seconds or less in order to achieve practical feasibility of semantic translation between peers.

We here present QOM (acronym for Quick Ontology Mapping), an approach that follows Herb Simon's model of men, where he argues that human decision making is not aiming at optimality, but at satisfying the decision maker by achieving a sufficient degree of quality. We show that QOM has lower run-time complexity than existing approaches. Then, we show in experiments that this theoretical investigation translates into practical benefits. While QOM gives up some of the possibilities for producing high-quality results in favor of efficiency, our experiments show that this loss of quality is marginal, hence satisficing (=satisfying + sufficient).

11.1 Introduction

Semantic mapping[1] between ontologies is a necessary precondition to establish interoperation between individual peers using different ontologies. In recent years we have seen a range of research work on methods proposing such mappings [1, 17, 6]. The focus of the previous work, however, has been laid exclusively on improving the *effectiveness* of the approach (i.e. the quality of proposed mappings, such as evaluated against some human judgement given either a posteriori or a priori).

When we tried to apply these methods to some of the real-world scenarios we address in applications like Bibster (Chap. 18) and Xarop (Chap. 17), we found that existing mapping methods were not suitable for the ontology integration task at hand, as they all neglected *efficiency*. To illustrate our requirements: We have been working in realms where light-weight ontologies are applied such as the ACM Topic hierarchy with its 10^4 concepts or folder structures of individual computers, which

---

[1] Frequently also called alignment.

corresponded to 10^4 to 10^5 concepts. When mapping between such light-weight ontologies, the trade-off that one has to face is between effectiveness and efficiency. For instance, in Bibster and Xarop it is not sufficient to provide its user with the best possible mapping, it is also necessary to identify identical objects within a few seconds — even if two peers use two different ontologies and have never encountered each other before. In Xarop the users extend their ontology by integrating ontologies from foreign peers. During this ontology editing process corresponding entities have to be quickly identified and presented to the user, who can then integrate them accordingly. In the Bibster scenario the mapping application differs. After query results have been retrieved from many peers, objects representing the same publication or person have to be automatically identified and merged. The user is to be presented an object only once. Again this has to occur within a few seconds.

Therefore, in this paper we present an approach that aims at producing sufficiently good ontology mappings, which satisfy the users, but which do not necessarily yield optimal results. Herb Simon coined the notion of "satisficing" in order to describe the typical human decision-making process. The process does not target optimality, but it aims at using limited resources of attention, time and efforts in order to come up with solutions that were just "good enough."

Correspondingly, we consider both the quality of mapping results as well as the run-time complexity incurred by mapping algorithms. Our hypothesis is that mapping algorithms may be streamlined such that the loss of quality (compared to a standard baseline) is marginal, but the improvement of efficiency is so tremendous that it allows for the ad-hoc mapping of large-size, light-weight ontologies. To substantiate the hypothesis, we outline a comparison of the worst-case run-time behavior (given in full detail in [8]) and we report on a number of practical experiments. The approaches used for our (unavoidably preliminary) comparison represent different classes of algorithms for ontology mapping. Comparing to these approaches we can observe that our new efficient approach QOM[9] achieves good quality. The complexity of QOM is of $O(n \cdot log(n))$ (measuring with n being the number of the entities in the ontologies) against $O(n^2)$ for approaches that have similar effective outcomes.

The remainder of this chapter on efficient ontology mapping starts with a clarification of terminology (Sect. 11.2). To compare the worst-case run-time behavior of different approaches, we then describe a canonical process for ontology mapping that subsumes the different approaches compared in this paper (Sect. 11.3). The process is a core building block for later deriving the run-time complexity of the different mapping algorithms. Sect. 11.4 presents our toolbox to analyze these algorithms. In Sect. 11.5, different approaches for proposing mappings are described and aligned to the canonical process, one of them being our approach QOM. The way to derive their run-time complexity is outlined in Sect. 11.6. Experimental results (Sect. 11.7) complement the comparison of run-time complexities. We close this paper with a short section on related work and a conclusion.

11.2 Terminology

11.2.1 Ontology

As we currently focus on light-weight ontologies, we build on RDF/S[1] to represent ontologies. To facilitate the further description, we briefly summarize its major primitives and introduce some shorthand notations. An RDF model is described by a set of statements, each consisting of a subject, a predicate and an object. An ontology O is defined by its set of Concepts C (instances of "rdfs:Class") with a corresponding subsumption hierarchy H_C (a binary relation corresponding to "rdfs:subClassOf"). Relations $\mathcal{R}$ (instances of "rdf:Property") exist between single concepts. Relations are arranged alike in a hierarchy H_R ("rdfs:subPropertyOf"). An entity $i \in \mathcal{I}$ may be an instance of a class $c \in C$ ("rdf:type"). An instance $i \in \mathcal{I}$ may have one j or many role fillers from $\mathcal{I}$ for a relation r from $\mathcal{R}$. We also call this type of triple (i, r, j) a property instance.

11.2.2 Mapping

We here define our use of the term "mapping." Given two ontologies O_1 and O_2, mapping one ontology onto another means that for each entity (concept C, relation R, or instance I) in ontology O_1, we try to find a corresponding entity, which has the same intended meaning, in ontology O_2.

Definition 1. *We define an ontology mapping function,* map, *based on the vocabulary,* $\mathcal{E}$, *of all terms* $e \in \mathcal{E}$ *and based on the set of possible ontologies,* $\mathcal{O}$, *as a partial function:*

$$\text{map} : \mathcal{E} \times \mathcal{O} \times \mathcal{O} \rightharpoonup \mathcal{E},$$

$$\text{with } \forall e \in O_1 (\exists f \in O_2 : \text{map}(e, O_1, O_2) = f \vee \text{map}(e, O_1, O_2) = \bot).$$

A term e interpreted in an ontology O is either a concept, a relation or an instance, i.e. $e_{|O} \in C \cup \mathcal{R} \cup \mathcal{I}$. We usually write e instead of $e_{|O}$ when the ontology O is clear from the context of the writing. We write $\text{map}_{O_1, O_2}(e)$ for $\text{map}(e, O_1, O_2)$. We derive a relation map_{O_1, O_2} by defining $\text{map}_{O_1, O_2}(e, f) \Leftrightarrow \text{map}_{O_1, O_2}(e) = f$. We leave out O_1, O_2 when they are evident from the context and write $\text{map}(e) = f$ and $\text{map}(e, f)$, respectively. Once a (partial) mapping, map, between two ontologies O_1 and O_2 is established, we also say *"entity e is mapped onto entity f"* iff $\text{map}(e, f)$. An entity can either be mapped to at most one other entity. A pair of entities (e, f) that is not yet in map and for which appropriate mapping criteria still need to be tested is called a *candidate mapping*.

11.2.3 Example

The following example illustrates a mapping from the tourism domain of the SWAP virtual enterprize scenario. Two ontologies O_1 and O_2 describing the domain of car retailing are given (Fig. 11.1). A reasonable mapping between the two ontologies is given in Table 11.1 as well as by the dashed lines in the figure.

---

[1] http://www.w3.org/RDFS/

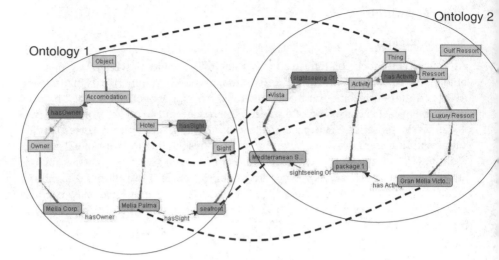

Fig. 11.1. Example Ontologies and their Mappings

Table 11.1. Mapping Table for Relation $\mathrm{map}_{O_1,O_2}(e, f)$

Ontology O_1	Ontology O_2
Object	Thing
Hotel	Ressort
Melia Palma	Gran Melia Victoria
Sight	Vista
seafront	Mediterranean Sea

11.3 Process

We briefly introduce a canonical process that subsumes all the mapping approaches we are aware of. Figure 11.2 illustrates its six main steps. It is started with two ontologies, which are going to be mapped onto one another, as its input:

1. Feature engineering transforms the initial representation of ontologies into a format digestible for the similarity calculations. For instance, the subsequent mapping process may only work on a subset of RDFS primitives.

2. Selection of Next Search Steps. The derivation of ontology mappings takes place in a search space of candidate mappings. This step may choose, to compute the similarity of a restricted subset of candidate concepts pairs $\{(e, f)|e \in O_1, f \in O_2\}$ and to ignore others.

3. Similarity Computation determines similarity values of candidate mappings.

4. Similarity Aggregation. In general, there may be several similarity values for a candidate pair of entities e, f from two ontologies O_1, O_2, e.g. one for the similarity of their labels and one for the similarity of their relationship to other terms. These different similarity values for one candidate pair must be aggregated into a single aggregated similarity value.

5. Interpretation uses the individual or aggregated similarity values to derive mappings between entities from O_1 and O_2. Some mechanisms here are to use thresholds for similarity mappings [17], to perform relaxation labelling [6], or to combine structural and similarity criteria.

6. Iteration. Several algorithms perform an iteration over the whole process in order to bootstrap the amount of structural knowledge. Iteration may stop when no new mappings are proposed. Note that in a subsequent iteration one or several of steps 1 through 5 may be skipped, because all features might already be available in the appropriate format or because some similarity computation might only be required in the first round.

Eventually, the output returned is a mapping table representing the relation map_{O_1,O_2}.

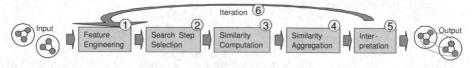

Fig. 11.2. Mapping Process

11.4 A Toolbox of Data Structures and Methods

The principal idea of this section is to provide a toolbox of data structures and methods common to many approaches that determine mappings. This gives us a least common denominator based on which concrete approaches instantiating the process depicted in Fig. 11.2 can be compared more easily.

11.4.1 Features of Ontological Entities

To compare two entities from two different ontologies, one considers their characteristics, i.e. their features. The features may be specific for a mapping generation algorithm, in any case the features of ontological entities (of concepts, relations, instances) need to be extracted from extensional and intensional ontology definitions. See also [10] and [11] for an overview of possible features and a classification of them. Possible characteristics include:

- *Identifiers*: i.e. strings with dedicated formats, such as unified resource identifiers (URIs) or RDF labels.
- *RDF/S Primitives*: such as properties or subclass relations.
- *Derived Features*: which constrain or extend simple RDFS primitives (e.g. most-specific-class-of-instance).

- *Aggregated Features*: i.e. aggregating more than one simple RDFS primitive, e.g. a sibling is every instance-of the parent-concept of an instance.
- *OWL Primitives*: such as an entity being the sameAs another entity.
- *Domain Specific Features* are features which only apply to a certain domain with a predefined shared ontology. For instance, in an application where files are represented as instances and the relation hashcode-of-file is defined, we use this feature to compare representations of concrete files.

Example. We again refer to the example in Fig. 11.1. The actual feature consists of a juxtaposition of relation name and entity name. The Hotel concept of ontology 1 is characterized through its (label, Hotel), the concept which it is linked to through (subclassOf, Accomodation), its (concept sibling, Campground), and the (direct property, hasSight). Hotel is also described by its instances through (instance, Melia Palma). The relation hasSight on the other hand is described through the (domain, Hotel) and the (range, Sight). An instance would be Melia Palma, which is characterized through the instantiated (property instance, (hasOwner, Melia Corp.)) and (property instance, (hasSight, seafront)).

11.4.2 Similarity Computation

Definition 2. *We define a similarity measure for comparison of ontology entities as a function as follows (cf. [2]):*

$$\text{sim} : \mathcal{E} \times \mathcal{E} \times \mathcal{O} \times \mathcal{O} \to [0,1]$$

Different similarity measures $\text{sim}_k(e, f, O_1, O_2)$ are indexed through a label k. Further, we leave out O_1, O_2 when they are evident from the context and write $\text{sim}_k(e, f)$.

The following similarity measures are needed to compare the features of ontological entities at iteration t.

- *Object Equality* is based on existing logical assertions — especially assertions from previous iterations: $\text{sim}_{obj}(a, b) := \{1 \text{ iff } \text{map}_{t-1}(a) = b, 0 \text{ otherwise}\}$
- *Explicit Equality* checks whether a logical assertion already forces two entities to be equal: $\text{sim}_{exp}(a, b) := \{1 \text{ iff } statement(a, \text{"}sameAs\text{"}, b), 0 \text{ otherwise}\}$
- *String Similarity* measures the similarity of two strings on a scale from 0 to 1 (cf. [14]) based on Levenshtein's edit distance, ed [13]. $\text{sim}_{str}(c, d) := max(0, \frac{min(|c|,|d|) - ed(c,d)}{min(|c|,|d|)})$
- *SimSet*: For many features we have to determine to what extent two sets of entities are similar. To remedy the problem, multidimensional scaling [4] measures how far two entities are from all other entities and assumes that if they have very similar distances to all other entities, they must be very similar: $\text{sim}_{set}(E, F) = \frac{\sum_{e \in E} \mathbf{e}}{|\sum_{e \in E} \mathbf{e}|} \cdot \frac{\sum_{f \in F} \mathbf{f}}{|\sum_{f \in F} \mathbf{f}|}$ with $\mathbf{e} = (\text{sim}(e, e_1), \text{sim}(e, e_2), \dots, \text{sim}(e, f_1), \text{sim}(e, f_2), \dots)$, $\mathbf{f}$ analogously.

These measures are all input to the similarity aggregation.

11.4.3 Similarity Aggregation

Similarities are aggregated by:
$$\text{sim}_{agg}(e, f) = \frac{\sum_{k=1\ldots n} w_k \cdot \text{adj}(\text{sim}_k(e,f))}{\sum_{k=1\ldots n} w_k}$$
with w_k being the weight for each individual similarity measure, and adj being a function to transform the original similarity value ($adj : [0, 1] \rightarrow [0, 1]$), which yields better results.

11.4.4 Interpretation

From the similarity values we derive the actual mappings. The basic idea is that each entity may only participate in one mapping and that we assign mappings based on a threshold t and a greedy strategy that starts with the largest similarity values first. Ties are broken arbitrarily by $arg\tilde{m}ax_{(g,h)}$, but with a deterministic strategy.

$$P(\bot, \bot, E \cup \{\bot\}, E \cup \{\bot\}).$$
$$P(g, h, U\backslash\{e\}, V\backslash\{f\}) \leftarrow P(e, f, U, V) \wedge \text{sim}(g, h) > t$$
$$\wedge (g, h) = arg\tilde{m}ax_{(g,h)\in U\backslash\{e\}\times V\backslash\{f\}}\text{sim}_{agg}(g, h).$$
$$\text{map}(e, f) \leftarrow \exists X_1, X_2 P(e, f, X_1, X_2) \wedge (e, f) \neq (\bot, \bot).$$

11.5 Approaches to Determine Mappings

In the following we now use the toolbox, and extend it, too, in order to define a range of different mapping generation approaches. In the course of this section we present our novel Quick Ontology Mapping approach — QOM.

11.5.1 Standard Mapping Approaches

Our Naive Ontology Mapping (NOM)[10] constitutes a straight forward baseline for later comparisons. It is defined by the steps of the process model as follows. Where appropriate we point to related mapping approaches and briefly describe the difference in comparison to NOM.

1. Feature Engineering. Firstly, the ontologies have to be represented in RDFS. We use features as shown in Sect. 11.4.1.

For PROMPT and Anchor-PROMPT [17] any ontology format is suitable as long as it can be used in the Protege environment. GLUE [6] learns in advance, based on a sample mapping set, a similarity estimator to identify equal instances and concepts.

2. Search Step Selection. All entities of the first ontology are compared with all entities of the second ontology. Any pair is treated as a candidate mapping. This is generally the same for other mapping approaches, though the PROMPT algorithm can be implemented more efficiently by sorting the labels first, thus only requiring the comparison of two neighboring elements in the list.

Table 11.2. Features and Similarity Measures for Different Entity Types Contributing to Aggregated Similarity in NOM. The corresponding ontology is indicated through an index.

Comparing	No.	Feature	Similarity Measure
Concepts	1	(label,X_1)	string similarity(X_1, X_2)
	2	(URI_1)	string equality(URI_1, URI_2)
	3	(X_1,sameAs,X_2) relation	explicit equality(X_1, X_2)
	4	(direct properties,Y_1)	SimSet(Y_1, Y_2)
	5	all (inherited properties,Y_1)	SimSet(Y_1, Y_2)
	6	all (super-concepts,Y_1)	SimSet(Y_1, Y_2)
	7	all (sub-concepts,Y_1)	SimSet(Y_1, Y_2)
	8	(concept siblings,Y_1)	SimSet(Y_1, Y_2)
	9	(direct instances,Y_1)	SimSet(Y_1, Y_2)
	10	(instances,Y_1)	SimSet(Y_1, Y_2)
Relations	1	(label,X_1)	string similarity(X_1, X_2)
	2	(URI_1)	string equality(URI_1, URI_2)
	3	(X_1,sameAs,X_2) relation	explicit equality(X_1, X_2)
	4	(domain,X_d1) and (range,X_r1)	object equality(X_{d1}, X_{d2}), (X_{r1}, X_{r2})
	5	all (super-properties,Y_1)	SimSet(Y_1, Y_2)
	6	all (sub-properties,Y_1)	SimSet(Y_1, Y_2)
	7	(property siblings,Y_1)	SimSet(Y_1, Y_2)
	8	(property instances,Y_1)	SimSet(Y_1, Y_2)
Instances	1	(label,X_1)	string similarity(X_1, X_2)
	2	(URI_1)	string equality(URI_1, URI_2)
	3	(X_1,sameAs,X_2) relation	explicit equality(X_1, X_2)
	4	all (parent-concepts,Y_1)	SimSet(Y_1, Y_2)
	5	(property instances,Y_1)	SimSet(Y_1, Y_2)
Property-Instances	1	(domain,X_d1) and (range,X_r1)	object equality(X_{d1}, X_{d2}), (X_{r1}, X_{r2})
	2	(parent property,Y_1)	SimSet(Y_1, Y_2)

3. Similarity Computation. The similarity computation between an entity of O_1 and an entity of O_2 is done by using a wide range of similarity functions. Each similarity function is based on a feature (Sect. 11.4.1) of both ontologies and a respective similarity measure (Sect. 11.4.2). For NOM they are shown in Table 11.2.

The PROMPT system determines the similarity based on the exact equality (not only similarity) of labels. Anchor-PROMPT adds structural components. In GLUE the similarity is gained using the previously learned Similarity Estimator. It further adds other features using Relaxation Labelling based on the intuition that mappings of a node are typically influenced by the node's neighborhood.

4. Similarity Aggregation. NOM emphasizes high individual similarities and deemphasizes low individual similarities by weighting individual similarity results with a sigmoid function first and summing the modified values then. To produce an aggregated similarity (cf. Sect. 11.4.2) NOM applies $adj(x) = \frac{1}{1+e^{-5(x-0.5)}}$. Weights w_k are assigned by manually maximizing the f-measure on overall training data from different test ontologies.

In systems with one similarity value such as PROMPT or GLUE this step does not apply.

5. Interpretation. NOM interpretes similarity results by two means. First, it applies a threshold to discard spurious evidence of similarity. Second, NOM enforces bijectivity of the mapping by ignoring candidate mappings that would violate this constraint and by favoring candidate mappings with highest aggregated similarity scores.

As PROMPT is semi-automatic this step is less crucial. It presents all pairs with a similarity value above a relatively low threshold value and the users can decide to carry out the merging step or not. The relaxation labelling process of GLUE can also be seen as a kind of interpretation.

6. Iteration. The first round uses only the basic comparison method based on labels and string similarity to compute the similarity between entities. By doing the computation in several rounds one can access the already computed pairs and use more sophisticated structural similarity measures. Therefore, in the second round and thereafter NOM relies on all the similarity functions listed in Table 11.2.

PROMPT also requires these iterations after feedback has been given by the user. The GLUE system heavily relies on iterations for the relaxation labelling process. Neither PROMPT nor GLUE changes the strategies during the iterations.

11.5.2 QOM — Quick Ontology Mapping

The goal of this chapter is to present an efficient mapping algorithm. For this purpose, we optimize the effective, but inefficient NOM approach towards our goal. The outcome is QOM — Quick Ontology Mapping. We would also like to point out that the efficiency gaining steps can be applied to other mapping approaches as well.

1. Feature Engineering. Like NOM, QOM exploits RDF triples.

2. Search Step Selection. A major ingredient of run-time complexity is the number of candidate mapping pairs which have to be compared to actually find the best mappings. Therefore, we use heuristics to lower the number of candidate mappings. Fortunately, we can make use of ontological structures to classify the candidate mappings into promising and less promising pairs.

In particular we use a dynamic programming approach [3]. In this approach we have two main data structures. First, we have candidate mappings which ought to be investigated. Second, an agenda orders the candidate mappings, discarding some of them entirely to gain efficiency. After the completion of the similarity analysis and their interpretation new decisions have to be taken. The system has to determine which candidate mappings to add to the agenda for the next iteration. The behavior of initiative and ordering constitutes a search strategy.

We suggest the subsequent strategies to propose new candidate mappings for inspection:

Random A simple approach is to limit the number of candidate mappings by selecting either a fixed number or percentage from all possible mappings.

Label This restricts candidate mappings to entity pairs whose labels are near to each other in a sorted list. Every entity is compared to its "label"-neighbors.

Change Propagation QOM further compares only entities for which adjacent entities were assigned new mappings in a previous iteration. This is motivated by the fact that every time a new mapping has been found, we can expect to also find similar entities adjacent to these found mappings. Furthermore, to prevent very large numbers of comparisons, the number of pairs is restricted.

Hierarchy We start comparisons at a high level of the concept and property taxonomy. Only the top level entities are compared in the beginning. We then subsequently descend the taxonomy.

Combination The combined approach used in QOM follows different optimization strategies: it uses a label subagenda, a randomness subagenda, and a mapping change propagation subagenda. In the first iteration the label subagenda is pursued. Afterwards we focus on mapping change propagation. Finally, we shift to the randomness subagenda, if the other strategies do not identify sufficiently many correct mapping candidates.

With these multiple agenda strategies we only have to check a fixed and restricted number of mapping candidates for each original entity. Please note that the creation of the presented agendas does require processing resources itself.

3. Similarity Computation. QOM, just like NOM, is based on a wide range of ontology feature and heuristic combinations. In order to optimize QOM, we have restricted the range of costly features as specified in Table 11.3. In particular, QOM avoids the complete pair-wise comparison of trees in favor of a (n incomplete) top-down strategy. The marked comparisons in the table were changed from features which point to complete inferred sets to features only retrieving limited size direct sets.

Table 11.3. Features and Similarity Measures for Different Entity Types Contributing to Aggregated Similarity in QOM. The lower case "a" indicates that the feature has been modified for efficiency considerations.

Comparing	Change	Feature	Similarity Measure
Concepts	5	all (inherited properties, Y_1)	$\text{SimSet}(Y_1, Y_2)$
	$\longrightarrow$ 5a	(properties of direct super-concepts, Y_1)	$\text{SimSet}(Y_1, Y_2)$
	6	all (inherited super-concepts, Y_1)	$\text{SimSet}(Y_1, Y_2)$
	$\longrightarrow$ 6a	(direct super-concepts, Y_1)	$\text{SimSet}(Y_1, Y_2)$
	7	all (inherited sub-concepts, Y_1)	$\text{SimSet}(Y_1, Y_2)$
	$\longrightarrow$ 7a	(direct sub-concepts, Y_1)	$\text{SimSet}(Y_1, Y_2)$
	10	all (inherited instances, Y_1)	$\text{SimSet}(Y_1, Y_2)$
	$\longrightarrow$ 10a	(instances of direct sub-concepts, Y_1)	$\text{SimSet}(Y_1, Y_2)$
Relations	5	all (inherited super-properties, Y_1)	$\text{SimSet}(Y_1, Y_2)$
	$\longrightarrow$ 5a	(direct super-properties, Y_1)	$\text{SimSet}(Y_1, Y_2)$
	6	all (inherited sub-properties, Y_1)	$\text{SimSet}(Y_1, Y_2)$
	$\longrightarrow$ 6a	(direct sub-properties, Y_1)	$\text{SimSet}(Y_1, Y_2)$
Instances	4	all (inherited parent-concepts, Y_1)	$\text{SimSet}(Y_1, Y_2)$
	$\longrightarrow$ 4a	(direct parent-concepts, Y_1)	$\text{SimSet}(Y_1, Y_2)$

4. Similarity Aggregation. The aggregation of single methods is only performed once per candidate mapping and is therefore not critical for the overall efficiency. Therefore, QOM works like NOM in this step.

5. Interpretation. Also the interpretation step of QOM is the same as in NOM.

6. Iteration. QOM iterates to find mappings based on lexical knowledge first and based on knowledge structures later.

In all our tests we have found that after ten rounds hardly any further changes occur in the mapping table. This is independent from the actual size of the involved ontologies. QOM therefore restricts the number of runs.

Assuming that ontologies have a fixed percentage of entities with similar lexical labels, we will easily find their correct mappings in the first iteration. These are further evenly distributed over the two ontologies, i.e. the distance to the furthest not directly found mapping is constant. Through the change propagation agenda we pass on to the next adjacent mapping candidates with every iteration step. The number of required iterations remains constant; it is independent from the size of the ontologies.

11.6 Comparing Run-time Complexity

We determine the worst-case run-time complexity of the algorithms to propose mappings as a function of the size of the two given ontologies. Thereby, we wanted to base our analysis on realistic ontologies and not on artifacts. We wanted to avoid the consideration of large ontologies with n leaf concepts but a depth of the concept hierarchy H_C of $n - 1$. [19] have examined the structure of a large number of ontologies and found that concept hierarchies on average have a branching factor of around 2 and that the concept hierarchies are neither extremely shallow nor extremely deep. The actual branching factor can be described by a power law distribution. Hence, in the following we base our results on their findings.

Theorem 1. *The worst case run-time behaviors of NOM, PROMPT, Anchor-PROMPT, GLUE and QOM are given by the following table:*

NOM	$O(n^2 \cdot log^2(n))$
PROMPT[1]	$O(n \cdot log(n))$
Anchor-PROMPT	$O(n^2 \cdot log^2(n))$
GLUE[2]	$O(n^2)$
QOM	$O(n \cdot log(n))$

Proof Sketch 1 *The different algorithmic steps contributing to complexity[3] are aligned to the canonical process of Sect. 11.3.*

---

[3] In this paper we assume that the retrieval of a statement of an ontology entity from a database can be done in constant access time, independent of the ontology size, e.g. based on sufficient memory and a hash function.

For each of the algorithms, one may then determine the costs of each step. First, one determines the cost for feature engineering (feat). The second step is the search step i.e. candidate mappings selection (sele). For each of the selected candidate mappings (comp) we need to compute k different similarity functions sim_k and aggregate them (agg). The number of entities involved and the complexity of the respective similarity measure affect the run-time performance. Subsequently the interpretation of the similarity values with respect to mapping requires a run-time complexity of inter. Finally we have to iterate over the previous steps multiple times (iter).

Then, the worst case run-time complexity is defined for all approaches by:

$$c = (feat + sele + comp \cdot (\sum_k sim_k + agg) + inter) \cdot iter$$

Depending on the concrete values that show up in the individual process steps the different run-time complexities are derived in detail in [8].

11.7 Empirical Evaluation and Results

In this section we show that the worst case considerations carry over to practical experiments and that the quality of QOM is only negligibly lower than the one of other approaches. The implementation itself was coded in Java using the KAON-framework[1] for ontology operations.

11.7.1 Test Scenario

Metrics

We use standard information retrieval metrics to assess the different approaches (cf. [5]):

Precision $p = \frac{\#correct\_found\_mapping}{\#found\_mappings}$

Recall $r = \frac{\#correct\_found\_mappings}{\#existing\_mappings}$

F-Measure $f_1 = \frac{2pr}{p+r}$

Data Sets

Three separate data sets were used for evaluation purposes. As real world ontologies and especially their mappings are scarce, students were asked to independently create and map ontologies.[2]

Russia 1. In this first set we have two ontologies describing Russia. The students created the ontologies with the objective of representing the content of two independent travel websites about Russia. These ontologies have approximately 400 entities each, including concepts, relations, and instances. The total number of possible mappings is 160, which the students have assigned manually.

---

[1] http://kaon.semanticweb.org/
[2] The datasets are available from http://www.aifb.uni-karlsruhe.de/WBS/meh/mapping/.

Russia 2. The second set again covers Russia, but the two ontologies are more difficult to map. After their creation they have been altered by deleting entities and changing the labels at random. They differ substantially in both labels and structure. Each ontology has 300 entities with 215 possible mappings, which were captured during generation.

Tourism. Finally, the participants of a seminar created two ontologies which separately describe the tourism domain of Mecklenburg-Vorpommern. Both ontologies have an extent of about 500 entities. No instances were modelled with this ontology though, they only consist of concepts and relations. The 300 mappings were created manually.

Strategies

We evaluated the mapping strategies described in the previous sections:

- PROMPT — As the PROMPT algorithm is rather simple and fast we use it as a baseline to evaluate the speed. The empirical evaluation is based on the actual implementation of PROMPT rather than its theoretic potential, as described in the previous section.
- NOM / Anchor-PROMPT — Naive Ontology Mapping is an approach making use of a wide range of features and measures. Therefore it reaches high levels of effectiveness and represents our quality baseline. In terms of structural information used and complexity incurred it is similar to Anchor-PROMPT.
- QOM — Quick Ontology Mapping is our novel approach focusing on efficiency.

To circumvent the problem of having semi-automatic merging tools (PROMPT and Anchor-PROMPT) in our fully automatic mapping tests, we assumed that every proposition of the system is meaningful and correct. Further, as we had difficulties in running Anchor-PROMPT with the size of the given data sets, we refer to the results of the somewhat similar NOM. For GLUE we face another general problem. The algorithm has a strong focus on example instance mappings. As we can not provide this, we refrained from running the tests on a poorly trained estimator which would immediately result in poor quality results.

11.7.2 Results and Discussion

We present the results of the strategies on each of the data sets in Fig. 11.3 and 11.4. The tourism dataset shows similar characteristics as Russia 1 and is therefore not plotted. The x-axis shows the elapsed time on a logarithmic scale, the y-axis corresponds to the f-measure. The symbols represent the result after each iteration step.

Depending on the scenario, PROMPT reaches good results within a short period of time. Please notice that for ontologies with a small number of similar labels (Fig. 11.4) this strategy is not satisfactory (f-measure 0.06). In contrast, the f-measure value of the NOM strategy rises slowly but reaches high absolute values of up to

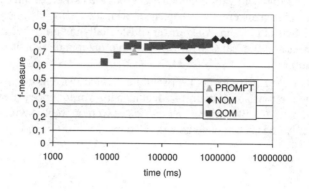

Fig. 11.3. Mapping quality reached over time with Russia 1 ontologies.

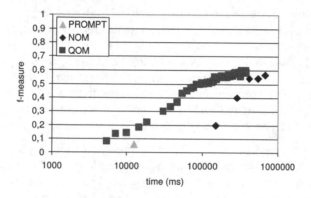

Fig. 11.4. Mapping quality reached over time with Russia 2 ontologies.

0.8. Unfortunately it requires a lot of time. Finally the QOM Strategy is plotted. It reaches high quality levels very quickly. In terms of absolute values it also seems to reach the best quality results of all strategies. This appears to be an effect of QOM achieving an about 20 times higher number of iterations than NOM within the given time frame.

Lessons Learned. We had the hypothesis that faster mapping results can be obtained with only a negligible loss of quality. We here briefly present the bottom line of our considerations in this paper:

1. Optimizing the mapping approach for efficiency — like QOM does — decreases the overall mapping quality. If ontologies are not too large one might prefer to avoid this.
2. Labels are very important for mapping, if not the most important feature of all, and alone already return very satisfying results.

3. Using an approach combining many features to determine mappings clearly leads to significantly higher quality mappings.
4. The Quick Ontology Mapping approach shows very good results. Quality is lowered only marginally, thus supporting our hypothesis.
5. QOM is faster than standard prominent approaches by a factor of 10 to 100 times.

Recapitulating, we can say that our mapping approach is very effective and efficient.

11.8 Related Work

We only present closely related work not yet mentioned in this paper.

Various authors have tried to find a general description of similarity with several of them being based on knowledge networks. [18] give a general overview of similarity.

Original work on mapping is presented by [16] in their tool ONION, which uses inferencing to execute mappings, but is based on manually assigned mappings or very simple heuristics. An interesting approach for schema and ontology mapping is presented in Chap. 9. Explicit semantic rules are added for consideration. A SAT solver is used to prevent mappings to imply semantical contradictions.

Despite the large number of related work on effective mapping already mentioned throughout this chapter, there are very few approaches raising the issue of efficiency.

Apart from the ontology domain research on mapping and integration has been done in various computer science fields. [1] present an approach to integrate documents from different sources into a master catalog. There has also been research on efficient schema and instance integration within the database community. [15] is a good source for an overview. Due to the different domain, comparisons with our approach are very difficult.

11.9 Conclusion

The problem of mapping two ontologies effectively and efficiently arises in many application scenarios [7, 12]. We have devised a generic process model to investigate and compare different approaches that generate ontology mappings. In particular, we have developed an original method, QOM, for identifying mappings between two ontologies. We have shown that it is on a par with other good state-of-the-art algorithms concerning the quality of proposed mappings, while outperforming them with respect to efficiency — in terms of run-time complexity ($O(n \cdot log(n))$ instead of $O(n^2)$) and in terms of the experiments we have performed (by a factor of 10 to 100). This technology has been successfully integrated into the SWAP applications Xarop and Bibster. As both applications have to provide mapping results on-the-fly and within a few seconds, QOM was the approach to use.

References

[1] Rakesh Agrawal and Ramakrishnan Srikant. On integrating catalogs. In *Proceedings of the tenth international conference on World Wide Web*, pages 603–612. ACM Press, 2001.

[2] G. Bisson. Why and how to define a similarity measure for object based representation systems. *Towards Very Large Knowledge Bases*, pages 236–246, 1995.

[3] M. Boddy. Anytime problem solving using dynamic programming. In *Proceedings of the Ninth National Conference on Artificial Intelligence*, pages 738–743, Anaheim, California, 1991. Shaker Verlag.

[4] T. Cox and M. Cox. *Multidimensional Scaling*. Chapman and Hall, 1994.

[5] H. Do, S. Melnik, and E. Rahm. Comparison of schema matching evaluations. In *Proceedings of the second int. workshop on Web Databases (German Informatics Society)*, 2002.

[6] A. Doan, P. Domingos, and A. Halevy. Learning to match the schemas of data sources: A multistrategy approach. *VLDB Journal*, 50:279–301, 2003.

[7] M. Ehrig, P. Haase, F. van Harmelen, R. Siebes, S. Staab, H. Stuckenschmidt, R. Studer, and C. Tempich. The SWAP data and metadata model for semantics-based peer-to-peer systems. In *Proceedings of MATES-2003. First German Conference on Multiagent Technologies*, LNAI, Erfurt, Germany, September 22-25 2003. Springer.

[8] M. Ehrig and S. Staab. Quick ontology mapping with QOM. Technical report, University of Karlsruhe, Institute AIFB, 2004. http://www.aifb. uni-karlsruhe.de/WBS/meh/mapping/.

[9] Marc Ehrig and Steffen Staab. QOM - quick ontology mapping. In Frank van Harmelen, Sheila McIlraith, and Dimitris Plexousakis, editors, *Proceedings of the Third International Semantic Web Conference (ISWC2004)*, LNCS, pages 683–696, Hiroshima, Japan, 2004. Springer.

[10] Marc Ehrig and York Sure. Ontology mapping - an integrated approach. In *Proceedings of the First European Semantic Web Symposium, ESWS 2004*, volume 3053 of *Lecture Notes in Computer Science*, pages 76–91, Heraklion, Greece, May 2004. Springer Verlag.

[11] J. Euzenat and P. Valtchev. An integrative proximity measure for ontology alignment. In Anhai Doan, Alon Halevy, and Natasha Noy, editors, *Proceedings of the Semantic Integration Workshop at ISWC-03*, 2003.

[12] A. Hotho, S. Staab, and G. Stumme. Ontologies improve text document clustering. In *Proceedings of the International Conference on Data Mining — ICDM-2003*. IEEE Press, 2003.

[13] I. V. Levenshtein. Binary codes capable of correcting deletions, insertions, and reversals. *Cybernetics and Control Theory*, 1966.

[14] Alexander Maedche and Steffen Staab. Measuring similarity between ontologies. In *Proceedings of the European Conference on Knowledge Acquisition and Management (EKAW)*. Springer, 2002.

[15] Andrew McCallum, Kamal Nigam, and Lyle H. Ungar. Efficient clustering of high-dimensional data sets with application to reference matching. In *Knowledge Discovery and Data Mining*, pages 169–178, 2000.

[16] Prasenjit Mitra, Gio Wiederhold, and Martin Kersten. A graph-oriented model for articulation of ontology interdependencies. *In Lecture Notes in Computer Science*, 1777:86+, 2000.

[17] Natalya F. Noy and Mark A. Musen. The PROMPT suite: interactive tools for ontology merging and mapping. *International Journal of Human-Computer Studies*, 59(6):983–1024, 2003.

[18] M. Andrea Rodríguez and Max J. Egenhofer. Determining semantic similarity among entity classes from different ontologies. *IEEE Transactions on Knowledge and Data Engineering*, 2000.

[19] Christoph Tempich and Raphael Volz. Towards a benchmark for semantic web reasoners - an analysis of the DAML ontology library. In York Sure, editor, *Evaluation of Ontology-based Tools (EON2003) at Second International Semantic Web Conference (ISWC 2003)*, October 2003.

12

Scalable, Peer-Based Mediation Across XML Schemas and Ontologies

Zachary G. Ives[1], Alon Y. Halevy[2], Peter Mork[2], Igor Tatarinov[2]

[1] Department of Computer and Information Science, University of Pennsylvania,
   Philadelphia, United States
   zives@cis.upenn.edu
[2] Department of Computer Science and Engineering, University of Washington, Seattle,
   United States
   {alon,pmork,igor}@cs.washington.edu

Summary. Research on the Semantic Web has focused on reasoning about data that is semantically annotated in the RDF data model, with concepts and properties specified in rich
ontology languages such as OWL. However, to flourish, the Semantic Web needs to provide
interoperability both between sites with different ontologies and with existing, non-RDF data
and the applications operating on them. To achieve this, we are faced with two problems. First,
most of the world's data is available not in RDF but in XML; XML and the applications consuming it rely not only on the domain structure of the data, but also on its document structure.
Hence, to provide interoperability between such sources, we must map between both their domain structures and their document structures. Second, data management practitioners often
prefer to exchange data through local point-to-point data translations, rather than mapping to
common mediated schemas or ontologies.

   In this chapter, we present the Piazza system, which addresses the challenges of medi-
ating between data sources on the Semantic Web by mapping both the domain structure and
document structure. A key aspect of Piazza is its support for mapping between XML data and
RDF data that is accompanied by OWL ontology definitions. Mappings in are provided at a
local scale between small sets of nodes, and Piazza's query answering algorithm is able to
chain sets mappings together to obtain relevant data from across the system. We describe our
experiences with the prototype Piazza system and a data sharing scenario implemented using
it.

12.1 Introduction

Much of the research focus on the Semantic Web is based on treating the Web as a
knowledge base defining meanings and relationships. In particular, researchers have
developed knowledge representation languages for representing *meanings* — relating them within custom ontologies for different domains — and *reasoning* about the
concepts. The best-known example is RDF and the languages that build upon it: RDF
Schema, DAML+OIL, and OWL [7].

The progress in developing ontologies and representation languages leaves us with two significant problems. The first problem (also noted by [17]) is that there is a wide disconnect between the RDF world and most of today's data providers and applications. RDF represents everything as a set of classes and properties, creating a graph of relationships. As such, RDF is focused on identifying the *domain structure*. In contrast, most existing data sources and applications export their data into XML, which tends to focus less on domain structure and more around important objects or entities. Instead of explicitly spelling out entities and relationships, they often nest information about related entities directly *within* the descriptions of more important objects, and in doing this they sometimes leave the relationship type unspecified. For instance, an XML data source might serialize information about books and authors as a list of book objects, each with an embedded author object. Although book and author are logically two related objects with a particular association (e.g., in RDF, author writes book), applications using this source may know that this *document structure* implicitly represents the logical writes relationship.

The vast majority of data sources (e.g., relational tables, spreadsheets, programming language objects, e-mails, and web logs) use hierarchical structures and references to encode both objects and domain structure-like relationships. Moreover, most application development tools and web services rely on these structures. Clearly, it would be desirable for the Semantic Web to be able to inter-operate with existing data sources and consumers — which are likely to persist indefinitely since they serve a real need. From the perspective of building Semantic Web applications, we need to be able to map not only between different domain structures of two sources, but also between their document structures.

The second challenge we face concerns the scale of ontology and schema mediation on the Semantic Web. Currently, it is widely believed that there will not exist a single ontology for any particular domain, but rather that there will be a few (possibly overlapping) ones. However, the prevailing culture, at least among users of data management tools, entails that the number of ontologies/schemas we will need to mediate among is actually substantially higher. Suppliers of data are not used to mapping their schemas to a select small set of ontologies (or schemas): it is very hard to build a consensus about what terminologies and structures should be used. In fact, it is for this reason that many data warehouse projects tend to fail precisely at the phase of schema design [20]. Interoperability is typically attained in the real world by writing translators (usually with custom code) among small sets of data sources that are closely related and serve similar needs, and then gradually adding new translators to new sources as time progresses. Hence, this practice suggests a practical model for how to develop a large-scale system like the Semantic Web: we need an architecture that enables building a web of data by allowing incremental addition of sources, where each new source maps to whatever sources it deems most convenient — rather than requiring sources to map to a slow-to-evolve and hard-to-manage standard schema. Of course, in the case of the Semantic Web, the mappings between the sources should be specified declaratively. To complement the mappings, we need efficient algorithms that can follow *semantic paths* to obtain data from distant but related nodes on the web.

The goal of the Piazza System is to pave the way for a fruitful combination of data management and knowledge representation techniques in the construction of the Semantic Web. As such, Piazza provides an infrastructure for building Semantic Web applications that is based on a *bottom-up* approach to the Semantic Web. The bottom-up approach begins with distributed sharing of XML data and building in expressive power from there.

A Piazza application consists of many nodes, each of which can serve either or both of two roles: supplying source data in its schema, or providing a schema (and later, an ontology) that can be queried. A very simple node might only supply data (perhaps from a relational database); at the other extreme, a node might simply provide a schema to which other nodes' schemas may be mapped. The semantic glue in Piazza is provided by *local* mappings between small sets (usually pairs) of nodes. When a query is posed over the schema of a node, the system will utilize data from any node that is transitively connected by semantic mappings, by *chaining* mappings. Piazza's architecture can accommodate both local point-to-point mappings between data sources, as well as collaboration through select mediated schemas. Since the architecture is reminiscent of Peer-to-Peer architectures, we refer to Piazza as a *peer data management system* (PDMS).

12.2 System Overview

We begin with an overview of the concepts underlying Piazza and our approach to building Semantic Web applications.

12.2.1 Data, Schemas, and Queries

Our ultimate goal with Piazza is to provide query answering and translation across the full range of data, from RDF and its associated ontologies to XML, which has a substantially less expressive schema language. The main focus of this paper is on sharing XML data, but we explain how RDF and OWL data instances can also be incorporated.

Today, most commercial and scientific applications have facilities for automatically exporting their data into XML form. Hence, for the purpose of our discussion, we can consider XML to be the standard representation of a wide variety of data sources (as do others [17]). In some cases, accessing the actual data may require an additional level of translation (e.g., with systems like [9, 18]). Perhaps of equal importance, many applications, tools, and programming languages or libraries have facilities for loading, processing, and importing XML data. In the ideal case, one could map the wealth of existing XML-style data into the Semantic Web and query it using Semantic Web tools; correspondingly, one could take the results of Semantic Web queries and map them back into XML so they can be fed into conventional applications.

RDF is neutral with respect to objects' importance: it represents a graph of interlinked objects, properties, and values. RDF also assigns uniform semantic meaning to certain reserved objects (e.g., containers) and properties (e.g., identifiers, object types, references). Relationships between pairs of objects are explicitly named. (This actually resembles what is done in entity-relationship diagrams, which are used to design relational databases.)

The main distinctions between RDF and unordered XML are that XML (unless accompanied by a schema) does not assign semantic meaning to any particular attributes, and XML uses hierarchy (membership) to implicitly encode logical relationships. Within an XML hierarchy, the central objects are typically at the top, and related objects are often embedded as subelements within the *document structure*; this embedding of objects creates binary relationships. Of course, XML may also include links and can represent arbitrary graphs, but the predominant theme in XML data is nesting. Whereas RDF names all binary relationships between pairs of objects, XML typically does not. The semantic meaning of these relationships is expressed within the schema (through keys, foreign keys, membership, and cardinality constraints) or simply within the interpretation of the data. Hence, it is important to note that although XML is often perceived as having only a syntax, it is more accurately viewed as a semantically grounded encoding for data, in a similar fashion to a relational database. Importantly, as pointed out by Patel-Schneider and Simeon [17], if XML is extended simply by reserving certain attribute names to serve as element IDs and IDREFs, one can maintain RDF semantics in the XML representation.

As with data, the XML and RDF worlds use different formalisms for expressing schema. The XML world uses XML Schema, which is based on object-oriented classes and database schemas: it defines classes and subclasses, and it specifies or restricts their structure and also assigns special semantic meaning (e.g., keys or references) to certain fields. In contrast, languages such as RDFS, DAML+OIL [12] and the various levels of OWL [7] come from the Knowledge Representation (KR) heritage, where ontologies are used to represent sets of objects in the domain and relationships between sets. OWL uses portions of XML Schema to express the structure of so-called *domain values*. In the remainder of this chapter, we refer to OWL as the representative of this class of languages.

Much of the functionality of KR descriptions and concept definitions can be captured in the XML world (and more generally, in the database world) using *views*. In the KR world, concept definitions are used to represent a certain set of objects based on constraints they satisfy, and they are compared via *subsumption* algorithms. In the XML world, queries serve a similar purpose, and furthermore, when they are named as views, they can be referenced by other queries or views. Since a view can express constraints or combine data from multiple structures, it can perform a role like that of the KR concept definition. Queries can be compared using *query containment* algorithms. There is a detailed literature that studies the differences between the expressive power of description logics and query languages and the complexity of the subsumption and containment problem for them (e.g., [14]). For example, certain forms of negation and number restrictions, when present in query expressions, make query containment undecidable, while arbitrary join conditions cannot be expressed and reasoned about in description logics.

12.2.2 Data Sharing and Mediation

Logically, a Piazza system consists of a network of different sites (also referred to as peers or nodes), each of which contributes resources to the overall system. The resources contributed by a site include one or more of the following: (1) ground or *extensional* data, e.g., XML or RDF data instances, (2) models of data, e.g., XML schemas or OWL ontologies. In addition, nodes may supply *computed data*, i.e., cached answers to queries posed over other nodes.

When a new site (with data instance or schema) is added to the system, it is semantically related to some portion of the existing network, as we describe in the next paragraph. Queries in Piazza are always posed from the perspective of a given site's schema, which defines the preferred terminology of the user. When a query is posed, Piazza provides answers that utilize all semantically related XML data within the system.

In order to exploit data from other sites, there must be *semantic glue* between the sites, in the form of semantic mappings. Mappings in Piazza are specified between small numbers of sites, usually pairs. In this way, we are able to support the two rather different methods for semantic mediation mentioned earlier: *mediated mapping*, where data sources are related through a mediated schema or ontology, and *point-to-point mappings*, where data is described by how it can be translated to conform to the schema of another site. Admittedly, from a formal perspective, there is little difference between these two kinds of mappings, but in practice, content providers may have strong preferences for one or the other.

12.2.3 Query Processing

Ultimately, the goal of a Semantic Web is to answer queries from users. In our system this means answering an XQuery when given a set of sites and the semantic mappings between them. There are two aspects to the query answering problem: (1) how to obtain a semantically correct set of operations for answering the query, and (2) how to process the resulting operations efficiently over the data. In this chapter we focus mostly on the first problem, called *query reformulation*. Section 12.5 describes a query answering algorithm for the Piazza mapping language: given a query at a particular site, we need to expand and translate it into appropriate queries over semantically related sites, as well. Query answering may require that we follow semantic mappings in both directions. In one direction, composing semantic mappings is simply query composition for an XQuery-like language. In the other direction, composing mappings requires using mappings in the reverse direction, which is known as the problem of answering queries using views [10]. These two problems are well understood in the relational database setting (i.e., when data is relational and mappings are specified as some restricted version of SQL), but they have only recently been treated in limited XML settings.

DTD for Source1.xml:	DTD for Source2.xml:	OWL definitions from Source3.rdf:
pubs	authors	`Class id = "book"`
book*	author*	`DataTypeProperty id = "bookTitle"`
title	full-name	`  domain = "#book"`
author*	publication*	`  range = "xsd:string"`
name	title	`DataTypeProperty id = "bookAuthor"`
publisher*	pub-type	`  domain = "#book"`
name		`  range = "#author"`
		`Class id = "author"`
		`DataTypeProperty id = "authorName"`
		`  domain = "#author"`
		`  range = "xsd:string"`

Fig. 12.1. Structures of three different data sources (two XML sources and one RDF source with an OWL ontology). Source1.xml contains books with nested authors; Source2.xml contains authors with nested publications. Indentation illustrates nesting and a * suffix indicates "0 or more occurrences of...", as in a BNF grammar. Source3.rdf is a set of OWL class and property definitions with a slightly simplified notation.

12.3 Mapping Requirements for Structured Data

Between any two independently developed ontologies or schemas, there is likely to be a significant variation in the representations of their data instances — partly because of unique preferences in different data modelers' approaches, and partly because of inherent differences in how data will be used. In this section, we briefly discuss some of the requirements for mapping schemas or ontologies on the Semantic Web, and we discuss how these fit into our framework.

We distinguish between modeling variations at the data-instance level from those at the schema/ontology level. At the data-instance level, values may have different representations (e.g., an address can be a single string or composed of several sub-fields; names can be represented differently). The common approach for handling such discrepancies are *concordance tables*, which use a binary relation of the form $(schema1\_attrib, schema2\_attrib)$ to describe associations between values in each of the representations. Note that concordance tables can represent $m : n$ correspondences as well as $1 : 1$ ones. Database query languages, including Piazza's mapping language, can easily make use of concordance tables by *joining* them with existing data items. Of course, the key question is how concordance tables are constructed. There is a significant work from both the artificial intelligence [16, 19] and database communities [2, 6]) on object matching, and recent work in [13] has looked at the problem of composing concordance table mappings. Piazza can make direct use of these existing matching algorithms and techniques, as well as any new ones that produce similar output.

At the schema level, the simplest form of a mapping is an attribute correspondence, where a property or attribute value in one representation corresponds to a different value in the other representation. This is the type of correspondence captured by OWL's owl:equivalentProperty construct. It is also possible to have correspondences at a higher level, that of the class (in ontologies) or view (in databases).

These can be very simple equivalences (as in owl:equivalentClass), or they can be more complex. For instance, a mapping may express containment (one view's results are contained in another's, or one class is subsumed by another), overlap (a subset of class 1 is equivalent to a subset of class 2), disjointness, and so on. An extra layer of complexity occurs when mapping concepts in an XML world: two classes may describe concepts that are semantically the same, but the XML representations may be structured differently. Mapping between such classes requires some form of *structural transformation*, one that includes both the ability to *coalesce* multiple entries and to *split* a single entry into multiple fragments. This particular type of structural mapping is the main innovation of Piazza's mapping language (see Sect. 12.4). Note that one class of XML we support is a serialization of RDF: here, we must convert from an RDF graph structure to an XML tree structure, or vice-versa. In the next section, we will illustrate mappings between XML sources and between XML and RDF. Our example XML DTDs and OWL ontology definition appear in Fig. 12.1.

Finally, there may be a need for so-called "higher-order" transformations, e.g., between a class in one ontology and a relationship in another. OWL has no capability for this, but most XML query languages, including XQuery, include support for *tag variables* that represent element or attribute tag names. We exploit this capability in Piazza to achieve certain kinds of higher-order mappings, e.g., between relationships and values.

12.4 Schema Mappings in Piazza

In this section, we describe the language we use for mapping between sites in a Piazza network. As described earlier, we focus on nodes whose data is available in XML (perhaps via a wrapper over some other system). For the purposes of our discussion, we ignore the XML document order. Each node has a schema, expressed in XML Schema, which defines the terminology and the structural constraints of the node. We make a clear distinction between the intended domain of the terms defined by the schema at a node and the actual data that may be stored there. Clearly, the stored data conforms to the terms and constraints of the schema, but the intended domain of the terms may be much broader than the particular data stored at the node. For example, the terminology for publications applies to data instances beyond the particular ones stored at the node.

Given this setting, mappings play two roles. The first role is as *storage descriptions* that specify which data is actually stored at a node. This allows us to separate between the intended domain and the actual data stored at the node. For example, we may specify that a particular node contains publications whose topic is Computer Science and have at least one author from the University of Washington. The second role is as *schema mappings*, which describe how the terminology and structure of one node correspond to those in a second node. The language for storage mappings is essentially indistinguishable from the language for schema mappings, hence our discussion focuses on the latter.

The ultimate goal of the Piazza system is to use mappings to answer queries; we answer each query by rewriting it using the information in the mapping. Of course, we want to capture structural as well as terminological correspondences. As such, it is important that the mapping capture maximal information about the relationship between schemas, but also about the data instances themselves — since information about content can be exploited to more precisely answer a query.

The field of data integration has spent many years studying techniques for precisely defining such mappings with relational data, and we base our techniques on this work. In many ways, the vision of Piazza is a broad generalization of data integration: in conventional data integration, we have a *mediator* that presents a *mediated schema* and a set of data sources that are mapped to this single mediated schema; in Piazza, we have a web of sites and semantic mappings.

The bulk of the data integration literature uses queries (views) as its mechanism for describing mappings: views can relate disparate relational structures, and can also impose restrictions on data values. There are two standard ways of using views for specifying mappings in this context: data sources can be described as views over the mediated schema (this is referred to as *local-as-view* or LAV), or the mediated schema can be described as a set of views over the data sources (*global-as-view* or GAV). The direction of the mapping matters a great deal: it affects both the kinds of queries that can be answered and the complexity of using the mapping to answer the query. In the GAV approach, query answering requires only relatively simple techniques to "unfold" (basically, macro-expand) the views into the query so it refers to the underlying data sources. The LAV approach requires more sophisticated query reformulation algorithms (surveyed in [10]), because we need to use the views in the *reverse* direction. It is important to note that in general, using a view in the reverse direction is not equivalent to writing an inverse mapping.

As a result of this, LAV offers a level of flexibility that is not possible with GAV. In particular, the important property of LAV is that it enables the description of data sources that organize their data *differently* from the mediated schema. For example, suppose the mediated schema contains a relationship Author, between a paper-id and an author-id. A data source, on the other hand, has the relationship CoAuthor that relates two author-id's. Using LAV, we can express the fact that the data source has the join of Author with itself. This description enables us to answer certain queries — while it is not possible to use the source to find authors of a particular paper, we can use the source to find someone's co-authors, or to find authors who have co-authored with at least one other. With GAV we would lose the ability to answer these queries, because we lose the association between co-authors. The best we could say is that the source provides values for the second attribute of Author.

This discussion has a very important consequence as we consider mappings in Piazza. When we map between two sites, our mappings, like views, will be directional. One could argue that we can always provide mappings in both directions, and even though this doubles our mapping efforts, it avoids the need for using mappings in reverse during query reformulation. However, when two sites organize their schemas differently, some semantic relationships between them will be captured only by the mapping in *one* of the directions, and this mapping cannot simply be inverted.

Instead, these semantic relationships will be exploited by algorithms that can reverse through mappings on a per-query basis, as we illustrated in our example above. Hence, the ability to use mappings in the reverse direction is a key element of our ability to share data among sites, and is therefore the focus of Section 12.5.

Our goal in Piazza has been to leverage both LAV and GAV algorithms from data integration, but to extend them in two important directions. First, we must extend the basic techniques from the two-tier data integration architecture to the peer data management system's heterogeneous, graph-structured network of interconnected nodes; this was the focus of our work in [11]. Our second direction, which we discuss in this chapter, is to move these techniques into the realms of XML and its serializations of RDF.

Following the data integration literature, which uses a standard relational query language for both queries and mappings, we might elect to use XQuery for both our query language and our language for specifying mappings. However, we found XQuery inappropriate as a mapping language for the following reasons. First, an XQuery user thinks in terms of the input documents and the transformations to be performed. The mental connection to a required schema for the output is tenuous, whereas our setting requires thinking about relationships between the input and output schemas. Second, the the user must define a mapping in its entirety before it can be used. There is no simple way to define mappings incrementally for different parts of the schemas, to collaborate with other experts on developing sub-regions of the mapping, etc. Finally, XQuery is an extremely powerful query language (it is, in fact, Turing-complete), and as a result some aspects of the language make it difficult or even impossible to reason about.

12.4.1 Mapping Language and Examples

Our approach is to define a mapping language that borrows elements of XQuery, but is more tractable to reason about and can be expressed in *piecewise* form. Mappings in the language are defined as one or more *mapping definitions*, and they are *directional* from a source to a target: we take a fragment of the target schema and annotate it with XML query expressions that define what source data should be mapped into that fragment. The mapping language is designed to make it easy for the mapping designer to visualize the target schema while describing where its data originates.

Conceptually, the results of the different mapping definitions are combined to form a complete mapping from the source document to the target, according to certain rules. For instance, the results of different mapping definitions can often be concatenated together to form the document, but in some cases different definitions may create content that should all be combined into a single element; Piazza must "fuse" these results together based on the output element's unique identifiers (similar to the use of Skolem functions in languages such as XML-QL [8]). A complete formal description of the language would be too lengthy for this paper. Hence, we describe the main ideas of the language and illustrate it via examples.

Each mapping definition begins with an XML template that matches some path or subtree of a legal instance of the target schema, i.e., a prefix of a legal string in the target DTD's grammar. Elements in the template may be annotated with query expressions (in a subset of XQuery) that bind variables to XML nodes in the source; for each combination of bindings, an instance of the target element will be created. Once a variable is bound, it can be referenced anywhere within its scope, which is defined to be the enclosing tags of the template. Variable bindings can be output as new target data, or they can be referenced by other query expressions to *correlate* data in different areas of the mapping definition. Figure 12.2(a) illustrates a simple initial mapping from the schema of Source2.xml of Fig. 12.1 to Source1.xml.

```
<pubs>
  <book>
    {: $a IN document("Source2.xml")/authors/author,
       $t IN $a/publication/title,
       $typ IN $a/publication/pub-type
       WHERE $typ = "book" :}
    <title>{ $t }</title>
    <author>
      <name> {: $a/full-name :} </name>
    </author>
  </book>
</pubs>
```

(a) Initial mapping

```
<pubs>
  <book piazza:id={$t}>
    {: $a IN document("Source2.xml")/authors/author,
       $t IN $a/publication/title,
       $typ IN $a/publication/pub-type
       WHERE $typ = "book" :}
    <title piazza:id={$t}>{ $t }</title>
    <author piazza:id={$t}>
      <name> {: $a/full-name :} </name>
    </author>
  </book>
</pubs>
```

(b) Refined mapping that coalesces entries

Fig. 12.2. Simple examples of mappings from the schema of Source2.xml in Fig. 12.1 to Source1.xml's schema.

We make variable references within { } braces and delimit query expression annotations by {: :}. This mapping definition will instantiate a new book element in the target for every occurrence of variables $a, $t, and $typ, which are bound to the author, title, and publication-type elements in the source, respectively. We construct a title and author element for each occurrence of the book. The author name contains a new query expression annotation ($a/full-name), so this element will be created for each match to the XPath expression (for this schema, there should only be one match).

The example mapping will create a new book element for each author-publication combination. This is probably not the desired behavior, since a book with multiple authors will appear as multiple book entries, rather than as a single book with multiple author subelements. To enable the desired behavior in situations like this, Piazza reserves a special piazza:id attribute in the target schema for mapping multiple binding instances to the same output: if two elements created in the target have the same tag name and ID attribute, then they will be *coalesced* — all of their attributes and element content will be combined. This coalescing process is repeated recursively over the combined elements.

Example 1. See Fig. 12.2(b) for an improved mapping that does coalescing of book elements. The sole difference from the previous example is the use of the piazza:id attribute. We have determined that book titles in our collection are unique, so every occurrence of a title in the data source refers to the *same* book. Identical books will be given the same piazza:id and coalesced; likewise for their title and author subelements (but not author names). Hence, in the target we will see all authors nested under each book entry. This example shows how we can *invert* hierarchies in going from source to target schemas.

Sometimes, we may have detailed information about the values of the data being mapped from the source to the target — perhaps in the above example, we know that the mapping definition only yields book titles starting with the letter "A." Perhaps more interestingly, we may know something about the possible values of an attribute present in the target but *absent* in the source — such as the publisher. In Piazza, we refer to this sort of meta-information as *properties*. This information can be used to help the query answering system determine whether a mapping is relevant to a particular query, so it is very useful for efficiency purposes.

Example 2. Continuing with the previous schema, consider the partial mapping:

```
<pubs>
  <book piazza:id={$t}>
    {: $a IN document("Source2.xml")/authors/author,
       $t IN $a/publication/title,
       $typ IN $a/publication/pub-type
       WHERE $typ = "book"
       PROPERTY $t >= 'A' AND $t < 'B'
    :}
    <title piazza:id={$t}>{ $t }</title>
    <author piazza:id={$t}>
      <name> {: $a/full-name :} </name>
    </author>
    [:
    <publisher>
      <name>
```

```
      {:PROPERTY $this IN {"PrintersInc", "PubsInc"}:}
      </name>
    </publisher>
    :]
  </book>
</pubs>
```

The first PROPERTY definition specifies that we know this mapping includes only titles starting with "A." The second defines a "virtual subtree" (delimited by [: :]) in the target. There is insufficient data at the source to insert a value for the publisher name; but we can define a PROPERTY restriction on the values it *might* have. The special variable $this allows us to establish a known invariant about the value at the current location within the virtual subtree: in this case, it is known that the publisher name must be one of the two values specified. In general, a query over the target looking for books will make use of this mapping; a query looking for books published by BooksInc will not. Moreover, a query looking for books published by PubsInc cannot use this mapping, since Piazza cannot tell whether a book was published by PubsInc or by PrintersInc.

Finally, while we have been focusing mostly on pure XML data to this point, our mappings are also useful in translating to and from XML serializations of RDF. (As in most real-world situations for data interchange, we assume that schema and class definitions have already been created, and our focus is on mapping the data from one representation to the other.) We now present an example that maps from XML to RDF and also uses value mappings from a concordance table.

Example 3. Suppose that we are attempting to map from Source2.xml of Fig. 12.1 and the OWL instance Source3.rdf. Furthermore, let us assume that the title of each book is specified differently in each of the sources (perhaps one source uses an all-caps format and the other uses mixed-case). Let us further assume that a concordance table, concordance.xml, has been populated and that it has a DTD of the following form:

```
table
  entry*
   source2-name
   source3-name
```

We can use the following mapping to map data from Source2.xml into Source3.rdf:

```
<book piazza:id={$s3}
rdf:id={"http://myorg.org/Source3/" + $s3}>
     {:  $a IN document("Source2.xml")/authors/author,
         $t IN $a/publication/title,
         $an IN $a/full-name
         $typ IN $a/publication/pub-type,
         $e IN document("concordance.xml")/table/entry,
```

```
              $s2 IN $e/source2-name,
              $s3 IN $e/source3-name
           WHERE $typ = "book" AND $t = $s2 :}
      <bookTitle rdf:resource={ "#" + $an } />
           <bookName>{$s3}</bookName>
      </bookTitle>
</book>
<author rdf:id={"http://myorg.org/Source3/" + $an}>
    {:  $a IN document("Source2.xml")/authors/author,
           $typ IN $a/publication/pub-type,
           $an IN $a/full-name
        WHERE $typ = "book" :}
    <authorName>{$an}</authorName>
</author>
```

This example highlights the ability to express a mapping between an XML data source and an RDF data source in Piazza. When an XML document adheres to a valid RDF serialization, it is accessible to Semantic Web applications. Piazza mappings can be used to convert arbitrary XML into valid RDF, and hence, and data that is available to Piazza (either directly or through following paths in Piazza) can be made accessible to Semantic Web applications. These mappings also capture semantic relationships between XML paths (like document("Source2.xml")/authors/author) and RDFS classes (e.g., author).

A more challenging question is to enable flow of data with richer semantics within Piazza. Specifically, Piazza mappings suffice for capturing equivalences between RDF classes and properties (including RDFS(FA) [15]), which means that in practice Piazza mappings cover most cases. Piazza mappings capture neither sub-/super-class relationships between elements (only between sources) nor do they capture the richness of description logics and therefore of data sources that employ OWL. In order for two sources in Piazza, both described using ontologies in OWL, to fully capture the semantics of each other's data, we need to extend our mapping language and query reformulation algorithms. While such extensions are beyond the scope of this chapter, techniques for answering queries using views described in description logics (e.g., [3, 5]) can be adapted to our context.

12.4.2 Semantics of Mappings

We briefly sketch the principles underlying the semantics of our mapping language. At the core, the semantics of mappings can be defined as follows. Given an XML instance, I_s, for the source node S and the mapping to the target T, the mapping defines a *subset* of an instance, I_t, for the target node. The reason that I_t is a subset of the target instance is that some elements of the target may not exist in the source (e.g., the publisher element in the examples). In fact, it may even be the case that required elements of the target are not present in the source. In relational terms, I_t is a *projection* of some complete instance I_t' of T on a subset of its elements and attributes. In fact, I_t defines a *set* of complete instances of T whose projection is

I_t. When we answer queries over the target T, we provide only the answers that are consistent with *all* such I_t's (known as the *certain answers* [1], the basis for specifying semantics in the data integration literature). It is important to note that partial instances of the target *are* useful for certain queries, in particular, when a query asks for a subset of the elements. Instances for T may be obtained from multiple mappings (and instances of the sources, in turn, can originate from multiple mappings), and as we described earlier, may be the result of coalescing the data obtained from multiple bindings using the piazza:id attribute.

A mapping between two nodes can either be an *inclusion* or an *equality* mapping (analogues of rdfs:subClassOf and owl:equivalentClass, respectively). In the former case, we can only infer instances of the target from instances of the source. In the latter case, we can also infer instances of the source from instances of the target. However, since the mapping is defined from the source to the target, using the mapping in reverse requires special reasoning. The algorithm for doing such reasoning is the subject of Section 12.5. Finally, we note that storage descriptions, which relate the node's schema to its actual current contents allow for both the *open-world assumption* or the *closed-world assumption*. In the former case, a node is not assumed to store all the data modeled by it schema, while in the latter case it is. In practice, very few data sources have complete information.

12.4.3 Discussion

To complete the discussion of our relationship to data integration, we briefly discuss how our mapping language relates to the LAV and GAV formalisms. In our language, we specify a mapping from the perspective of a particular *target schema* — in essence, we define the target schema using a GAV-like definition relative to the source schemas. However, two important features of our language would require LAV definition in the relational setting. First, we can map data sources to the target schema even if the data sources are missing attributes or subelements required in the source schema. Hence, we can support the situation where the source schema is a projection of the target. Second, we support the notion of data source *properties*, which essentially describes scenarios in which the source schema is a selection on the target schema.

Hence, our language combines the important properties of LAV and GAV. It is also interesting to note that although query answering in the XML context is fundamentally harder than in the relational case, specifying mappings between XML sources is more intuitive. The XML world is fundamentally semistructured, so it can accommodate mappings from data sources that lack certain attributes — without requiring null values. In fact, during query answering we allow mappings to pass along elements from the source that do not exist in the target schema — we would prefer not to discard these data items during the transitive evaluation of mappings, or query results would always be restricted by the lowest-common-denominator schemas along a given mapping chain. For this reason, we do not validate the schema of answers before returning them to the user.

While we have been discussing the relationship between our techniques and those of data integration, we remark that there are similar parallels in the knowledge representation community. Specifically, asserting that a derived (or complex) concept or property defined in the target ontology corresponds to a base property or class in a source ontology is similar in spirit to LAV, whereas asserting that a base property or class in the target ontology corresponds to a derived (or complex) concept or property in the source ontology corresponds to GAV.

12.5 Query Answering Algorithm

This section describes Piazza's query answering algorithm, which performs the following task: given a network of Piazza nodes with XML data, a set of semantic mappings specified among them, and a query over the schema of a given node, efficiently produce *all* the possible *certain answers* that can be obtained from the system.

From a high level, an algorithm proceeds along the following lines. Given a query Q posed over the schema of node P, we first use the storage descriptions of data in P (i.e., the mappings that describe which data is actually stored at P) to rewrite Q into a query Q' over the data stored at P. Next, we consider the *semantic neighbors* of P, i.e., all nodes that are related to elements of P's schema by semantic mappings. We use these mappings to expand the reformulation of query Q to a query Q'' over the neighbors of P. In turn, we expand Q'' so it only refers to stored data in P and its neighbors; then we union it with Q', eliminating any redundancies. We repeat this process recursively, following all mappings between nodes' schemas, and the storage mappings for each one, until there are no remaining useful paths.

Ignoring optimization issues, the key question in designing such an algorithm is how to reformulate a query Q over its semantic neighbors. Since semantic mappings in Piazza are directional from a source node S to a target node T, there are two cases of the reformulation problem, depending on whether Q is posed over the schema of S or over that of T. If the query is posed over T, then query reformulation amounts to query composition: to use data at S, we compose the query Q with the query (or queries) defining T in terms of S. Our approach to XML query composition is based on that of [9], and we do not elaborate on it here.

The second case is when a query is posed over S and we wish to reformulate it over T. Now both Q and T are defined as queries over S. In order to reformulate Q, we need to somehow use the mapping in the *reverse* direction, as explained in the previous section. This problem is known as the problem of answering queries using views (see [10] for a survey), and it is conceptually much more challenging. The problem is well understood for the case of relational queries and views, and we now describe an algorithm that applies to the XML setting. The key challenge we address for the context of XML is the nesting structure of the data (and hence of the query) — relational data is flat.

DTD for S1.xml: DTD for S2.xml: Query over S1.xml:

```
people        people       <result> {
 faculty*      faculty*      for $faculty in
  name          student        document("S1.xml")/people/faculty,
  advisee*      name           $name in $faculty/name/text(),
 student*      advisor*       $advisee in $faculty/advisee/text()
                             where $name = "Ullman"
                             return
                               <student> {$advisee} </student>
                           } </result>
```

Fig. 12.3. Two schemas about advisors and students, and a query posed over one of the schemas.

12.5.1 Query Representation

Our algorithm operates over a graph representation of queries and mappings. Suppose we start with the schemas of Fig. 12.3, which differ in how they represent advisor-advisee information. S1 puts advisee names under the corresponding faculty advisor whereas S2 does the opposite by nesting advisor names data under corresponding students. Now suppose we are provided with a mapping from S1 to S2, and we are attempting to answer the XQuery of Fig. 12.3.

The query is represented graphically by the leftmost portion of Fig. 12.4. Note that the `result` element in the query simply specifies the root element for the resulting document. Each box in the figure corresponds to a query block, and indentation indicates the nesting structure. With each block we associate the following constructs that are manipulated by our algorithm:

A set of tree patterns: XQuery uses XPath expressions in the FOR clause to bind variables, e.g., `$faculty in document("S1.xml")/people/faculty` binds the variable `$faculty` to the nodes satisfying the XPath expression. The bound variable can then be used to define new XPath expressions such as `$faculty/name` and bind new variables. Our algorithm consolidates XPath expressions into logically equivalent *tree patterns* for use in reformulation[1]. For example, the tree pattern for our example query is indicated by the thick forked line in the leftmost portion of Fig. 12.4.

For simplicity of presentation, we assume here that every node in a tree pattern binds a single variable; the name of the variable is the same as the tag of the corresponding tree pattern node. Hence, the node `advisee` of the tree pattern binds the variable `$advisee`.

A set of predicates: a predicate in a query specifies a condition on one or two of the bound variables. Predicates are defined in the XQuery WHERE clause over the variables bound in the tree patterns. The variables referred to in the predicate can be bound by different tree patterns. In our example, there is a single predicate:

---

[1] We focus on the subset of XPath that corresponds to regular path expressions, so tree patterns capture the required semantics.

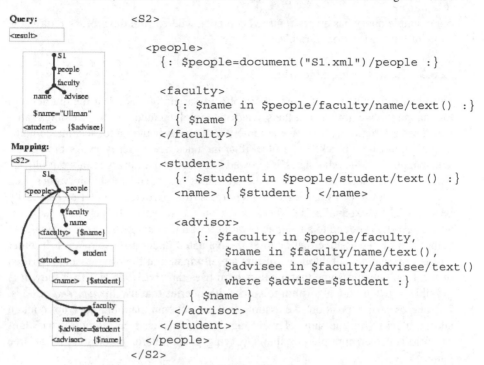

```
Query:                           <S2>
<result>
                                   <people>
      S1                             { : $people=document("S1.xml")/people : }
        people
        faculty                      <faculty>
   name    advisee                     { : $name in $people/faculty/name/text() : }
                                        { $name }
    $name="Ullman"                   </faculty>
   <student>   {$advisee}

Mapping:                             <student>
<S2>                                   { : $student in $people/student/text() : }
                                       <name> { $student } </name>
      S1
   <people>   people                   <advisor>
                                          { : $faculty in $people/faculty,
         faculty                              $name in $faculty/name/text(),
           name                               $advisee in $faculty/advisee/text()
   <faculty>  {$name}                         where $advisee=$student : }
                                          { $name }
          student                        </advisor>
   <student>                           </student>
                                     </people>
   <name>  {$student}              </S2>

           faculty
      name    advisee
      $advisee=$student
   <advisor>  {$name}
```

Fig. 12.4. Matching a query tree pattern into a tree pattern of a schema mapping. The matching tree patterns are shown in bold. The schema mapping corresponding to the middle graph is shown on the right.

name="Ullman". If a predicate involves a comparison between two variables, then it is called a *join* predicate, because it essentially enforces a relational join.

A set of variable equivalence classes: the equality predicates in a query define the equivalence classes (ECs) between query variables. EC information allows for "substituting" a variable for an equivalent one. Note that the ECs of a query block contain the ECs of the outer blocks. In other words, if a block has the condition $x = $y, the same condition applies in all of the inner blocks (but not vice versa).

Output results: output, specified in the XQuery RETURN clause, consists of element or attribute names and their content. An element tag name is usually specified in the query as a string literal, but it can also be the value of a variable. This is an important feature, because it enables transformations in which data from one source becomes schema information in another. In our query graph of Fig. 12.4, an element tag is shown in angle brackets. Hence, the element tag of the top-level block is result. The element tag of the inner block is student. The contents of the returned element of a query block may be a sequence of elements, attributes, string literals, or variables. (Note that our algorithm does not support "mixed content," in which subelements and data values may be siblings, as this makes reformulation much harder). We limit our discussion to the case of a single returned item. In the figure, the variable/value returned by a query block is enclosed in curly braces. Thus, the top level block of our example query has empty returned contents, whereas the inner block returns the value of the $advisee variable.

12.5.2 The Rewriting Algorithm

Our algorithm makes the following simplifying assumptions about the queries and the mappings (we note that in the scenario we implemented, all the mappings satisfied these restrictions). First, we assume the query over the target schema contains a single non-trivial block, i.e., a block that includes tree patterns and/or predicates. The mapping, on the other hand, is allowed to contain an arbitrary number of blocks. Second, we assume that all "returned" variables are bound to atomic values, i.e., text() nodes, rather than XML element trees (this particular limitation can easily be removed by expanding the query based on the schema). In Fig. 12.4 the variable $people is bound to an element; variables $name and $student are bound to values. Third, we assume that queries are evaluated under a set semantics. In other words, we assume that duplicate results are eliminated in the original and rewritten query. Finally, we assume that a tree pattern uses the *child* axis of XPath only. It is possible to extend the algorithm to work with queries that use the *descendant* axis. For purposes of exposition, we assume that the schema mapping does not contain sibling blocks with the same element tag. Handling such a case requires the algorithm to consider multiple possible satisfying paths (and/or predicates) in the tree pattern.

The pseudocode for the algorithm is shown in Fig. 12.5. In the rest of this section we describe the algorithm in more detail. Intuitively, the rewriting algorithm performs the following tasks (see the *rewriteQueryBlock* function in the pseudocode). Given a query Q, it begins by comparing the tree patterns of the mapping definition with the tree pattern of Q — the goal is to find a corresponding node in the mapping definition's tree pattern for every node in the Q's tree pattern. Then the algorithm must restructure Q's tree pattern to parallel the way the mapping restructures its input tree patterns (Q must be rewritten to match against the *target* of the mapping rather than its source). That is done in the function *rewriteTreePattern*. Next, the algorithm considers the variable(s) returned by the query and makes sure that the variables are still available in the rewritten query. The function *rewriteVar* is used here. Finally, the algorithm must ensure that the predicates of Q can be satisfied using the values output by the mapping, see function *rewritePredicates*. The steps performed by the algorithm are:

Step 1: Pattern matching and rewriting. This step (function *rewriteTreePattern*) considers the tree patterns in the query, and finds corresponding patterns in the target schema. Intuitively, given a tree pattern, t in Q, our goal is to find a tree pattern t' on the target schema such that the mapping guarantees that an instance of that pattern could only be created by following t in the source. The algorithm first matches the tree patterns in the query to the expressions in the mapping and records the corresponding nodes. In Fig. 12.4, the darker lines in the representation of the schema mapping denote the tree pattern of the query (far left) and its corresponding form in the mapping (second from left). The algorithm then creates the tree pattern over the

```
Query rewriteQuery(Query q, Mapping m) {
        // we assume q contains only one non-trivial block
        return new Query(rewriteQueryBlock(q.queryBlock, m));
}


// return a single rewriting; we note when multiple rewritings are possible
QueryBlock rewriteQueryBlock(QueryBlock qb, Mapping m) {

        // assume a single tree pattern in the query; the case of multiple tree patterns can be reduced to a single pattern
        TreePattern rtp = rewriteTreePattern(qb.treePattern, m);

        // may need to extend the rewritten tree pattern (rtp) to rewrite the content variable
        // multiple rewritings are possible here due to many equivalent vars and different ways of extending rtp.
        Set eqVars = qb.eqClassMap[qb.contentVar];
        Var rContentVar = rewriteVar(eqVars, rtp, m);
        If failure, return failure — not possible to rewrite the content variable.

        For each pred in qb.predicates {
                Check if the predicate is already enforced in the mapping (1) // see text
                If success, no need to add the predicate to the rewritten query block
                Else
                        // rewrite the predicate; multiple rewritings are possible. (2)
                        Predicate rPred = rewritePredicate(pred, rtp, m).
                        If success add rPred to the rewritten query block and consider next predicate.
                        Else
                                Try extending rtp so that an equivalent predicate in the mapping applies. (3)
                                If success, no need to add the predicate to the rewritten query block.
                                Else
                                        Try "folding" rtp to enforce pred as described in text (4)
                                        If success, no need to add the predicate to the rewritten query block
                                        Else return failure.

        }
        return new QueryBlock(rtp, rPreds, rContentVar);
}

// this function rewrites a given query tree pattern using a mapping.
TreePattern rewriteTreePattern(TreePattern tp, Mapping m) {
        Map m.tp into tp; m.tp may have extra branches (path expressions) in all possible ways
        Return a rewritten tp that navigates through the matching block structure of m
}

// rewrite one of the given equivalent vars; extend the given rtp if necessary
Var rewriteVar(Set vars, TreePattern rtp, Mapping m) {
        // pick one of the equivalent vars; in general every equiv. var will result in a different rewriting
        Find if any of the mapping blocks corresponding to rtp return a variable that is the image
        of one of the "vars"; if so, return the original var.

        Try extending rtp so that one of the "var" images is returned.
        If success, return the original var;
        Else return failure — no way to get any of the equiv. variables using the mapping
}

// rewrite a given query predicate; make sure all vars are available
Predicate rewritePredicate(Predicate pred, TreePattern rtp, Mapping m) {
        Rewrite each of pred's variables using rewriteVar(); if success, return rPred.
        // can't rewrite the predicae
        return failure;
}
```

Fig. 12.5. The algorithm for rewriting a single-block query using a mapping.

target schema as follows: starting with the recorded nodes in the mapping, it recursively marks all of their ancestor nodes in the output template. It then builds the new tree pattern over the target schema by traversing the mapping for all marked nodes.

Note that t' may enforce additional conditions beyond those of t, and furthermore, there may be several patterns in the target that match a pattern in the query, ultimately yielding several possible queries over the target that provide answers to Q. If no match is found, then the resulting rewriting will be empty (i.e., the target data does not enable answering the query at the source).

Step 2: Handling returned variables and predicates. In this step the algorithm ensures that all of the variables required in the query can be returned, and that all of the predicates in the query have been applied. Here, the nesting structure of XML data introduces subtleties beyond the relational case.

To illustrate the first potential problem, recall that our example query returns advisee names, but the mapping does not actually return the advisee, and hence the output of Step 1 does not return the advisee. We must extend the tree pattern to reach a block that actually outputs the $advisee element, but the <advisor> block where $advisee is bound does not have any subblocks, so we cannot simply extend the tree pattern. Fortunately, the <advisor> block includes an equality condition that puts the $advisee and $student variables in the same equivalence class. Since $student is output by the <name> block we can rewrite the tree pattern as $student in document("S2.xml")/people/student, $advisor in $student/advisor, $name in $student/name. Of course, it is not always possible to find such equalities, and in those cases there will be no rewriting for that pattern.

Query predicates raise another problem. Predicates can be handled in one of the four ways as noted in the pseudocode. First, case (1), a query predicate (or one that subsumes it) might already be applied by the relevant portion of the mapping (or it might be a known property of the data being mapped). In this case, the algorithm can consider the predicate to be satisfied. Case (2) occurs when the mapping does not impose the predicate, but returns all variables necessary for testing the predicate. Here, the algorithm simply inserts the predicate into the rewritten query. The third possibility, case (3), is more XML-specific: the predicate is not applied by the portion of the mapping used in the query rewriting, nor can the predicate be evaluated over the mapping's output — but a different sub-block in the mapping may impose the predicate. If this occurs, the algorithm can *add a new path* into the rewritten tree pattern, traversing into the sub-block. Now the rewritten query will only return a value if the sub-block (and hence the predicate) is satisfied. Finally, case (4) applies when the mapping contains the required predicate, but the rewritten tree pattern has to be "massaged" or folded as described below in order for case (1) to be applicable.

In our example query, the predicate can be reformulated in terms of the variables bound by the replacement tree pattern as follows: $advisor="Ullman". Hence, case (2) applies and the resulting rewritten query is the following:

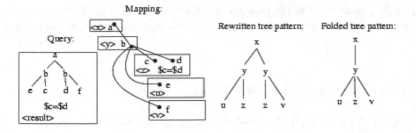

Fig. 12.6. Folding the rewritten tree pattern for predicate rewriting. The result of rewriting the query tree pattern (on the left) using the mapping, cannot be used to enforce the predicate of the query. The folded tree pattern on the right can.

```
<result> {
  for $student in document("S2.xml")/people/student,
      $advisor in $student/advisor/text(),
      $name in $student/name/text()
  where $advisor = "Ullman"
  return
    <student> { $name } </student>
}
</result>
```

In order to test if a given predicate in the mapping can be used to enforce a query predicate as in case (1), the following condition needs to be satisfied. For each variable in the mapping predicate, we find the node in the rewritten tree pattern that corresponds to that variable. If the resulting set of nodes lie on a single path from the root, the mapping predicate is applicable; otherwise, it is not. To illustrate this rule, consider the example query shown as a tree in Fig. 12.6. The single-block query in this example contains a predicate $c=$d. The mapping does not return the variables matching $c and $d, however. Hence, the only way to enforce the predicate is to exploit a predicate in the query. Unfortunately, the rewritten tree pattern does not allow for that as the two z nodes corresponding to the query variables $c and $d do not lie on one path from the root. To fix this problem, the tree pattern needs to be "folded," see case (4) in the pseudocode, along the $y and $z nodes as shown on the right in this Figure. The resulting tree pattern is more restrictive but it allows for exploiting the predicate in the mapping. Note that because folding results in a more restrictive tree pattern, it should only be applied when it is necessary for predicate enforcement. Otherwise, some answers may be lost.

Note that in the above discussion, we always made the assumption that a mapping is useful if and only if it returns all output values and satisfies all predicates. In many cases, we may be able to loosen this restriction if we know more information about the relationships within a set of mappings, or about the properties of the mappings. For instance, if we have two mappings that share a key or a parent element, we may be able to rewrite the query to use both mappings if we add a join predicate on the key or the parent element ID, respectively. Conversely, we may be able to make use of properties to determine that a mapping cannot produce any results satisfying the query.

12.6 Conclusions and Future Work

The vision of the Semantic Web [4] is compelling and will certainly lead to significant changes in how the Web is used, but we are faced with a number of technical obstacles in realizing this vision. Knowledge representation techniques and standardized ontologies will undoubtedly play a major role in the ultimate solution. However, we believe that the Semantic Web cannot succeed if it requires everything to be rebuilt "from the ground up": it must be able to make use of structured data from non-Semantic Web-enabled sources, and it must inter-operate with traditional applications. This requires the ability to deal not only with domain structure, but also with document structures that are used by applications. Moreover, mediated schemas and ontologies can only be built by consensus, so they are unlikely to scale.

The Piazza peer data management architecture addresses these two problems with the following innovations. First, we designed a language for mapping between sets of XML source nodes with different document structures (including those with XML serializations of RDF). Second, we deployed an architecture that uses the transitive closure of mappings to answer queries. Third, we implemented an algorithm for query answering over this transitive closure of mappings, which is able to follow mappings in both forward and reverse directions, and which can both remove and reconstruct XML document structure.

Our prototype suggests that our architecture provides useful and effective mediation for heterogeneous structured data, and that adding new sources is easier than in a traditional two-tier environment. Furthermore, the overall Piazza system gives us a strong research platform for uncovering and exploring issues in building a semantic web.

References

[1]   Serge Abiteboul and Oliver Duschka. Complexity of answering queries using materialized views. In *Proceedings of the Seventeenth ACM SIGMOD-SIGACT-SIGART Symposium on Principles of Database Systems, June 1-3, 1998, Seattle, Washington, USA*, pages 254–263, Seattle, WA, 1998.

[2]   Rohit Ananthakrishna, Surajit Chaudhuri, and Venkatesh Ganti. Eliminating fuzzy duplicates in data warehouses. In *VLDB 2002, Proceedings of 28th International Conference on Very Large Data Bases, Hong Kong, China*, 2002.

[3]   Catriel Beeri, Alon Y Levy, and Marie-Christine Rousset. Rewriting queries using views in description logics. In *Proceedings of the Sixteenth ACM SIGACT-SIGMOD-SIGART Symposium on Principles of Database Systems*, page 99Ű108, Tucson, AZ, 1997. ACM Press.

[4]   Tim Berners-Lee, James Hendler, and Ora Lassila. The semantic web. *Scientific American*, May 2001.

[5]   Diego Calvanese, Giuseppe De Giacomo, and Maurizio Lenzerini. Answering queries using views in description logics. In *Working notes of the KRDB Workshop*, 1999.

[6]   Surajit Chaudhuri, Kris Ganjam, Venkatesh Ganti, and Rajeev Motwani. Robust and efficient fuzzy match for online data cleaning. In *SIGMOD 2003, Proceedings of the ACM SIGMOD International Conference on Management of Data, June 9-12, 2003, San Diego, California, USA*, 2003.

[7]   Mike Dean, Dan Connolly, Frank van Harmelen, James Hendler, Ian Horrocks, Deborah L. McGuinness, Peter F. Patel-Schneider, and Lynn Andrea Stein. OWL web ontology language 1.0 reference. Available from http://www.w3c.org/TR/2002-WD-owl-ref-20020729/, 29 July 2002. W3C Working Draft.

[8]   Alin Deutsch, Mary F. Fernandez, Daniela Florescu, Alon Levy, and Dan Suciu. A query language for XML. In *Proceedings of the Eighth International Word Wide Web Conference, Toronto, CA, 1999*. World-Wide Web Consortium, 1999.

[9]   Mary Fernandez, Weng-Chiew Tan, and Dan Suciu. SilkRoute: Trading between relations and XML. In *Proceedings of the Ninth International World Wide Web Conference, Amsterdam, NL, 2000*. World-Wide Web Consortium, November 1999.

[10] Alon Y. Halevy. Answering queries using views: A survey. *VLDB Journal*, 10(4):270–294, 2001.

[11] Alon Y. Halevy, Zachary G. Ives, Dan Suciu, and Igor Tatarinov. Schema mediation in peer data management systems. In *Proceedings of the 19th International Conference on Data Engineering, March 5-8, 2003, Bangalore, India*. IEEE Computer Society, March 2003.

[12] Ian Horrocks, Frank van Harmelen, and Peter Patel-Schneider. DAML+OIL. http://www.daml.org/2001/03/daml+oil-index.html, March 2001.

[13] Anastasios Kementsietsidis, Marcelo Arenas, and Renée J. Miller. Mapping data in peer-to-peer systems: Semantics and algorithmic issues. In Alon Y. Halevy, Zachary G. Ives, and AnHai Doan, editors, *SIGMOD 2003, Proceedings of the ACM SIGMOD International Conference on Management of Data, June 9-12, 2003, San Diego, California, USA*. ACM, June 2003.

[14] Alon Levy and Marie-Christine Rousset. Combining Horn rules and description logics in CARIN. *AIJ*, 104:165–209, September 1998.

[15] Jeff Z Pan and Ian Horrocks. Metamodeling architecture of web ontology languages. In *Proc. of the 2001 International Semantic Web Working Symposium*, page 131Ű149, 2001.

[16] Hanna Pasula and Stuart J. Russell. Approximate inference for first-order probabilistic languages. In *IJCAI '01*, pages 741–748, 2001.

[17] Peter Patel-Schneider and Jerome Simeon. Building the Semantic Web on XML. In *International Semantic Web Conference 2002, Sardinia, Italy, June 9-12, 2002*, June 2002.

[18] Michael Rys. Bringing the internet to your database: Using SQLServer 2000 and XML to build loosely-coupled systems. In *Proceedings of the 17th International Conference on Data Engineering, April 2-6, 2001, Heidelberg, Germany*, pages 465–472. IEEE Computer Society, 2001.

[19] Sheila Tejada, Craig A. Knoblock, and Steven Minton. Learning object identification rules for information integration. *Information Sys ems Journal Special Issue on Data Extraction, Cleaning, and Reconciliation*, December 2001.

[20] Paul Westerman. *Data Warehousing: Using the Wal-Mart Model*. Morgan Kaufmann Publishers, 2000.

13

Semantic Gossiping: Fostering Semantic Interoperability in Peer Data Management Systems

Karl Aberer, Philippe Cudré-Mauroux, Manfred Hauswirth

School of Computer and Communication Sciences, Ecole Polytechnique Fédérale de Lausanne (EPFL), Switzerland
{karl.aberer,philippe.cudre-mauroux,manfred.hauswirth}@epfl.ch

Summary. Until recently, most data integration techniques revolved around central approaches, e.g., global schemas, to enable transparent access to heterogeneous databases. However, with the advent of the Internet and the democratization of tools facilitating knowledge elicitation in machine-processable formats, the situation is quickly evolving. One cannot rely on global, centralized schemas anymore as knowledge creation and consumption are getting increasingly dynamic and decentralized. Peer Data Management Systems (PDMS) address this problem by eliminating centralization and instead applying compositions of local, pair-wise mappings to propagate queries among databases. We present a method to foster global semantic interoperability in PDMS settings in a totally decentralized way based on the analysis of the semantic graph linking data sources with pairwise semantic mappings. We describe how quality measures for the mappings can automatically be derived by analyzing transitive closures of mapping operations. The information obtained from these analyses are then used by the peers to route queries in a network of semantically heterogeneous sources, and to iteratively correct erroneous mappings in a self-organizing way. Additionally, we present heuristics to analyze semantic interoperability in large and heterogeneous communities. Finally, we describe Grid-Vine which implements our approach and provides a semantic overlay to demonstrate how our approach can be deployed in a practical setting.

13.1 Introduction

Ubiquitous availability of digital equipment has transformed end-users into industrious producers of digital content. As a matter of fact, electronic devices not only produce content, but also metadata — for example date and time when a picture was taken, technical information on the quality of a photo, or even GPS coordinates. Additionally, users often annotate their information with further metadata to increase usability. From an information systems point of view, this means that the information producers, the "domain experts," augment automatically produced metadata with high-quality domain-specific metadata at the data source.

As digital content is shared over the Internet, enormous amounts of data suddenly become available, additionally to the local data already available anyway. This proliferation of digital content calls for the development of large-scale infrastructures to share, integrate, and process massive amounts of data in a meaningful way. For example, it would be highly interesting to connect photos which are annotated with GPS coordinates to descriptions of the locations. This is just a simple, yet rather useful example, e.g., when it comes to travel planning. Many other interesting applications can be imagined. All of them, however, require the availability of metadata and their integration, as no universal metadata schema exists and is unlikely to exist ever.

Peer-to-Peer (P2P) systems already enable the efficient sharing of information on a global scale. Integration and use of metadata, however, falls short in these systems. Current P2P systems either impose a simple semantic structure a-priori (e.g., Napster or Kazaa) and leave the burden of semantic annotation and integration to the user, or do not address the issue of semantics at all (e.g., Gnutella, standard DHT-based infrastructures) but simply support a semantically unstructured data representation and leave the burden of "making sense" to the skills of the user, e.g., by providing pseudo-structured file names such as *Enterprise-2x03-Mine-Field* that encapsulate very simple semantics.

This situation exemplifies again a key problem in current Internet information systems: the lack of semantic interoperability. Semantic interoperability is a crucial element for making distributed information systems usable. It is a prerequisite for structured, distributed search, data exchange, and data integration, and provides the foundations for higher level services and processing. Classical attempts to make information resources semantically interoperable, in particular in the domain of database integration, do not scale well to global information systems such as P2P systems. Despite a large number of approaches and concepts, such as federated databases, the mediator concept [8], or ontology-based information integration approaches [5, 6], practically engineered solutions are still frequently hard-coded and require substantial support from human experts. Typical examples of such systems are domain-specific portals such as CiteSeer (*citeseer.ist.psu.edu*, publication data), SRS (*srs.ebi.ac.uk*, biology) or *streetprices.com* (e-commerce). They integrate data sources on the Internet and store them in a central warehouse. The data is converted to a common schema, which usually is of simple to medium complexity. This approach adopts a simple form of wrapper-mediator architecture and typically requires substantial development efforts for the automatic or semi-automatic generation of mappings from the data sources into the central schema.

Following the P2P paradigm, new architectures addressing the issue of semantic interoperability without relying on central coordination/knowledge have recently appeared. These architectures, today commonly referred to as *peer data management systems* (PDMS), rely on pair-wise mappings (e.g., views) to foster semantic interoperability among heterogeneous information parties. In the following, we present an approach for obtaining semantic interoperability in PDMS as a result of an iterative process. We assume that users who are interested in information from other users provide mappings between their own metadata (schema) and other metadata (schemas). Also we assume that users make these pair-wise, local mappings accessible. We then build on the principle of gossiping, which has been successfully applied for creating useful global behaviors in P2P systems.

In any P2P system, search requests are routed in a network of interconnected information systems. We extend the operation of these systems as follows: When different schemas are involved, local mappings are used to further distribute a search request to other semantic domains. The quality of search results in a gossiping-based approach clearly depends on the quality of the local translations in the translation graph. To take this into account, *our fundamental assumption is that the translation links/schema mappings may be incorrect*. Thus, our mechanisms try to determine which translations can be trusted and which cannot and take this into consideration to guide the search process.

In the following we will present our model in detail and identify different methods that can be applied to estimate the quality of local mappings. We elaborate the details of each of these methods for a simple example. The information obtained from these analyses are then used by the peers to direct searches in the network of semantically heterogeneous information sources, and to iteratively correct erroneous mappings in a self-organizing way. Also, we develop heuristics to analyze semantic interoperability in large and heterogeneous communities. Finally, we present our *GridVine* system, which implements our approach and provides a semantic overlay to demonstrate how our approach can be deployed in a practical setting.

We believe that this radically new approach to semantic interoperability shifts the attention from problems that are inherently difficult to solve in an automated manner at the global level (*"How do humans interpret information models in terms of real world concepts?"*), to a problem that leaves vast opportunities for automated processing and for increasing the value of existing information sources, namely the processing of existing local semantic relationships in order to raise the level of their use from local to global semantic interoperability.

13.2 Motivation: Sharing Images Meaningfully

Scanners, digital cameras, webcams or new generations of cell phones: Over the last few years, we have witnessed a constant evolution and miniaturization of digital imaging equipment. Digital technologies have superseded traditional imaging technologies in most aspects of our everyday life. As a result, it is today not uncommon for end-users to store hundreds of megabytes or even gigabytes of images on their personal devices. The ways of sharing these images remain, however, rather primitive. Thus, most pictures remain local while only a small fraction get shared, either through simple web galleries or point-to-point communication (e.g., SMTP or MMS). Distributed search capabilities are equally flawed, as they often revolve around keyword searches on the filename of the image (often a serial number nowadays) or take advantage of low-level features (color moments, textures) barely connected to higher-level semantics.

Digital imaging devices offer a real opportunity for creating large-scale sharing infrastructures by leveraging on local metadata production. An increasing number of approaches use metadata to organize images locally: The Extensible Metadata Platform (XMP), Adobe Photoshop Album or Microsoft WinFS are just a few examples of this new trend. The question is: Why are these local metadata not exploited in the large? Because of two fundamental hurdles (see Fig. 13.1):

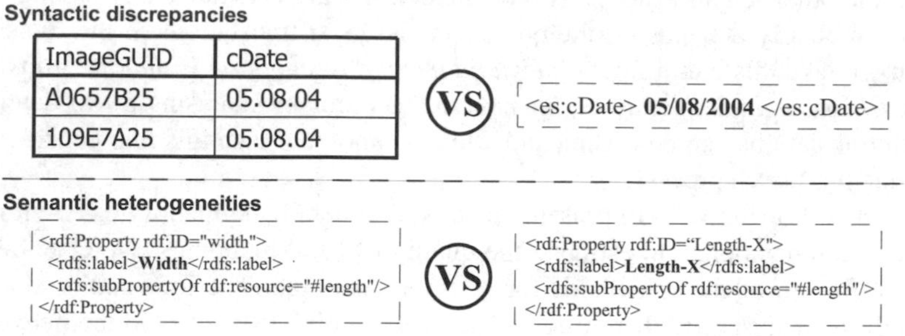

Syntactic discrepancies

ImageGUID	cDate
A0657B25	05.08.04
109E7A25	05.08.04

VS   `<es:cDate> 05/08/2004 </es:cDate>`

Semantic heterogeneities

```
<rdf:Property rdf:ID="width">
    <rdfs:label>Width</rdfs:label>
    <rdfs:subPropertyOf rdf:resource="#length"/>
</rdf:Property>
```

VS

```
<rdf:Property rdf:ID="Length-X">
    <rdfs:label>Length-X</rdfs:label>
    <rdfs:subPropertyOf rdf:resource="#length"/>
</rdf:Property>
```

Fig. 13.1. Two hurdles preventing the exploitation of local metadata in the large

Syntactic discrepancies: Data models can differ among tools. Even for a single data model, radically different encoding schemes often coexist. Although well-documented, reconciling different formats is still a tedious and error-prone task in practice. For example, in the upper part of Fig. 13.1, a relational representation is used on the left side while the right side uses a semi-structured model to encode the same information. Orthogonal to this issue, there is also the problem of translating items which cannot be represented in another format. This may lead to significant loss of information, especially while translating a query from one semantic domain into another (see Sec. 13.4).

Semantic heterogeneities: It is worth noticing that all the aforementioned metadata platforms are extensible, i.e., they all expect end-users to define their own vocabulary to describe data. In such a context, common agreements on the data model and encoding scheme cannot alone guarantee semantic interoperability. Some ontological commitment on the various concepts introduced by the peers is required to ensure meaningful communication. For example, in the lower part of Fig. 13.1, both sides define the same concept but use different concept names. Of course, this is just a very simple example, yet it would already impair integration and query forwarding in current P2P systems.

The second problem is particularly difficult to tackle in decentralized environments like the one we are considering. Indeed, standard semantic reconciliation techniques (e.g., LAV or GAV) rely on a predefined, global schema, which would be impossible to enforce in a world-wide P2P context. In the following, we explore a different avenue by considering local schemas and schema mappings only, incrementally integrating them and guiding the integration with quality measures.

13.3 Of Semantic Neighborhoods and Schema Translations

Without constraining general applicability, we assume that there exists a P2P communication facility among the participants that enables sending and receiving of information, i.e., queries, data, and schema information. In the P2P system, groups of peers may have agreed on common semantics, i.e., a common schema. We denote these groups as *semantic neighborhoods*. The size of a neighborhood may range from a single individual peer up to any number. If two peers located in two disjoint neighborhoods meet, they can exchange their schemas and provide mappings between them (how peers meet and how they exchange this information depends on the underlying system but does not concern our approach). Figure 13.2 shows a simple mapping graph assuming each of the peers (denoted by circles) uses its own schema.

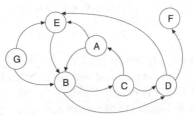

Fig. 13.2. Mapping graph among semantic neighborhoods

The direction of the mapping and the peer providing a mapping are not necessarily correlated. For example, peers A and B might both provide a mapping from $schema(A)$ to $schema(B)$, and they may exchange these mappings upon discretion. Figure 13.3 shows an example of how mappings among heterogeneous schemas can be applied to support query forwarding. In this example we use XML and XQuery as one possible way to encode the mappings. In fact, our approach works irrespective of the data model (see Sec. 13.7 for an application based on triples), mapping or query language used.

By providing a mapping translation ($T12$) among the Photoshop and the WinFS schema (see figure), queries against the Photoshop database ($Q1$) can also be posed against a WinFS database ($Q2$). Both the queries and the translation are expressed in XQuery. Assuming that the two databases reside at two different peers, this setup enables data integration and query forwarding.

During the life-time of the system, each peer has the possibility to learn about existing mappings and may add new ones. This means that a directed graph of mappings as shown in Fig. 13.2 will be built between the neighborhoods along with the normal operation of the system, e.g., query processing and query forwarding in a P2P system.

The mapping graph has two interesting properties: (1) based on the already existing mappings and the ability to learn about existing mappings, new mappings can be

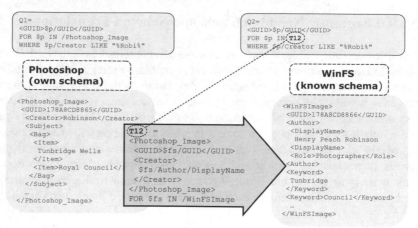

Fig. 13.3. A translation link using a mapping in XQuery to transform queries

added automatically by means of transitivity, for example, $D \rightarrow E \rightarrow B \Rightarrow D \rightarrow B$ and (2) the graph has cycles. (1) means that we can propagate queries towards peers for which no direct translation link exists. This is what we call *Semantic Gossiping*. (2) gives us the possibility to assess the degree of *semantic agreement* along a cycle, i.e., to measure the quality of the translations and the degree of semantic agreement in a community.

In such a system, we expect peers to perform several task: (1) upon receiving a query, a peer has to decide where to forward the query to, based on a set of criteria that will be introduced below; (2) upon receiving results or feedback (cycle), it has to analyze the quality of the results at the schema and at the data level and adjust its criteria accordingly; and (3) it has to update its view of the overall semantic agreement.

The criteria to assess the quality of translations — which in turn is a measure of the semantic agreement — can be categorized as *syntactic* and *semantic*. Syntactic criteria relate only to the processed query and to the required translation. For example, by *syntactic similarity* we denote the extent to which a query is preserved after translation (lost attributes, etc.). Semantic criteria relate to the degree of agreement that can be achieved among different peers upon specific translations. Such degrees of agreement may be computed using feedback mechanisms, for example from cycles in the translation graph or from results returned. This means that a peer will locally obtain both returned queries and data through multiple cycles. In case a disagreement is detected (e.g., a wrong attribute mapping at the schema level or the violation of a constraint at the data level), the peer has to suspect that at least some of the mappings involved in the cycle were incorrect, including the mapping it has used itself to propagate the query. Even if an agreement is detected, it is not clear whether this is not accidentally the result of compensating mapping errors along the cycle. Thus, analyses are required that assess which are the most probable sources of errors along cycles, to what extent the own mapping can be trusted and therefore how to use these mappings in future routing decisions. At a global level, we can view the problem as follows: The translations among domains of semantic homogeneity (i.e., sets of related schemas) form a directed graph. Within that directed graph we find cycles. Each cycle allows to return a query to its originator which in turn can make the analysis described above.

Assuming all the peers implement this approach, we expect the network to converge to a state where a query is only forwarded to the peers that most-likely understand it ("can understand it") and where the correct mappings are increasingly reinforced by adapting the per-hop forwarding behaviors of the peers. Implicitly, this is a state where a *global agreement* on the semantics of the different schemas has been reached.

13.4 Semantic Query Routing

To assess the quality of schema translations we use a set of measures which guide the query forwarding process. The analysis includes (1) a syntactic assessment that covers issues such as loss of attributes, combination of attributes, etc., and (2) semantic analyses that address correctness of translations at the schema and the data level. If the combination of these measures is above a certain threshold, then a query will be forwarded over a certain link, otherwise it will be dropped. The analysis is done continuously, such that query routing paths will change dynamically over time, mirroring the situation in the network.

The query forwarding algorithm itself looks as follows:

1. When a query is first received, return potential results.
2. In case the local neighborhood has not received the query, forward it to the local neighborhood.
3. Detect any semantic cycles and do the necessary bookkeeping.
4. When a query is first received, perform the following operations for each of the outgoing links for which a translation is known:
   a) Apply the translation to the query.
   b) Update the similarity measures for the transformed query.
   c) Test the similarity measures against predefined thresholds.
   d) Forward the query if all similarity measure tests succeed, i.e., if the transformed query can still be considered as close enough to the original query.

In the following we give an informal overview of the measures we use and how to compute them. Complete mathematical definitions and derivations are given in [1].

13.4.1 Syntactic Measures

When forwarding a query through a translation link, parts of the query may be lost since the schema which the query is mapped onto may not have a representation for the information contained in the original schema. *Syntactic similarity* provides a measure which is related to this type of information loss during translation. This measure is context-independent since its evaluation relies exclusively on the inspection of the syntactic features of the translated queries. A high syntactic similarity does not ensure that forwarding a query is useful, but conversely a low syntactic similarity implies that it might not be useful to further forward a query.

Let us suppose we have a relational query q, originally applied to database DB_1 with schema S_1. Assume a transformation T of query q is given, such that q can be evaluated against database DB_2 with schema S_2, i.e., $T(q)(DB_2)$, which again can be given in the form of a query. T is the schema mapping we have discussed in the previous section. The problem we need to assess in analyzing the quality of T in respect to syntactic similarity is that it might occur that attributes used in q are no longer available after applying T to q, i.e., they are lost. These losses may be of varying degrees as the importance of attributes is query dependent. We have two issues to consider after applying a composite transformation $T = T_1 \circ \ldots \circ T_n$.

Not all attributes in selection predicates are preserved. In terms of SQL, these are the attributes used in the predicates of the WHERE clause of the statement. If some of these attributes cannot be mapped, some of the predicates will not be correctly evaluated (in our case, the predicates will simply be dropped). Depending on the selectivity of the predicate, this might be harmful to different degrees. We capture this by assigning selectivity values $\in [0, 1]$ to all selection predicates. High values indicate highly selective attributes, i.e., attributes whose predicates select a small proportion of the database. Thus dropping highly selective and thus more critical attributes will lead to lower the value of this measure. In conjunction with additional user-defined importance weights we can derive a syntactic similarity measure in respect to selection. The overall similarity measure combines all attribute measures and will decrease proportionally to the relative weight and selectivity of every attribute lost in the selection.

Not all projection attributes are preserved. In terms of SQL, these are the attributes used in the SELECT clause of the statement. If not all projection attributes are preserved, the results returned may be incomplete or even erroneous. Following the method used above for selection, we capture this by calculating a value $\in [0, 1]$. Again, this similarity measure combines the individual attribute measures and decreases with the number of translations applied to the query, until it reaches 0 when all the projection attributes are lost.

13.4.2 Semantic Measures

The context-independent measure of syntactic similarity is based on the assumption that the query transformations are semantically correct, which in general might not be the case. A better way to view semantics is to consider it as an agreement among peers. If two peers agree on the meaning of their schemas, then they will generate compatible translations. From that basic observation, we will clearly need context-dependent measures of *semantic similarity*. These measures will allow us to assess the quality of attributes that are preserved in the translations. We use two mechanisms for deriving the quality of a translation. One mechanism, *cycle analysis*, is based on analyzing the correctness of translations at the schema level, the other one, *result analysis*, is based on analyzing the quality of query results at the data level.

Cycle Analysis

For the first mechanism, we exploit the fact that in forwarding queries, circles may occur. A translation T applied to a query actually means that a peer p_1 applies a translation T to a query and forwards it to a peer p_2. For this we use the abbreviated notation $T_{p_1 \to p_2}$. A circle then simply means that there exists a sequence $T_{p_1 \to p_2}, T_{p_2 \to p_3}, \ldots T_{p_n \to p_1}$ for some $n > 1$. The returning query q_n is of the form $q_n = (T_{p_1 \to p_2} \circ T_{p_2 \to p_3} \circ \ldots \circ T_{p_n \to p_1})(q_1)$. p_1 may now analyze the differences between the original query q and the returning query q_n. It could attempt to check whether the composed transformation is equivalent to the identity transformation. identity, but the approach we propose here appears to be more practical. We inspect all attributes present in the original query distinguishing three cases:

1. The attribute is maintained throughout the cycle. This indicates that all the peers along the cycle agree on the meaning of the attribute, which increases the confidence in the correctness of the translations used (*positive feedback*).
2. The attribute is lost. This means that someone along the cycle had no representation for the attribute which is thus not part of the common semantics; This case is handled by the syntactic analyses. This leaves the semantic confidence in the translations unchanged (*neutral feedback*).
3. The attribute is mapped onto another attribute in the returning query. This indicates some semantic confusion along the cycle. Subcases can occur depending on the cases. This lowers the confidence in the translations (*negative feedback*).

Clearly p_1 may receive multiple cycle messages from different cycles and we have derived heuristics which allow p_1 to assess the correctness of the translation $T_{p_1 \to p_2}$ it has used based on the different cycle messages it receives. These heuristics also have to take into account *compensating errors*, i.e., series of independent translation errors resulting in a correct overall translation that may occur along the cycle of foreign links without being noticed by p_1, which only has the final result q_n at its disposal. Again, we come up with an overall measure whose value starts from 1 (in the semantic domain which the query originates from) and decreases as the query traverses increasingly semantically heterogeneous domains. A detailed mathematical derivation of this similarity measure, along with longer explanations, is given in [1].

Result Analysis

The second mechanism for analyzing the semantic quality of the translations is based on the analysis of the results returned. Although the results returned to a peer may be correct at the schema level, the data returned may not necessarily make sense. By using low-level analyses on the returned content, a peer can determine whether or not it received what it was expected to receive. Queries in our metadata model are an intensional way of expressing semantic concepts, whereas extensionally the concepts are related to sets of documents. By relating the intensional notion of a concept from the query it sent to the extensional notion of the concept as conveyed by the results it received, a peer can try to assess the semantic quality of the translation links which have been used to forward the query.

These analyses also result in positive and negative feedback which can be combined into an overall measure for the quality of the translation links. Again, we refer the interested reader to [1] for the low-level conceptual and mathematical details.

13.4.3 An illustrating example

To illustrate query forwarding and the application of the syntactic and semantic measures, let us consider the simple semantic network depicted in Fig. 13.4.

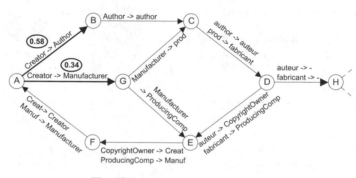

Fig. 13.4. A simple semantic network

The network is composed of eight peers $(A \dots H)$ sharing digital pictures that have been annotated independently. Peer A wants to retrieve images based on the name of their creator. A can use two translation links to forward its query: the translation link between A and B, mapping A's *Creator* onto B's *Author*, and the translation link between A and G, mapping *Creator* to *Manufacturer*.

A runs the analyses to assess the quality of its outgoing translation links for its *Creator* attribute. It issues a simple query which gets propagated to all the nodes except H, which has no representation for the attribute in question (thus, the syntactic similarity drops to zero and the query is not forwarded). A detects three cycles involving *Creator*: $A \rightarrow B \rightarrow C \rightarrow D \rightarrow E \rightarrow F \rightarrow A$, which yields positive feedback (as the transitive closure of the translations maps *Creator* onto itself), and $A \rightarrow G \rightarrow E \rightarrow F \rightarrow A$ and $A \rightarrow G \rightarrow C \rightarrow D \rightarrow E \rightarrow F \rightarrow A$, which both yield negative feedback. By applying our heuristics, A gets 0.58 and 0.34 for the semantic quality measure of the first and the second mapping respectively. Clearly, there is some disagreement on the mappings involving G. Thus, A chooses to discard the second link and forwards the query through B only, where the semantics of its query are more likely to be preserved.

13.5 Self-Healing Semantic Networks

So far, we have applied Semantic Gossiping techniques to evaluate the quality of various mappings and selectively forward queries to groups of peers. Going one step further, we now take advantage of the semantic similarity results to attempt to detect mapping errors and incrementally correct them. In this way, Semantic Gossiping can be used to automatically refine semantic agreements in a large community of heterogeneous information parties.

We conducted series of experiments to evaluate this approach. We proceeded iteratively as follows: We construct a network of peers (representing each a semantic domain) interconnected with translation links using a small-world topology. We start with a certain percentage of erroneous translation links (i.e., erroneous mappings). For each iteration step, peers first have to randomly select one of their local attributes and send out a probe query for this attribute. Probe queries are routed irrespective of the syntactic analysis with a Time-To-Live (TTL) value indicating how many translation links they can traverse. Peers can evaluate the correctness of their outgoing translation links on the basis of the positive or negative feedback they receive or detect. Peers then attempt to modify their mappings in order to maximize the similarity results. They finally adopt the most probably correct mapping according to our analyses.

What is the result of this process in the long run? It depends of course on the initial setting but in the end, our method attempts to obtain a mapping consensus based on the feedback received from the rest of the network. Considering a high density of links and relatively few erroneous links, the method converges (i.e., repairs all erroneous mappings) rapidly, since peers can base their decisions on numerous and meaningful feedback cycles or documents. For settings where links are scarce, peers do not have sufficient information for making sensible choices, and results may diverge.

We give below a few examples illustrating this point. Complete experimental results may be found in [1]. Figure 13.5 shows the sensitivity to the number of translation links l connected to each peer (cycle analysis only): the higher the number of links, the greater the number of cycles which can be detected. We start with $eRate = 10\%$ of erroneous links (Y-axis) and iteratively conduct series of cycle analyses (X-axis). For low numbers of translation links, peers simply do not get sufficient feedback information to correct mappings. For high values (e.g., 5 translation links per domain), peers receive sufficient information to correct most (or even all) of the erroneous mappings after nine iterations. Thus, the importance of the density of the translation links in a network of heterogeneous peers.

Figure 13.6 below shows some scalability results. Given that the peers apply the methods we have presented in their vicinity only and that we do not rely on any

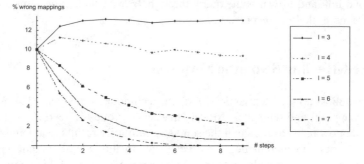

Fig. 13.5. Sensitivity to the number l of translation links/peer (cycle analysis only) for 25 peers, 4 attributes/peer and $TTL = 5$ hops

central component or computation, it is not surprising to see that the results are rather insensitive to the network size.

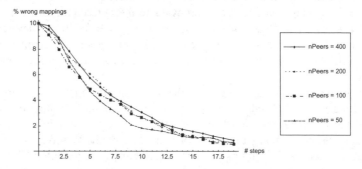

Fig. 13.6. Scalability (result analysis only) for 4 attributes/peer, 2 translation links/peer, $TTL = 3$ hops, 10% of misclassified documents, 2 documents/peer on average and a varying number of peers

Combining both the cycle and the result analyses, we can push the evaluation further and apply our healing process on very faulty topologies. Figure 13.7 reports on an experiment where at each step, every peer first performs a result analysis step (modifying the mappings depending on the results returned) and then performs a cycle analysis step (trying to reach some local agreement on mappings based on cycle feedback). This method takes longer to converge than the two analyses applied separately; This is because the analyses keep interfering with each other until some state is reached that is consistent from both a cycle and a feedback analysis point of view.

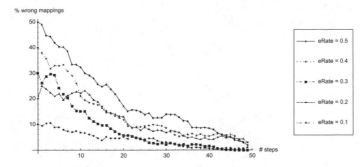

Fig. 13.7. Combined results for 25 peers, 4 attributes/peer and 2 translation links/peer, $TTL = 3$ hops (results), $TTL = 6$ hops (cycles), 10% of misclassified documents, 2 documents/peer on average and a varying percentage of erroneous mappings

13.6 Analyzing Semantic Interoperability in the Large

Considering the results from the previous section, one can observe some correlation between the topology of the network of translation links and the quality of the semantic agreement which can be achieved. This observation inspired us to develop new techniques to analyze semantic interoperability in very large networks.

Imagine a large set of peers creating and mapping schemas through translation links. The degree of interconnection of the resulting network of schemas may vary depending on the location and the number of translation links: It can be in a state where schemas are largely disconnected (subcritical state) or in a state where there are enough translation links to actually interconnect most of the schemas (supercritical state). Based on the degree distribution and some statistical aspects of the graph, and by applying a recent graph-theoretic framework, we were able to determine (see [4]) the point at which the network of translations starts to percolate, i.e., the point at which the number of translation links is such that most peers are connected to each other through transitive closures of translation links. This is highly important as a large network of peers simply cannot be semantically interoperable before this point, due to the lack of translation links.

This result also enables us to predict to what extent a query can be propagated through the P2P network. Figure 13.8 shows the size of the out-component—the maximal fraction of the overall network a peer is able to reach by forwarding a query through series of translation links—in a randomly generated directed graph of *10 000* heterogeneous peers (vertices) with an increasing number of translation links (edges).

The two curves represent the relative size of the component (a) as evaluated using our graph-theoretic method and (b) as really found in the graph. As can be seen the two curves nearly perfectly match which indicates the correctness of our prediction method. As a practical application, this method can be used to measure the minimum

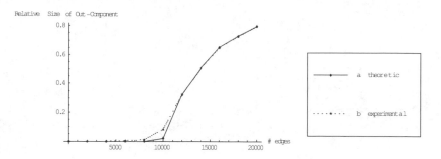

Fig. 13.8. Size of the out-component in a random network of *10 000* vertices

number of translations required in a network so that it can start to self-organize and further optimize integration. It can also be used to predict an upper-bound on the number of semantic neighborhoods a query can reach.

13.7 GridVine: Implementing Semantic Gossiping on top of a DHT

To demonstrate the applicability of our approach, we implemented it in our Grid-Vine [2] system. The Semantic Gossiping approach maps quite naturally onto unstructured P2P systems as they can gossip at the physical layer. In fact, most existing proposals for schema integration and query forwarding are based on some form of unstructured P2P system offering this capability. In contrast to that, we based GridVine on a structured P2P system, which is more scalable and use considerably less resources in terms of networking bandwidth. Distributed hash tables (DHTs) as Chord, CAN, Pastry or P-Grid, which are all variants of the approach suggested by Plaxton [7], are considered as the most promising candidates for next-generation P2P systems. They typically offer $\mathcal{O}(log(n))$ search complexity, with n being the number of participating peers. Although the performance and scalability of these systems are much better than that of unstructured P2P systems, they impose new problems for P2P data management approaches as broadcasting is replaced by more efficient search mechanisms.

We based GridVine on the P-Grid (http://www.p-grid.org) P2P system. In Grid-Vine, we address the problem of building scalable semantic overlay networks by following the principle of data independence and separate the logical from the physical layer (see Fig. 13.9).

At the logical layer, we support various operations necessary for the use and maintenance of a semantic overlay network within the standard syntactic framework of RDF/OWL. We let end-users derive new schemas to annotate the content they

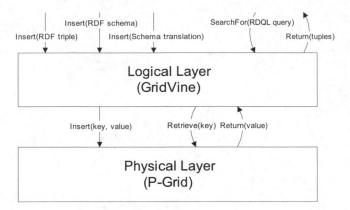

Fig. 13.9. GridVine: separating the logical from the physical layer

want to share and define simple mappings to relate their schemas to other schemas. Annotations are encoded in RDF, schemas use RDFS, while translation links are expressed in OWL. All semantic data get indexed into the underlying DHT infrastructure, which supports efficient location of resources based on their identifiers (i.e., keys).

Figure 13.10 below gives a simplified example of query resolution in GridVine. One of the peers poses a query against a local schema called *NewYearPic* (1), as it wants to retrieve New Year's Day images taken in Lausanne. The query can be resolved in $\mathcal{O}(log(n))$ messages by routing a couple of messages through the P-Grid infrastructure, where all triples are indexed based on their *subject*, *property* and *object* values. To retrieve more results, the peer starts a Semantic Gossiping process: it searches for similar schemas, and finds a related schema, *EoYearJPEG*, with a high semantic similarity value for the property in question (2). It decides to use this schema as well and issues a transformed query, which retrieves in turn the location of a picture, *DSC000045*, whose annotations match the transformed query (3). The peer can then route a final messages through the P-Grid to retrieve the desired picture (4).

This kind of search process is totally automated in GridVine, as both multi-triples RDQL queries and Semantic Gossiping are supported. The separation of the physical from the logical layer allows us to process these logical operations with different physical execution strategies. In particular, we identified and implemented two alternatives for the traversal of the semantic overlay network: iterative forwarding, where the requesting peer itself repeatedly resolves and transforms the query, and recursive forwarding, where query forwarding and translation are delegated to intermediate peers.

As we rely on end-users to create schemas in GridVine, fostering interoperability among sets of independently created but semantically related schemas is crucial. To do so, we rely on schema inheritance and semantic cycle analysis. Schema inheritance enforces reuse of conceptualizations and monotonic inheritance of properties

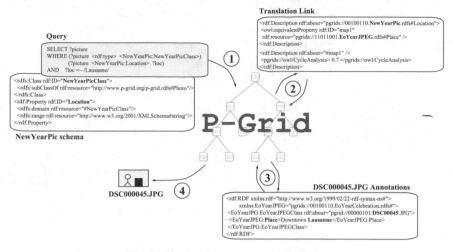

Fig. 13.10. Resolving a query in GridVine

through schema hierarchies. By letting users derive subschemas from other schemas, we bootstrap semantic interoperability on small sets of properties shared by all the descendants of a (potentially very popular) base schema. Semantic cycle analysis operates as previously explained: It analyzes compositions of user-defined mappings to selectively forward queries through relevant translation links only.

To test the large-scale applicability of our approach under real-world conditions, we deployed our software on PlanetLab. PlanetLab [3] is a global testbed for large-scale experiments with distributed systems. The goal of our experiments on Planet-Lab was to validate the analytical and simulation results for our semantic overlay under realistic conditions using a concrete and fully functional implementation. The results of the experiments we conducted so far match the theoretical predictions quite accurately and show that the system scales gracefully both with the number of peers and schemas.

13.8 Conclusions

Semantic interoperability is a key issue on the way to the Semantic Web, which can push the usability of the web considerably beyond its current state. Its success, however, depends heavily on the degree of global agreement that can be achieved, i.e., on global semantics. We have presented a possible approach facilitating the fulfillment of this requirement by deriving global semantics from purely local interactions. We see our approach as a complementary effort to the on-going standardization processes in the area of semantics which may help to improve their acceptance and application by augmenting their top-down approach with a dual bottom-up strategy. We have developed our approach in a formal model that is built around a set of instruments which enable us to assess the quality of the inferred semantics. Also, we have conducted series of simulations and experiments with a concrete infrastructure legitimating our claims and provided a number of techniques aiming at a better understanding of network-related properties fostering semantic interoperability.

References

[1]   Aberer K, Cudré-Mauroux P, Hauswirth M (2003) — Start making sense: The Chatty Web approach for global semantic agreements. In: Journal of Web Semantics, 1(1).

[2]   Aberer K, Cudré-Mauroux P, Hauswirth M, van Pelt T (2004) — GridVine: Building Internet-Scale Semantic Overlay Networks. In International Semantic Web Conference (ISWC04):107–121.

[3]   Chun B, Culler D, Roscoe T, Bavier A, Peterson L, Wawrzoniak M, Bowman M (2003) — PlanetLab: An Overlay Testbed for Broad-Coverage Services. In: ACM SIGCOMM Computer Communication Review, 33(3).

[4]   Cudré-Mauroux P, Aberer K (2004) — A Necessary Condition For Semantic Interoperability In The Large. In International Conference on Ontologies, DataBases, and Applications of Semantics for Large Scale Information Systems (ODBASE04):859–872.

[5]   Hull R (1997) — Managing Semantic Heterogeneity in Databases: A Theoretical Perspective. In Symposium on Principles of Database Systems (PODS97):51–61.

[6]   Ouksel A, Ahmed I (1999) — Ontologies are not the Panacea in Data Integration: A Flexible Coordinator to Mediate Context Construction. In Distributed and Parallel Databases, 7(1):7–35.

[7]   Plaxton C, Rajaraman R, Richa A (1997) — Accessing Nearby Copies of Replicated Objects in a Distribute Environment In ACM Symposium on Parallel Algorithms and Architectures (SPAA97): 311-320.

[8]   Wiederhold G (1992) — Mediators in the Architecture of Future Information Systems. In IEEE Computer, 25(3):38–39.

Part IV

Methodology and Systems

Overview: Methodology and Systems

Steffen Staab

Deploying a Semantic Web and Peer-to-Peer application is more than just providing a technical solution. It is well known from technical history that some technology that worked in one organizational and social environment could not be brought to work under similar, but slightly different, social constraints. In disciplines like knowledge engineering and e-commerce, people have thought about how the organizational environment needed to be modelled so that a knowledge management system would work in a specific setting or how a business model needed to look in order to be commercially successful.

Compared with such disciplines, the study of human behavior using either Semantic Web or Peer-to-Peer technologies (see e.g. [9, 3] and [2, 1], respectively) is only a recent endeavour. At the same time, the solution that we target with Semantic Web and Peer-to-Peer solutions is particularly challenging with regard to people's motivations, organizational constraints or — sometimes — legal issues. Let us first consider each of the two technologies in isolation. We will find that each requires substantial thinking about how to deploy them in order make them a success.

With regard to Peer-to-Peer solutions, there are some well-known problems that need to be considered:

- *The tragedy of the commons* [5] describes a situation where a common good (e.g., fishs in the open sea) is exploited by individuals. The individuals can individually optimize their gains by unlimited use (e.g., fishing as much as possible), but together they deplete the resource (e.g., overfishing leads to scarcity of fish). In a Peer-to-Peer system, *free riding* [2, 6] constitutes a corresponding behavior, because peers that just exploit the network (but that do not contribute resources) optimize their individual gain, but degrade the network to an extent that it becomes unusable. Such behavior is encouraged by factors like anonymity[1] or lack of intrinsic or extrensic motivation to share computing resources.

---

[1] Even if true anonymity may not apply for file sharing in an organization, there is still the issue that individual actions, whether good or bad for the network as a whole, already seem to go undetected for a middle-sized network.

- *Incentives* to share computing resources (cf. [10]) may thus become inevitable in order to make a Peer-to-Peer system workable; however, developing a successful incentive system is tricky and some of the earlier proposals (e.g. Mojo Nation http://mojonation.net/) are seldom heard of today.
- *Security* concerns (see, e.g. [7]): By their very nature, Peer-to-Peer systems offer potential for security breaches. Peer-to-Peer systems need to interact across firewalls and, hence, if programmed or administered with mistakes, may constitute a potential technical security hole. Because Peer-to-Peer systems open another channel for communication, they may be misused, e.g. if people are negligent about data access restrictions.

Likewise, Semantic Web applications presume requirements concerning the way their community of users behaves:

- *Agreeing on Ontology*: To fully exploit semantic metadata it is necessary that a group of users agrees on ways to view the world [4]. Though there are some resources that do that with enormous success,[1] such success is far from being guaranteed automatically.
- *Semantic Metdata* needs to be provided, or in more traditional terms, the *Knowledge Base* for an ontology needs to be filled by users to make the ontology effective for finding and retrieving knowledge. The provisioning of semantic metadata is a challenge that requires particular thought by knowledge engineers and domain experts [8].
- *Managing Change* of an ontology remains a challenge, because such change has effects on the community as well as on the corresponding metadata. For example a removal of a concept definition may invalidate metadata definitions.

Thus, for the success of a Semantic Web application, it is also necessary to comprehensively treat the deployment and maintenance of the ontology as well as their corresponding systems and (meta)data.

When we come to the focus of this book and apply the joint communities for information sharing and knowledge management, common problems include:

- *Costs for Early Adopters*: Information sharing and knowledge management as well as Peer-to-Peer solutions in general tend to come with considerable costs for early adopters and little or late payoff. Thus, it is necessary to plan for sufficient seed content *and* seed systems in order to create a community of contributors that receive instantaneous gratification when using the system. Such planning is a prerequisite for successful management. *Hope*, which is a methodology tailored for Semantic Web and Peer-to-Peer solutions, provides necessary guidance for meeting such prerequisites (Chap. 14).
- *Distributed Definition of Ontologies*: While the Semantic Web must deal with the evolution of ontologies in general, the problem is aggravated by *dynamic*

---

[1] Cf., e.g., UMLS http://www.nlm.nih.gov/research/umls/ with its 10^7 concept descriptions.

systems, such as a Semantic Web that is driven on top of a Peer-to-Peer platform. In such an environment, it is not sufficient to provide a technical solution for ontology evolution, but this solution must be adapted in order to allow for methodology-oriented definition and evolution of ontologies. *Diligent* is a methodology that approaches the methodological problem of distributed definition of ontologies and substantiates its findings by initial empirical studies (cf. Chap. 15).

- *Understanding the technology by its users*: Finally, we need to mention that the technology that is deployed cannot only be evaluated based on its technical abilities, but also by its usability aspects. A large problem for Semantic-Web *and* P2P-based solutions is that they are more sophisticated than what is easily understood by the average user. Therefore, the pros and cons of such technology need to be evaluated against organizational constraints, metaphors of use, or similar parameters — and they need to be evaluated in living systems. In this book, we present three living systems that have been deployed in various organizations:
  1. KEx: A system for P2P knowledge management within organisations (Chap. 16).
  2. Xarop: A system for P2P knowledge management across organisations (Chap. 17).
  3. Bibster: A P2P system for world-wide sharing of bibliographic information in the field of computer science (Chap. 18).

In summary, this part addresses the problem of deploying Semantic Web and P2P-based systems for information sharing and knowledge management *in realiter*. It does so by presenting two methodologies and three applications that have been run over several months (or longer — as is the case with the commercially available software, KEx).

References

[1] *Third Workshop on the Economics of Peer-to-Peer Systems*, 2005. http://p2pecon.cs.cornell.edu/.

[2] E Adar and B. Huberman. Free riding in gnutella. *First Monday*, Oct. 2000. http://citeseer.nj.nec.com/adar00free.html.

[3] J. Davies, A. Duke, and Y. Sure. OntoShare - An Ontology-based Knowledge Sharing System for virtual Communities of Practice. *Journal of Universal Computer Science*, 10(3):262–283, March 2004.

[4] A. Gomez-Perez, M. Fernandez-Lopez, and O. Corcho. *Ontological Engineering with examples from the areas of Knowledge Management, e-Commerce and the Semantic Web*. Springer, 2004.

[5] Garrett Hardin. The tragedy of the commons. *Science*, pages 1243–1248, 1968.

[6] D. Hughes, G. Coulson, and J. Walkerdine. Free riding on gnutella revisited: The bell tolls? *IEEE Distributed Systems Online*, 6(6), 2005.

[7] J. Schmücker and W. Müller. Praxiserfahrungen bei der Einführung dezentraler Wissensmanagement Löosungen. *Wirtschaftsinformatik*, 45:307–311, 2003.

282   Steffen Staab

[8]   G. Schreiber et al. *Knowledge Engineering and Management — The CommonKADS Methodology*. The MIT Press, Cambridge, Massachusetts; London, England, 1999.

[9]   York Sure, Asunción Gómez-Pérez, Walter Daelemans, Marie-Laure Reinberger, Nicola Guarino, and Natalya Fridman Noy. Why evaluate ontology technologies? because it works!. *IEEE Intelligent Systems*, 19(4):74–81, 2004.

[10] M. Yang, Z. Zhang, X. Li, and Y. Dai. An empirical study of free-riding behavior in the maze p2p file-sharing system. In *IPTPS-2005, 4th Int. Workshop on Peer-to-Peer Systems*, 2005. http://iptps05.cs.cornell.edu/.

14

A Methodology for Distributed Knowledge Management Using Ontologies and Peer-to-Peer

Peter Mika

Section Business Informatics, Vrije Universiteit Amsterdam, The Netherlands
pmika@cs.vu.nl

Summary. While Knowledge Management solutions designed for the traditional organization achieve knowledge transfer by establishing central repositories of information and global procedures for knowledge flow, Distributed Knowledge Management aims to support the local processes of knowledge creation and puts the emphasis on limited, ad-hoc co-operations based on shared goals instead of global control. Peer-to-peer architectures offer an ideal technological match for the theory of DKM and may be the only choice in many practical cases, e.g. when dealing with personal knowledge that needs to be controlled locally. In the following we present the case for DKM and the methodology that was used in the SWAP project to develop and deploy the P2P applications described elsewhere in this book.

14.1 Introduction

While organizations have long been managing their human and intellectual assets, the business discipline of Knowledge Management (KM) was eventually formed in the early 1990s to meet these specific challenges [5, 14, 4]. Unfortunately, there is hardly any consensus on the definition of Knowledge Management, mostly due to the varied views of the practitioners on what knowledge is on the first place. For our purposes, we will define Knowledge Management by its goal and present it as an umbrella term covering all measures taken by an organization to ascertain that its members have relevant, actionable and timely knowledge at their disposal for carrying out knowledge-intensive tasks.

Ontologies of various complexity (from simple vocabularies and taxonomies to complex knowledge bases) have been successfully applied in several Knowledge Management applications in the past, particularly in the area of Content Management [1]. The role of ontologies in these systems is to replace the hidden, hardwired conceptual schemas used in the past with an explicit but still machine processable knowledge model that can be directly manipulated by the users and the system alike. The benefit is mainly easier, more flexible management of community knowledge and the possible reuse of ontologies and metadata when expressed in standard languages such as RDF and OWL.

The methods that have emerged through a number of industrial cases studies have focused mainly on supporting relatively small, homogeneous communities [22], where creating an ontology required merely codifying an existing consensus with hardly any need for negotiation. This ontology could then be stored and managed at a central location and use a centralized process, such as one that involves a single person or a small committee managing the ontology on behalf of the community.

The scenario of distributed ontology-based KM is different: it targets situations where the scale and heterogeneity of the community[1] does not allow such a centralized approach. The social difference is best highlighted by Berners-Lee, when he writes:

In a company with six employees, everybody can sit around a table, share their visions of where they're going, and reach a common understanding of all the terms they are using. In a large company, somebody defines the common terms and behaviour that makes the company work as an entity. Those who have been through this transition know it only too well: It typically kills diversity. It's too rigid a structure. And it doesn't scale... At the other extreme is the utopian community with no structure, which doesn't work either because nobody actually takes out the garbage. [2]

A distributed approach to ontology-based KM means letting loose of the idea of a central ontology and centralized control. While it does not represent a shift in world-view, it concerns a different segment of reality than existing work and thus requires a methodology on its own.

In the following we introduce some of the elements of this methodology in the order suggested by the methodology pyramid introduced by Schreiber et al. [17]. The methodology pyramid is a graphical representation of the defining elements of every methodology: a unique world view (paradigm), a theory, a set of methods, tools and practice with their use. In time, the best practice provides continuous feedback to the methodology, which can be amended until fundamental changes in the world will lead to a paradigm shift and the need for a new methodology. (See Fig. 14.1.)

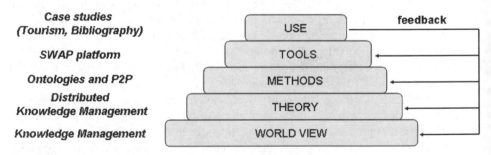

Fig. 14.1. The general concepts of the methodology pyramid

---

[1] In case of large scale and heterogeneity, we may not be able to talk of a single community any more, but of a society, woven together from individual communities.

Our proposed methodology is structured according to the this pyramid and the remaining of the paper also follows this organization. While we consider no fundamental changes in the world view of Knowledge Management, we argue that changing theories on the nature of knowledge and a shift toward distributed organizational structures require the introduction of new methods. The theory of Distributed Knowledge Management (DKM) will be introduced in Sect. 14.2. Our proposed method, the use of Peer-to-Peer as a technical implementation of DKM, is treated in detail in Sect. 14.3. Lastly, we describe how the software platform developed in the SWAP project can be adapted to create knowledge sharing environments tailed to particular use cases. Two of these use cases and the specific solutions developed in the SWAP project are introduced elsewhere in this volume. In particular, Chap. 16 introduces Bibster, a SWAP-based Peer-to-Peer platform for sharing bibliographic information in scientific communities. The SWAP-based XAROP system, developed for a virtual organization in the tourism sector, is described in Chap. 18 of this book.

14.2 The Theory of Distributed Knowledge Management

Advanced information technology has played prominent role in applied Knowledge Management since the early days of the discipline. The technology-driven approach to KM was based on the idea that information systems would connect knowledge workers to repositories of explicit knowledge or other members of the organization for exchanging tacit knowledge through online discussion and shared action. Not much attention has been paid to methodologies, however, as vendors hastily rolled out Enterprise Content Management solutions, Business Intelligence systems, intranets, workflow, HR and project management systems, collaborative workspaces and online communities all in the name of Knowledge Management. Most of these deployments have been abandoned by their users after an initial period of excitement and left behind a sense of disillusionment in stakeholders. This in turned triggered a serious backlash against an IT centric view of Knowledge Management and the field in general.

Looking closer we find that almost without exception the reason for failure was an ignorance toward the embeddedness of Knowledge Management into the wider context in which is to be applied, in particular the psychological, social, cultural, organizational environment that surrounds the systems and their users, the knowledge workers. After the failings of applying technology out-of-the-box, it was soon realized that adapting KM to the organizational context requires a methodological approach and that such a methodology needs to be built on organization theory as well as a theory of knowledge and its diffusion.

This wisdom is already reflected in early methodologies of knowledge-based systems engineering such as CommonKADS [17]. In CommonKADS, the analysis proceeds from an overview of the organization and its business environment, to the analysis of the business process and the selection of a relevant knowledge-intensive task within that process that can be effectively automated by reusing standard problem-solving components. By taking the organizational context as a starting point it is possible to rule out technology as a solution in cases where the problem lies elsewhere in the organization (e.g. when dealing with a business process inefficiency, human resource problem, structural deficiency, exclusive corporate culture etc.) Also, the organizational model can be used during the design of the knowledge system.

While centralized knowledge-based systems continue to perform important tasks in many application areas, there are both theoretical and organizational arguments for moving towards a distributed approach to Knowledge Management.

First, critics argue that centralized approaches to KM neglect the subjective nature of personal knowledge and the social characteristic of collective knowledge [3, 9]. In their view, knowledge is inherently subjective as the interpretation of explicit knowledge is dependent on the context of the interpreter and his mental schemata and thus necessarily subjective. Collective knowledge can only arise through the continuous process of negotiating interpretations with people from similar or different contexts. (The goal in the first case is to improve performance through cognitive similarity, while the absorption of knowledge from different contexts sustains innovation.)

In this view of the world there is no place for a central repository or a central mediator. A central repository would require coming to an agreement over the representation of collective knowledge, which is likely to be costly and result in significant loss of knowledge. A central point of control, on the other hand, is likely to be inefficient in tracking the needs for coordination and exchange between actors.

According to the emerging discipline of Distributed Knowledge Management, the most we can do in terms of management is establishing and supporting the systems, structures and processes needed for knowledge exchange to take place. Instead of the centralization and normalization of knowledge, DKM is concerned with supporting the local processes of knowledge management within independent, autonomous units (individual or close community), so that knowledge is managed in the context where it is created and used. Local knowledge management is complemented with creating opportunities for dynamic exchange of knowledge across units on the basis of need, instead of control.

Organizational arguments also support the move towards Distributed Knowledge Management. In many areas of business, organizational structures are shifting away from the bureaucratic organization of Weber toward more flexible, horizontal structures in order to increase efficiency in the face of rapid change. The process of the empowerment of the individual versus the collective takes place at both the personal, group and organizational levels:

- **Personal Knowledge Management.** Personal Knowledge Management refers to the management of personal knowledge, stored and managed online in personal spaces (e.g. blogs), on desktop computers and especially on the array of embedded or mobile devices ("gadgets") that we integrate into our environment for more convenient access to information or computing resources such as PDA, mobile phones, etc. Due to the highly trusted nature of the devices in our immediate environment, we are more likely to entrust sensitive, personal knowledge on them. Technologically, these devices are organized in ad-hoc, distributed network architectures where participation and sharing can be controlled by the owner of the device.

- **Virtual and Distributed Communities of Practice.** Distributed Communities of Practice are groups of professionals active in the same field who exchange knowledge or carry out their work in coordination, while separated geographically from each other [8]. (These professionals may not necessarily belong to the same organization, as in the notion of international workteams.) DCoPs are most often virtual in that they are supported by information technology in their communication. Examples of DCoP are the communities of software developers who use a particular tool and share their experiences in virtual spaces over the Web and may even engage in shared development as in the case of open source software. A further example are scientific communities that share information online (homepages, blogs, wikis, portals etc.) as well as offline through journals, conferences etc. The membership of these communities is often large and very dynamic. Without fixed boundaries or an established leadership, such communities need to rely on distributed mechanisms to establish trust in (the expertise of) newcomers and their work, i.e. based on a peer review. In case of self-organized communities the lack of controlling authority makes centralized solutions undesirable.

- **Virtual and Network Organizations.** With the opening of markets, today's businesses compete in an increasingly international and dynamic environment. A Virtual Organization is a consortium of organizations that are geographically apart while appearing to others to be a single, unified organization with a real physical location. Network organizations are a form of production network based on strategic alliances [7]. The lack of identity and the dynamic nature of strategic alliances makes them even more susceptible to change than virtual organizations. (Strategic alliances are typically short-term arrangements designed for specific purposes, e.g., produce a component, establish a joint venture, enter a new market). Common to Virtual Organizations and networks is that most resources (including organizational knowledge) remain under the control of the individual members, who coordinate their efforts based on shared short term interests. In this case a centralized solution to Knowledge Management is often undesirable due to a lack of trust and impractical due to the dynamic nature of the organization.

In case of a horizontal organizational structure at any of these levels, the argument for DKM is largely an architectural one: while certain technological architectures can shape social/organizational structures, when it comes to Knowledge Management the result of a misfit between technological and human architectures is likely to result in resistance or quick abandonment.

14.3 Methods for Distributed Knowledge Management

The theoretical underpinnings for Distributed Knowledge Management provide a strong argument for the use of ontology-based Peer-to-Peer systems: such systems provide a technical solution for balancing autonomy and the need for coordination.

Ontologies are representations of shared conceptualizations used to capture the collective understanding of a group [6]. When there is some emerging need for the exchange of knowledge, the relevant parts of the ontologies can be mapped so that it becomes possible to interpret queries and answers from other communities. Ontology mapping is a task that can be at least partially automated with today's technology.

Instead of being created, global ontologies (semantic networks) are expected to gradually emerge from the bottom-up process of making bilateral connections between the conceptualizations of single communities. (This process is often referred to as *emergent semantics*.) Note that this network is not likely to be static over time as it follows both the dynamics of the interaction needs of the communities and the natural evolution of their ontologies. (For discussions on ontology evolution, see e.g. [10, 21].)

Peer-to-peer provides the ideal technological platform for the implementation of such a knowledge network in cases where the expected semantic network also follows a Peer-to-Peer pattern, i.e. most of the exchanges are localized to a relatively small "semantic" neighborhood of the peer and that queries and answers are evenly distributed. (This is the case in the scenarios described above.)

A semantic network, however, does not need to be a completely horizontal structure. In fact, if interactions in the Peer-to-Peer network map the underlying social structure of the community, it is likely to exhibit small-world properties over time, a common characteristic of social networks [13]. This means that there will always be a small number of super-peers or hubs in such networks that have an extraordinarily high number of connections. Nevertheless, small-world networks are still localized in that they exhibit a very high clustering compared to grids or random networks. (In other words, hubs have a high number of connections, but those are likely to lead to their immediate neighborhood.)

If the assumptions of Peer-to-Peer exchange are violated, the structure of the semantic network may also drift from the horizontal organization of the underlying Peer-to-Peer architecture. This is the case if their is some implicit hierarchy in terms of either the knowledge or the goals of the peers. For example, if a node (or a small set of nodes) holds knowledge that is relevant to the entire network (e.g. some kind of general knowledge) then most of the queries will be directed to them and a hierarchy will emerge. Similarly, if there is a hierarchy in terms of tasks and goals (as in the organizational chart of traditional organizations), the network will assume that structure as it evolves to maximize its efficiency.

A semantics-based Peer-to-Peer system may contain mechanisms that enforce that the semantic network maintains a certain structure. The key methodological choice here is what the initial structure is and how much the system allows the ontologies of the peers to drift away from each other. Since this is one of the important questions to answer in deployment, we treat the topic here and reference this discussion in Sect. 14.4.

The first, extreme case (shown in Fig. 2(a)) is that all peers share the same ontology. This architecture is only suitable for the artificial (ideal) case where no sub-communities (local structures) can be identified, i.e. all peers use and share the same conceptualization of the domain. This arrangement is also the most rigid, as all peers need to agree on changes to the ontology and conversely changes to the ontology effect all peers. Unless a distributed voting mechanism can be established, this will require a central point of control for collecting requests for changes and propagating new versions of the ontology. An advantage of this scenario is that no ontology mapping is required.

The second case (shown in Fig. 2(b)) is an architecture where alternative community ontologies exist in the system, each shared by a subset of peers. This arrangement maps the realistic setting where each community has a different (but possibly overlapping) conceptualization of the same (or overlapping) domains. Change management will still likely to require coordination, however, in this case the effects are limited to the set of peers involved. Ontology mapping is required only when knowledge needs to be exchanged across communities. In this case, mapping may be performed by knowledgeable peers on the "edge" of communities who share commitment to both ontologies in question.

The third, extreme alternative (shown in Fig. 2(c)) is the situation where each peer has its own ontology of the domain, i.e. the ontologies may capture similar intentions (i.e. similar sets of possible worlds, but the knowledge is modelled in a different way.[1] This is the most flexible scenario for ontology management, since each ontology is managed by a single peer. On the other hand, at least partial mappings are required whenever knowledge is transferred.

The two extreme cases represent the alternatives described by Berners-Lee (see Sect. 14.1): the first has to be based on central control and the other is the utopian commune. While the first case is incompatible with the ideal of Peer-to-Peer due to the need of central control, the third case often presents difficulties in practice: automated technologies for ontology mapping work best when there is at least some overlap on the syntactical level as well, besides overlaps in semantics. For these reasons, the second case and variations on it offer the best alternatives. For example, it is often practical to work with a single top level ontology shared by all peers and only allow peers to define extensions to this ontology. This idea may be applied hierarchically for peers or sub-communities within communities, e.g. community ontologies may be shared by groups of peers, but peers within the communities can maintain personal extensions to the community ontology.

Its worth noting that Peer-to-Peer is not only different from client-server architectures (which is often considered as the antonym of P2P), but also represents a break from the traditional web architecture. On the negative side, this means that content in Peer-to-Peer networks is not accessible (and not even addressable) from the Web

---

[1] A better name would be a *context* for these structures, since the definition of an ontology requires it to be shared by a community of agents.

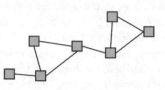

(a) The case of a single ontology
shared by all peers.

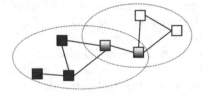

(b) The case of multiple ontologies
shared by (sub)communities.

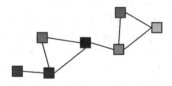

(c) The case of separate ontologies
(contexts) for each peer.

Fig. 14.2. Three alternative ontology architectures for distributed systems

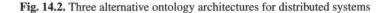

nor vice versa. The reasons are mainly historical: the first P2P networks used for exchanging illegal content have seen an advantage for not being traceable the same way that they would have been on the Web. (The technology still develops in a way to minimize liability of the "owners" of P2P networks, if there are owners at all.) This technological gap between the Web and P2P networks is very unfortunate and occurred despite the wishes of the original inventor of the Web, who imagined a future where the Web could have filled much of the functionality we attributed above to P2P systems.[1] In practice, it means that organizations implementing Peer-to-Peer are likely to duplicate their information architectures if no special provisions are made.

On the positive side, the break from the publisher/browser model of the Web means that P2P lowers the effort to knowledge contribution and generates more interactivity. Publishing is made as easy as determining what data to share; peers can also immediately share the content that is downloaded from other peers. (The resulting duplication means that P2P is also more robust to the appearance/disapperance of individual peers or content.) Two way exchanges of files stimulate other forms of interaction: P2P applications often combine messaging, chatting and other forms of social interaction such as reviews of peers and content.

In the following, we introduce the application methodology developed in the SWAP project for building applications using the generic P2P platform of SWAP. Together the SWAP platform and the methodology enable the development of targeted applications for specific domains and organizational contexts. Although some of the steps in this application development process relate to particular features of the SWAP platform, most of the steps (and the questions raised in each step) are likely to be applicable to all Knowledge Management systems based on a distributed architecture.

14.4 Tools for Distributed Knowledge Management

The HOPE[2] process provides a step-by-step guideline for implementing and deploying P2P systems based on SWAP technology. SWAP provides a basic platform for developing semantic-based Peer-to-Peer systems for specific domains and applications contexts. Development using the SWAP platform is guided by the HOPE process. Two of the systems built using SWAP technology are introduced elsewhere in this volume.

HOPE is firmly embedded in a stream of application development methodologies applied in the area of Knowledge Engineering and Management. In this field a distin-

---

[1] Berners-Lee imagined the Web to provide more interactivity as well as ad-hoc organization: "Perhaps the Web will enable more organic styles of management, in which groups within a company form in a local, rather ad hoc fashion... They could be made self-forming like a newsgroup, but with constraints that ensure that whoever joins is needed for the work of the company and is covered by sufficient budget. Beyond that, the company doesn't have much traditional structure. When someone has a task to perform, they associate with whomever they need to get it done." [2]

[2] HOPE stands for Harnessing Ontologies and Peer-to-Peer

guished role is played by the CommonKADS methodology, which was the result of a series of international research and application projects in knowledge engineering dating back as far as 1983 [17]. CommonKADS is a methodology for the development of Knowledge-based Systems (KBS) through the re-use of abstract methods of problem solving.

HOPE incorporates the organizational analysis of CommonKADS, which has the role to ensure early in the analysis phase that the system addresses a real knowledge problem (or opportunity) within the enterprise, that the benefits are understood by all stakeholders alike, the project is feasible to carry out with given resources etc. A difference to CommonKADS is that the methodology does not address distributed knowledge-based systems and therefore does not deal with problems related to distributed ontology creation, ontology mapping or evolution. The expert knowledge to be modelled in a KBS is also much more complex than the simple knowledge structures of the ontologies employed in a Peer-to-Peer system such as SWAP. For our purposes, we will reuse the organizational context modelling of CommonKADS, but refer to more recently developed methodologies for ontology engineering.

The activities of HOPE are naturally grouped in five *phases* of development, namely 1. Analysis, 2. Design, 3. Development, 4. Deployment and 5. Evaluation. Phases are ordered in the sense that each phase results in well-defined deliverables used by subsequent phases of development. In order to avoid the pitfalls of a flat, linear, "waterfall" style process, HOPE advocates an evolutionary approach, where development is an iteration of the development *cycle* rather than a one-shot execution of a sequential process. The cycle of phases is visualized in Fig. 14.3.

Evolutionary or prototyping approaches are especially appropriate in the development of innovative knowledge systems. With such systems it is important to maintain the confidence of stakeholders and control their expectations by showing visible results early on [17]. Also, in explorative projects the requirements are often unclear on the outset and the results of early evaluations are a thus major factor in planning for the next development cycles. The combination of a linear process with a prototyping approach is also called the *spiral model* to development: while the cycles are identical, each execution of the cycle leads to an advance in both understanding and addressing the problem.

In the following, we describe each phase (with the exception of Development) in a separate section.

14.4.1 Analysis

The goal of the analysis phase is twofold: first, to provide information for executive decision-making, and second to provide the necessary information for system design. Common to these goals is the need to build a model of the organizational context in which the future platform is to be deployed. The organizational model should contain enough details about the knowledge-related problem and foreseeable solutions to be the basis of executive decision-making about the project, i.e. whether the project should proceed as planned or to be discarded. It should pay particular attention to those parts of the organization that will come into interaction with the system or will

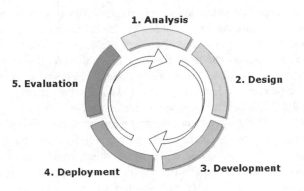

Fig. 14.3. Overview of the five phases of system development with HOPE

be impacted by its use in any way (the organizational context). In terms of ontology-based P2P systems, this means a strong focus on the existing knowledge communities and their goals and intentions.

For creating a concise organizational a model, we adapt the CommonKADS organizational context analysis [17]. Using CommonKADS, organizational analysis is carried out in four main steps:

1. Carry out a scoping and feasibility study, consisting of two parts:
   - Identifying problem/opportunity[1] areas and potential solutions, and putting them into a wider organizational perspective.
   - Deciding about economic, technical and project feasibility, in order to select the most promising focus area and target solution.
2. Carry out an impact and improvements study for the selected target solution, again consisting of two parts:
   - Gathering insights into the relationships between the task, agents involved and use of knowledge for successful performance, and what improvements may be achieved here.
   - Deciding about organizational measures and task changes, in order to ensure organizational acceptance and integration of the knowledge-system solution.

Thus analysis and decision making are divided in two stages. The first stage, the scope and feasibility study builds on a large-scale overview of the organization. A problem and matching solution[2] are selected, based on promised return and feasibil-

---

[1] Problems are often perceived as opportunities and vice versa: a missed opportunity can turn into a problem in face of competition.

[2] By solution at this point we mean an idea or direction for a potential solution rather than an actual choice on technologies or implementations.

ity. This stage is supported by the Organizational Model worksheets: OM-1, OM-2, OM-3, OM-4, OM-5.

The second stage, the impacts and improvement study builds on a more thorough analysis of the selected area, detailed on the level of agents, tasks, processes, knowledge assets and other resources used. For the management, this analysis is the basis for deciding on additional measures to facilitate the adoption of the new system (see Deployment in Sect. 14.4.3). For the engineers, the detailed analysis is used as input for the knowledge system design (Sect. 14.4.2) and for planning the evaluation (Sect. 14.4.4). This second stage is supported by the Task and Agent modelling worksheets: TM-1, TM-2, AM-1, and the summary worksheet OTA-1.

In cases where knowledge sharing is largely driven by the social networks of individuals or no formal organization exists at all, other techniques of organizational analysis may be considered. In particular, HOPE proposes the use of intentional analysis and social network analysis for mapping the informal organizational chart.

Intentional Analysis is a method in Multi-Agent Systems design for the analysis of the intentional dimension of the organizational setting: the interests, intents, and strategic relationships among actors[1]. Intentional Analysis is also applied in a KM setting, where an agent-oriented mindset is particularly useful in exploring the underlying motivations for knowledge sharing (or the lack thereof) [11].

Social Network Analysis is a branch sociology concerned with relational data. Unlike other fields of sociology, SNA focuses on relationships between actors rather than attributes of actors, takes a network view rather than an atomistic view [18, 23]. SNA can be effectively applied to map the informal organization chart by simple questionnaire or interview methods (see e.g. [12]). Analysis of the resulting networks can give insight into the social structure of the community and the potential effects of this structure on individual and collective performance.

14.4.2 Design

The Design phase consists of the steps required for adapting the underlying knowledge management solution for the particular domain and the problem area selected in the phase of analysis.

Design, much like the analysis, should be carried out in close collaboration with domain experts, end-users and other stakeholders. It is our experience that participants should be familiar with the system early on: users are often be biased by their own conceptions about what the system will offer to them, often based on experiences with "similar" software used before. Mockups or prototypes can be used to align expectation of the users with the system design. This will help in pinpointing the features that the users are expecting, but not planned for the system; but also finding those features that the users would not expect, but will be provided to them.

In the following we go through the design options based on the facilities offered by the SWAP system. SWAP has the specific advantage of a highly modularized design, which means that most components of the system can be replaced with relative ease.

---

[1] See http://www.cs.toronto.edu/km/istar/

1. **Design the ontology architecture.** This step refers to choosing between one of the alternatives described in Sect. 14.3 with respect to control over the ontologies of the peers and their evolution. In case there is a need for developing community ontologies or a single top level ontology to bootstrap the system, the following step needs to be taken.

2. **Develop the ontologies of knowledge communities [Optional].** In case of an ontology architecture with subcommunities, domain ontologies need to be developed for the communities identified during analysis. The recommended approach to ontology engineering in HOPE is the DILIGENT method (see Chap. 17 in this volume).

   The approach of DILIGENT is that of loose coordination, midway between central control and free evolution. A central ontology exists from which peers are allowed to derive local adaptations. Drift is prevented by continuously updating the central ontology with the consensus emerging from these local adaptations. Updates to the central ontology are managed by a central control board consisting of representatives of domain experts and ontology engineers. Although it is not possible to fully automate this consensus building process, the various steps of the methodology are supported by automated tools in order to enhance scalability.

3. **Prepare the metadata (instance knowledge) and content to be shared.** The SWAP platform contains the necessary support for exchanging metadata as well as files through the system. This is the case in the tourism case study introduced in Chap. 18, where documents, emails and bookmarks are shared. (Note that the folder structures in which these items are organized by the user provide can be considered as simple classification structures.) It is also possible that only metadata is shared through the system. An example for that is the Bibster system (Chap. 16), where only bibliographic references are exchanged between peers.

   It is advisable to reuse existing sources of content and metadata in order to bootstrap the system, so that even the very first users of the application would not have to encounter an "empty" system. Unstructured information in the form of text or multimedia collections need to be indexed or classified according to the ontology. Structured information in the form of databases (DBMS, ODBMS, XML but also Bibtex) can be wrapped as *passive peers*[1] by aligning their schema to the ontology and converting the data to either instances[2] or content (e.g. text documents). In both cases, the metadata or the files may be either generated by the passive peer on the fly as requests come in or in advance.[3]

---

[1] Passive peers are peers which only act as knowledge provider, but not as knowledge requester, i.e. they don't make queries themselves.

[2] Generic tools are available for this purpose, e.g. D2R (http://www.wiwiss.fu-berlin.de/suhl/bizer/d2rmap/D2Rmap.htm) and KAON-Reverse http://kaon.semanticweb.org/alphaworld/reverse/view.

[3] The trade-off is between query answering time and the storage space required. Also, one should keep in mind that all duplication of information leads to update problems (how and when to update the duplicate when the data source changes).

4. **Decide on automated vs. manual classification.** If a single ontology or a set of community ontologies are used to annotate textual content, metadata may be generated by using automated classifiers. (Automated classification of multimedia content is not feasible in practice.) Automated methods to classification are expected to provide poorer results than manual efforts, but can still lower the effort required from the users (who only need to reclassify misplaced items). One should also take into account that changes in the ontology are likely to require changes to the classifiers (new rules or new training sets, depending on the method).

5. **Develop template queries [Optional].** Based on the task analysis (see previous chapter), template queries may be developed for user convenience. Template queries are parameterized queries represented as forms on the user interface, where the values of the parameters are provided by the user.

6. **Customize the peer selection routine.** The semantics-based peer selection component needs customization, in particular the expertise model, the initial expertise topology, the content and frequency of advertisements, etc. (see Chap. 6). Besides automatic peer selection, users may be also allowed to manually select the peers where the queries are sent.

7. **Customize the user interface.** Visualization options are open in the basic platform. The best interface for knowledge providing, query formulation and the visualization of the result set depends on the kind of knowledge that is stored in the system, the specific use cases (user tasks) that need to be supported, the level of expertise of the expected users, etc. The interface can be used to reveal or conceal certain advanced features of the system, such as the manual peer selection or manual classification mentioned before.

   In case a single ontology is used within the system or within a community, the ontology may be also used to drive the design of the user interface. For example, if a geographic ontology is provided to users, their interface may be customized with user interface elements for entering and visualizing geographic locations. Nevertheless, this adaptation needs to be handled with care: if the ontology is "engineered into the interface," the interface may become overly dependent on the particular ontology. (This, of course, is only a problem if the ontology is expected to change more frequently than versions of the software.)

8. **Prepare the system for internationalization [Optional].** In cases the system has to support users with different languages, the user interface needs to be translated into those languages. Multilinguality also affects all internal components where natural language technology is used, e.g. for classifications and ontology mapping.

9. **Clarify security and legal issues [Optional].** Security and legal questions are particularly acute for systems that naturally cross lines of authority such as organizational lines. Where peers from multiple authorities are involved, the access to the individual peer's documents and metadata need to be controlled. Secure channels are also necessary for preventing eavesdropping. Finally, public key infrastructures may be required for authentication and non-repudiation.

Legal questions surrounding the use of the Peer-to-Peer system also need to clarified before deployment. An individual or organization using a P2P network may be held liable for transferring the intellectual property of third parties (i.e. those who are neither users nor providers of the system). We propose that an agreement limiting the responsibility of the system provider should be distributed to all users and that the signing of this agreement should be a condition of using the system.

14.4.3 Deployment

Deployment (or roll-out) of the system consists of activities required to install and support the system from a technical point of view as well as activities required to make sure that the system is used in a way that is consistent with the goals established during analysis and design.

Minimally, this requires performing the following steps:

1. **Training users in system use.** Training can take many forms, but help should be available at least in the software and in the form of a users manual.
2. **Installing and supporting the system.** In a P2P environment, it may be a requirement to avoid centralized solutions. If the goal is to avoid centralized distribution and support, the system should be made easy enough to install by users on their own. Users in this case should also use other peers as resources if they run into problems during installation or while using the system. Alternatively, installation and support may be carried out by a dedicated person at each location or by a central point in the network.
   Feedback (experience in system use) should be gathered in some way as input for a next cycle of system design.
3. **Motivating users.** Motivation is the most important challenge in the deployment of a distributed knowledge-based system. With only local control or no control at all, the danger is reproducing the utopian community of Berners-Lee where "no one takes out the garbage."
   In the first period after deployment users should be actively motivated in using the system, especially in contributing knowledge. Particular attention should be paid to convince managers and key experts to work with the system: others will follow suit if they see that the formal or informal leadership of the community approves the system.
   Encouraging system use is important because the usefulness of the system at any time depends on how many users are actively using it to provide knowledge. Users should be guided to contribute knowledge while installing the system or immediately after and to keep running the system in the background even when they are not using it to make queries themselves. The goal is to reach a *critical mass* of knowledge early on so that new members joining the network are able to derive benefits from the system from the moment they install the system ("instant gratification").

Incentives may be necessary to reward active users and to punish free-riders.[1] It is important to realize that free-riding is a natural phenomenon that results from users trying to conserve their own resources (in particular, bandwidth) by not sharing files. For example, in the Gnutella file-sharing system, over 70% of the content was provided by just 5% of the users [15]. In open, anonymous P2P systems successful reward mechanisms appeal to the altruism and idealism of the users (the free-spirit ideals behind the P2P system). In closed membership systems incentives may play with the social pressures from the community such as the will of the users to achieve good standing within the community.

A fair use policy or etiquette can be established to describe the social conventions around the system and to prevent softer abuses such as taking up resources by using the system for non work-related activities.

14.4.4 Evaluation

Every real-world system needs to be evaluated to ascertain properties of the system that can not be proved by theoretical means. In practice, most of the goals set out for complex socio-technological systems during analysis and design are examples of such soft properties. Soft goals represent expectations that can only be evaluated in an approximate way by monitoring a set of system parameters that describe the expectations in terms of system behavior. Evaluation therefore poses many of the same challenges as analysis and should be carried out in cooperation with those involved in the analysis.

In the following we propose a skeletal evaluation plan that can be extended to fit particular use cases of the technology. We note that evaluation methodology in general is out of the scope for the present work. For a broader treatment of these issues, we refer the reader to [16].

The skeletal evaluation plan follows a top-down approach to planning (see Fig. 14.4.) First, the goals of the evaluation are established. These goals are then used to extract specific measures to investigate. Some of these measures concern only the characteristics of the system and are collected through automated methods (System Evaluation). Other measures concern the external, human experience, which need elicited through User Evaluation. Finally, these measures are processed and correlated in the Analysis phase.

In the following, we briefly describe each of these steps in more detail. For a more detailed example, we refer the reader to the user evaluation of the Bibster system [19, 20].

1. **Goals of the evaluation**

   The first step is to clarify the goals of the evaluation, based on the expected benefits established in the analysis phase. As with the project plan, the goals should be formulated using terms that are easily understood by the stakeholders.

---

[1] There is some danger in alienating users, many of whom join Peer-to-Peer networks because they find the lack of control and the free spirit of these systems attractive. Designing an overly restrictive system would be against these ideals.

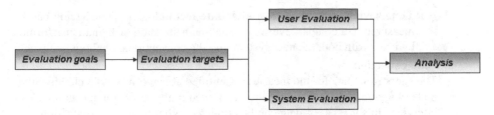

Fig. 14.4. Structure of the evaluation plan

Having these statements beforehand helps to maintain focus on the overall goal of the evaluation, especially how the results will be used once the evaluation is carried out. These statements will be operationalized in the next step in order to make a list of the measures that need to be observed, either by monitoring system parameters or carrying out a user survey.

Some examples are included below.

a) *We expect the system to improve knowledge sharing resulting in more efficiency in carrying out task X.*

b) *We would like to find out if the system represents an improvement over system X in terms of Y.*

c) *We would like to find out how the users value feature X in order to improve the system in a next project cycle.*

d) *We would like to find out more about the knowledge networks in our organization in order to take additional measures in the next project cycle.*

2. **Evaluation Measures**

The values to be measured are characteristics of the key concepts in the above goals that can be objectively measured. Some examples are shown below.

a) **Knowledge transfer and knowledge topology.** Knowledge transfer is manifested by the system as the download and saving of an instance (document) from a remote user of the system. Such actions make up the knowledge transfer network. An indicator of real knowledge sharing activity is the emergence of a knowledge topology that reflects the expected social network of users based on their formal and informal relations.

b) **User activity and user satisfaction.** The user's attitude can be measured with respect to the system as a whole or with respect to specific features. Standard questionnaires such as the SUMI survey[1] offer reliability and the advantage of providing standardized scores. Activity of system use can also be considered as a simple indicator of user satisfaction and can be measured, for example, by the time spent with the system (per week, for example), the number of queries made per week or per session, the number of instances shared, etc. These measures are also interesting to explore in time. Did the user's rely on the system more and more, or did they abandoned it after an initial phase of enthusiasm?

---

[1] http://www.ucc.ie/hfrg/questionnaires/sumi/

c) **Time saving with respect to alternate technologies.** Time saving can be measured in a comparative way by taking a standard task that is performed by users with both the new system and the conventional methods.

3. **Data collection**

The supporting data for the measures identified above can be collected by automated logging, while others need to be elicited in the form of a questionnaire or interview. In some cases, data can be collected either way, e.g. satisfaction may be measured by asking the user in a survey or by monitoring system activity or even including an "i'm happy" button in the interface. If there is some heterogeneity in the data (e.g. different identifiers for the same item) then the data also needs to be aggregated and normalized before analysis.

Automated logging is preferred when both methods are available, because it requires less human effort and rules out much of the human bias in measurement. As an example for such an implementation one may look at the Bibster system (see Chap. 16), where logging is implemented as part of the client application. The client application also has the task of periodically transferring the collected log files to a central point for evaluation and debugging purposes.

4. **Data Analysis**

In the analysis phase, the preestablished evaluation measures are calculated and reported in an evaluation document.

14.5 Summary

In the above we have introduced the theory of Distributed Knowledge Management and its realization in practice using ontologies and Peer-to-Peer technology. Lastly, we have shown the process of designing, implementing, deploying and evaluating such a system based on the platform and tools developed in the SWAP project.

While these elements cover all layers of a methodology, more feedback will be required in the future to validate our methods. For example, alternative models based on Multi Agent Systems (MAS) could verify the overall approach of Distributed Knowledge Management, just as alternative implementations of ontology-based P2P systems have provided important feedback to the design of the SWAP platform. Further case studies of different scales in various domains and organizational settings would also be necessary to attest to the extent that we can generalize the results.

Lastly, we note that Knowledge Management will remain the clashing point of alternative views on knowledge due to the variety of backgrounds held by its practitioners, ranging from work psychology and sociology to library sciences and cognitive studies. In such an multi-disciplinary context the use of advanced information technology is likely to be debated as a solution on its own, but it will prove its value as part of more complex approaches to handling knowledge bottlenecks in the modern enterprise.

References

[1] Andreas Abecker and Ludger van Elst. *Handbook on Ontologies*, chapter 22: Ontologies for Knowledge Management, pages 436–454. International Handbooks on Information Systems. Springer Verlag, 2003.

[2] Tim Berners-Lee, Mark Fischetti, and Michael L. Dertouzos. *Weaving the Web : The Original Design and Ultimate Destiny of the World Wide Web by its Inventor*. Harper San Francisco, 1999.

[3] Matteo Bonifacio, Paolo Bouquet, and Paolo Traverso. Enabling Distributed Knowledge Management: Managerial and Technological Implications. *Novatica and Informatik/Informatique*, III(1), 2002.

[4] Th.H. Davenport and L. Prusak. *Working Knowledge*. Harvard Business School Press, Boston, MA, 1998.

[5] P.F. Drucker. *Post-Capitalist Society*. Butterworth-Heinemann, Oxford, UK, 1993.

[6] Tom R. Gruber. Towards Principles for the Design of Ontologies Used for Knowledge Sharing. In N. Guarino and R. Poli, editors, *Formal Ontology in Conceptual Analysis and Knowledge Representation*, Deventer, The Netherlands, 1993. Kluwer Academic Publishers.

[7] Ranjay Gulati. Social structure and alliance formation patterns: A longitudinal analysis. *Administrative Science Quarterly*, 40:619–652, 1995.

[8] Paul Hildreth, Chris Kimble, and Peter Wright. Communities of practice in the distributed international environment. *Journal of Knowledge Management*, 4(1):27–38, 2000.

[9] Marleen Huysman and Volker Wulf, editors. *Social Capital and Information Technology*. MIT Press, 2004.

[10] Michel Klein. *Change Management for Distributed Ontologies*. PhD thesis, Vrije Universiteit Amsterdam, 2004.

[11] Alessandra Molani, Anna Perini, Eric Yu, and Paolo Bresciani. Analyzing the Requirements for Knowledge Management using Intentional Analysis. In *Proceedings of the AAAI Spring Symposium on Agent-Mediated Knowledge Management (AMKM-03)*, Lecture Notes in Artificial Intelligence. Springer, 2003.

[12] José Luis Molina. The informal organizational chart in organizations: An approach from the social network analysis. *Connections*, 24(1):78–91, 2001.

[13] Mark Newman. Models of the Small World: A Review. *Journal of Statistical Physics*, 101:819–841, November 2000.

[14] Ikujiro Nonaka and Hirotaka Takeuchi. *The Knowledge-Creating Company*. Oxford University Press, 1995.

[15] Kavitha Ranganathan, Matei Ripeanu, Ankur Sarin, and Ian Foster. To share or not to share: An analysis of incentives to contribute in collaborative file sharing environments. In *In Workshop on Economics of Peer-to-Peer Systems*, Berkeley, CA, 2003.

[16] Colin Robson. *Real World Research: A Resource for Social Scientists and Practitioner-researchers*. Blackwell Publishers, 2001.

[17] Guus Schreiber, Hans Akkermans, Anjo Anjewierden, Robert de Hoog, Nigel Shadbolt, Walter van de Velde, and Bob Wielinga. *Knowledge engineering and management. The CommonKADS Methodology.* MIT Press, 1999.

[18] John P. Scott. *Social Network Analysis: A Handbook.* Sage Publications, 2nd edition, 2000.

[19] Ronny Siebes, Peter Mika, Maarten Menken, and Peter Haase. Evaluation plan. SWAP Deliverable 10.2, 2004.

[20] Ronny Siebes, Peter Mika, Maarten Menken, and Peter Haase. Evaluation Report. SWAP Deliverable 10.4, 2004.

[21] Ljiljana Stojanovic, Alexander Maedche, Boris Motik, and Nenad Stojanovic. User-driven Ontology Evolution Management. In *Proceedings of the 13th European Conference on Knowledge Engineering and Knowledge Management (EKAW2002), Siguenza, Spain,* 2002.

[22] York Sure and Rudi Studer. On-To-Knowledge Methodology Ů Final Version. On-To-Knowledge Deliverable 18, 2002.

[23] Stanley Wasserman, Katherine Faust, Dawn Iacobucci, and Mark Granovetter. *Social Network Analysis: Methods and Applications.* Cambridge University Press, 1994.

Distributed Engineering of Ontologies (DILIGENT)

H. Sofia Pinto[1], Steffen Staab[2], Christoph Tempich[3], York Sure[3]

[1] Instituto Superior Tecnico, Universidade Tecnica de Lisboa, Portugal
   `sofia.pinto@dei.ist.utl.pt`
[2] ISWeb, University of Koblenz-Landau, Germany
   `staab@uni-koblenz.de`
[3] AIFB, University of Karlsruhe, Germany
   `{sure,tempich}@aifb.uni-karlsruhe.de`

Summary. Ontology engineering processes in truly distributed settings like the Semantic Web or global Peer-to-Peer systems may not be adequately supported by conventional, centralized ontology engineering methodologies. In this chapter, we present our work towards the DILIGENT methodology, which is intended to support *domain experts* in a *distributed* setting to *engineer and evolve* ontologies. We show partial results on how the DILIGENT process model has been applied in two case studies, in particular (1) in a computer science department where we investigated a fine-grained methodological approach for argumentation, and (2) in a virtual organizational setting in the tourism domain with the support of a Peer-to-Peer system.

15.1 Introduction and Motivation

It has been a widespread conviction in knowledge engineering that methodologies for building knowledge-based systems help knowledge engineering projects to successfully reach their goals in time (cf. [16] for one of the most widely deployed methodologies). With the arrival of ontologies in knowledge-based systems the same kind of methodological achievement for structuring the ontology-engineering process has been pursued by approaches like [4, 18, 21] and their application has been proposed in such areas as the Semantic Web, too. At this point, however, we have found some mismatches between these proposals (including our own) and the requirements we meet in the Semantic Web:

1. Classical development of knowledge-based systems and of corresponding ontologies is mostly *centralized* like the targeted knowledge-based system itself. In contrast, we consider the general tendency to support *distributed information processing with ontologies*, *e.g.* the Semantic Web, agents, web services or ontology-based Peer-to-Peer (P2P). Stakeholders in an ontology development process will hardly ever gather in one place. Yet they have an interest to fruitfully contribute toward the ongoing development of their ontologies.
2. Existing methodologies support knowledge engineering (KE) by using check lists that guide the engineering process. The check lists have been shaped by the

needs of *knowledge engineers* to comprehensively cope with nearly arbitrarily complex processes. In contrast, in the distributed cases we consider, the participation of a knowledge engineer is often restricted to a (possibly complex) core ontology. Beyond the core, these cases involve extensive participation and, comparatively simple, concept formation by *domain experts*.

3. KE has mostly focused on an *up- and running system* with some moderate effort for maintenance. In contrast, ontologies for distributed information processing must permanently *evolve* in order to reflect the widely diverging needs of their users.

4. KE methodologies remain rather *coarse* and the gap between their description and concrete actions to be taken is filled by the KE. In contrast, for Semantic Web ontologies and comparable use cases, we ask the question whether we could provide the domain experts with *fine-grained* guidance in order to improve their effectiveness and efficiency in ontology engineering.

To account for some of the differences between classical knowledge engineering and ontology engineering methodologies derived from there, we have started to develop a methodology for DIstributed (cf. item 1 above), Loosely-controlled (cf. item 2) and evolvInG (cf. item 3) Engineering of oNTologies, the validity of which has been partially checked and is still being checked against experiences in two case studies (cf. [15]).

In this chapter, we focus on the last consideration (cf. item 4): Could ontology engineering benefit from a more fine-grained methodological support? To answer this question we have applied this process framework in two case studies. In the first case study, we specifically investigated whether some argumentation structures dominate the progress in the ontology engineering task and should therefore be accounted for in a fine-grained methodology. We tested the methodological hypothesis by an *in vivo* experiment of collaborative ontology engineering — once with and once without fine-grained methodological guidance. In the second case study, we have investigated how this kind of process framework can be realized in a virtual organizational setting in the tourism domain with the support of a P2P network.

In the remainder of this chapter, we start by explaining the methodological framework of DILIGENT (Sect. 15.2). Then, we present the experiences that helped finding a DILIGENT ontology engineering argumentation framework (Sect. 15.3). In Sect. 15.4 we show the technical solutions developed to support the realization of a DILIGENT process in an organizational setting.

Before concluding, we compare to some related work not contrasted in the introduction here.

15.2 DILIGENT Process

We here sketch the overall framework, in which it is embedded, i.e. the overall DILIGENT process (cf. [15]).

Scenario

In *distributed* development there are several experts, with different and complementary skills, involved in collaboratively building the same ontology. For instance, in Virtual Organizations, Open Source, and Standardization efforts, experts belong to different competing organizations and are geographically dispersed. In these cases, builders typically are also users and, although some users are not directly involved in changing the ontology, they take part in the process by using the ontology.

Process

We will now describe the general process, roles and functions in the DILIGENT process. It comprises five main activities: (1) **build**, (2) **local adaptation**, (3) **analysis**, (4) **revision**, (5) **local update** (*cf.* Fig. 15.1). The process starts by having *domain experts,users*, *knowledge engineers*, and *ontology engineers* **build** an initial ontology. In contrast to known ontology engineering methodologies available in the literature [3, 4, 13, 21] our focus is distributed ontology development involving different stakeholders, who have different purposes and needs and who usually are not at the same location. Therefore, they require online ontology engineering support. The team involved in building the initial ontology should be relatively small, in order to more easily find a small and consensual first version of the shared ontology. Moreover, we do not require completeness of the initial shared ontology with respect to the domain.

Once the product is made available, users can start using it and **locally adapting** it for their own purposes. Typically, due to new business requirements, or user and organization changes, their local ontologies evolve in a similar way as folder hierarchies in a file system. In their local environment they are free to change the reused shared ontology. However, they are not allowed to directly change the ontology shared by all users. Furthermore, the control board collects change requests to the shared ontology.

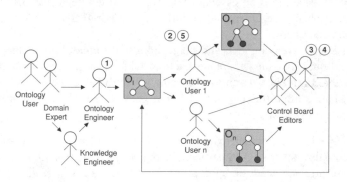

Fig. 15.1. Roles and functions in distributed ontology engineering

The board **analyzes** the local ontologies and the requests and tries to identify similarities in users' ontologies. Since not all of the changes introduced or requested by the users will be introduced,[1] a crucial activity of the board is deciding which changes are going to be introduced in the next version of the shared ontology. The input from users provides the necessary arguments to underline change requests. A balanced decision that takes into account the different needs of the users and meets user's evolving requirements[2] has to be found. The board should regularly **revise** the shared ontology, so that local ontologies do not diverge too far from the shared ontology. Therefore, the board should have a well-balanced and representative participation of the different kinds of participants involved in the process.

Once a new version of the shared ontology is released, users can **update** their own **local** ontologies to better use the knowledge represented in the new version. Even if the differences are small, users may rather reuse *e.g.* the new concepts instead of using their previously locally defined concepts that correspond to the new concepts represented in the new version.

15.3 AIFB Case Study: An Argumentation Framework for DILIGENT

In this section we describe how we specifically investigated whether some argumentation structures dominate the progress in the ontology engineering task and should therefore be accounted for in a fine-grained methodology.

15.3.1 Threads of Arguments

A central issue in the DILIGENT process is keeping track of threads of exchanged arguments. We can identify several stages in which arguments play an essential part:

- An ontology is defined as "a shared specification of a conceptualization" [5]. Although "shared" is an essential feature, it is often neglected. In DILIGENT experts exchange arguments while **build**ing the initial shared ontology in order to reach consensus.
- When users make comments and suggestions to the control board, based on their **local adaptations,** they are requested to provide the arguments supporting them.
- While the control board **analyzes** the changes introduced and requested by users, and balances the different possibilities, arguments are exchanged and balanced to decide how the shared ontology should change.

There is evidence that distributed ontology development can be rather time consuming, complex, and difficult, particularly in getting agreement among domain experts. Therefore, one needs an appropriate framework to assure it in a speedier and

---

[1] The idea in this kind of development is not to merge all user ontologies.

[2] This is actually one of the trends in modern software engineering methodologies (see Rational Unified Process).

easier way. In order to provide better support, one needs to identify which kind of arguments are more relevant and effective to reach consensus. The Rhetorical Structure Theory can be used to classify the kinds of arguments most often used and identify the most effective ones.

Rhetorical Structure Theory

The aim of Rhetorical Structure Theory (RST) [10] is to offer an explanation of the coherence of texts. It is assumed that for every part of a coherent text there is some function. RST focuses on showing an evident role for every part of a text. A text is usually divided into structures, building blocks. These blocks are of 2 levels: nuclearity and relations. The most frequent structure is two spans of text (virtually adjacent). These are usually related such that one of them has a specific role relative to the other: the span making the claim is the nucleus (N) and the span with the evidence is the satellite (S). Thirty relations between 2 spans of text have already been identified and loosely defined. Usually the connection between both spans of text is provided by an expression.

In the examples provided within the case study section we will use the following typefaces to highlight the different elements.

span nucleus ... relation indicator ...
`span satellite`   **Relation**

On the one hand we have presentational relations, such as **background** that increases the ability of the reader to comprehend an element in N, **evidence**, where reader's comprehension of S increases his/her belief of N, **justify**, **restatement**, **summary**, etc. On the other hand we have subject-matter relations, such as **elaboration**, where S presents additional detail about what is presented in N, for instance set::member; abstraction::instance; whole::part, object::attribute, etc., **evaluation**, **purpose**, **solutionhood**, etc. There are also other relations that do not carry a definite selection of one nucleus, such as **contrast**, where the reader recognizes the comparability and differences in situations described in two N, etc.

The analysis process is intended to give a structured, definite way for a person to understand the text to state a part of what that understanding includes. Sometimes one may not find some structural role for every element of the text. A text may have more than one analysis, either because the observer finds ambiguity or finds that a combination of analyses best represents the author's intent. The analysis gives an account of textual coherence that is independent of the lexical and grammatical forms of the text. The available tools are tables that explain the relations between spans of text. Therefore, the analysis process is manual, intensive and requires full NL-understanding.

15.3.2 Hypothesis

In this section we report how the hypothesis underlying the DILIGENT argumentation model has been developed. We have found in the field of Biology a taxonomy that has been evolving since 1735 and following a DILIGENT 5-step process.

It was initially proposed by Linnaeus based on phenetics (observable features). At that time two kingdoms were proposed: animals and plants. As more and more detailed knowledge about them was discovered, new kingdoms were proposed by users of the system. Once a consensus was reached, the new definitions of the kingdoms were introduced by the boards controlling the taxonomy. For instance, when microorganisms were discovered the moving ones were classified in the animals kingdom and the colored (non moving) ones in the plant kingdom. A few were classified in both kingdoms. Users were locally adapting the taxonomy for their own purposes. To more easily identify organisms in both classes, Haeckel (1894) proposed a new kingdom to more easily identify them, the Protista kingdom. Other examples showing the parallel with DILIGENT template process are described in [14]. One can summarize the major force for reorganization of the taxonomy over time as the identification of important classifying features and gathering all beings sharing a given value for that feature into that class.

Based on the RST analysis of real arguments that are exchanged and used to support changes in this taxonomy, we formulated as a hypothesis that there is a subset of arguments that can focus, speed, and ease this kind of ontology engineering.

EXAMPLE When analyzing the arguments exchanged by taxonomists to change the names and organization of the taxonomy one can perceive its vast array and complexity.[1]

> ...*Acinetosporaceae*, including the genera `Acinetospora, Feldmannia`, ... **Elaboration**
> *This group* forms a well-supported clade in molecular trees based on `rbcL data`. **Evidence**
> So far, trees from nuclear ribosomal data do not reveal `them` as *a well-supported group* **Antithesis**
> but are not contradictory to *their* recognition. **Concession**
> ...

DISCUSSION The analysis of the arguments driving the evolution of the taxonomy of life on earth led to the assumption that RST could be useful to analyze arguments exchanged in ontology building processes in distributed environments.

From an argumentative point of view, the focus of this section, we can see that although elaborated, there are a few arguments in the biology case study which play a major role, such as examples/evidence, counter examples, elaboration, alternatives, and comparisons to convey a certain decision.

15.3.3 Hypothesis Validation

In order to substantiate our hypothesis, that an appropriate argumentation framework can facilitate the ontology engineering process, we pursued an *in vivo* experiment in a computer science department. Arguments in collaborative, distributed settings take

---

[1] Example from http://www.ncbi.nlm.nih.gov/Taxonomy/taxonomyhome.html/index.cgi?chapter=CHANGETOCLASS

place in a social environment. Therefore, organizational issues are non-negligible and were also taken into account.

We performed two experiments: in the first, participants were not constrained in any way; in the second, participants were asked to (1) use a subset of arguments, those that that had been found more effective in the first round,(2) and were given stricter rules to conduct their discussions. The task in both sessions was to build an ontology, which (1) represents the knowledge available in the research group, (2) can be used for internal knowledge management, (3) and makes the research area comprehensible for outsiders. Both experiments lasted each for **one hour and a half**. From the eleven participants — all from the computer science department, thus domain experts — three were unexperienced in ontology engineering. Seven were very active in both discussions. Concepts were only added after argumentation and some consensus was achieved.

First Experiment

The goal of the first experiment was to identify the dominant arguments used to push forward ontology development.

SETTING The participants met in a virtual chat room. Each had their own client and all of them could see the current ontology. All arguments were exchanged via the chat room, no other forms of communication were allowed. A moderator was responsible for reminding people to stay on the subject and to include the modelling decisions into the formal ontology which was visualized on a web page. At this stage very few procedural and methodological restrictions were a-priori imposed. The subjects were instructed of the high level goal of the experiment, of the procedure, and of their goals.

EXAMPLE [1] An excerpt from the real dialogues taking place:

...

sa : i dont care whether *someone* plays baseball or not when I am modelling *research domain*.   **Evaluation**

cs : sa just an example...   **Circumstance**

ct : maybe it is the purpose of *the website*, that people get also *informed about hobbys*   **Purpose**

cs : so we have person   **Restatement**

jt : what I find a bit more interesting is *the conference problem*   **Motivation**

...

RESULT In the beginning participants brought forward different kinds of arguments, like background knowledge, examples, elaboration and so on. This led to different argumentation threads where participants were discussing different topics at the same time. At some points there were four threads at the same time, most of the time there was more than one, including procedural and noise. Therefore, discussion was very tangled and at some points rather difficult to follow. Topics which were discussed included: the appropriate formalism to model the ontology, detailed

---

[1] We have changed the transcripts a bit, for the sake of readability.

elaboration of leaf concepts, which top level concepts to begin with, philosophical modelling decisions (roles vs. multi inheritance), which are the main modules, topic lists, etc. From time to time participants called for a vote. However, a decision was seldom reached. The moderator only rarely interacted in the discussion, because timely moderating of multiple threads is very difficult: by the time an intervention was issued two or three other interventions from participants had already been issued. As a result, a core ontology with two concepts, Role and Topic, was agreed upon.

CONCLUSION We analyzed the discussion with the help of RST. Table 15.1 lists the frequency of the different arguments exchanged during the experiment. We could identify the arguments which had most influence on the creation of the ontology, *viz.* **elaboration, evaluation/justification, examples, counter examples, alternatives**.

With respect to the experimental setup we identified the following problems: (1) Participants started too many discussion threads and lost the overview, (2) the discussion proceeded too fast, hence not everybody could follow the argumentation, (3) the moderator was too reluctant to intervene, (4) there was no explicit possibility to vote or make decisions. Even in this setting, where participants shared a very similar background knowledge, the creation of a shared conceptualization without any guidance is almost impossible, or at least very time consuming. We concluded that a more controlled approach is needed with respect to the process and moderation.

Table 15.1. Arguments used and outcome

Arguments	First Round	Second round
Elaboration	24	36
Eval. & Just.	14	33
Contrast & Alternative	12	17
Example	12	9
Counter Example	10	8
Background knowledge	9	3
Motivation	5	
Summary	5	3
Solutionhood	4	8
Restatement	3	6
Purpose	3	
Condition	2	
Preparation	1	
Circumstance	1	
Result	1	
Enablement	1	
List	1	1
Concepts agreed on	2	10
Relations agreed on	3	0

Second Experiment

The goals of the second experiment were to underline that with an appropriate argumentation framework the ontology creation proceeds faster and more effectively and the resulting ontology represents a shared view.

SETTING In the second experiment participants were asked to extend the ontology built in the first round. In this phase the formalism to represent the ontology was fixed. The most general concepts were also initially proposed, to avoid philosophical discussions. The initial ontology defined the modelling primitives for topics and the different roles people are involved in. For the second round the arguments **elaboration**, **examples**, **counter examples**, **alternatives**, and **evaluation/justification** were allowed.

The participants in the second case study joined two virtual chat rooms. One was used for providing topics for discussion, hand raising, and voting. The other one served to exchange arguments. When the participants — the same as in the first experiment — wanted to discuss a certain topic *e.g.* the introduction of a new concept, they had to introduce it in the first chat room. The topics to discuss were published on a web site, and were processed sequentially. Each topic could then be expatiated with the allowed arguments. Participants could provide arguments only after hand raising and waiting for their turn. The participants decided autonomously when a topic was sufficiently discussed, called for a vote and thus decided how to model a certain aspect of the domain. The evolving ontology was again published on a web site. The moderator had the same tasks as in the first experiment, but was more restrictive. Whenever needed, the moderator called for an example of an argument to enforce the participants to express their wishes clearly.

EXAMPLE An example from the arguments window:

> . . .
>
> **cs :** We have done quite a bit of research in distributed knowledge management (DKM) lately. So I suggest DKM as a topic plus a subtopic "Peer-to-Peer" (P2P)   **Elaboration**
>
> **ah :** I suggest *knowledge management (KM)* as super concept of DKM because every DKM is a kind of *KM*   **Elaboration, Justification**
>
> **jt :** Well I am now wondering whether *P2P is DKM*, because File exchange is not always KM is it?   **Counterexample**
>
> **ph :** I suggest *Distributed Comp. (DC)* with P2P and Grid as subtopics; *DKM* as subtopic of DC and KM   **Elaboration**
>
> **do :**   PRO **ph** : because his approach *separates KM* and distributiveness   **Justification, Evaluation**
>
> **cs :** I'd like to agree to **ph** and **do** suggestion. . . .

RESULT As expected, the discussion was more focused, due to the stricter procedural rules. Agreement was reached more quickly. A total of ten new concepts were agreed on. With the stack of topics which were to be discussed (not all due to time constraints), the focus of the group was kept. Some relations were proposed, but they were not agreed upon.

From a methodological point of view, one can classify the ontology engineering approach followed as **middle-out**. The restricted set of arguments is easy to classify and thus the ontology engineer was able to build the ontology in a straightforward way. It is possible to explain to new attendees why a certain concept was introduced and modelled in such a way. It is even possible to state the argumentation line used to justify it. The participants truly shared the conceptualization and did understand it. In particular, in conflict situations when opinions diverged the restriction of arguments was helpful. In this way participants could either prove their view, or were convinced. **LESSONS LEARNED** Our experiments provide strong indication – though not yet full-fledged evidence – that a restriction of possible arguments can enhance the ontology engineering effort in a distributed environment. In addition the second experiment underlines the fact that appropriate social management procedures and tool support help to reach consensus more smoothly.

The process could certainly be enhanced with better tool support. Besides the argumentation stack, an alternatives stack would be helpful. Arguments in particular **elaboration, evaluation & justification**, and **alternatives** were discussed heavily. However, the lack of appropriate evaluation measures made it difficult, at some times, for the contradicting opinions to achieve an agreement. The argumentation should then be focused on the evaluation criteria. As to the use of the RST to analyze real dialogues, instead of carefully written texts, one should mention, in particular in the first round where the discussion was rather tangled, that it was rather difficult to classify at some parts. However, the restricted set is easy to identify and we conjecture that the provision of template arguments will ease the task further.

15.4 IBIT Case Study: a running DILIGENT Process

We are now going to describe how a DILIGENT ontology engineering process is taking place in the IBIT case study. In this case the process template is being realized in an organizational setting supported by a P2P system. Moreover, we here show how the chosen tool, OntoEdit was adapted to support it.

15.4.1 Organizational Setting

In the SWAP project, one of the case studies is in the tourism domain of the Balearic Islands. The needs of the tourism industry there, which is 80% of the islands' economy, are best described by the term "coopetition". On the one hand, the different organizations *compete* for customers against each other. On the other hand, they must *cooperate* in order to provide high quality for regional issues — like infrastructure, facilities, clean environment, or safety — that are critical for them to be able to compete against other tourist destinations.

To collaborate on regional issues a number of organizations now collect and share information about *Indicators* reflecting the impact of growing population and tourist fluxes in the islands, their environment, and their infrastructures. Moreover, these indicators can be used to make predictions and help planning. For instance, organizations that require *Quality & Hospitality Management* use the information to better plan, *e.g.*, their marketing campaigns. As another example, the governmental agency

IBIT[1], the Balearic Government's co-ordination center of telematics, provides the local industry with information about *New Technologies* that can help the tourism industry better perform their tasks.

Due to the different working areas and objectives of the collaborating organizations, it proved impossible to set up a centralized knowledge management system or even a centralized ontology. They explicitly asked for a system without a central server, where knowledge sharing is integrated into the normal work, but where very different kinds of information could be shared with others.

To this end the SWAP consortium — including we at the University of Karlsruhe, IBIT, Free University of Amsterdam, Meta4, and Empolis — have been developing the SWAP generic platform and we have built a concrete application on top that satisfies the information sharing needs just elaborated.

15.4.2 Technical Setting

The SWAP environment (Semantic Web And Peer-to-Peer; short SWAPSTER) [1] is a generic platform which was designed to enable knowledge sharing in a distributed network. Nodes wrap knowledge from their local sources (files, e-mails, etc.) and they ask for and retrieve knowledge from their peers. For communicating knowledge SWAPSTER transmits RDF structures, which are used to convey conceptual structures (e.g., the definition of what a document is) as well as corresponding data (e.g., data about Documents-on-Indicators-2002). For structured queries, as well as for keyword queries, SWAPSTER uses SeRQL (Chap. 1), an SQL-like query language that allows for queries combining the conceptual and the data level and for returning newly constructed RDF-structures.

15.4.3 Realizing a DILIGENT Process

The work reported here involved one organization with seven peers and lasted for two weeks.

Building. In the IBIT case study two knowledge engineers were involved in building the first version of the shared ontology with the help of two ontology engineers. In this case, the knowledge engineers were at the same time also knowledge providers. In addition, they received additional training such that when the P2P network was up and running on a bigger scale, they were able to act as ontology engineers on the board — which they are already doing in later stages of this case study not reported here.

The ontology engineering process started by identifying the main concepts of the ontology through the analysis of competency questions and their answers. The most frequent queries and answers exchanged by peers were analyzed. The identified concepts were divided into three main modules: "Sustainable Tourism Development", "New Technologies and Innovation", and "Quality&Hospitality Management". From the competency questions we quickly derived a first ontology with

---

[1] http://www.ibit.org

22 concepts and 7 relations for the "Sustainable Tourism Development" ontology. This was the domain of the then participating organizations. Recently the other modules have been further elaborated.

Based on previous experience of IBIT with the participants, we could expect that users would mainly specialize the modules of the shared ontology corresponding to their domain of expertise and work. Thus, it was decided by the ontology engineers and knowledge providers involved in building the initial version that the shared ontology should only evolve by addition of new concepts, and not from other more sophisticated operations, such as restructuring or deletion of concepts.

Local Adaptation. The developed core ontology for "Sustainable Tourism Development" was distributed among the users and they were asked to extend it with their local structures. With the assistance of the developers, they extracted on average 14 folders. The users mainly created sub concepts of concepts in the core ontology from the folder names. In other cases they created their own concept hierarchy from their folder structure and aligned it with the core ontology. They did not create new relations. Instance assignment took place, but was not significant. We omitted the use of the automatic functions to get a better grasp of the actions the users did manually.

Analyzing. The members of the board gathered the evolving structures and analyzed them with help of the OntoEdit plug-in. The following observations were made:

Concepts matched: A third of the extracted folder names was directly aligned with the core ontology. A further tenth of them was used to extend existing concepts.

Folder names indicate relations: In the core ontology a relation inYear between the concept Indicator and Temporal was defined. This kind of relation is often encoded in one folder name *e.g.* the folder name "SustInd2002" matches the concepts Sustainable Indicator and Year[1]. It also points to a modelling problem, since Sustainable Indicator is a concept while 2002 is an instance of concept Year.

Missing top level concepts: The concept project was introduced by more than half of the participants, but was not part of the initial shared ontology.

Refinement of concepts The top level concept Indicator was extended by more than half of the participants, while other concepts were not extended.

Concepts were not used: Some of the originally defined concepts were never used. We identified concepts as used, when the users created instances, or aligned documents with them. A further indicator of usage was the creation of sub concepts.

Folder names represent instances: The users who defined the concept project used some of their folder names to create instances of that concept *e.g.* Sustainable Indicators Project.

Different labels: The originally introduced concept Natural Spaces was often aligned with a newly created concept Natural Environments and never used itself.

---

[1] Year is sub class of class Temporal.

Ontology did not fit: One user did create his own hierarchy and could use only one of the predefined concepts. Indeed, his working area was forgotten in the first ontology building workshop.

From the discussions with the domain experts we have the impression that the local extensions are a good indicator for the evolution direction of the core ontology. However, since the users made use of the possibility to extend the core ontology with their folder names, as we expected, the resulting local ontologies represent the subjects of the organized documents. Therefore, a knowledge engineer is still needed to extend the core ontology, but the basis of his work is being improved significantly. From our point of view there is only a limited potential to automate this process.

Revision. The board extended the core ontology where it was necessary and performed some renaming. More specifically the board introduced (1) one top level concept (Project), and (2) four sub concepts of the top level concept Indicator and one for the concept Document. The users were further pointed to the possibility to create instances of the introduced concepts. *E.g.* some folder names specified project names, thus could be enriched by such an annotation.

Local update. The extensions to the core ontology were distributed to the users. The general feedback of the users was generally positive. However, a prolonged evaluation of the user behavior and second cycle in the ontology engineering process is still being performed.

15.4.4 Lessons Learned from the Realization

The case study helped us to generally better comprehend the use of ontologies in a P2P environment. First of all our users did understand the ontology mainly as a classification hierarchy for their documents. Hence, they did not create instances of the defined concepts. However, our expectation that folder structures can serve as a good input for an ontology engineer to build an ontology was met.

Currently, we doubt that our manual approach to analyse local structures will scale to cases with many more users. Therefore, we will look into technical support to recognize similarities in user behavior. Furthermore, the local update will be a problem when changes happen more often. Last, but not least, we have so far only addressed the ontology creation task itself — we are currently measuring if users get better and faster responses with the help of DILIGENT-engineered ontologies. All this is current work.

In spite of the technical challenges, user feedback was very positive since (i) the tool was integrated into their daily work environment and could be easily used, and (ii) the tool provided very beneficial support to perform their tasks. However, it will require the introduction of some new features in order to ease ontology editing tasks by users without a knowledge engineering background.

15.4.5 Tool Support for DILIGENT Steps

We support the participants in the DILIGENT process with a tool (*cf.* Fig. 15.2). It is an implementation of the *Edit* component of the SWAP environment, thus it works on the information stored in the local node repository, and is realized as an OntoEdit plug-in. We will now describe in detail how the tool supports the actions **building**, **locally adapting**, **analyzing**, **revising**, and **locally updating**.

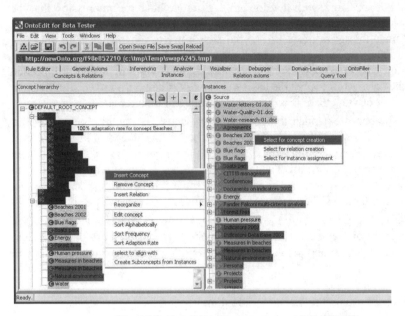

Fig. 15.2. OntoEdit plug-in to support DILIGENT

Build

The first step of the ontology engineering task is covered by established methodologies and by common OntoEdit functions. Some major tool functionality includes support for knowledge elicitation from domain experts by means of competency questions and mind maps, and further support for the refinement process.

In contrast to a common full ontology engineering cycle, the objective of this **build** task is not to generate a complete and evaluated ontology, but rather to *quickly* identify and formalize the main concepts, and main relations.

Local Adaptation

We distinguish two main types of users. The less frequent type is the user with ontology engineering competence who analyzes his personal needs, conceptualizes, and formalizes them. He uses established ontological guidelines [6] in order to maintain soundness and validity. Besides, he annotates his knowledge according to his locally extended ontology.

The more common type of user reuses the categorizations he had defined in his daily work before (*e.g.*his folder structures) and just aligns them with the shared ontology. To illustrate this use case we must point forward to some issues we found in the case study. In the case study, users primarily expect from a P2P system the possibility to share their documents with others. Users already organize their files in folder structures according to their individual views. Hence, they extend the core ontology with concepts and relations corresponding to folder structures found in their file or email system.

Concept creation

Our tool supports the creation of concepts and thus the extension of the shared ontology in two ways. The reader may note that both methods have been heavily influenced by our targeted system, SWAPSTER, and may be supplemented or overridden by other methods for other target systems:

1. OntoScrape — part of the SWAPSTER knowledge source integrator — can extract information from the user's local file and email system. OntoScrape extracts *e.g.*the folder hierarchy and builds up an RDFS representation in which the folder names are used to create instances of class Folder. This information is stored in the local node repository. Then, the user can pick a set of instances of Folder and create concepts or relations using the folder names. In case of "concept creation" he can select a certain concept and the system can subclass that concept using the names of the previously selected folders.
   The user may also reuse the folder hierarchy given by the inFolder relation to construct a subClassOf hierarchy.
2. Furthermore, a user can query other participants for their local subconcepts of the core ontology. He can use the gathered information to directly extend his own structures by integrating retrieved information. Alternatively, he may use the query result only for inspiration and create own extensions and modifications.
   SWAPSTER integrates a component for semi-automatic alignment. Alignment detection is based on similarities between concepts and relations(cf., *e.g.*, [11]). The user may either select a set of classes and ask for proposed alignment for these classes, or he can look for alignments for the entire class hierarchy. The reader may note that even the best available alignment methods are not very accurate and hence some user involvement is required for aligning ontologies.

We are well aware of the drawbacks of this approach since the created structures will not be "clean" ontologies. However, as our case study indicates, the created structures are good enough to be a fair input for the revision phase.

Instance assignment

Besides instances of the created concepts the user has mainly instances of concept Source *e.g.*Folder and File and wants to relate them to his concepts. In particular, documents play a predominant role in our case study. Since the global ontology certainly differs from existing local structures, we face the typical bootstrapping problem that the documents need to be aligned with the defined concepts. Our tool offers two possibilities to facilitate the assignment of documents to classes.

Manual Assignment: Instances of concept Source can manually be selected and assigned to any concept in the ontology.

Automatic Assignment: Automatic text classification is nowadays very effective. Hence we provide an interface for classifiers to suggest document classifications. Classifier training can take place remotely for the core ontology or according to established procedures [17]. The classifier has to produce a set of RDFS statements, stating which files should be classified where in the concept hierarchy.

Analyzing

As described in the methodology, the board comes together in fixed time lines or when a certain threshold of change requests has been reached. They subsequently analyze the activities which have taken place. They gather the ontologies from all participating peers on one central peer. The main task of the board is to incorporate the change requests into the core ontology and to identify common usage patterns. Our tool supports the board members in different ways to fulfill their task.

View selection

The number of newly created concepts within the peer network can be large. The board members can use queries to select only parts of the ontology to be visualized. Instead of loading the entire local node repository, a SeRQL query can be used to generate a view on the repository. Queries can be defined manually, or predefined ones — visualizing certain branches of the ontology — can be selected.

Colors

The board needs to separate extensions made by different users and is interested in their relative activity. Since each peer uses its own name space to create URIs, extensions to the core made by different peers can be distinguished. The tool highlights the concepts, relations and instances of different peers by changing their background color. The saturation and brightness of the color indicates the number of concepts coming from a particular peer.[1] White is preserved for name spaces which the users can chose not to highlight (e.g. the local, swap-peer and swap-common name space are excluded from highlighting by default).

---

[1] Brighter and less saturated means less concepts than darker and more saturated.

Adaptation rate

The averaged adaptation rate[1] of concepts from the core ontology and also of concepts from different users is an indicator of how well a concept fits the user needs. If a concept of the core ontology was not accepted by the users it probably has to be changed. Alternatively, a concept introduced by a user which has been reused by many other users can easily be integrated into the core ontology. The adaptation rate is visualized as a tool tip. In our case study *e.g.* the concept **beaches** was adapted by all users. It is calculated from the information stored in the SWAP data model.

Visualizing alignments

Instead of reusing concepts from other users, they can align them. The semantics of both actions is very similar. However, alignment implies, in most cases, a different label for the concept, which is determined by the board.

Sorting

To facilitate the analysis process, concepts, relations, and instances may be sorted alphabetically, according to their adaptation rate or the peer activity. Concepts with the same label, but from different peers, can be identified. Equally, the concepts reused by most peers may be recognized.

Revision

The analysis is followed by the revision of the core ontology. The change requests, as well as the recognized common usage patterns, are integrated. In a traditional scenario the knowledge engineer introduces the new concepts and relations or changes the existing ones while the system meets the requirements described in [19]. The ontology changes must be resolved taking into account that the consistency of the underlying ontology and all dependent artifacts are preserved and may be supervised.

Additionally we require that the reasons for any change do not require too much effort from the individual user. In particular, changes to the core ontology made because of overarching commonalities should be easy to integrate for users who created the concepts in the first place.

Local update

The changes to the core ontology must be propagated to all peers afterwards. The list of changes is transmitted to the different peers by the *Advertisement* component. Maedche et al. describe in [9] the necessary infrastructure to enable consistent

---

[1] The adaptation rate of a concept indicates how many users have included the concept into their local ontology:
adaptation rate :=
   No of participants who have locally included the concept / No of participants.

change propagation in a distributed environment. We do not require that all users adapt their ontology to the changes introduced by the board members. Furthermore, we allow that they use different evolution strategies when they accept changes (see [19] for an overview of different strategies).

After the *local update* takes place, the iteration continues with *local adaptation*. During the next *analysis* step the board will review which changes were actually accepted by the users.

15.5 Related Work

Collaborative ontology engineering has been examined in recent years from different perspectives. We see three research areas as related to our work. The first deals with ontology engineering in general, the second is the work done on methodologies for collaborative ontology engineering, and the third deals with remote collaboration. We have outlined the differences between the general ontology engineering methodologies and our approach already in Sect. 15.1, and 15.2 and do not refer to them here. In [7] a methodology for collaborative ontology engineering is proposed. The aim of their work is to support the creation of a static ontology. A knowledge engineer defines an initial ontology which is extended, and changed based on the feedback from a panel of domain experts. In contrast to their work, we support on-line discussion for a distributed group, thus the participants can interact. Moreover, our process deals with evolving ontologies rather than static ones. [20] describes a system to collect feedback on different ontological decisions. However, the feedback is not analysed in the structured way as we do.

There are a number of technical solutions to tackle problems of remote collaboration, *e.g.* ontology editing with mutual exclusion [2], inconsistency detection with a voting mechanism [12], or evolution of ontologies by different means [9]. All these solutions address the issue of keeping an ontology consistent. Obviously, none supports (and do not intend to) the work process of the ontology engineers by way of a methodology. Our process could also benefit from the incorporation of appropriate argument visualization (cf. [8]).

15.6 Conclusion

It is now widely agreed that ontologies are a core enabler for the Semantic Web. The development of ontologies in centralized settings is well studied, and established methodologies exist. However, current experiences from projects and the analysis of the evolution of the classification of life forms in Biology, suggest that ontology engineering should be subject to continuous improvement rather than a one time action, and that ontologies promise the most benefits in decentralized rather than centralized systems. Hence, a methodology for distributed, loosely-controlled and evolving ontology engineering settings is needed. DILIGENT is a step towards such a methodology. DILIGENT comprises the steps **Build, Local Adaptation, Analysis,**

Revision, and **Local Update** and introduces a board to supervise changes to a shared core ontology.

In this chapter we present a fine-grained argumentation framework to be used in evolving distributed environments. We use RST to analyze the arguments exchanged when consensus is sought in evolving distributed ontology engineering processes. We have strong evidence from an *in vivo* experiment that our argumentation framework decisively contributed for speeding the process, and for finding a truly shared ontology. This is a particularly important conclusion when one foresees the development of shared ontologies in distributed settings, such as the Semantic Web. The arguments which we identified as most useful in an ontology building process are: **elaboration**, **evaluation/justification**, **alternatives**, **examples**, and **counter examples**. Having provided evidence for the applicability of our methodology it would be interesting to assess if other distributed ontology engineering efforts like the IEEE SUO will benefit from our findings.

In this chapter we also present a realization of a complete DILIGENT process cycle in an organizational setting. We have applied the methodology with good results in a case study at IBIT, one of the partners of the SWAP project. We found that the local extensions are very document centered. Though we are aware that this may often lead to unclean ontologies, we believe it to be one (of many) step(s) towards creating a practical Semantic Web in the near future.

References

[1] M. Ehrig et al. The swap data and metadata model for semantics-based peer-to-peer systems. In *Proceedings of MATES-2003. First German Conference on Multiagent Technologies*, LNAI, Erfurt, Germany, September 22-25 2003. Springer.

[2] A. Farquhar et al. The ontolingua server: A tool for collaborative ontology construction. Technical report KSL 96-26, Stanford, 1996.

[3] A. Gangemi et al. Ontology integration: Experiences with medical terminologies. In Nicola Guarino, editor, *Formal Ontology in Information Systems*, pages 163–178, Amsterdam, 1998. IOS Press.

[4] A. Gómez-Pérez et al. *Ontological Engineering*. Advanced Information and Knowlege Processing. Springer, 2003.

[5] T. R. Gruber. Towards Principles for the Design of Ontologies Used for Knowledge Sharing. In N. Guarino and R. Poli, editors, *Formal Ontol. in Conc. Analysis and Knowl. Rep.* Kluwer Acad. Pub., 1993.

[6] N. Guarino and C. Welty. Evaluating ontological decisions with OntoClean. *Communications of the ACM*, 45(2):61–65, February 2002.

[7] C. W. Holsapple and K. D. Joshi. A collaborative approach to ontology design. *Commun. ACM*, 45(2):42–47, 2002.

[8] P. A. Kirschner et al., editors. *Visualizing Argumentation: Software Tools for Collaborative and Educational Sense-Making*. Springer, 2003.

[9] A. Maedche et al. Managing multiple and distributed ontologies on the seman-
     tic web. *The VLDB Journal*, 12(4):286–302, Nov 2003.

[10] W. C. Mann and S. A. Thompson. Rhetorical structure theory: A theory of
     text organization. In L. Polanyi, editor, *The Structure of Discourse*. Ablex Pub.
     Corp., Norwood, N.J., 1987.

[11] N.F. Noy and M.A. Musen. The PROMPT suite: Interactive tools for ontology
     merging and mapping. Technical report, SMI, Stanford University, CA, USA,
     2002.

[12] A. Pease and J. Li. Agent-mediated knowledge engineering collaboration. In
     L. van Elst et al., editors, *"Agent-Mediated Knowledge Management" Interna-
     tional Symposium AMKM 2003*. Springer, 2003.

[13] H. S. Pinto and J.P. Martins. A Methodology for Ontology Integration. In
     K-CAP2001, pages 131–138, New York, 2001. ACM Press.

[14] Helena Sofia Pinto, Steffen Staab, and Christoph Tempich. DILIGENT: To-
     wards a fine-grained methodology for distributed, loosely-controlled and evolv-
     ing engineering of ontologies. In *Proceedings of the 16th European Conference
     on Artificial Intelligence, ECAI'2004*, pages 393–397. IOS Press, 2004.

[15] S. Pinto et al. OntoEdit empowering SWAP: a case study in supporting DIs-
     tributed, Loosely-controlled and evolvInG Engineering of oNTologies (DILI-
     GENT). In *1st ESWS 2004*. Springer, 2004.

[16] G. Schreiber et al. *Knowledge Engineering and Management — The Com-
     monKADS Methodology*. The MIT Press, Cambridge, Massachusetts; London,
     England, 1999.

[17] Fabrizio Sebastiani. Machine learning in automated text categorization. *ACM
     Computing Surveys*, 34(1):1–47, 2002.

[18] S. Staab et al. Knowledge processes and ontologies. *IEEE Intelligent Systems*,
     16(1), 2001.

[19] L. Stojanovic et al. User-driven ontology evolution management. In
     EKAW2002, Madrid, Spain, Oct 2002.

[20] J. Tennison and N. R. Shadbolt. APECKS: a Tool to Support Living Ontologies.
     In BR Gaines and MA Musen, editors, *11th KAW*, 1998.

[21] M. Uschold and M. King. Towards a methodology for building ontologies. In
     Proc. of IJCAI95 WS, Montreal, Canada, 1995.

A Peer-to-Peer Solution for Distributed Knowledge Management

Matteo Bonifacio

Dept. of Informatics and Business Studies - University of Trento, Italy
matteo.bonifacio@economia.unitn.it

Summary. Distributed Knowledge Management is an approach to Knowledge Management based on the principle that the multiplicity (and heterogeneity) of perspectives within complex organizations should not be viewed as an obstacle to knowledge exploitation, but rather as an opportunity that can foster innovation and creativity. Despite a wide agreement on this principle, most current KM systems are based on the idea that all perspectival aspects of knowledge should be eliminated in favor of an objective and general representation of knowledge. In this chapter we propose a Peer-to-Peer architecture (called KEx), which embodies the principle above in a quite straightforward way: (i) each peer (called a K-peer) provides all the services needed to create and organize "local" knowledge from an individual's or a group's perspective, and (ii) social structures and protocols of meaning negotiation are defined to achieve semantic coordination among autonomous peers (e.g., when searching documents from other K-peers).

16.1 Introduction

Distributed Knowledge Management (DKM), as described in [6], is an approach to KM based on the principle that the multiplicity (and heterogeneity) of perspectives within complex organizations should not be viewed as an obstacle to knowledge exploitation, but rather as an opportunity that can foster innovation and creativity. The fact that different individuals and communities may have very different perspectives, and that these perspectives affect their representation of the world (and therefore of their work) is widely discussed — and generally accepted — in theoretical research on the nature of knowledge. Knowledge representation in artificial intelligence and cognitive science have produced many theoretical and experimental evidences of the fact that what people know is not a mere collection of facts; indeed, knowledge always presupposes some (typically implicit) interpretation schema, which provide an essential component in sense-making (see, for example, the notions of context [18, 7, 13], mental space [12], partitioned representation [10]; studies on the social nature of knowledge stress the social nature of interpretation schemas, viewed as the outcome of a special kind of "agreement" within a community of knowing (see, for example, the notions of scientific paradigm [16], frame [15]), thought world [11], perspective [3]). Despite this large convergence, it can be observed that the high level architecture of most current KM systems in fact does not reflect this vision of knowledge (see [5, 6, 4] for a detailed discussion of this claim). The fact is that most KM systems embody the assumption that, to share and exploit knowledge, it is necessary to implement a process of knowledge-extraction-and-refinement, whose aim is to eliminate all subjective and contextual aspects of knowledge, and create an objective and general representation that can then be reused by other people in a variety of situations. Very often, this process is finalized to build a central knowledge base, where knowledge can be accessed via a knowledge portal. This centralized approach — and its underlying objectivist epistemology — is one of the reasons why so many KM systems are deserted by users, who perceive such systems either as irrelevant or oppressive [9]. In this chapter we propose a Peer-to-Peer (P2P) architecture, called KEx, which is coherent with the vision of DKM. Indeed, P2P systems seem particularly suitable to implement the two core principles of DKM, namely the principle of autonomy (communities of knowing should be granted the highest possible degree of semantic autonomy to manage their local knowledge), and the principle of coordination (the collaboration between autonomous communities must be achieved through a process of semantic coordination, rather than through a process of semantic homogenization) [6]. In KEx, each community of knowing (or Knowledge Nodes [KN], as they are called in [4]) is represented by a peer, and the two principles above are implemented in a quite straightforward way: (i) each peer provides all the services needed by a knowledge node to create and organize its own local knowledge (autonomy), and (ii) by defining social structures and protocols of meaning negotiation in order to achieve semantic coordination (e.g., when searching documents from other peers). The chapter is organized as follows. In Sect. 2, we describe the main features of KEx, and argue why they provide a useful support to DKM; in [3], we describe its implementation in a Peer-to-Peer platform called JXTA; finally, we draw some conclusions and future work.

16.2 KEx: a P2P Architecture for DKM

KEx is a P2P system that allows a collection of KNs to search and provide documents on a semantic basis without presupposing a beforehand agreement on how documents should be categorized, or on a common language for representing semantic information within the system. In the following sections, we describe the high-level architecture of KEx, and explain what role each element plays in a DKM vision.

16.2.1 K-peers

KEx is defined as a collection of peers, called knowledge peers (K-Peers), each of which represents a KN, namely an individual's or a group's perspective on a given body of knowledge. Each K-peer can play two main roles: provider and seeker. A K-peer acts as a provider when it "publishes" in the system a body of knowledge, together with an explicit perspective on it (called a context, e.g. a topic hierarchy used to categorized local documents [8]); a K-peer acts as a seeker when it searches for information by making explicit part of its own perspective, and negotiates it with other K-peers. Each K-peer has the structure shown in Fig. 16.1. Below we illustrate the main modules and functionalities.

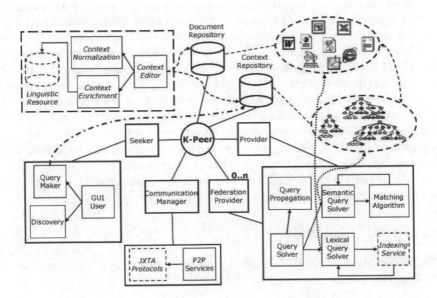

Fig. 16.1. The KEx's main components

Document Repository

A *Document Repository* is where each KN stores its own local knowledge. We can imagine a private space in which the KN maintains its document and data, possibly using a local semantic schema (e.g., a file-system structure, or a database schema), or a document management system in order to organize and access them.

Context Repository

Following [2], we define a context as a partial and approximate representation of the world from an individual's or a group's perspective. The reason why we adopt this notion of context is that it provides a robust formal framework (called Local Models Semantics [13]) for modeling both contexts and their relationships. In order to use contexts in KEx, we adopted a web-oriented syntax for contexts, called CTXML. It provides an XML-Schema specification of context for document organization and classification[1]. In KEx, each context plays the role of a category system for organizing and classifying documents, or any other kind of digital information identifiable by a URI, stored in a document repository. Each peer can use more than one context to classify local knowledge; a K-peer's contexts are stored in a context repository. From the standpoint of DKM, contexts are relevant in two distinct senses: on the one hand, they have an important role within each KN, as they provide a dynamic and incremental explicitation of its semantic perspective. Once contexts are reified, they become cognitive artifacts that contribute to the process of perspective making [3], namely the consolidation of a shared view in a KN, continuously subject to revision and internal negotiation among its members; on the other hand, contexts offer a simple and direct way for a KN to make public its perspective on the information that that KN can provide. Therefore, as we will see, contexts are an essential tool for semantic coordination among different KN. It is important to observe that contexts provide only a common syntax for classification structures. Indeed, we could see them as a language for wrapping any classification structure (e.g., like directory systems, databases schemas, web directories). This means that in principle people can continue to work with their preferred document management system, provided it can be wrapped using CTXML.

Context Management Module

The context management module allows users to create, manipulate, and use contexts in KEx. The module has two main components:

- **Context editor**: provides users with a simple interface to create and edit contexts, and to classify information with respect to a context. This happens by allowing users to create links from a resource (identified by a URI) to a node in a context. Examples of resources are: documents in local directories, the address of a database access services, addresses of other K-peers that provide information that a KN wants to explicitly classify in its own context;
- **Context browser**: is part of Seeker component (GUI User in Fig. 16.1) and allows users to navigate contexts in the context repository. The main reasons for navigating a context in KEx are two. The first is obviously to find document in the local knowledge repository by navigating the semantic structure. The second, and more important reason, is to build queries. The intuitive idea is that users can make context dependent queries (namely, from their perspective) by selecting a category in one of the available contexts. Once a category is selected, the context browser builds a *focus*[2] — namely a contextual interpretation of the user's query — by automatically extracting the relevant portion of the context to which the category belongs. The focus is then used as a basis for meaning coordination and negotiation with other K-peers during the search.

---

[1] Currently, contexts are trees, whose nodes are labelled with words defined in some name space. Arcs are Is-A, Part-Of or generic relations between nodes. Details can be found in [8].

[2] See [17] for a formal definition of focus.

16.2.2 Roles of K-peers in KEx

Each K-peer can play two main roles: seeker and provider. Their interactions are represented in Fig. 16.2, and described in detail in the following two sections.

Seeker

As a seeker, a K-peer allows users to search for documents (and other information) from other K-peers and federations (see Sect. 16.2.3). The seeker supports the user in the definition of context-dependent queries through the context browser.

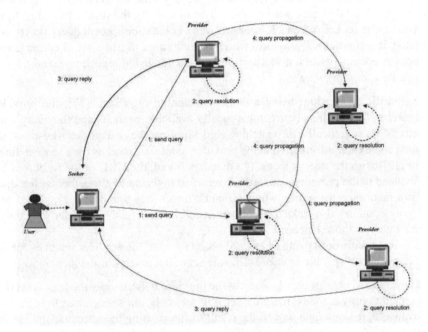

Fig. 16.2. The KEx system: interaction between Seeker and Provider roles

A query is composed by a query expression and a focus. A query expression is a list (possibly empty) of one or more keywords provided by a user; a focus is a portion of a context determined by the category that the user has selected. Moreover, the seeker provides the discovery mechanism, used to find resources to which the query is to be sent. The user decides to send the query to some of the available K-peers and federations. When the user submits the query, the seeker activates a session associated to that query (there can be only one active session for each seeker). In a session, a seeker can receive several asynchronous replies from the providers which resolved the query (through the meaning negotiation protocol, see below) and called back the seeker. The results returned to the user are composed by the aggregation of all the results received from the providers; each result is made up of a list of document descriptors (i.e., name of the document, short description, and so on). Each result is presented together with the part of context that the provider has matched against the current query. This relationship between contexts can be used as an opportunity for learning relationships across contexts of different KNs that the seeker can store and reuse for future queries (see Sect. 16.2.3). Finally, if one or more interesting documents are found, the seeker can contact the K-peers that have the documents and, if possible, download them.

Provider

The provider is the second main role in the KEx system. It contains the functionalities required to take and resolve a query, and to identify the results that must to be returned to the seeker. When a K-peer receives a context-dependent query (keywords + focus), it instantiates a provider (which is configured to use a set of contexts and to provide documents in a given portion of the knowledge repository), and tries to resolve the query in two ways:

- **Semantic resolution**: using a context matching algorithm [17], the provider searches for relations between the locally available contexts and the query's focus. More specifically, the matching algorithm searches categories whose associated contextual information in the providers contexts matches (in a sense defined in [17]) with the querys focus. If a match is found, the URIs of the resources associated to the provider's context are returned to the seeker, together with a short information on the reason why a semantic match was found. If the matched category contains also links to resources in other K-peers, the provider propagates the query to those Kpeers;
- **Lexical resolution**: using a keyword-based indexer, the provider searches for the occurrence of specific keywords into the set of documents of the local repository.

If the query contains only keywords, the provider will use only the lexical search; if it contains only a focus, the provider will use only the semantic search; if both are available, the outcome will be the result of intersecting the semantic and lexical results.

16.2.3 K-Services

KEx provides a collection of services which have an important role in supporting knowledge exchange (that is why they are called K-services). The main K-services are described in the following sections.

Context Normalization and Enrichment

This service allows to perform a linguistic normalization (e.g., deleting stop words, tokenizing, part-of-speech tagging, etc.) on user defined contexts, and to use knowledge from an external linguistic resource (e.g., WordNet) to add semantic information to the categories in a context. Normalization uses pretty standard NLP techniques, so we do not discuss it here. As to enrichment, it is applied offline to a context defined by a user (see [17] for details). It takes a user-defined context (e.g., a context built with the context editor) as input and returns a semantically enriched context as output. In our current implementation, the result is that linguistic knowledge (e.g., senses, synonyms, hierarchical relations with other categories, and so on) is extracted from WordNet and is "attached" to each context node label.

- It is important to say why enrichment is not equivalent to introduce a shared ("objective") semantics in KEx. Indeed, the intuition is that the meaning of a label in each context node has two components: the first is the linguistic component, which means that the words used as labels have a meaning (or, better, a set of meanings) in a "dictionary." This is used to record that many words have different meaning (e.g., "apple" as a fruit, "apple" as a tree, and "apple" as a computer brand), even if only one of them is likely to be the relevant one in a given context;
- The second is a sort of pragmatic component, which is given by its position in a context (e.g., its position in the path from the context root). This helps in understanding what the user means on a particular occasion with a word (e.g., "apple" in a path like "computer/software/apple" is different from "apple" in a path like "computer/hardware/printers/apple", even though "apple" has the same dictionary "meaning").

The first component of meaning is dealt with in the normalization and enrichment phase (for example, given a context, some potential senses are deleted because of the position of a label in that context); the second is dealt with in the meaning negotiation protocol, and cannot be computed beforehand, as it expresses a user's perspective in making a query (so this is the more "perspectival" aspect of meaning). It is extremely important to stress that different linguistic resources can be used to enrich a context. So far, we have been using only WordNet, but there is no reason why other resources (like CYC or any other domain-specific ontology) cannot be used to replace WordNet. Of course, this introduces a further problem, as the enriched contexts cannot be compared as directly as in the case of a shared resource. In this case, what happens is that each provider, after receiving a query from a context which is normalized with a different linguistic resource, applies a runtime normalization-and-enrichment of the query's focus, this way interpreting the query from its perspective. Then the query can be matched against local contexts. Of course, this introduces a further degree of semantic heterogeneity, and the returned results could be unsatisfactory for the seeker even if the semantic match good from the provider's perspective.

K-federation

A *K-federation* is a group of K-Peers that agree to appear as a unique entity to K-peers that perform a search. Each K-federation can be though as a "social" aggregation of K-peers that display some synergy in terms of content (e.g., as they provide topic-related content, or decided to use the same linguistic resource to create a common "vocabulary," thus providing more homogeneous and specific answers), quality (certify content) or access policies (certify members). Seekers can send queries directly to K-federations, and the query is managed internally at the federation. In our current implementation, the query is simply distributed to all the members of the federation (and therefore the result is the same as if the query was sent directly to each member of the federation, the only difference being that Kpeers explicitly answer as members of the federation), but the idea is that in general each K-federation can implement different methods to process queries. To become a member of a K-federation, a K-Peer must provide a K-federation Service (the Federation Provider in Fig. 1). It implements the required federation protocol (reply to queries sent to the K-federation) and observes the federation membership policy.

Discovery

Discovery is a mechanism that allows the user to discover resources in the P2P network. The user needs to discover K-peers and K-federations available in the network to contact and query them. A peer advertises the existence of resources by publishing an XML document (called Advertisement). In the KEx system, two types of resources are advertised:

- **K-peers** that have a provider service to solve queries. The main elements of the advertisement are a description of the peers contexts, and the peer address to contact it, to send it queries, and to retrieve documents.
- **K-federations**, namely sets of peers that have a federation service to solve queries. The federation assures that a query sent to a federation is propagated to all active peers that are member of the federation. In this case the main elements of the advertisement are the federation topic, its address and information for joining the federation. To discover resources, a peer sends a discovery request to another known peer, or sends a multi-cast request over the network, and receives responses (a list of advertisements) that describe the available services and resources. It is possible to specify search criteria (currently only keywords or textual expression) that are matched against the contents provided by the advertisement related to each peer or federation description.

Query Propagation

This functionality allows the KEx system to distributed queries in a highly dynamic environment. When a provider receives a query, it can forward it to other providers. To decide to which peers the query is to be forwarded, a peer has two possibilities:

- *Physical proximity:* The query is sent to peers known through the discovery functionality. This way, peers or providers that are non directly reachable from a seeker, or have just joined the system, can advertise their presence and contribute to the resolution of queries;
- *Semantic proximity:* This functionality exploits the fact that contexts can be used not only to classify resources like documents or database records, but also other peers. Thus, if the provider computes some matching between a query and a concept in its own context, and other peers are classified under that concept, the

provider forwards the query to these other peers, thus increasing the chances that other relevant peers are reached.

The propagation algorithm is based upon a cost function which allows choosing peers that are regarded as providing more relevant information (assigning a higher value to peers discovered through the semantic method than to peers reached through physical proximity one). Obviously, several parameters and mechanisms controlling the scope of the search can be implemented to prevent a "message flood." For example, the time-to-live (TTL), the number of hops, the list of peers already reached, and so on.

Learning

When the matching algorithm finds a semantic correspondence between concepts of different contexts, the provider can store this information for future reuse. This information is represented as a semantic "mapping" between concepts (see [8]), and can be used in three ways:

- When the K-Peer receives a query from a seeker, it can reuse stored mappings to facilitate (and possibly to avoid executing) the matching algorithm.
- A provider can use the existing mapping to forward a query to other peers that have a semantic relation with the query's focus.
- The seeker can search into the available mappings to suggest the user a set of providers with which it already had previous interactions and are considered qualified with respect to the semantic meaning of the concept selected in a query.

Using this mechanism, the K-peer network defines and increases the number and quality of the semantic relations among its members, and becomes a dynamic web of knowledge links.

16.3 Development Framework

In this section we briefly show how the non-functional requirements of a DKM system drive the choice of a particular architectural pattern design (a Peer-to-Peer system) and an underlying technology framework (the Jxta Project). In particular, KEx is under development within the business setting of an Italian national bank, and of an international insurance company[1]. From an implementation point of view, we started from JXTA[2], a set of open, generalized Peer-to-Peer protocols that allow devices to communicate and collaborate through a connecting network. This P2P framework

---

[1] This architecture is under development as part of EDAMOK (*Enabling Distributed and Autonomous Management of Knowledge*), a joint project of the Institute for Scientific and Technological Research (IRST, Trento) and of the University of Trento.

[2] JXTA is a P2P open source project started in 2001 and supported by Sun Microsystems. See http://www.jxta.org/ for details.

provides also a set of protocols and functionality: such as a decentralized discovery system, an asynchronous point-to-point messaging system, and a group membership protocol. A peer is a software component that runs some or all the JXTA protocols; every peer needs to agree upon a common set of rules to publish, share and access resources (like services, data or applications), and communicate among each others. Thus, a JXTA peer is used to support higher level processes (based, for example, on organizational considerations) that are built on top of the basic Peer-to-Peer network infrastructure; they may include the enhancement of basic JXTA protocols (e.g. discovery) as well as user-written applications. JXTA tackles these requirements with a number of mechanisms and protocols: for instance the publishing and discovery mechanisms, together with a message-based communication infrastructure (called "pipe") and peer monitoring services, supports decentralization and dynamism. Security is supported by a membership service (which authenticates any peer applying to a peer group) and an access protocol (for authorization control). The flexibility of this framework allows to design distributed systems that cover all the requirements of a DKM application, using the JXTA P2P capabilities, completed and enhanced through the implementation of user-defined services. As shown in the previous sections, in the KEx system we combine the P2P paradigm (characterizing a network of knowledge nodes as a network of distributed peers) and JXTA as an implementation infrastructure.

16.4 Conclusions and Research Issues

In this chapter, we argued that technological architectures, when dealing with processes in which human communication is strongly involved, must be consistent with the social architecture of the process itself. In particular, in the domain of KM, technology must embody a principle of distribution that is intrinsic to the nature of organizational cognition. Here, we suggest that P2P infrastructures are especially suitable for KM applications, as they naturally implement meaning distribution and autonomy. It is perhaps worth noting at this point that other research areas are moving toward P2P architectures. In particular, we can mention the work on P2P approaches to the Semantic Web [1], to databases [14], and to web services [19]. We believe this is a general trend, and that in the near future P2P infrastructure will become more and more interesting for all areas where we cannot assume a centralized control. A number of research issues need to be addressed to map aspects of distributed cognition into technological requirements. Here we propose two of them:

- **Social discovery and propagation:** In order to find knowledge, people need to discover who is reachable and available to answer a request. On the one hand, broadcasting messages generates communication overflow, on the other hand talking just to physically available neighbors reduces the potential of a distributed network. A third option could be for a seeker to ask his neighbors who they trust on a topic and, among them, who is currently available. Here the question is about social mechanisms through which people find — based on trust and rec-

ommendation — other people to involve in a conversation. A similar approach
could be used in order to support the propagation of information requests;

- **Building communities:** If we consider communities as networks of people that,
  to some extent, tend to share a common perspective [3], mechanisms are needed
  to support the bottom-up emergence of semantic similarities across interacting
  KNs. Through this process, which are based on meaning negotiation protocols,
  people can discover and form virtual communities, and within organizations,
  managers might monitor the evolving trajectories of informal cognitive networks.
  Then, such networks, can be viewed as potential neighborhoods to support social
  discovery and propagation.

References

[1]   M. Arumugam, A. Sheth, and I. Budak Arpinar: The peer-to-peer semantic
      web: A distributed environment for sharing semantic knowledge on the web.
      In: *WWW2002 Workshop on Real World RDF and Semantic Web Applications.*
      Honolulu, Hawaii, USA, 2002.
[2]   M. Benerecetti, P. Bouquet, and C. Ghidini: Contextual Reasoning Distilled.
      Journal of Theoretical and Experimental Artificial Intelligence, **12**, 3:279-305,
      July (2000).
[3]   J.R. Boland and R.V.Tenkasi: Perspective making and perspective taking in
      communities of knowing. Organization Science, **6**, 3:350-372, (1995).
[4]   M. Bonifacio, P. Bouquet, and R. Cuel. Knowledge Nodes: the Building Blocks
      of a Distributed Approach to Knowledge Management. Journal of Universal
      Computer Science, **8**, 6:652-661, (2002).
[5]   M. Bonifacio, P. Bouquet, and A. Manzardo: A distributed intelligence
      paradigm for knowledge management. In: *Working Notes of the AAAI Spring
      Symposium Series 2000 on Bringing Knowledge to Business Processes.* AAAI,
      March 18-20 2000.
[6]   M. Bonifacio and P. Bouquet and P. Traverso: Enabling Distributed Knowl-
      edge Management. Managerial and Technological Implications. Novatica and
      Informatik/Informatique **III**, 1 (2002).
[7]   P. Bouquet: *Contesti e ragionamento contestuale. Il ruolo del contesto in una
      teoria della rappresentazione della conoscenza,* (Pantograph, Genova Italy
      1998).
[8]   P. Bouquet, A. Donà, and L. Serafini: ConTeXtualized local ontology spec-
      ification via ctxml. In: *MeaN-02 - AAAI workshop on Meaning Negotiation.*
      Edmonton, Alberta, Canada, 2002.
[9]   G. C. Bowker and S. L. Star: *Sorting things out: classification and its conse-
      quences,* (MIT Press, 1999).
[10] J. Dinsmore: *Partitioned Representations,* (Kluwer Academic Publishers,
      1991).
[11] D. Dougherty: Interpretative barriers to successful product innovation in large
      firms. Organization Science, **3**, 2 (1992).

[12] G. Fauconnier: *Mental Spaces: aspects of meaning construction in natural language*, (MIT Press, 1985).

[13] C. Ghidini and F. Giunchiglia: Local Models Semantics, or Contextual Reasoning = Locality + Compatibility. Artificial Intelligence, **127**, 2:221-259, April (2001).

[14] Giunchiglia and I. Zaihrayeu: Making peer databases interact - a vision for an architecture supporting data coordination. In: *6th International Workshop on Cooperative Information Agents (CIA-2002)*. Universidad Rey Juan Carlos, Madrid, Spain, 2002.

[15] I. Goffaman: *Frame Analysis*, (Harper & Row, New York, 1974).

[16] T. Kuhn: *The structure of Scientific Revolutions*, (University of Chicago Press, 1979).

[17] B. Magnini, L. Serafini, and M. Speranza: Linguistic based matching of local ontologies. In: P. Bouquet, editor, *Working Notes of the AAAI-02 workshop on Meaning Negotiation*. Edmonton, Canada, 2002.

[18] J. McCarthy: Notes on Formalizing Context. In: *Proc. of the 13th International Joint Conference on Artificial Intelligence, pages 555-560*. Chambery, France, 1993.

[19] M.P. Papazoglou, J. Jang, and B.J.Kraemer: *Leveraging web-services and peer-to-peer networks*, (2002).

Xarop, a Semantic Peer-to-Peer System for a Virtual Organization

Esteve Lladó, Immaculada Salamanca

Fundación IBIT, España
{esteve,isalamanca}@ibit.org

Summary. Tourists' demands are increasingly exigent in terms of quality product and environment. Thus, the tourism industry in the Balearic Islands depends on a preserved environment and on keeping local identity and quality of life (so-called Sustainable Development). Sustainable Development will be achieved after a process of effective communication and co-operation among the main actors of the tourism industry. The IST project SWAP (IST-2001-34103), financed by the EU, brought the opportunity to implement an effective and reliable knowledge-based network to enable communication and co-operation among the main players of the tourism industry in the Balearic Islands, as a supporting tool to direct current social and economical challenges towards Sustainable Development. In this chapter we will describe XAROP, a semantic and P2P based knowledge management solution developed in SWAP project to satisfy the requirements of the case study.

17.1 Introduction

Tourism is the single most important sector of the economy in the Balearic Islands, with over 80% share of the GDP. Tourism, however, while packaged and sold to the outside as a product, is a very complex offering: the overall satisfaction of the tourist is determined by all experiences he gains while spending his time on the islands. This means that the Balearic product can only succeed in the market if the actions of all parties (public or private) are well coordinated. Since the product is a result of a composite process involving multiple independent actors, we may even talk of a Virtual Organization [1] in the Balearic Islands created by shared interests and mutual dependencies.

17.1.1 The Tourism Sector in the Balearic Islands

The Balearic Islands have been recognised worldwide as the leading holiday centre in the Western Mediterranean [5]. The main reasons for this are its sunny and balmy climate, the tranquillity of its coves, its landscape and diversity, its geographical situation (two-three hours trip from main European cities), good infrastructures and good value. They are one of the destinations with great experience in the zone and many destinations see the Islands as a model of economic development.

The Balearic economy got into tourism in the late fifties, faciliating the entrance of the Islands in the world economy and a starting point for initiating relations with the rest of Europe. This emerging economy had a positive impact on local people quality of life.

The competitive advantage of the Balearic Islands has been to offer the nice and sunny beach resorts in a pleasant environment, at a good price and close emission markets. This strategy has been functioning well until now, but the market changes continuously. New beach resorts and sunny destinations have come with better price offers as the main changes of the last decade. Such destinations had remained out of the market place due to internal problems and conflicts (the Balkan wars, unstable political situations, etc.). The tourist in general has become much more demanding than ever before, and therefore they have better knowledge of the product and services offer. The Balearic Islands can not longer survive with only the ongoing claim of a nice and sunny beach resort.

The competitiveness of the Balearic Islands must be based on variables other than price: quality, security, specialisation, uniqueness, cultural activities, preserved environment, etc. The synthesis of these variables is Sustainable Development, and the scope of this term refers not only to tourism sector, but also to the whole of Balearic Society.

17.1.2 Decision making in the Destination

Achieving a Sustainable Development is not immediate; it is about a cultural change in long term premises. The responsibility of leading this change is in the hands of the public administration policy makers and also the tourism industry managers through the design and development of policies and enterprise strategies able to balance social, economical and environmental aspects.

Decision making needs well founded support and judgement elements, which can be provided by different actors/institutions. The illustration (see Fig. 17.1) explains, in a simple way, the knowledge process in decision making at destination level. The actors are mainly exchanging documents in order to develop their functions. In the following, we describe each step of the knowledge process.

1 Data and information sources

The first step of the process consists of gathering of information from intranets, research databases, catalogues, and other resources providing documents and files in different formats and supports, about one or more relevant aspects of the tourism sector.

2 Analysis of information

The basic process that occurs at this stage is the analysis of the gathered information, which is carried out by the following actors:

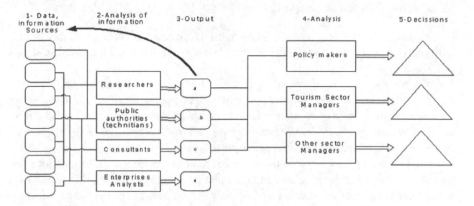

Fig. 17.1. Knowledge process and decision making in the tourism sector

- Researchers in public and private research institutions, which do a diligent and systematic inquiry into a subject in order to discover or revise facts, theories, etc.
- Technicians and/or civil servants, working in Public Administrations (PPAA), whose main task is to assist and support policy makers decisions, via elaborating reports, statistics, indicators and other analysis work.
- Consultants specialised on giving professional or expert advice, usually to a client (PPAA, enterprises) on a specific subject.
- Enterprise Analysts, who carry out the same task of technicians in PPAA but at private enterprises.

3 Output

After analysis of information, researchers, technicians, consultants and enterprise analysts elaborate specialised documents (public ones are incorporated to sources): Papers, studies, thesis, articles, reports, indicators, plans, newsletters, etc. in order to divulge their findings and conclusions.

4 Analysis

Decision makers analyse selected outputs, in order to secure and support their decisions (5 - Decisions) on strategy and medium and long planning.

17.1.3 Domains of Knowledge

We have identified three domains of knowledge that will lead the case study and the creation of a common ontology: Sustainable Tourism Development, Quality and Hospitality Management, and New Technologies and Innovation. Sustainable Tourism Development will be the most important one, as it is clearly the base of future economic and environmental policies of the Balearic Islands in the upcoming years. The following subsections describe these domains of knowledge (for details about ontology creation, see Chap. 16 describing the DILIGENT process).

Sustainable Tourism Development

In the case of the Balearic Islands, Sustainable Development [2] is inevitably linked with tourism, where we find the definition of the World Tourism Organisation stated in 1996:

Sustainable Tourism Development meets the needs of present tourists and host regions while protecting and enhancing opportunities for the future. It is envisaged as leading to management of all resources in such a way that economic, social and aesthetic needs can be fulfilled while maintaining cultural integrity, essential ecological processes, biological diversity and life support systems.

The present approach to Sustainable Tourism Development is to consider the tourist activity at a regional scope, and it can help to establish the relations and interactions between tourism, territory and society. Thus, actors will exchange information on sustainable indicators, studies, analysis, etc. on relevant subjects.

Information and knowledge shared within Sustainable Development has three main factors: Demographic, socio-economic and environmental [3],even though its differentiation can not be clearly stated because many of the elements are shared, complementary or even merging. This gives an idea of the complexity and the interdisciplinary of the elements involved in the Sustainable Development.

Quality and Hospitality Management

Tourism is a highly competitive industry, and the European tourism sector can no longer compete on the basis of cost alone. Quality is therefore a key element for the competitiveness of the tourism industry. It is also important for the sustainable development of the industry and for creating and improving jobs.

An integrated approach to quality management is necessary because so many different elements affect tourists perception of a destination (such as transport, accommodation, information, attractions, the environment, etc.). Integrated Quality Management (IQM) needs to take into account tourist businesses, tourists interests, the local population and the environment, and to have a positive impact on all of them. Quality is the perception by the tourist of the extent to which his expectations are met by his experience of the product. Quality is not to be equated to luxury, and must not be exclusive, but must be available to all tourists, including those with special needs.

Hospitality Industry is usually related to products that satisfy demand for food, drink and accommodation (but it excludes food and drink manufacture and retailing). Tasks involved in Hospitality Management are related to planning, organising, motivating and controlling according to policy requirements: Provision of facilities for a defined market; provision system (modifying the operational cycle); total customer satisfaction; formulation, establishment and maintenance of control systems to monitor costs, prices and sales; providing management information for performance reconciliation, and other tasks.

New Technologies and Innovation

Technology is an essential part of company competitiveness, with some 80% of instances of improved productivity being a result of new technologies. The ability to identify and incorporate technologies into business processes plays a critical role in the tourism sector of the Balearic Islands.

We do not regard technology as simply pieces of machinery, equipment, materials or tools, but include their impact on quality of design, production processes, the materials used, business organisation, and ultimately, the application and market share of a product.

There are identifiable drivers of both Innovation and Technology. These drivers can be mapped, measured and managed through methodologies, which can be both learned and practised.

17.2 Requirements Analysis

The tourism sector in the Balearic Islands can potentially benefit from a system whose architecture reflects the autonomy of the actors and the locality of the knowledge accumulated [6]. This architecture will be achieved by linking the participating organizations by a P2P network. As such a system has no central point of control, it is also expected to fare better in cases of realignments in the private sector (e.g. due to changes in the marketplace) or reorganizations in the public sector (e.g. due to changes in government).

On the other hand, the existence of a shared domain, overlapping or related competences within organizations and the need for carrying out certain functions in cooperation, suggests that it is possible to develop (or merge) ontologies shared by the different sub-communities (graphically represented in Fig. 17.2).

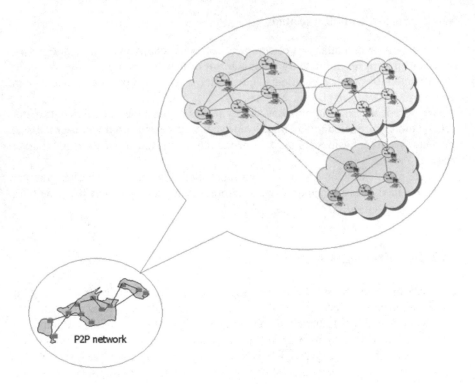

Fig. 17.2. Architecture based on linking participating organizations by a P2P network

17.2.1 Organizational Context Analysis

To analyse the organizations involved in the case study we have used *CommonKADS* [4], a complete methodological framework for the development of knowledge based systems. It supports most aspects of a KBS development project, such as: Project management, organisational analysis (including problem/opportunity identification), knowledge acquisition (including initial project scoping), knowledge analysis and modeling, capture of user requirements, analysis of system integration issues, and knowledge system design.

The modeling process is supported by worksheets. In seven organizations of the case study we have analysed the following worksheets:

Organisational Model (OM1-OM5)

- Worksheet OM-1: Identify knowledge-oriented problems and opportunities in the organization.
- Worksheet OM-2: Description of organisational aspects that have an impact on and/or are affected by chosen knowledge solutions.

- Worksheet OM-3: Description of the process in terms of the tasks it is composed of, and their main characteristics.
- Worksheet OM-4: Description of the knowledge component of the organisation model and its major characteristics.
- Worksheet OM-5: Checklist for the feasibility decision.

Task Model (TM1-TM2)

- Worksheet TM-1: Refined description of the tasks within the target process.
- Worksheet TM-2: Specification of the knowledge employed for a task, and possible bottlenecks and areas for improvement.

Agent Model (AM1)

- Worksheet AM-1: Agent specification according to the *CommonKADS* agent model.

Organisation-Task-Agent Model (OTA1)

- Worksheet OTA-1: Impacts and improvements decisions.

And from the analysis results we extracted as functional requirements the use cases described in the next section.

17.2.2 Use Cases Description

Searching for Information

The basic use case of the system is searching for information. One way of doing this is manual browsing of other peer folders. The system works in this scenario in a way similar to filesystems, with the particularity of using P2P technology and unifying views from different sources (like different peers and, from the other hand, from folders/files and bookmarks from Web browser).

More advanced information search is possible using full-text search. This way the user can easily find all documents containing words, e.g. typing *tourism* results in finding all documents containing the word *tourism* in its content.

The most powerful mechanism is *topic search*. In this case, the user is interested in some topic and asks for all documents related to that topic (e.g. *tourist arrivals*). The system allows this, delivering mechanism of automatic assignment of documents into topics. This mechanism is multi-lingual, so the query takes into consideration documents in any of supported languages, namely English, Spanish or Catalan. As automatic mechanism may not be perfectly accurate, the user is able to manually change document-topic alignments, and these alignments are considered when performing the search.

User has the possibility to restrict the scope of the query search (eg. local search, search to all connected peers, search to some selected peers only). Additionally, user has the possibility to combine results of all these search methods, to identify e.g. documents matching all of his criteria.

Sharing Information

Information sharing is publishing some of peers' local resources into the system. This function is easy to use, like e.g. selecting files, directories, Web bookmarks etc. from the list and marking them as shared.

Additionally, some security mechanism is needed to increase number of shared documents, otherwise non-public documents would be not shared. So this use case also covers use cases for giving or revoking permissions on resources to other peers and organizations.

Using Shared Information

Information is shared in form of documents and similar resources like e-mail and Web bookmarks.

Using shared data means something different for different types of resources. For Web bookmarks, it means opening a Web browser and redirecting it into bookmarked URL. In other cases it means downloading content into the requesting machine and opening it.

Using shared information is restricted by security permissions given by resource owners.

Ontology Editing

All peers are sharing a common ontology, containing some concept hierarchy. The basic use case for most users is assigning documents into topics (stating that this document is about this topic). More powerful users have possibility to change the ontology itself and all the knowledge contained in the system, e.g. extracted from folder structures or file metadata.

17.3 XAROP platform description

We have developed a semantic and P2P based knowledge management solution appropriate for the use cases sketched above. The platform is called XAROP i.e. Catalan for *syrup*. In this section we will describe the functionalities developed in the XAROP platform [7]. We can distinguish between the functionalities developed in XAROP as a generic Virtual Organization prototype, and specific developments for the Balearic case study.

Developed functionalities for a generic Virtual Organization prototype:

- Knowledge Providing functionalities:
    - Sharing folders and Web bookmarks
    - Full indexing and classification of documents
- Knowledge Searching functionalities:

- Browsing folders and Web bookmarks (on local and remote peers)
- Manual peer selection
- Keyword-based search (on local and remote peers)
- Conceptual search (on local and remote peers)
- Presenting/Visualizing results
- Duplicate detection on results
- Downloading files
- Managing Security Permissions:
  - Granting or revoking access permissions on documents and folders to individual peers or organizations (groups of peers)
  - Defining organizations and their members
  - Assigning an administrator to delegate the task of defining organizations
- Ontology Editing (see Chap. 16 for details about *OntoEdit* plug-in):
  - Editing concepts
  - Querying for subconcepts to other peers

Specific functionalities and developments for the Balearic case study are:

- Multilanguage user interfaces: English, Spanish and Catalan
- Definitions of a common ontology to conceptualize the domains of knowledge described in Sect. 17.1.3. (see Chap. 16 for details about the creation of the common ontology)

17.3.1 Knowledge Providing functionalities

The first step for a XAROP user is to select the local resources that the user wants to share with other peers. After starting the client the user can share folders, documents and Web bookmarks. Selecting from *Tools* menu *Share folders* item the user will be presented with the following window:

The user can navigate the local folder structure and choose the folders that he/she wants to share with other peers, and select *Extract to Repository* (see Fig. 17.3). The shared resources will appear in the *Peer Folders* panel (see Fig. 17.4). Alternatively, the user can select the *Write rdf file* option to export the selected content to a RDF file.

After sharing documents, it is possible to index the shared contents. This is a necessary task to perform keyword and concept searches. During the indexing process, following a multi-lingual mechanism, the documents are classified automatically under concepts of the concept hierarchy (common ontology), presented in the *Concept Search* panel (see Fig. 17.4). Some classification refinements can be done manually after the automatic classification process. Files or Web bookmarks can be manually classified by dragging them from the *Details* panel to a concept in the concept hierarchy.

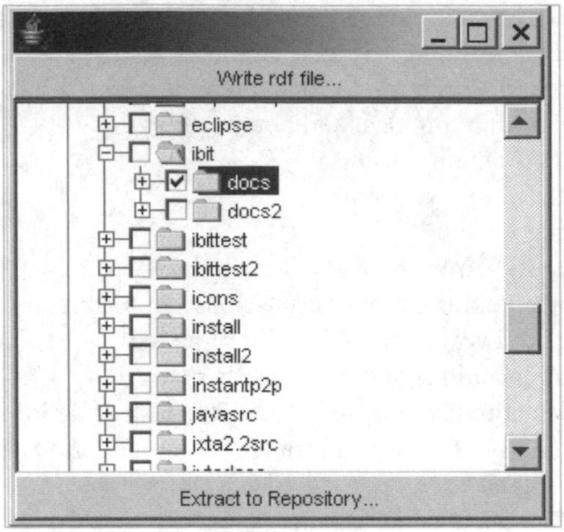

Fig. 17.3. Sharing documents window

17.3.2 Knowledge Searching Functionalities

Main searching user interface is shown in Fig. 17.4. On the top left, the user has the *Peer Folders* panel for browsing peer folders. The list of peers is there, with local and remote peers differentiated by color. The user can open a tree of shared folders of each peer. Selecting one of them and pressing *Show* brings its visualization into the *Cluster Map* panel.

On the bottom left, there is the *Queries* panel for posing keyword and concept queries. Concept queries are sent in similar manner as folder browsing the user browses the concept tree (*Concept Search* panel), selects a node and presses *Show* button. Keyword queries are sent by typing keywords in the text field and choosing language, and submitting the query. Both concept and keyword queries scope can be restricted to: the local peer or all peers (no restrictions) or a list of peers selected manually by user (the list is visible after pressing the *Specify...* button).

The central panel is the cluster map visualization of query results and folders. The user may freely select, move and delete nodes from the visualization. The *Details* panel shows details of the current selection names of files and their metadata. The user can try to download and open a file by right clicking on it in the *Details* panel, but he will fail when the user has no permissions to do that. Files can also be saved to a local shared folder by dragging them from the *Details* panel to a local folder in the *Peer Folders* tree. The files will automatically be saved to that folder and additional user input is only required when the application is about to overwrite an existing file (these files are not automatically shared).

Query results are analyzed in order to detect duplicate documents in different peers. When the same document is obtained in a query from two different peers, the corresponding entry for the document in the *Details* panel indicates the two peer

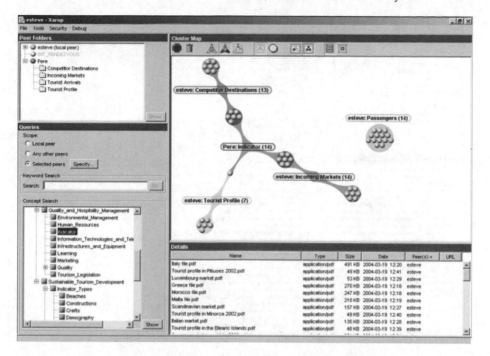

Fig. 17.4. Main searching user interface of XAROP

names in the *Peer(s)* column. Also, on the cluster map, a new cluster containing the duplicated documents will be represented.

17.3.3 Managing Security Permissions

Security window is shown in Fig. 17.5. The user is able to grant or revoke permissions on folders and documents to individual peers or organizations (group of peers). The user may also define organizations and their members, or he may delegate his trust to some other *admin peer* and let him or her define them.

17.4 Conclusions

In this chapter we have described the XAROP platform, a semantic Peer-to-Peer system building on a Virtual Organization of government agencies and tourist industry companies on the Balearic Islands. The evaluation results indicated that the XAROP platform satisfied the requirements and the major expectations of the virtual organization case study. The results were positive in terms of usability and about the functionalities for structuring and searching knowledge.

We concluded that, even though the system can contribute significantly to save time when exchanging knowledge within and between organizations, we have to

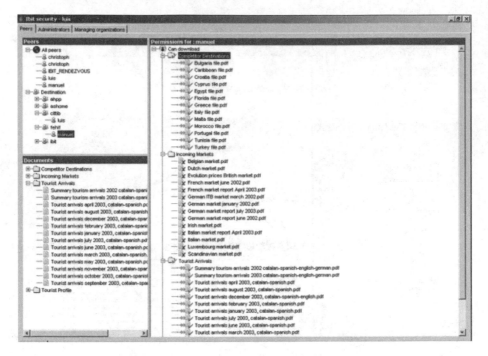

Fig. 17.5. Security window

find mechanisms to incentive peers to share knowledge. One possible solution in the future to increase the number of active peers could be to establish some passive and permanent active peers in some organizations, putting available documents of public interest (indicator reports emitted by public institutions).

Also, the definition of a common ontology contributed to the creation of a common understanding of the tourist destination management domain among organizations.

References

[1]   Luis M. Camarinha-Matos and Hamideh Afsarmanesh, editors. Processes and Foundations for Virtual Organizations. volume 262 of IFIP International Federation for Information Processing. Kluwer Academic Publishers, 2003.

[2]   WCED (1987) Our common future. Oxford University Press.

[3]   Blàzquez, M., Murray, I. and Garau, J.M. (2002), El tercer boom. Indicadors de sostenibilitat del turisme de les Illes Balears 1989-1999. Palma de Mallorca. CITTIB. Spain.

[4]   A. Th. Schreiber, J. Akkermans, A. Anjewierden, R. De Hoog, N. Shadbolt,W. Van De Velde & B. Wielinga. Knowledge Engineering and Management: The CommonKADS Methodology (2000), MIT Press.

[5] SWAP EU IST-2001-34103 Project Deliverable D7.1, First User Environment Definition.
[6] SWAP EU IST-2001-34103 Project Deliverable D7.2, Refined User Environment Definition.
[7] SWAP EU IST-2001-34103 Project Deliverable D7.3, Virtual Enterprise SWAP Prototype.

Bibster — A Semantics-Based Bibliographic Peer-to-Peer System

Peter Haase[1], Björn Schnizler[1], Jeen Broekstra[3], Marc Ehrig[1], Frank van Harmelen[2], Maarten Menken[2], Peter Mika[2], Michal Plechawski[4], Pawel Pyszlak[4], Ronny Siebes[2], Steffen Staab[5], Christoph Tempich[1]

[1] Institute AIFB, University of Karlsruhe, Germany
    {haase,ehrig,tempich}@aifb.uni-karlsruhe.de,
    schnizler@iw.uka.de
[2] Vrije Universiteit Amsterdam, The Netherlands
    {mrmenken,pmika,ronny}@cs.vu.nl
[3] Aduna, Amersfoort, The Netherlands
    jeen@aduna.biz
[4] Empolis, Warsaw, Poland
    {pap,mpl}@empolis.pl
[5] ISWeb, University of Koblenz-Landau, Germany
    staab@uni-koblenz.de

Summary. This chapter describes the design, implementation, and evaluation of Bibster, a Peer-to-Peer system for exchanging bibliographic data among researchers. Bibster exploits ontologies in data-storage, query formulation, query-routing and answer presentation: When bibliographic entries are made available for use in Bibster, they are structured and classified according to two different ontologies. This ontological structure is then exploited to help users formulate their queries. Subsequently, the ontologies are used to improve query routing across the Peer-to-Peer network. Finally, the ontologies are used to post-process the returned answers in order to do duplicate detection. The chapter describes each of these ontology-based aspects of Bibster.

18.1 Introduction

The advantages of Peer-to-Peer architectures over centralized approaches have been well advertised, and to some extent realized in existing applications: no centralized server (thus avoiding a bottleneck for both computational performance and information update), robustness against failure of any single component, scalability both in data volumes and the number of connected parties.

However, besides being the solution to many problems, the large degree of distribution of Peer-to-Peer systems is also the cause of a number of new problems: the lack of a single coherent schema for organizing information sources across the Peer-to-Peer network hampers the formulation of search queries, duplication of information across the network results in many duplicate answers to a single query, and answers to a single query often require the integration of information residing at different, independent and uncoordinated peers. Finally, query routing and network topology are significant problems.

The research community has recently turned to the use of semantics in Peer-to-Peer networks to alleviate these problems [3], [7]. The use of semantic descriptions of datasources stored by peers and indeed of semantic descriptions of peers themselves helps in formulating queries such that they can be understood by other peers. In particular, the use of ontologies and of Semantic Web technologies has been identified as promising for Peer-to-Peer systems.

The scenario that we have envisioned is that researchers share bibliographic metadata in a community with a Peer-to-Peer system. The data may have been obtained from local BibTeX files or from bibliography servers like the DBLP database[1] or CiteSeer[2]. As one may easily recognize, this scenario exhibits two characteristics that strongly require a semantics-based Peer-to-Peer system.

First, a centralized solution does not exist and cannot exist, because of the multitude of informal workshops that researchers refer to, but that do not show up in centralized resources such as DBLP. Any such centralized resource will only cover a limited scientific community. For example, DBLP covers a lot of Artificial Intelligence, but almost no Knowledge Management, whereas a lot of work is being done in the overlap of these two fields. At the same time, many individual researchers are willing to share their resources, provided they do not have to invest work in doing so.

Second, the use of Semantic Web technology is crucial in this setting. Although a small common-core ontology of bibliographic information exists (title, author/editor, etc), much of this information is very volatile and users define arbitrary add-ons, for example to include URLs of publications.

18.2 Major Use Cases for Bibster

Bibster is aimed at researchers that share bibliographic metadata. Requirements for Bibster must include capabilities that support their daily work. Researchers may want to:

1. Query a single specific peer (e.g. their own computer, because it is sometimes hard to find the right entry there), a specific set of peers (e.g. all colleagues at an institute) or the entire network of peers (to obtain the maximal recall at the price of low precision).
2. Search for bibliographic entries using simple keyword searches, but also more advanced, semantic searches, e.g. for publications of a special type, with specific attribute values, or about a certain topic.

---

[1] http://dblp.uni-trier.de/
[2] http://citeseer.org/

3. Integrate results of a query into a local knowledge base for future use. Such data may in turn be used to answer queries by other peers. They may also be interested in updating items that are already locally stored with additional information about these items obtained from other peers.

The screenshot in Fig. 18.1 partially indicates how these use cases are realized in Bibster. The *Scope* widget allows for defining the targeted peers, the *Search* and *Search Details* widgets allow for keyword and semantic search; *Results Table* and *BibtexView* widgets allow for browsing and re-using query results. The query results are visualized in a list grouped by duplicates. They may be integrated into the local repository or exported into formats such as BibTeX and HTML.

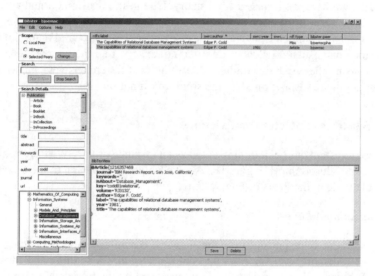

Fig. 18.1. Searching for publications about database management authored by Codd

18.3 Design of Bibster

18.3.1 Ontologies in Bibster

Ontologies are crucial throughout the usage of Bibster, viz. for importing data, formulating queries, routing queries, and processing answers.

Firstly, the system enables users to import their own bibliographic metadata into a local repository. Bibliographic entries made available to Bibster by a user are automatically aligned to two common ontologies: The first ontology (SWRC[1]) describes different generic aspects of bibliographic metadata (and would be valid across many

---

[1] http://www.semanticweb.org/ontologies/swrc-onto-2001-12-11.daml

different research domains), the second ontology (ACM Topic Hierarchy[1]) describes specific categories of literature for the Computer Science domain.

Secondly, queries are formulated in terms of the two ontologies: Queries may concern fields like author, publication type, etc. (using terms from the SWRC ontology) or queries may concern specific Computer Science terms (using the ACM Topic Hierarchy).

Thirdly, queries are routed through the network depending on the expertise models of the peers describing which concepts from the ACM ontology a peer can answer queries on. A matching function determines how closely the semantic content of a query matches the expertise model of a peer. Routing is then done on the basis of this semantic ranking.

Finally, answers are returned for a query. Due to the distributed nature and potentially large size of the Peer-to-Peer network, this answer set might be very large and contain many duplicate answers. Because of the semistructured nature of bibliographic metadata, such duplicates are often not exactly identical copies. Ontologies help to measure the semantic similarity between the different answers and to remove apparent duplicates as identified by the similarity function.

18.3.2 Bibster Architecture and Modules

The Bibster system has been implemented as an instance of the SWAP System architecture as introduced in [3]. Figure 18.2 shows a high-level design of the architecture of a single node in the Peer-to-Peer system.

Communication Adapter

This component is responsible for the network communication between peers. It serves as a transport layer for other parts of the system, for sending and forwarding queries. It hides and encapsulates all low-level communication details from the rest of the system. In the specific implementation of the Bibster system we use JXTA as the communication platform.

Knowledge Sources

The knowledge sources in the Bibster system are sources of bibliographic metadata, such as BibTeX files stored locally in the file system of the user.

Knowledge Source Integrator

The Knowledge Source Integrator is responsible for the extraction and integration of internal and external knowledge sources into the Local Node Repository. In Sect. 18.4 we describe the process of semantic extraction from BibTeX files. In Sect. 18.7 we explain how the knowledge of local and remote sources can be merged, i.e. how duplicate query results are detected.

---

[1] http://www.acm.org/class/1998/

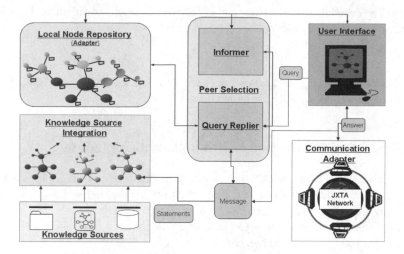

Fig. 18.2. SWAP System Architecture

Local Node Repository

In order to manage its information models and views as well as information acquired from the network, each peer maintains a Local Node Repository providing the following functionality: (1) Mediate between views and stored information, (2) support query formulation and processing, (3) specify the peer's interface to the network, and (4) provide the basis for peer ranking and selection. In the Bibster system, the Local Node Repository is based on the RDF-S Repository Sesame [4]. The query language SeRQL is used to formulate semantic queries against the Local Node Repository, as described in Sect. 18.5.

Informer

The task of the Informer is to proactively advertise the available knowledge of a peer in the Peer-to-Peer network and to discover peers with knowledge that may be relevant for answering the user's queries. This is realized by sending advertisements about the expertise of a peer. In the Bibster system, these expertise descriptions contain a set of topics that the peer is an expert on. Peers may accept – i.e. remember – these advertisements, thus creating a semantic link to the other peer. These semantic links form a semantic topology, which is the basis for intelligent query routing (cf. Sect. 18.6 for details).

Query Replier

The Query Replier is the coordinating component controlling the process of distributing queries. It receives queries from the User Interface or from other peers. Either way it tries to answer the query or distribute it further according to the content of the query. The decision to which peers a query should be sent is based on the knowledge about the expertise of other peers.

User Interface

The User Interface (Fig. 18.1) allows the user to import, create, and edit bibliographic metadata as well as to easily formulate queries.

18.4 Semantic Extraction of Bibliographic Metadata

Many researchers have accumulated extensive collections of BibTeX files for their bibliographic references. However, these files are semi-structured and thus single attributes may be missing or may not be interpreted correctly.

For interchanging bibliographic data in a semantically based Peer-to-Peer network it has to be represented in a structured and formal way.

BibToOnto is a component of Bibster for extracting explicit knowledge of bibliographic items. Plain BibTeX files are transformed into an ontology based knowledge representation.

The target ontology is the Semantic Web Research Community Ontology (SWRC), which models among others a research community, its researchers, topics, publications, tools, and properties between them. The SWRC ontology defines a shared and common domain theory which helps users and machines to communicate concisely and supports the exchange of semantics.

BibToOnto automatically classifies bibliographic entries according to the ACM topic hierarchy. Additionally, it is possible to reclassify the entries manually in the user interface of Bibster. The ACM topic hierarchy is a standard schema for describing and categorizing computer science literature. It covers 1287 topics of the computer science domain. In addition to the sub- and supertopic relations, it also provides information about related topics.

The following example shows a transformation of a BibTeX entry to a SWRC ontology based item. The result[1] is represented as an RDF graph in Fig. 18.3.

Example 1.
```
@ARTICLE{codd70relational
   author    = "Edgar F. Codd",
   year      = "1970",
   title     = "A relational model for large
                 shared data banks",
   journal   = "Communications of ACM",
   volume    = "13",
   number    = "6",
   pages     = "377--387"}
```

---

[1] For better readability we used a concatenation of the author name and the title of the publication as a URI in this example. In the Bibster system, however, we calculate hash codes over all attribute values to guarantee the uniqueness of URIs.

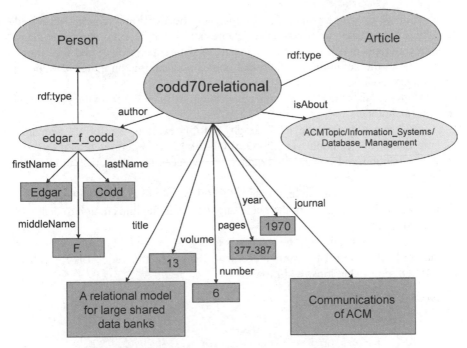

Fig. 18.3. SWRC Sample Metadata

18.5 Semantic Querying

Each peer node in the Bibster system manages a local RDF repository with bibliographic data extracted by BibToOnto or integrated from other peers. The query language interface to the local RDF repository is SeRQL (Chap. 1).

SeRQL (Sesame RDF Query Language) is an RDF/RDF-S query language that was developed in the context of the SWAP project to address practical requirements that were not sufficiently met by other query languages (Chap. 1).

Several characteristics are urgently required in the context of Bibster (but also of many other systems) for an RDF/RDF-S query language like SeRQL. In particular, it must:

1. be functional such that each query returns an RDF graph, which may be integrated into the local repository or queried again,
2. be aware of the (optional) schema,
3. let the user formulate path expressions for navigating the RDF graph, e.g. the combination of SWRC and ACM topic hierarchy,
4. be able to deal with *optional* values, e.g. a publisher field may be given or not.

Without showing all capabilities of SeRQL in full detail, the composition of SeRQL queries and the way how Bibster specific tasks are performed using SeRQL will be described:

(1) SeRQL uses a `select-from-where` or `construct-from-where` filter, where the `select` or `construct` clauses specify projections, the `from` clause specifies a graph match template (by means of path expressions), and the `where` clause allows the definition of additional boolean constraints on matched values in the path expressions.

(2) SeRQL takes the RDF schema into account by mapping from the given graph to its formal model.

(3) When navigating the RDF graph, SeRQL exploits the formal semantics of path labels. For example, `<rdfs:subClassOf>` is interpreted as a reflexive transitive relation and upward inheritance of instances is interpreted (through the `<rdf:type>` relation.

(4) Bibtex entries may be incomplete. SeRQL allows to distinguish between optional and required elements in the query and, hence, is flexible enough to deal with these circumstances.

In our running example, a researcher is querying for journal articles written by the author Codd about database management. Internally, this request is formulated as a SeRQL query that looks as follows:

Example 2.
```
construct distinct
    {s} prop {val};
        <rdf:type> {t};
        <swrc:author> {x} <rdf:type> {<rdf:Seq>};
                         <rdfs:member> {author} prop_author {val_author}
from
    {s} <serql:directType> {t};
        <rdf:type> {<swrc:Article>};
        prop {val};
        <swrc:isAbout> {<acm:ACMTopic/Information_Systems/Database_Management>};
        <swrc:author> {x} <rdfs:member> {} <swrc:lastName> {lname},
        [{x} <rdfs:member> {author} prop_author {val_author} ]
where prop != <rdf:type> and lname like "Codd" using namespace
    swrc = <!http://www.semanticweb.org/ontologies/swrc-onto-2001-12-11.daml#>,
    acm =  <!http://daml.umbc.edu/ontologies/classification#>
```

Compare the structure of the from-clause to the representation of the RDF graph given in Fig. 18.3. The from-clause retrieves not only the identifier for the particular journal entry ("codd70relational", matched by s), but also the graph structure surrounding it, which essentially gives the entry its meaning: the name of the author, the type of publication, the year it was published, the number of pages, etc. Also, if the first and middle names of an author are known, the query retrieves those (but it does not fail if these are not known).

The use of schema-awareness is evident in the use of typing information on s: s need not only be of type swrc:Article, also its *specific* (or *direct*) type are retrieved. Being functional plays a role as well: a graph transformation is used to create a query result that can be easily processed to be given back to the user through the GUI.

18.6 Expertise Based Peer Selection

The scalability of a Peer-to-Peer network is essentially determined by the way how queries are propagated in the network. Peer-to-Peer networks that broadcast all queries to all peers do not scale — intelligent query routing and network topologies are required to be able to route queries to a relevant subset of peers that are able to answer the queries. Here we give an overview of the model of expertise based peer selection and how it is used in the Bibster system. A detailed description can be found in Chap. 6.

In this model, peers use a shared ontology to advertise semantic descriptions of their expertise in the Peer-to-Peer network. The knowledge about the expertise of other peers forms a semantic topology, independent of the underlying network topology. If the peer receives a query, it can decide to forward it to peers about which it knows that their expertise is similar to the subject of the query.

Semantic Description of Expertise

The Peer-to-Peer network consists of a set of peers P. Every peer $p \in P$ has a Local Node Repository, which stores the bibliographic metadata.

The peers share an ontology O, which is used for describing the expertise of peers and the subject of queries. In Bibster, O is the ACM topic hierarchy that contains a set of topics T.

An expertise description is an abstract, semantic description of the Local Node Repository of a peer based on the shared ontology O. The expertise E of a peer is thus defined as $E \subseteq 2^T$, where each $e \in E$ denotes a set of ACM topics, for which a peer provides classified instances.

Advertisements $A \subseteq P \times E$ are used to promote descriptions of the expertise of peers in the network. An advertisement $a \in A$ associates a peer p with an expertise e. Peers decide autonomously — without central control — whom to promote advertisements to and which advertisements to accept. This decision is based on the semantic similarity between expertise descriptions.

Matching and Peer Selection

Queries $q \in Q$ are posed by a user and are evaluated against the local node repositories of the peers. First a peer evaluates the query against its local node repository and then decides which peers the query should be forwarded to.

A subject is an abstraction of a given query q expressed in terms of the common ontology. The subject specifies the required expertise to answer the query. In our scenario, the subjects of queries are defined as $S \subseteq 2^T$, each s is the set of ACM topics that are referenced in the query. For instance, the extracted subject of the query in Example 2 would be *Information Systems/Database Management*.

The similarity function $Sim : S \times E \mapsto [0, 1]$ yields the semantic similarity between a subject $s \in S$ and an expertise description $e \in E$. An increasing value indicates increasing similarity. If the value is 0, s and e are not similar at all, if the value is 1, they match exactly. Sim is used for determining to which peers a query should be forwarded. In Bibster, the similarity function Sim_{Topics} is based on the idea that topics which are close according to their positions in the topic hierarchy are more similar than topics that have a larger distance. For example, an expert on the ACM topic *Information Systems/Information Storage and Retrieval* has a higher chance of giving a correct answer on a query about *Information Systems/Database Management* than an expert on a less similar topic like *Hardware/Memory Structures*.

To be able to define the similarity of a peer's expertise and a query subject, which are both represented as a set of topics, we first define the similarity for individual topics. [5] have compared different similarity measures and have shown that for measuring the similarity between concepts in a hierarchical structured semantic network, like the ACM topic hierarchy, the following similarity measure yields the best results:

$$
sim_{Topic}(t_1, t_2) = \begin{cases} e^{-\alpha l} \cdot \frac{e^{\beta h} - e^{-\beta h}}{e^{\beta h} + e^{-\beta h}} & \text{if } t_1 \neq t_2, \\ 1 & \text{otherwise.} \end{cases}
$$

Here l is the length of the shortest path between topic t_1 and t_2 in the graph spanned by the *SubTopic* relation. h is the level in the tree of the direct common subsumer from t_1 and t_2. $\alpha \geq 0$ and $\beta \geq 0$ are parameters scaling the contribution of shortest path length l and depth h, respectively. Based on their benchmark data set, the optimal values are: $\alpha = 0.2$, $\beta = 0.6$.

The peer selection algorithm returns a ranked set of peers, where the rank value is equal to the similarity value provided by the similarity function. Therefore, peers that have an expertise more similar to that of the subject of the query will have a higher rank. From this set of ranked peers one can select the best n peers or all peers whose rank value is above a certain threshold. In the Bibster system we select the best n peers that have not yet received the query along the message path, where n can be specified. A detailed description is given in Chap. 6.

Semantic Topology

The knowledge of the peers about the expertise of other peers is the basis for a semantic topology. Here it is important to state that this semantic topology is independent of the underlying network topology. At this point, we do not make any assumptions about the properties of the topology on the network layer.

The semantic topology can be described by the following relation:

$Knows \subseteq P \times P$, where $Knows(p_1, p_2)$ means that p_1 knows about the expertise of p_2.

The relation $Knows$ is established by the selection of which peers a peer sends its advertisements to. Furthermore, peers can decide to accept an advertisement, e.g. to include it in their registries, or to discard the advertisement. The semantic topology in combination with the expertise based peer selection is the basis for intelligent query routing.

18.7 Semantic Duplicate Detection

When querying the Bibster network one receives a large number of results with an often high number of duplicates. This is due to the fact that no centralized but many distributed local repositories have been used. Furthermore, the representation of the metadata is very heterogeneous and possibly even contradicting. To enable an efficient and easily usable system, Bibster presents query results grouping duplicates together. Duplicates in Bibster are bibliographic entries which refer to the same publication, person, or organization in the real world, but are modelled as different resources. Bibster uses specific similarity functions to recognize two resources as being duplicates.

A similarity function for RDF resources R of the local node repository is a function $sim : R \times R \to [0..1]$.

For each resource type (publication, person, organization), a set of specific features used to assess the similarity between two of its instances has been compiled. For instance, publications are assessed based on their titles, publication types, authors, years, ACM topics, etc. For each of the features we use different *individual similarity functions*, which are grouped as follows:

Individual similarity functions have been used on a *data value level*, an *ontology level*, and *background knowledge about the bibliographic domain* as described in detail in Chap. 7. From the variety of individual similarity functions, an overall value is obtained with an aggregated similarity function, using a weighted average over the individual functions.

However, unlike in the recommender scenario in Chap. 7, specific weights and specific thresholds have been used to identify duplicates to pose semantic similar results.

For Bibster, the weights have been assigned based on experiments with sample data. More precisely, several duplicates were detected manually. From these training duplicates the weights were adjusted to achieve a maximal f-measure (combination of precision and recall) value.

Those pairs of resources are considered as duplicates, whose similarity is larger than a certain threshold:

$$t \in [0..1] : D_t := \{(x,y)|sim(x,y) \geq t\}.$$

Assuming that the duplicate relation is transitive, the transitive closure can be defined as:

$$TC(D_t) := \{(x,z)|(x,y) \in D_t \land (y,z) \in D_t\}.$$

This transitive closure essentially represents clusters of semantically similar resources.

Instead of presenting all individual resources of the query result, duplicates are visualized as one, merged, resource. The merged resources comprise the union of statements of the individuals identified as duplicates. In the case of conflicting property values, heuristics for the merging of resources are applied (e.g. for booktitles to select the most detailed value with the least abbreviations).

18.8 Results

The Bibster system has been evaluated by means of a public field experiment. The user actions and system events were continuously logged and analyzed to evaluate the user behavior and system performance. Analyzing the results for a period of three months (June to August 2004) and the following interesting results have been obtained:

A total number of 398 peers from various organizations spread mainly over Europe and North America used the Bibster system. The users shared nearly 100,000 bibliographic entries. While 62% (248 peers) were free riding and therefore shared no content, 6% (24 peers) shared at least 1000 entries each, accounting for 79% of the total shared content.

The users performed a total of 3319 queries. The two ontologies (SWRC and ACM) were used for about half of the queries, whereas the other half used the generic search over all attributes. The SWRC ontology was mainly used for the purpose of querying for special types of publications (e.g. for Articles) or for publications of a given author. In 720 queries the users asked for topics of the ACM topic hierarchy. Thereby it is obvious that the users are accepting the ontology based searching capabilities and that there is a benefit for them in using these ontologies. Furthermore, the frequent queries for ACM topics justify the chosen topic-based expertise model as the basis for peer selection.

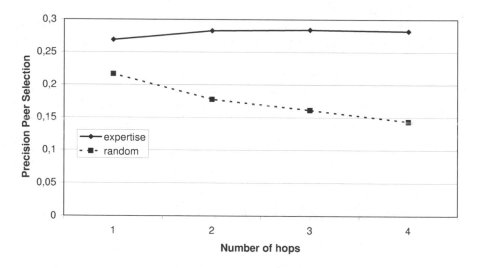

Fig. 18.4. Precision of the peer selection algorithm

With respect to query routing, the expertise based peer selection reduced the number of query messages by more than 50 percent, while retaining the same recall of documents compared to a naive broadcasting approach. Figure 18.4 shows the precision of the peer selection (the percentage of the reached peers that actually provided answers to a given query): While the expertise based peer selection results in an almost constant high precision of 28%, the naive algorithm results in a lower precision decreasing from 22% after 1 hop to 14% after 4 hops. The decrease is due the redundancy of relevant peers found on different message paths: Only distinct relevant peers are considered.

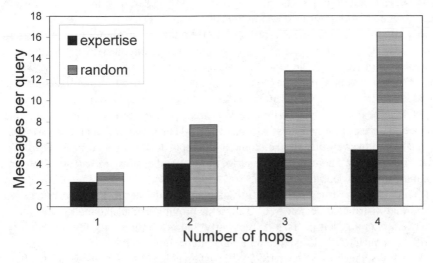

Fig. 18.5. Number of Messages

Figure 18.5 shows the number of forwarded query messages sent per query. It can be seen that with an increasing number of hops, the number of messages sent with the expertise based peer selection is considerably lower than with the naive algorithm. Although this shows an improvement in the performance, the results also show that with a network of the size as in the field experiment, a naive approach is also acceptable. On the other hand, with a growing number of peers, query routing and peer selection becomes critical: In simulation experiments with larger peer networks with thousands of peers, improvements in the order of one magnitude in terms of recall of documents and relevant peers could be shown in Chap. 6.

Summarizing some experiences gained from the development and application of Bibster, it is obvious that for Bibster and similar applications the usage of Semantic Web technologies and ontologies provide an *added value*. Semantic structures serve important user concerns like high quality duplicate detection or comprehensive searching capabilities.

Unsurprisingly, in small networks with *small user groups*, intelligent query routing is not a major issue. While it is beneficial to direct queries to specific peers known to the user, advanced routing algorithms may only be beneficial for a much larger number of users in a network. Based on our experience we now conjecture that content-based routing and trust issues will have to converge for such larger networks, too.

18.9 Related Work

In the previous sections, related work on the individual aspects of semantics-based Peer-to-Peer technology has already been discussed. Therefore in this section the study of related work focuses on complete systems.

Edutella [6] is a Peer-to-Peer system based on the JXTA platform, which offers similar base functionality as the SWAP system. The Edutella network focuses on the exchange of learning material. Super-peer based topologies are used, in which peers are organized in hypercubes to route queries. In contrast to Edutella, Bibster is embedded in the general SWAP architecture and a running application.

[2] describes the design of a Peer-to-Peer network for open archives, where data providers, i.e. research institutes, form a Peer-to-Peer network which supports distributed search over all the connected metadata repositories. This scenario is similar to the bibliographic Peer-to-Peer scenario. However, their system has not been implemented up to this point.

P-Grid [1] is a structured, yet fully-decentralized Peer-to-Peer system based on a virtual distributed search tree. It aims at providing load-balancing and fault-tolerance, assuming that peers fail frequently and are online with low probability. P-Grid also considers updates with an update algorithm based rumor spreading.

The DFN Science-to-Science (S2S) [9] system enhances content based searching by using Peer-to-Peer technology to make locally generated indexes accessible in an ad hoc manner. Whereas Bibster is fully distributed, S2S uses a kind of super peers (Search Hubs) to route queries and cache information.

Various systems address the issue of heterogeneity in Peer-to-Peer systems on the schema level, such as the Piazza peer data management system (Chap. 12),which allows for information sharing with different schemas relying on local mappings between schemas.

18.10 Conclusion

In this chapter, the design and implementation of Bibster, a semantics-based Peer-to-Peer system for the exchange of bibliographic metadata between researchers has been described. For this purpose, Bibster exploits lightweight ontologies, expressed in RDF Schema in all its crucial aspects: data-organisation, query formulation, query routing, and duplicate detection. To our knowledge, Bibster now constitutes the first ontology-based Peer-to-Peer systems ready for fielded deployment.

The next steps in the development of Bibster are, *(i)* its optimization (e.g., manual query optimization), *(ii)* its spreading to further user groups and, *(iii)* the extension of Bibster to better account for personalized semantic structures, based on the two common core ontologies, e.g. peer-local extensions of the ACM topic hierarchy.

The reader may find further reading material on Bibster, its underlying technologies and related material in the open available project deliverable documentation at `http://swap.semanticweb.org/` and `http://bibster.semanticweb.org/`.

References

[1] Aberer, K., P. C. Mauroux, A. Datta, Z. Despotovic, M. Hauswirth, M. Punceva, and R. Schmidt (2003). P-Grid: a self-organizing structured p2p system. *ACM SIGMOD Record 32*(3), 29–33.

[2] Ahlborn, B., W. Nejdl, and W. Siberski (2002). OAI-P2P: A peer-to-peer network for open archives. In *Proceedings of the Workshop on Distributed Computing Architectures for Digital Libraries - ICPP2002.*

[3] Broekstra, J., M. Ehrig, P. Haase, F. van Harmelen, A. Kampman, M. Sabou, R. Siebes, S. Staab, H. Stuckenschmidt, and C. Tempich (2003). A metadata model for semantics-based peer-to-peer systems. In *Proceedings of the WWW'03 Workshop on Semantics in Peer-to-Peer and Grid Computing.*

[4] Broekstra, J., A. Kampman, and F. van Harmelen (2001). Sesame: An architecture for storing and querying rdf data and schema information.

[5] Li, Y., Z. A. Bandar, and D. McLean (2003, July/August). An approach for measuring semantic similarity between words using multiple information sources. *Transactions on Knowledge and Data Engineering 15*(4), 871–882.

[6] Nejdl, W. et al. (2003, May). Super-peer-based routing and clustering strategies for rdf-based peer-to-peer networks. In *Proceedings of the Twelfth International World Wide Web Conference (WWW 2003)*, Budapest, Hungary.

[7] Nejdl, W., B. Wolf, C. Qu, S. Decker, M. Sintek, A. Naeve, M. Nilsson, M. Palmér, and T. Risch (2002, May). Edutella: A P2P networking infrastructure based on rdf. In *Proceedings to the Eleventh International World Wide Web Conference.*

[8] Tatarinov, I., Z. Ives, J. Madhavan, A. Halevy, D. Suciu, N. Dalvi, X. Dong, Y. Kadiyska, G. Miklau, and P. Mork (2003). The piazza peer data management project. *SIGMOD Record 32*(3).

[9] Wertlen, R. (2003). Dfn science-to-science: Peer-to-peer scientific research. In *Proceedings of the Terena Networking Conference (TNC 2003)*, Zagreb, Croatia.

Author Index